BUNNY**DROP**
yumi unita

STORY

Ten years have passed since Daikichi, a single guy with no experience in child-rearing, made the decision to take in Rin, his grandfather's love child, and create a family life together. Rin now attends the same high school as her childhood friend Kouki, who asks her to be his girlfriend. She doesn't take him seriously, but his profession seems to have something to do with his former girlfriend, Akari...

MAIN CHARACTERS

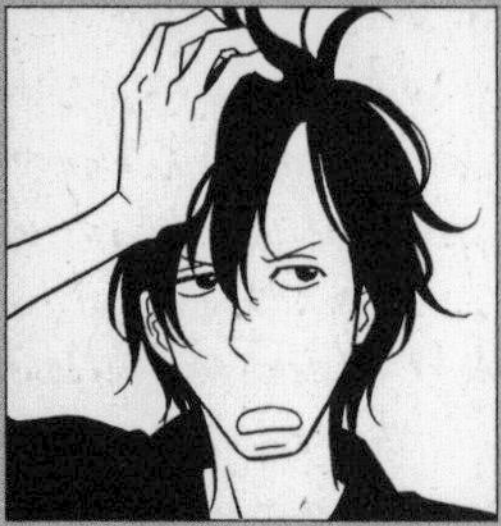

KOUKI NITANI

Rin's childhood friend from daycare days. High school first-year. Professed his love to Rin.

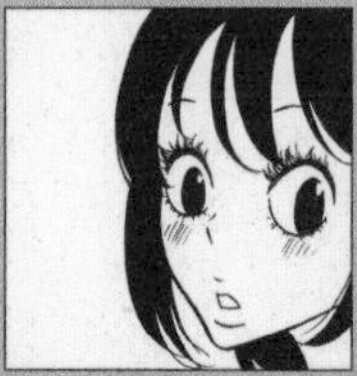

REINA

Daikichi's cousin Haruko's daughter. High school first-year.

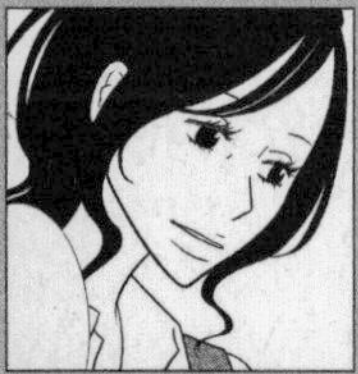

NITANI-SAN

Kouki's mother and a single mom. Was proposed to by Daikichi but hasn't made a decision yet.

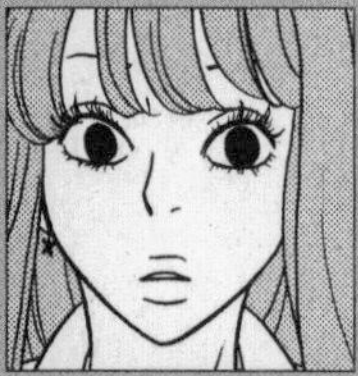

AKARI

Kouki's former girlfriend. Has delinquent tendencies.

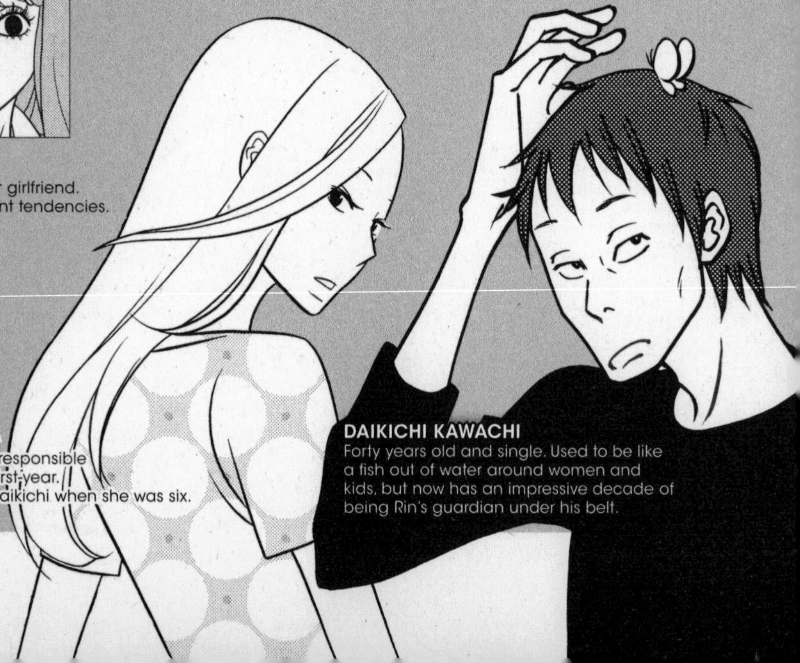

RIN KAGA

A smart and responsible high school first-year. Taken in by Daikichi when she was six.

DAIKICHI KAWACHI

Forty years old and single. Used to be like a fish out of water around women and kids, but now has an impressive decade of being Rin's guardian under his belt.

c o n t e n t s

BUNNY**DROP**

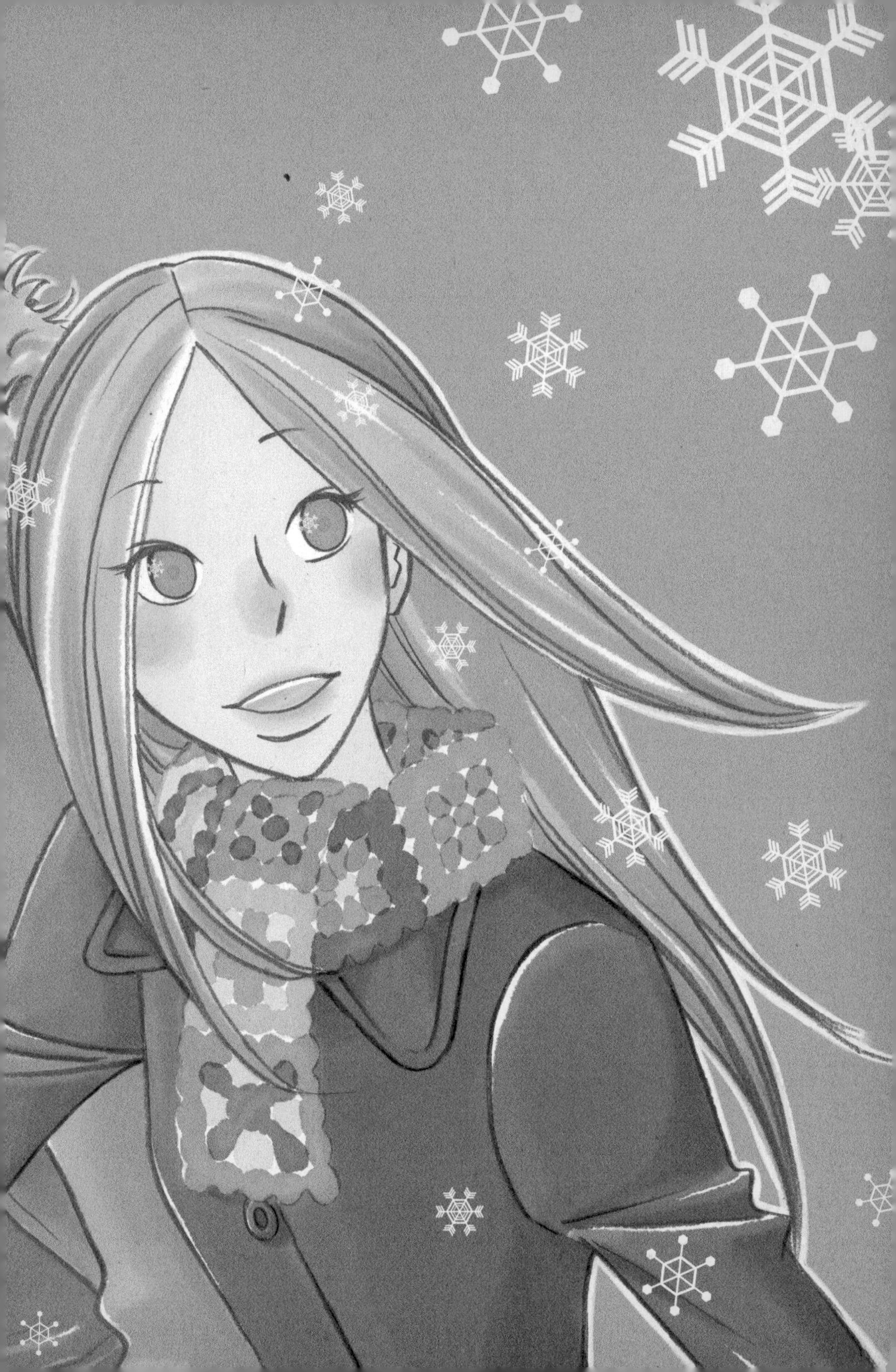

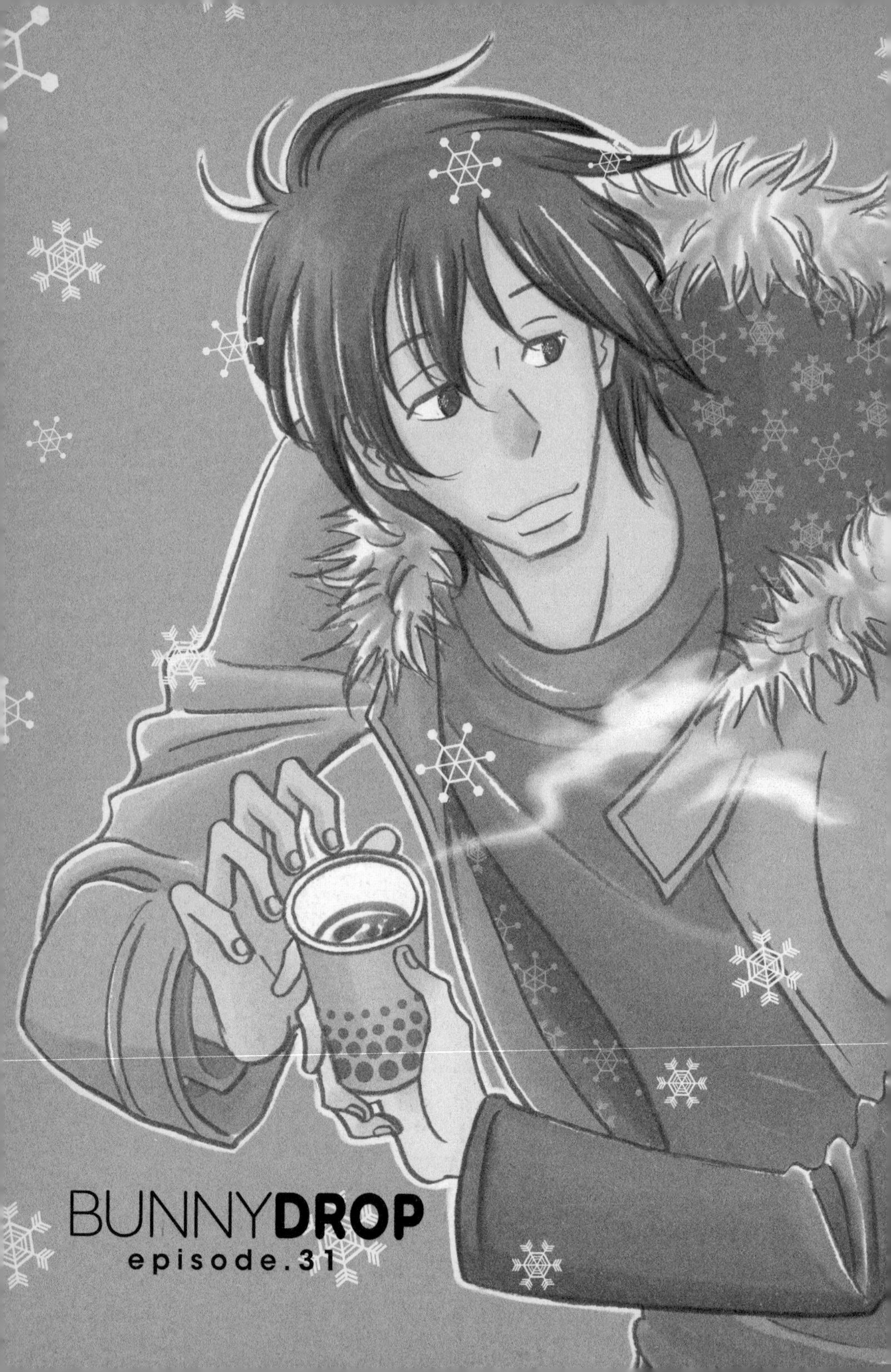
BUNNY**DROP**
episode.31

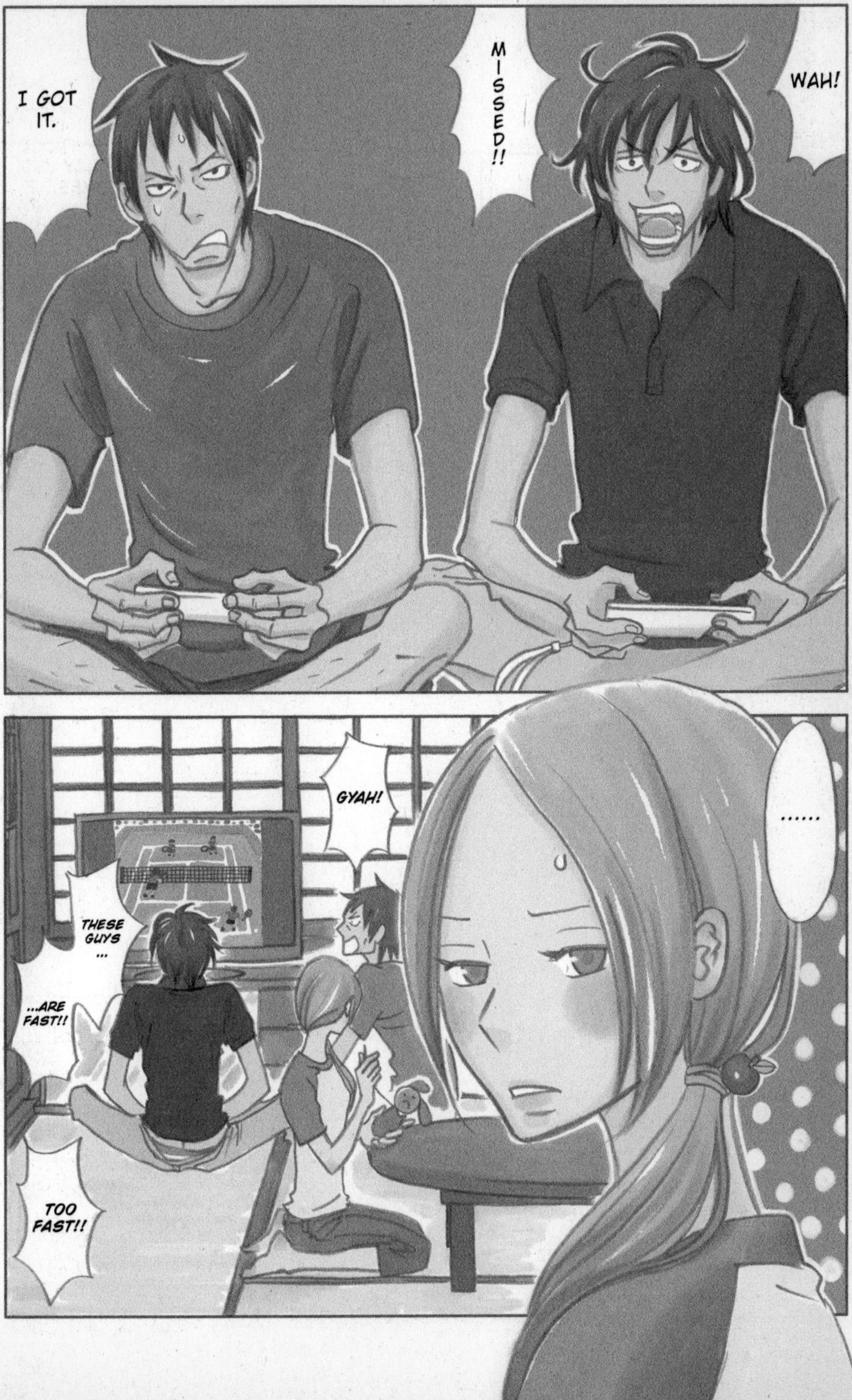
WAH!
MISSED!!
I GOT IT.
......
GYAH!
THESE GUYS ...
...ARE FAST!!
TOO FAST!!

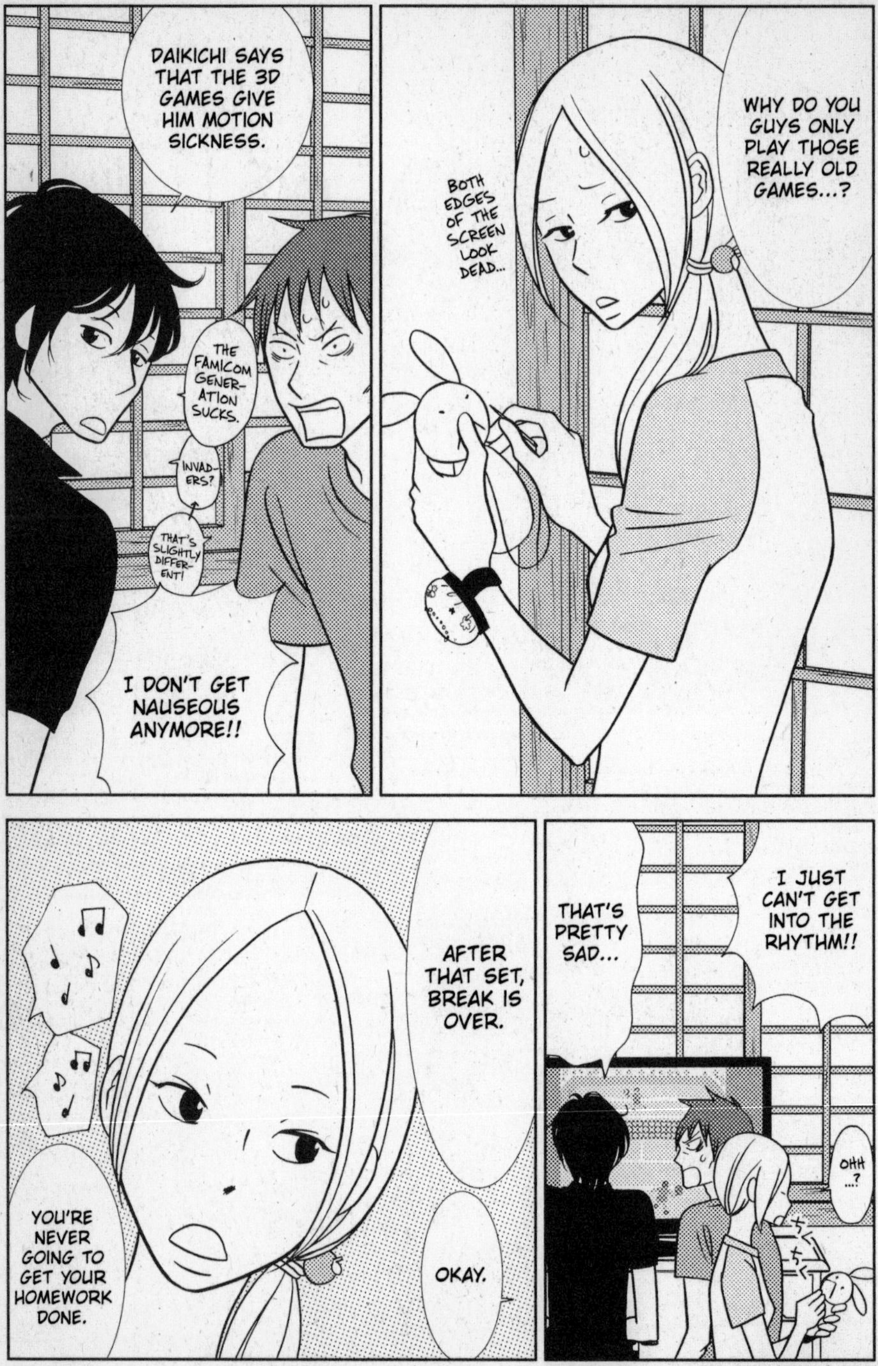
WHY DO YOU GUYS ONLY PLAY THOSE REALLY OLD GAMES...?
BOTH EDGES OF THE SCREEN LOOK DEAD...
DAIKICHI SAYS THAT THE 3D GAMES GIVE HIM MOTION SICKNESS.
THE FAMICOM GENERATION SUCKS.
INVADERS?
THAT'S SLIGHTLY DIFFERENT!
I DON'T GET NAUSEOUS ANYMORE!!
I JUST CAN'T GET INTO THE RHYTHM!!
THAT'S PRETTY SAD...
OHH ...?
AFTER THAT SET, BREAK IS OVER.
OKAY.
YOU'RE NEVER GOING TO GET YOUR HOMEWORK DONE.
SFX: CHIKU (STITCH) CHIKU

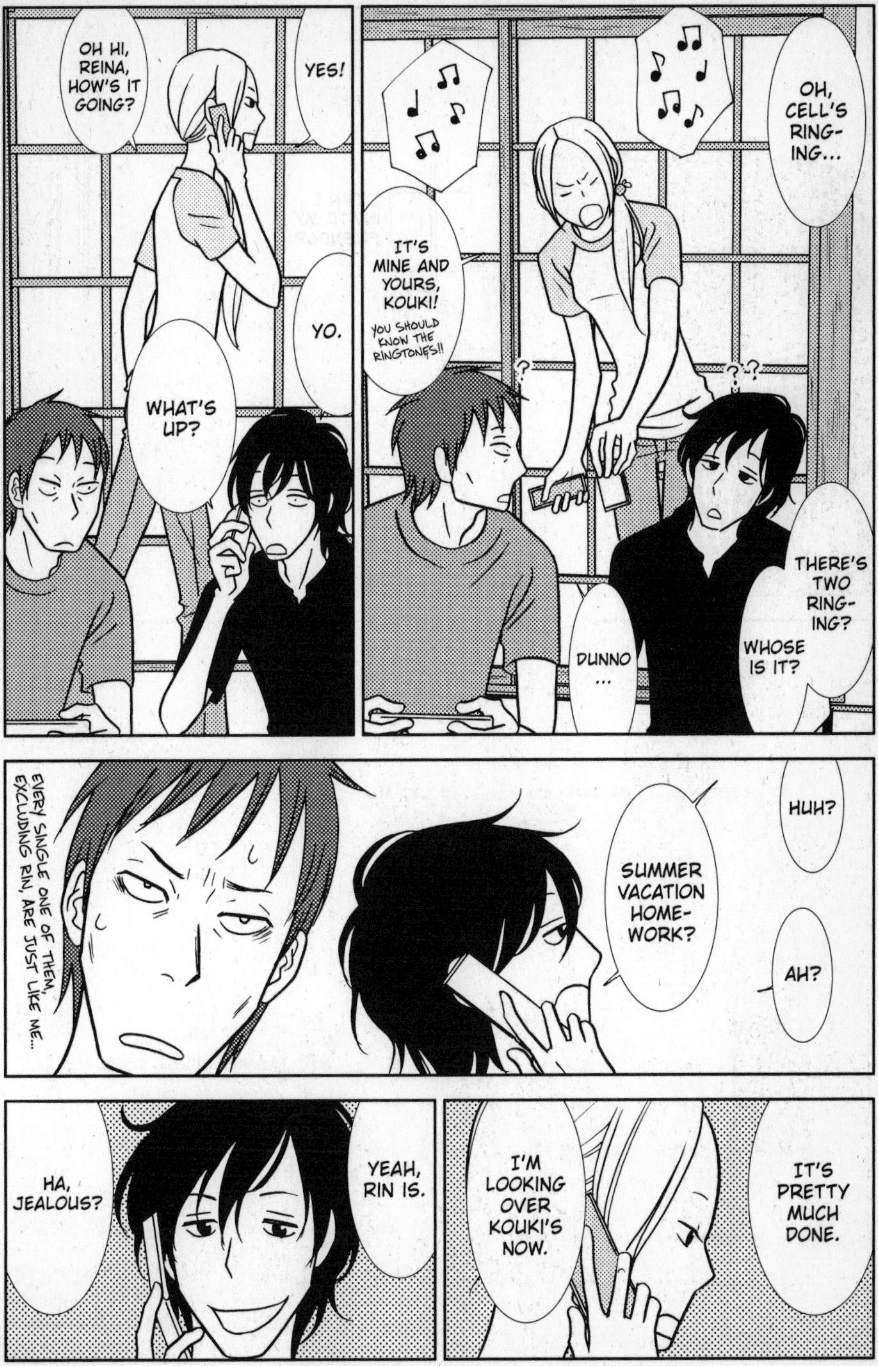
OH, CELL'S RING-ING...
IT'S MINE AND YOURS, KOUKI!
YOU SHOULD KNOW THE RINGTONES!!
THERE'S TWO RING-ING?
WHOSE IS IT?
DUNNO ...
YES!
OH HI, REINA, HOW'S IT GOING?
YO.
WHAT'S UP?
HUH?
AH?
SUMMER VACATION HOME-WORK?
EVERY SINGLE ONE OF THEM, EXCLUDING RIN, ARE JUST LIKE ME...
IT'S PRETTY MUCH DONE.
I'M LOOKING OVER KOUKI'S NOW.
YEAH, RIN IS.
HA, JEALOUS?

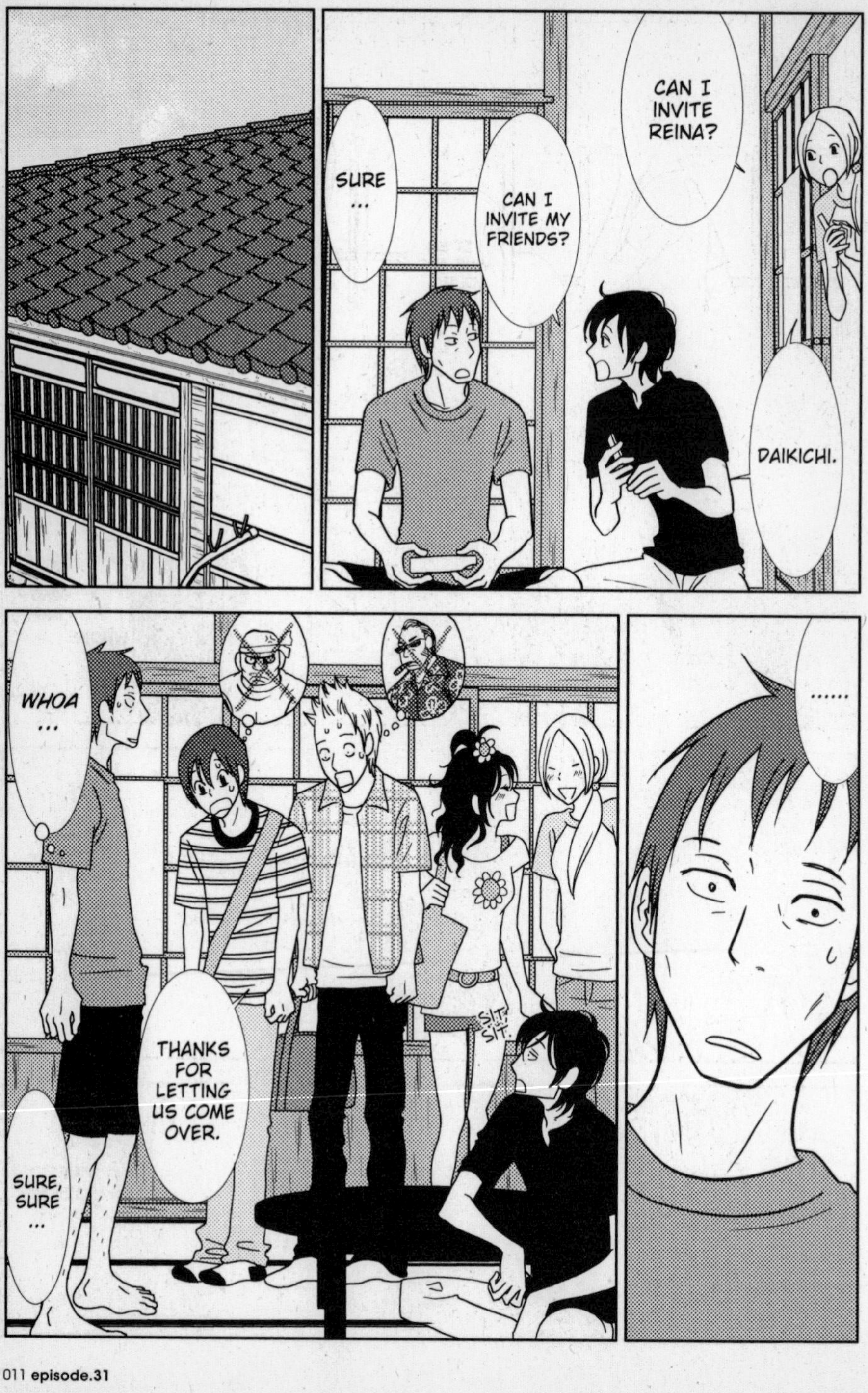
CAN I INVITE REINA?
DAIKICHI.
CAN I INVITE MY FRIENDS?
SURE ...
......
WHOA ...
THANKS FOR LETTING US COME OVER.
SIT SIT.
SURE, SURE ...

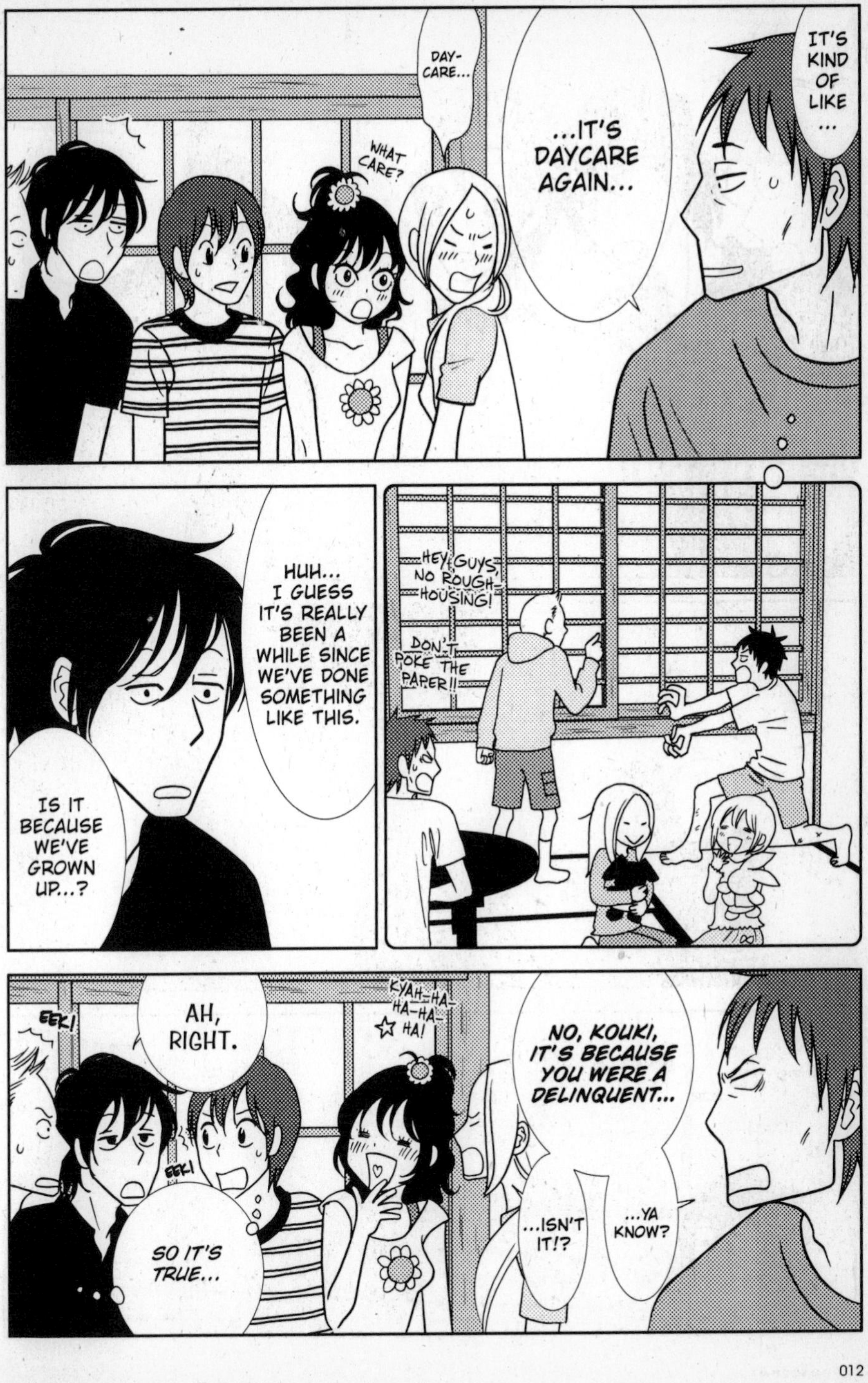
IT'S KIND OF LIKE ...
...IT'S DAYCARE AGAIN...
DAY-CARE...
WHAT CARE?
HEY, GUYS, NO ROUGH-HOUSING!
DON'T POKE THE PAPER!!
HUH... I GUESS IT'S REALLY BEEN A WHILE SINCE WE'VE DONE SOMETHING LIKE THIS.
IS IT BECAUSE WE'VE GROWN UP...?
NO, KOUKI, IT'S BECAUSE YOU WERE A DELINQUENT...
...YA KNOW?
...ISN'T IT!?
KYAH-HA-HA-HA-HA!
AH, RIGHT.
EEK!
EEK!
SO IT'S TRUE...

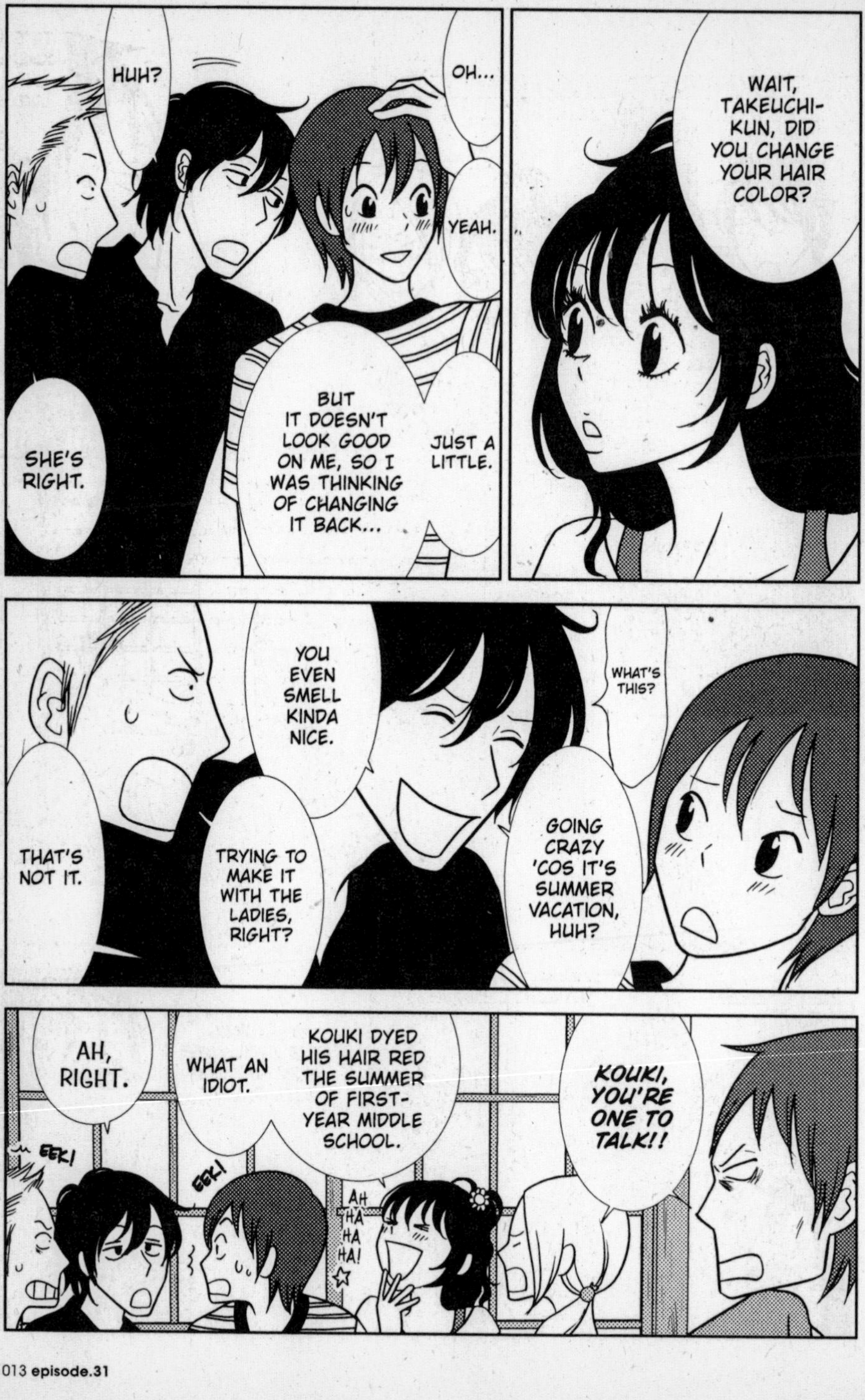
WAIT, TAKEUCHI-KUN, DID YOU CHANGE YOUR HAIR COLOR?
OH...
YEAH.
HUH?
JUST A LITTLE.
BUT IT DOESN'T LOOK GOOD ON ME, SO I WAS THINKING OF CHANGING IT BACK...
SHE'S RIGHT.
WHAT'S THIS?
YOU EVEN SMELL KINDA NICE.
GOING CRAZY 'COS IT'S SUMMER VACATION, HUH?
TRYING TO MAKE IT WITH THE LADIES, RIGHT?
THAT'S NOT IT.
KOUKI, YOU'RE ONE TO TALK!!
KOUKI DYED HIS HAIR RED THE SUMMER OF FIRST-YEAR MIDDLE SCHOOL.
WHAT AN IDIOT.
AH, RIGHT.
AH HA HA HA!
EEK!
EEK!

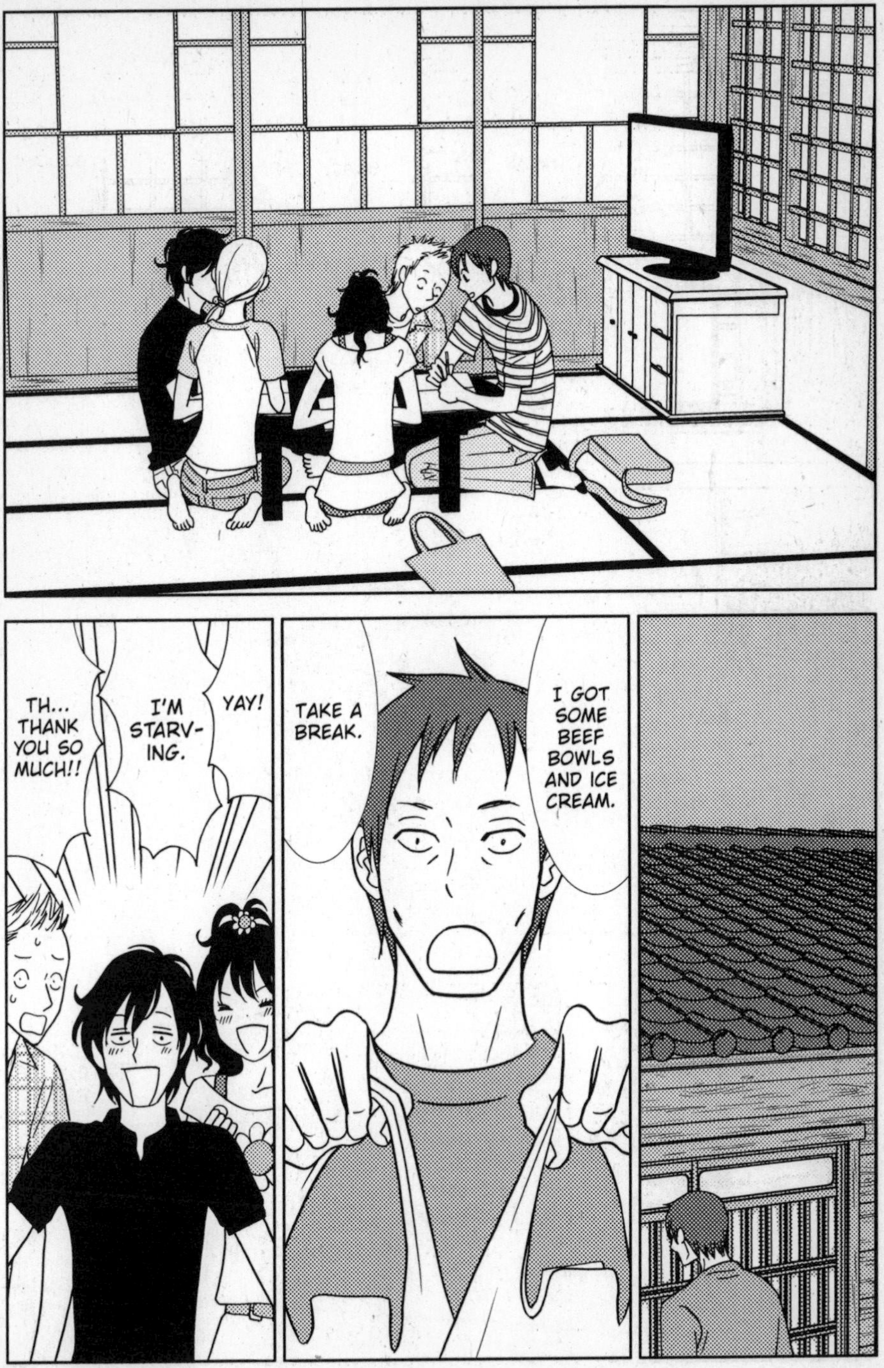
I GOT SOME BEEF BOWLS AND ICE CREAM.
TAKE A BREAK.
YAY!
I'M STARVING.
TH... THANK YOU SO MUCH!!

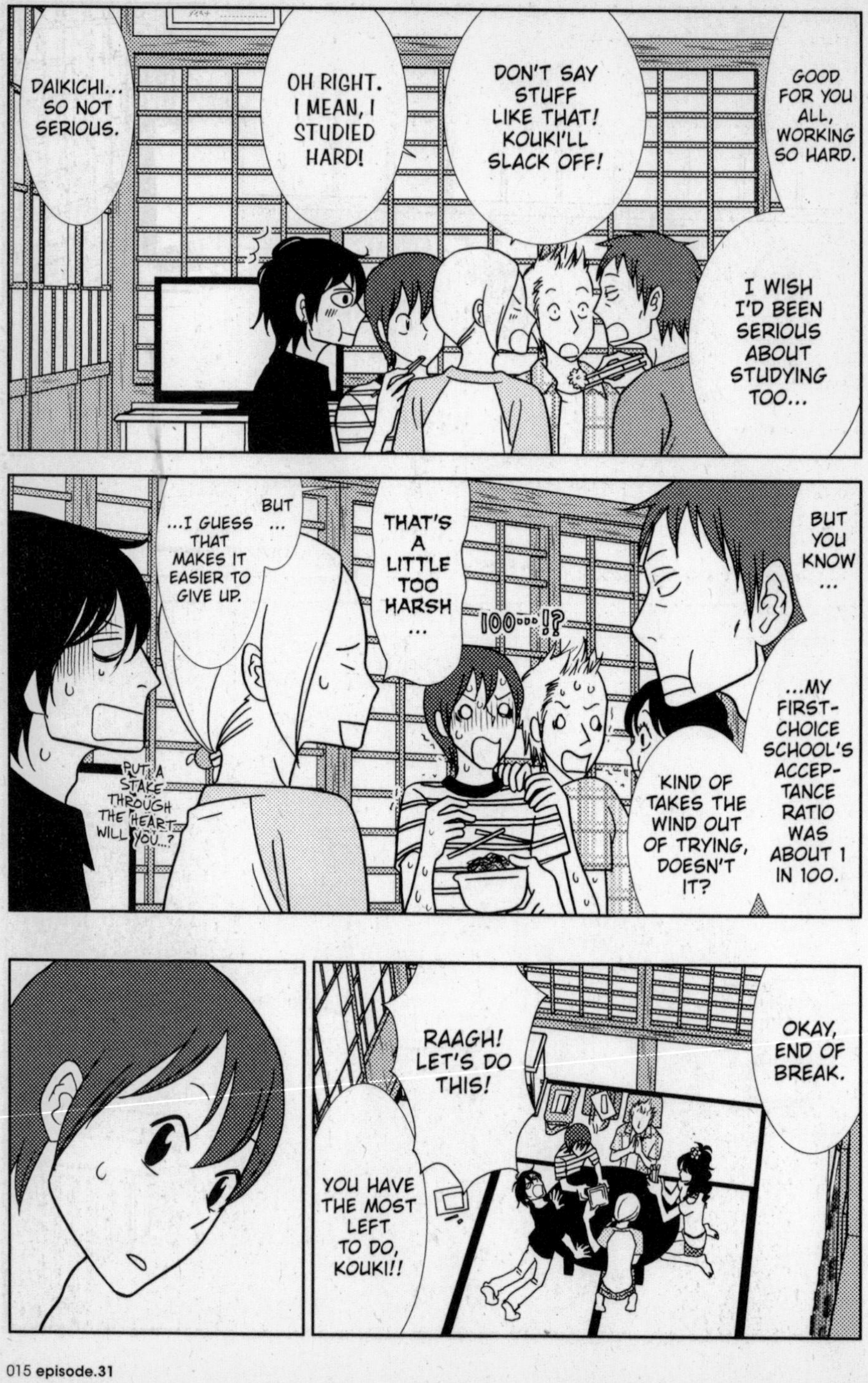
GOOD FOR YOU ALL, WORKING SO HARD.
I WISH I'D BEEN SERIOUS ABOUT STUDYING TOO...
DON'T SAY STUFF LIKE THAT! KOUKI'LL SLACK OFF!
OH RIGHT. I MEAN, I STUDIED HARD!
DAIKICHI... SO NOT SERIOUS.
BUT YOU KNOW ...
...MY FIRST-CHOICE SCHOOL'S ACCEPTANCE RATIO WAS ABOUT 1 IN 100.
KIND OF TAKES THE WIND OUT OF TRYING, DOESN'T IT?
100...!?
THAT'S A LITTLE TOO HARSH ...
BUT ...
...I GUESS THAT MAKES IT EASIER TO GIVE UP.
PUT A STAKE THROUGH THE HEART, WILL YOU...?
OKAY, END OF BREAK.
RAAGH! LET'S DO THIS!
YOU HAVE THE MOST LEFT TO DO, KOUKI!!

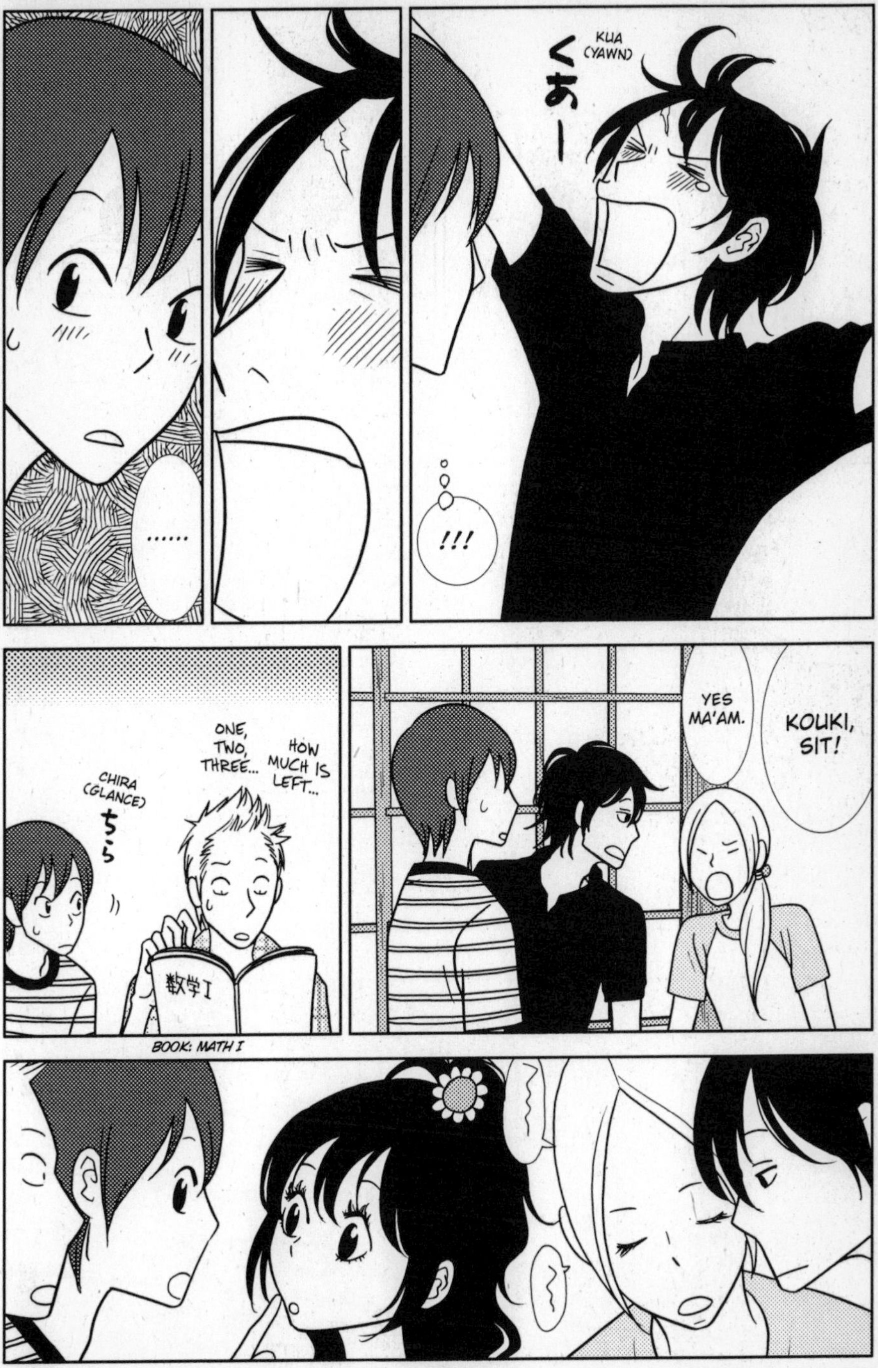
KUA (YAWN)
くあー
!!!
......
KOUKI, SIT!
YES MA'AM.
HOW MUCH IS LEFT...
ONE, TWO, THREE...
CHIRA (GLANCE)
ちら
数学I
BOOK: MATH I

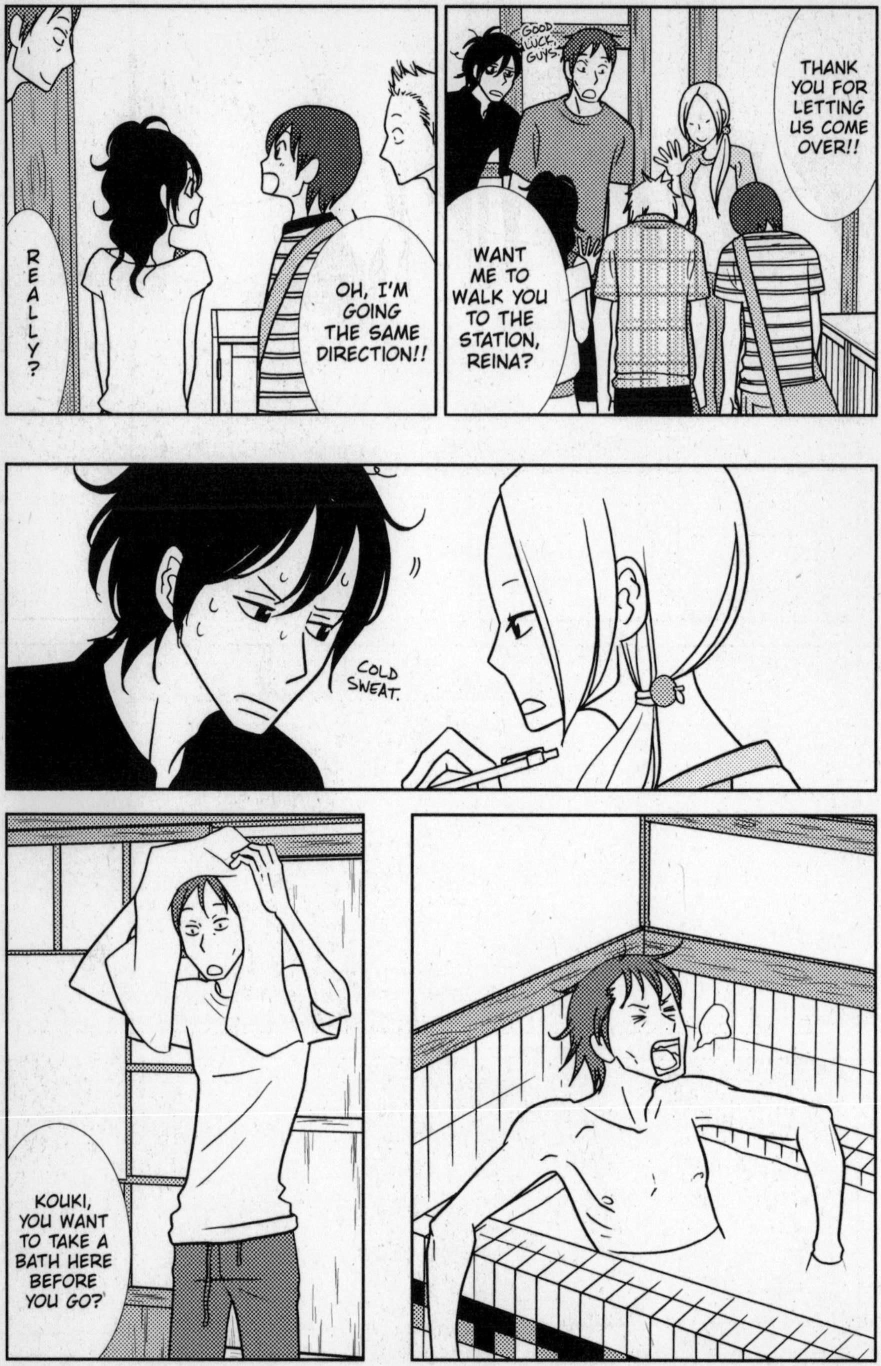
THANK YOU FOR LETTING US COME OVER!!
GOOD LUCK, GUYS.
WANT ME TO WALK YOU TO THE STATION, REINA?
OH, I'M GOING THE SAME DIRECTION!!
REALLY?
COLD SWEAT.
KOUKI, YOU WANT TO TAKE A BATH HERE BEFORE YOU GO?

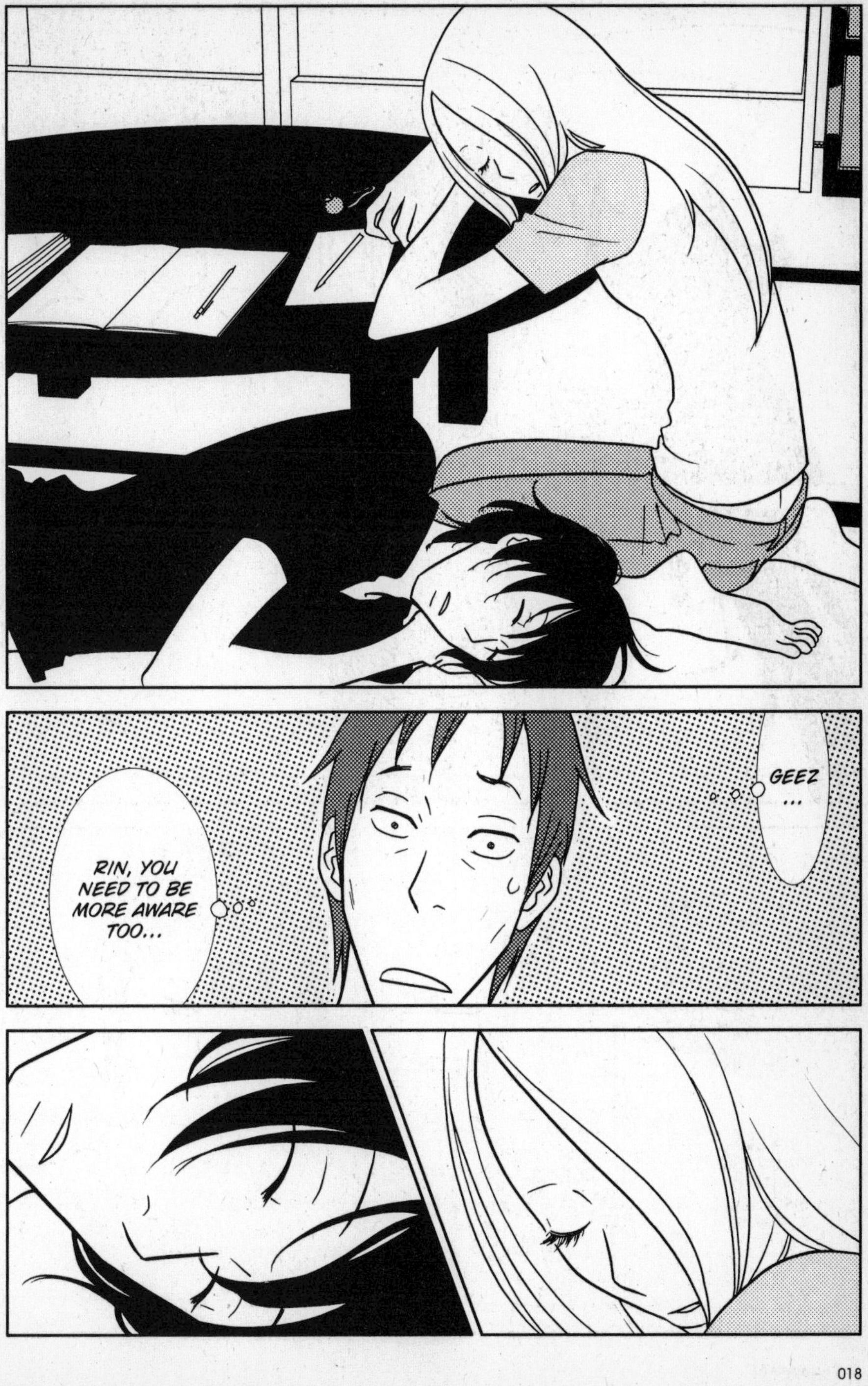
GEEZ ...
RIN, YOU NEED TO BE MORE AWARE TOO...

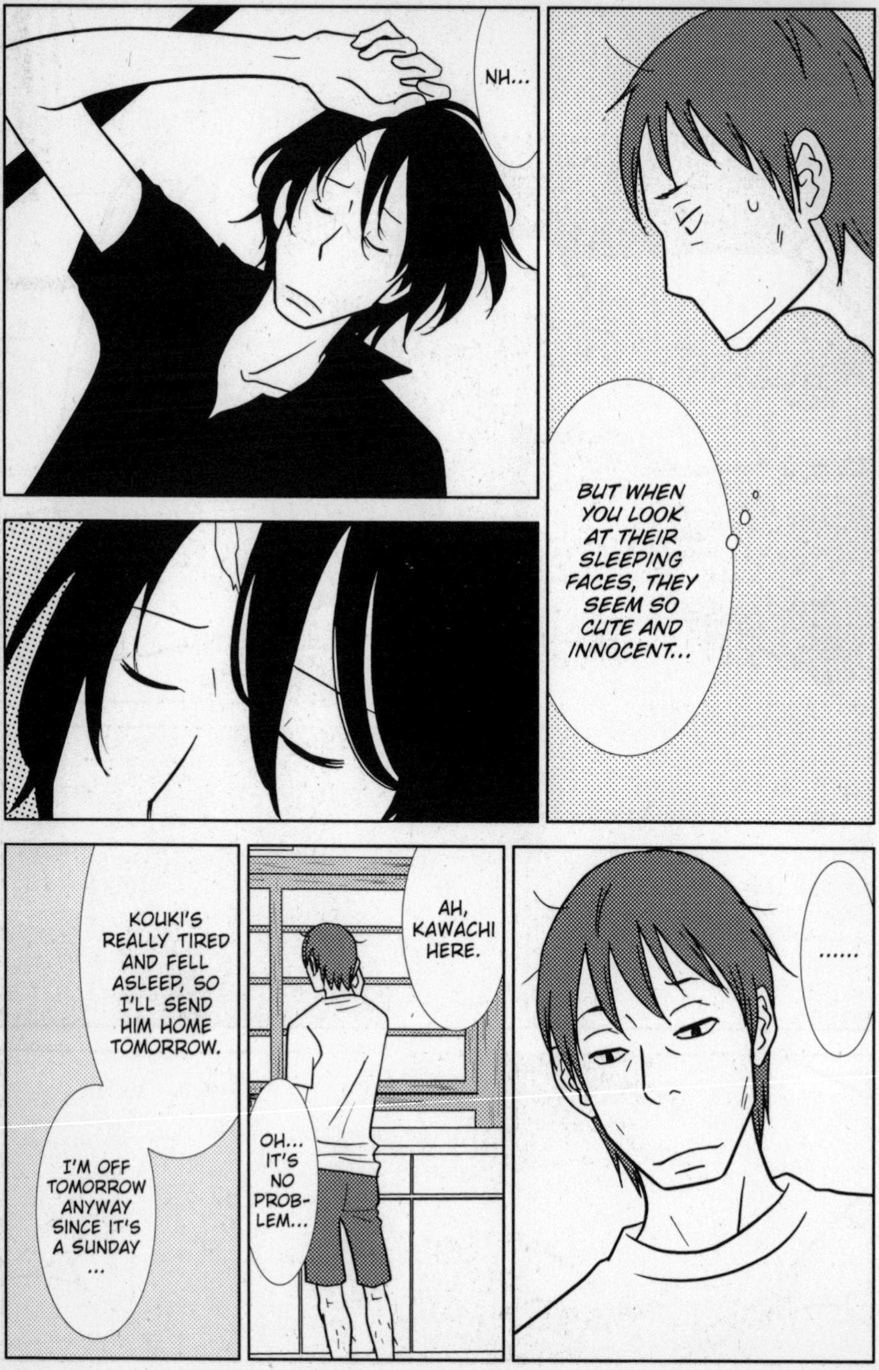
BUT WHEN YOU LOOK AT THEIR SLEEPING FACES, THEY SEEM SO CUTE AND INNOCENT...
NH...
......
AH, KAWACHI HERE.
OH... IT'S NO PROB-LEM...
KOUKI'S REALLY TIRED AND FELL ASLEEP, SO I'LL SEND HIM HOME TOMORROW.
I'M OFF TOMORROW ANYWAY SINCE IT'S A SUNDAY ...

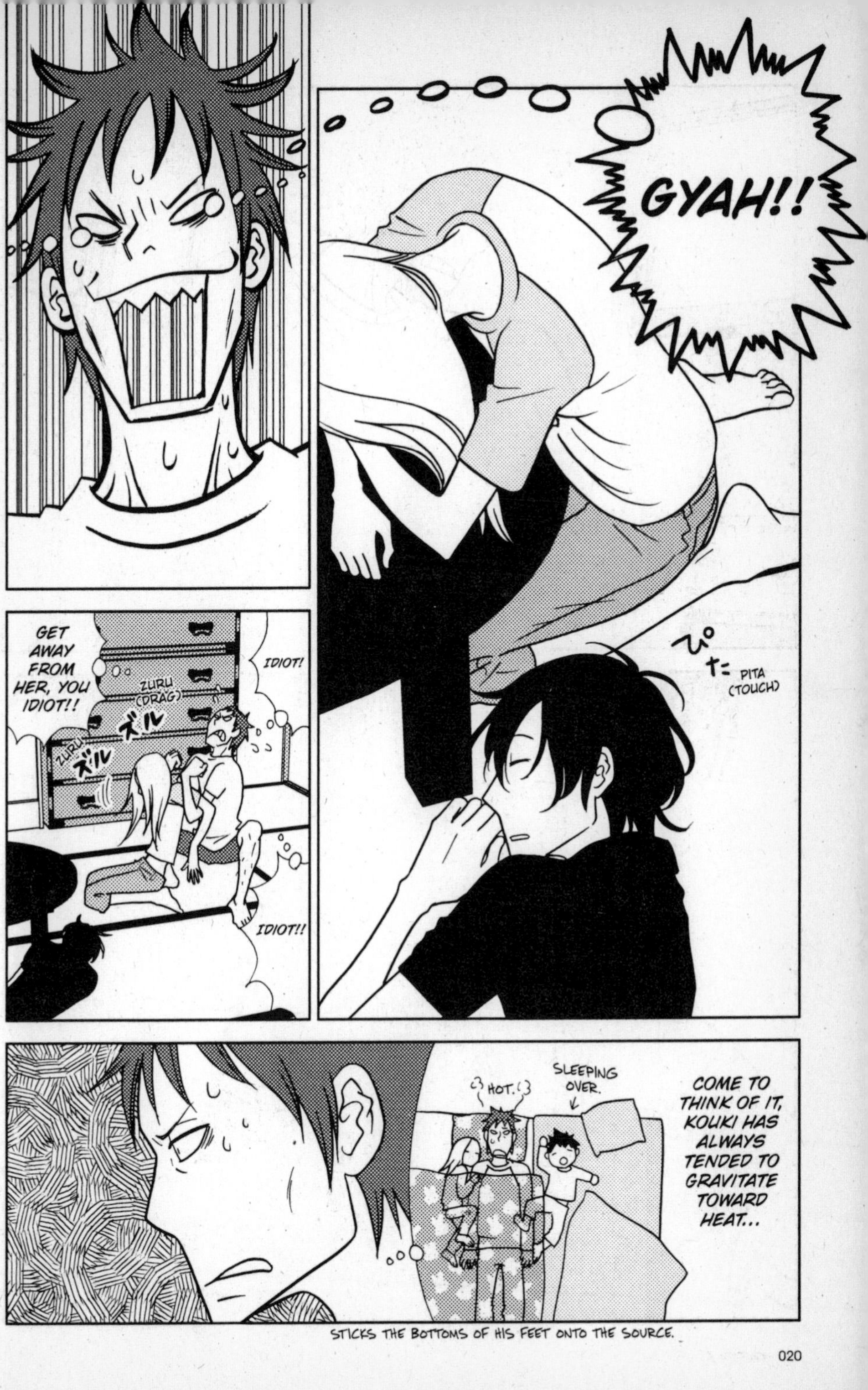
GYAH!!
ぴた
PITA (TOUCH)
IDIOT!
GET AWAY FROM HER, YOU IDIOT!!
ズル
ZURU (DRAG)
ズル
ZURU
IDIOT!!
COME TO THINK OF IT, KOUKI HAS ALWAYS TENDED TO GRAVITATE TOWARD HEAT...
SLEEPING OVER.
HOT.
STICKS THE BOTTOMS OF HIS FEET ONTO THE SOURCE.

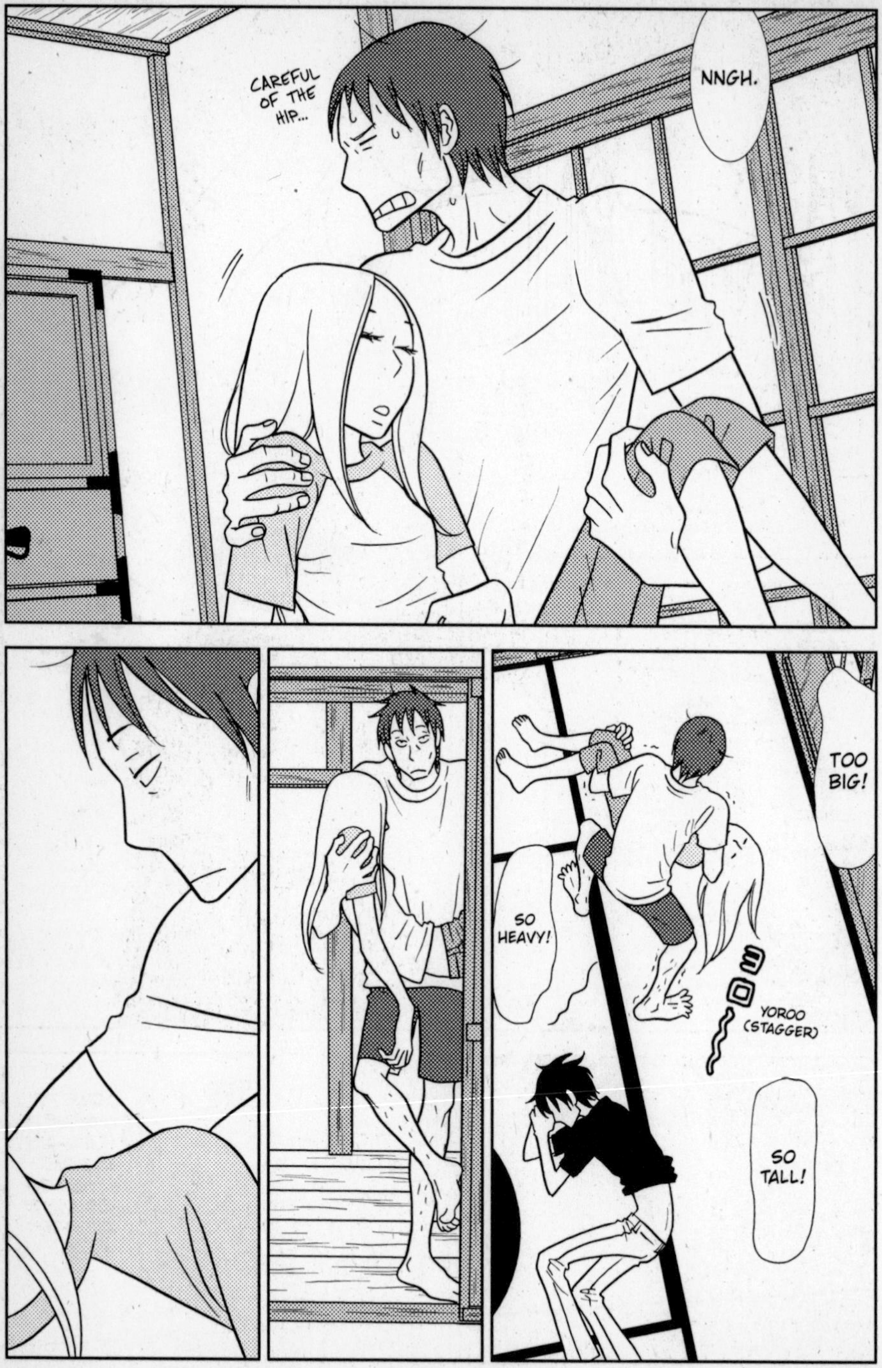
NNGH.
CAREFUL OF THE HIP...
TOO BIG!
SO HEAVY!
ヨロ~
YOROO (STAGGER)
SO TALL!

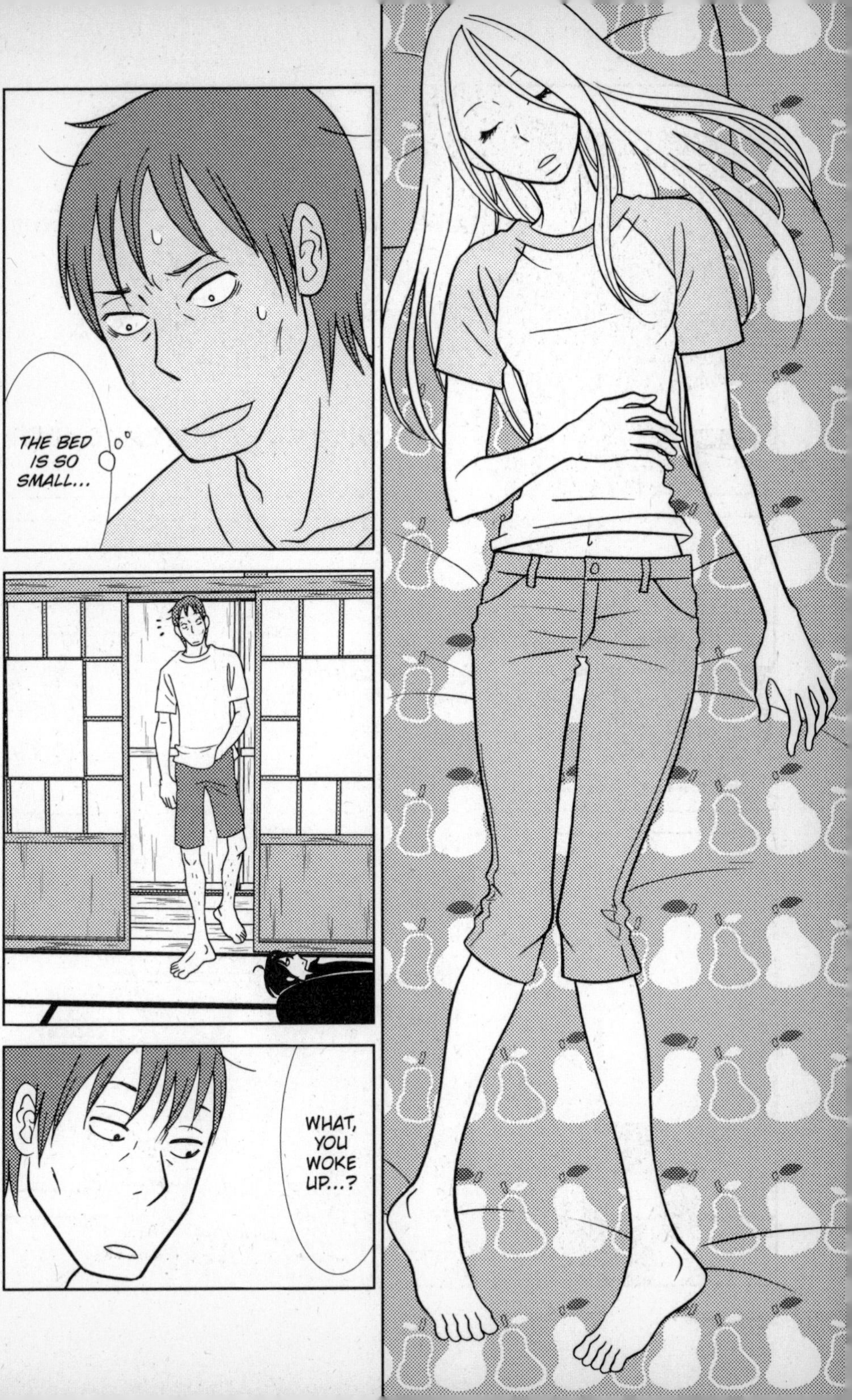
THE BED IS SO SMALL...
WHAT, YOU WOKE UP...?

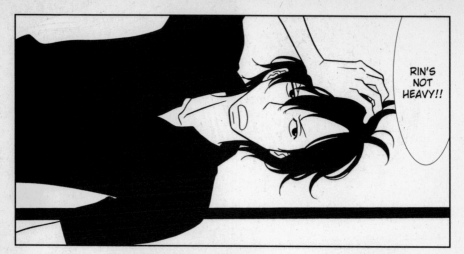

RIN'S NOT HEAVY!!
HA HA...
YOU'RE LIVING IN DREAM-LAND!
EVEN IF SOMEONE IS THIN, IF THEY'RE BIG, THEY END UP FEELING HEAVY.
IT'S HARDER TO CARRY IF THEY'RE TALL TOO
HARDER TO CARRY...?
PLUS...
...YOU'RE LOOKING AT THIS AS A GUY.
I'M LOOKING AT THIS AS A DAD.

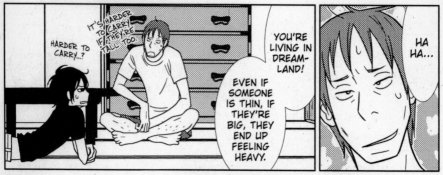

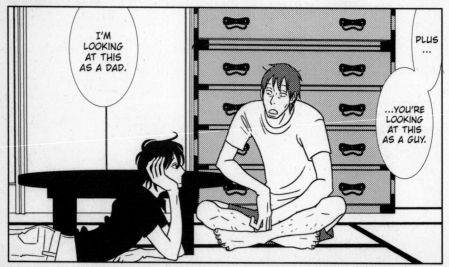

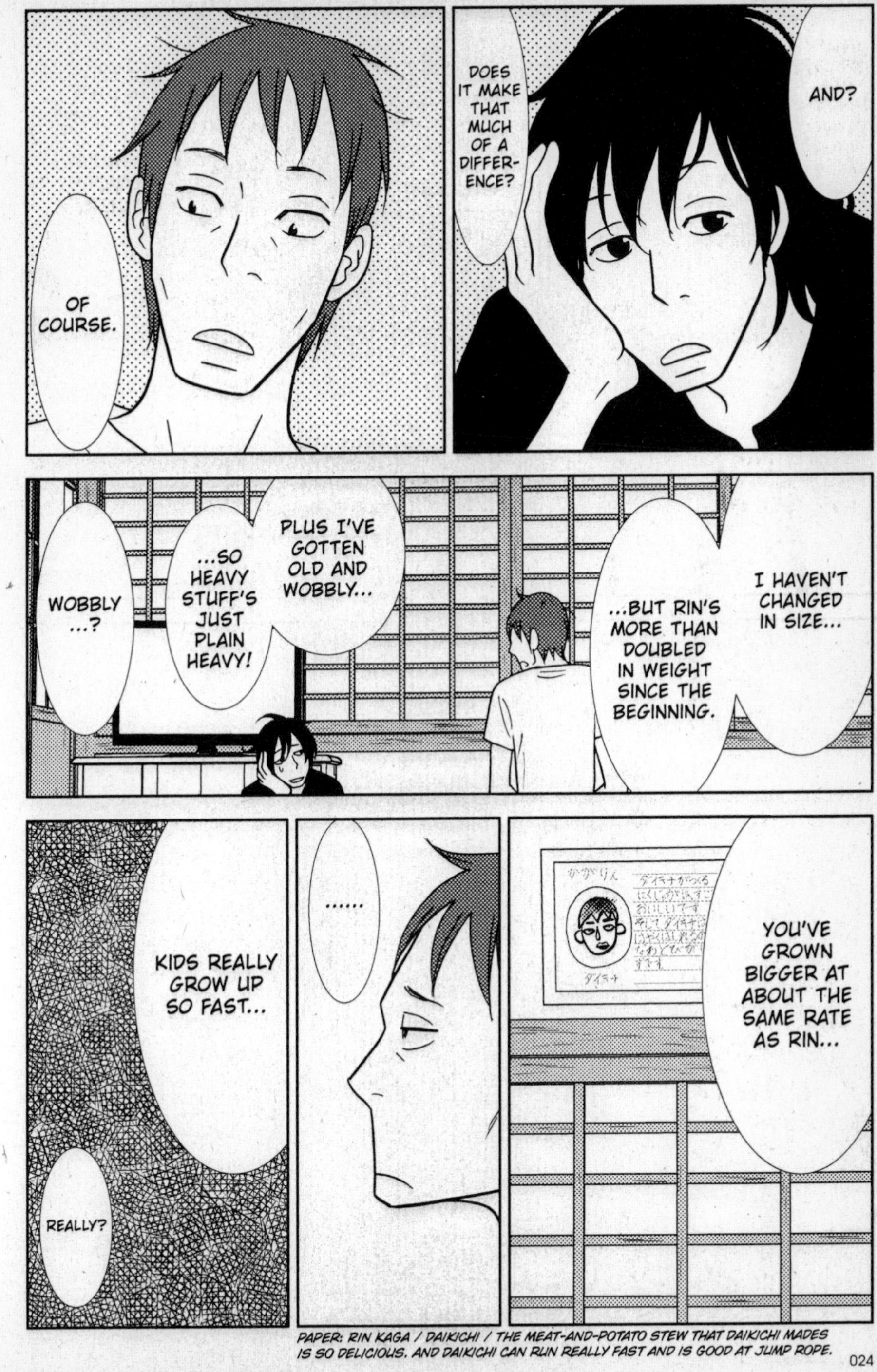
AND?
DOES IT MAKE THAT MUCH OF A DIFFERENCE?
OF COURSE.
I HAVEN'T CHANGED IN SIZE...
...BUT RIN'S MORE THAN DOUBLED IN WEIGHT SINCE THE BEGINNING.
PLUS I'VE GOTTEN OLD AND WOBBLY...
...SO HEAVY STUFF'S JUST PLAIN HEAVY!
WOBBLY...?
YOU'VE GROWN BIGGER AT ABOUT THE SAME RATE AS RIN...
......
KIDS REALLY GROW UP SO FAST...
REALLY?

PAPER: RIN KAGA / DAIKICHI / THE MEAT-AND-POTATO STEW THAT DAIKICHI MADES IS SO DELICIOUS. AND DAIKICHI CAN RUN REALLY FAST AND IS GOOD AT JUMP ROPE.

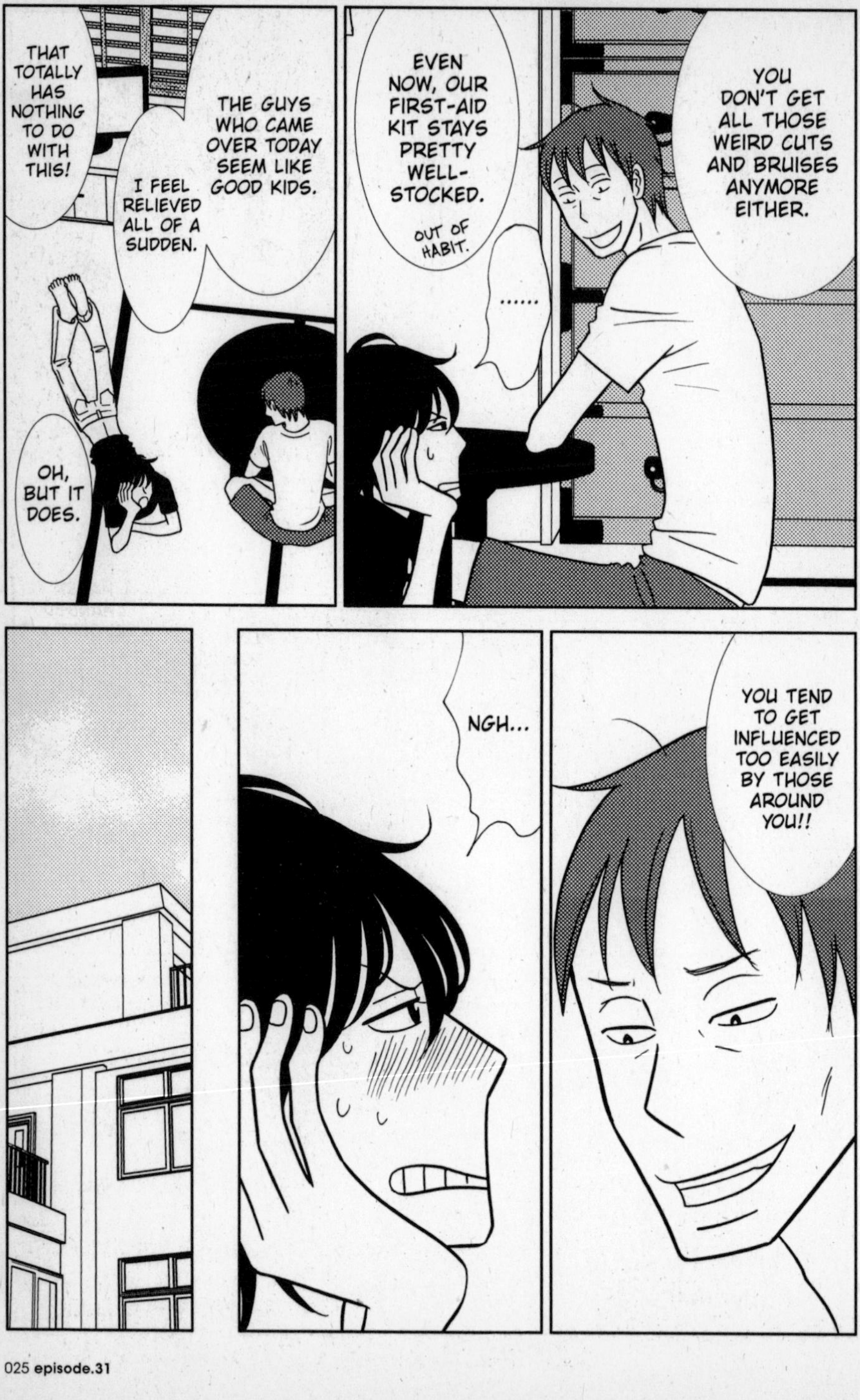
YOU DON'T GET ALL THOSE WEIRD CUTS AND BRUISES ANYMORE EITHER.
EVEN NOW, OUR FIRST-AID KIT STAYS PRETTY WELL-STOCKED.
OUT OF HABIT.
......
THE GUYS WHO CAME OVER TODAY SEEM LIKE GOOD KIDS.
I FEEL RELIEVED ALL OF A SUDDEN.
THAT TOTALLY HAS NOTHING TO DO WITH THIS!
OH, BUT IT DOES.
YOU TEND TO GET INFLUENCED TOO EASILY BY THOSE AROUND YOU!!
NGH...

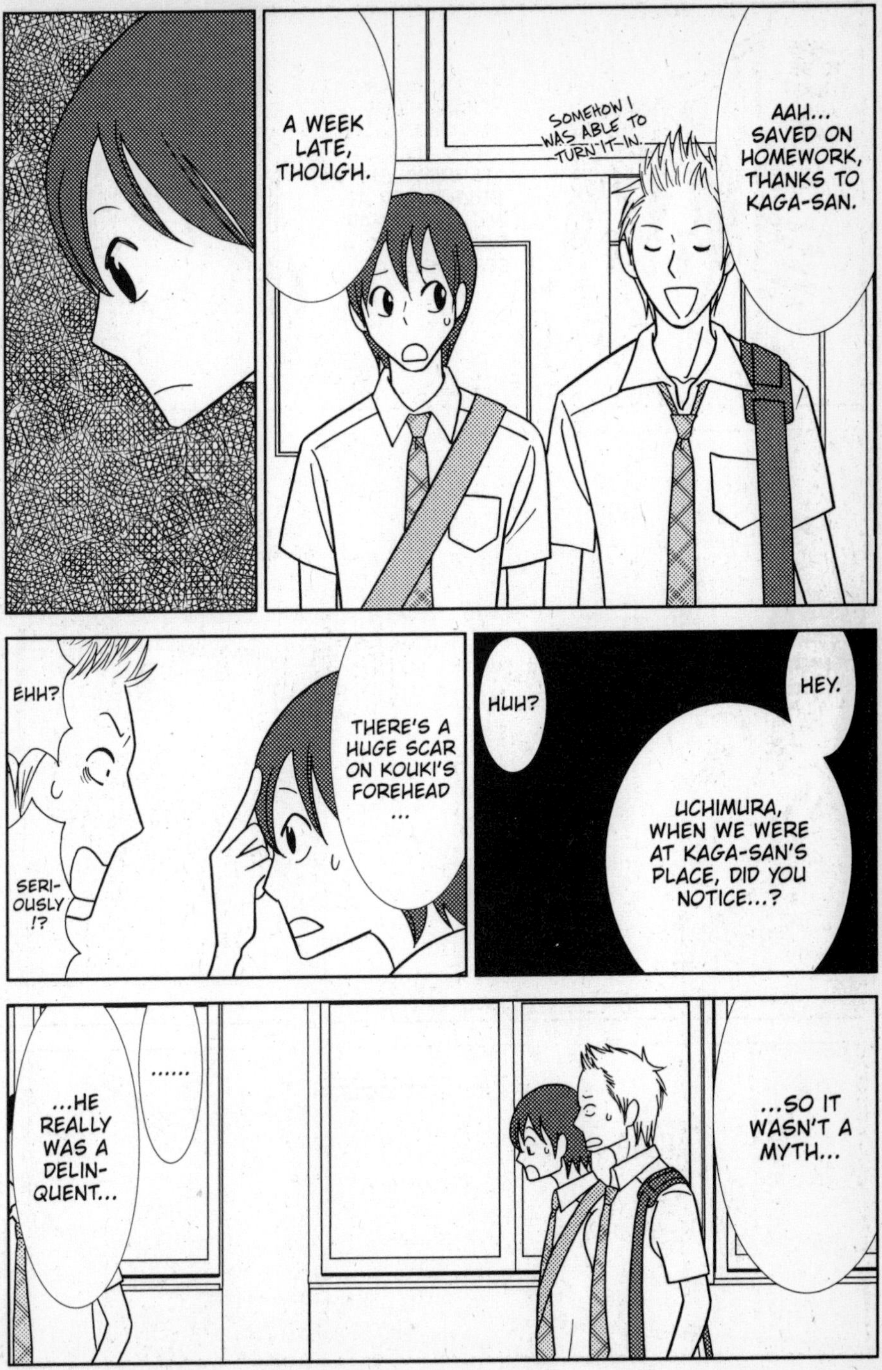
AAH... SAVED ON HOMEWORK, THANKS TO KAGA-SAN.
SOMEHOW I WAS ABLE TO TURN IT IN.
A WEEK LATE, THOUGH.
HEY.
HUH?
UCHIMURA, WHEN WE WERE AT KAGA-SAN'S PLACE, DID YOU NOTICE...?
THERE'S A HUGE SCAR ON KOUKI'S FOREHEAD ...
EHH?
SERI-OUSLY !?
...SO IT WASN'T A MYTH...
......
...HE REALLY WAS A DELIN-QUENT...

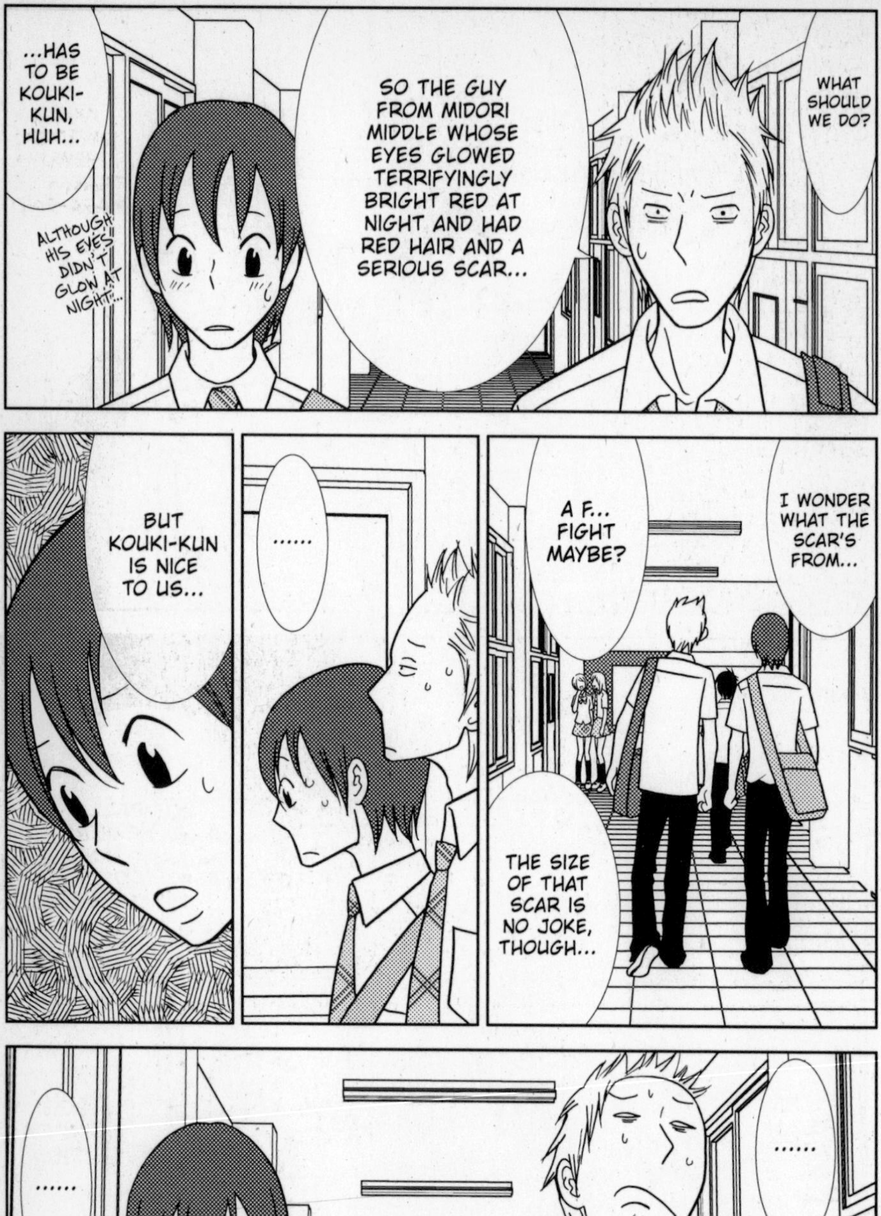
WHAT SHOULD WE DO?
SO THE GUY FROM MIDORI MIDDLE WHOSE EYES GLOWED TERRIFYINGLY BRIGHT RED AT NIGHT AND HAD RED HAIR AND A SERIOUS SCAR...
...HAS TO BE KOUKI-KUN, HUH...
ALTHOUGH HIS EYES DIDN'T GLOW AT NIGHT...
I WONDER WHAT THE SCAR'S FROM...
A F... FIGHT MAYBE?
THE SIZE OF THAT SCAR IS NO JOKE, THOUGH...
......
BUT KOUKI-KUN IS NICE TO US...
......
......

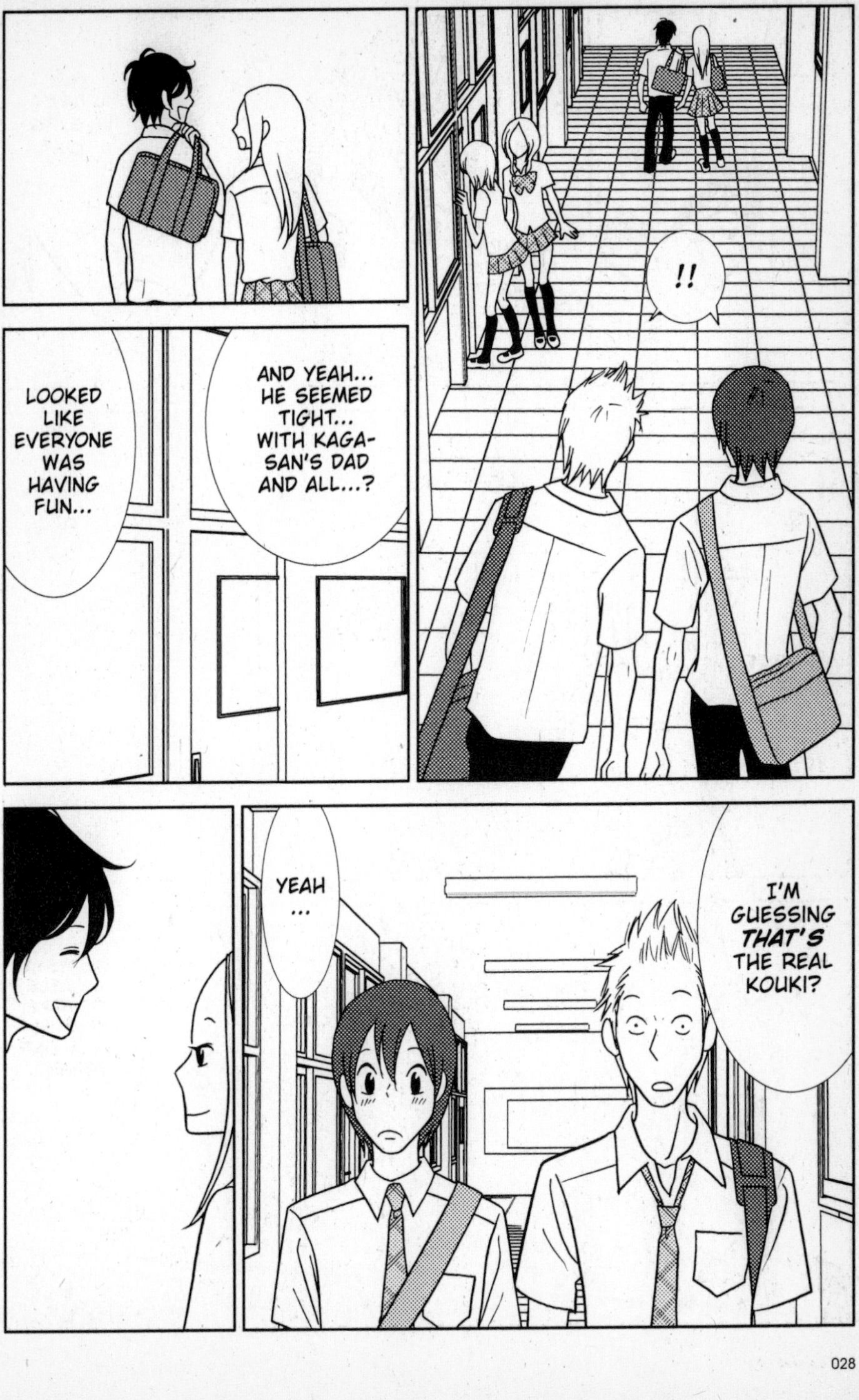
!!
AND YEAH... HE SEEMED TIGHT... WITH KAGA-SAN'S DAD AND ALL...?
LOOKED LIKE EVERYONE WAS HAVING FUN...
I'M GUESSING THAT'S THE REAL KOUKI?
YEAH ...

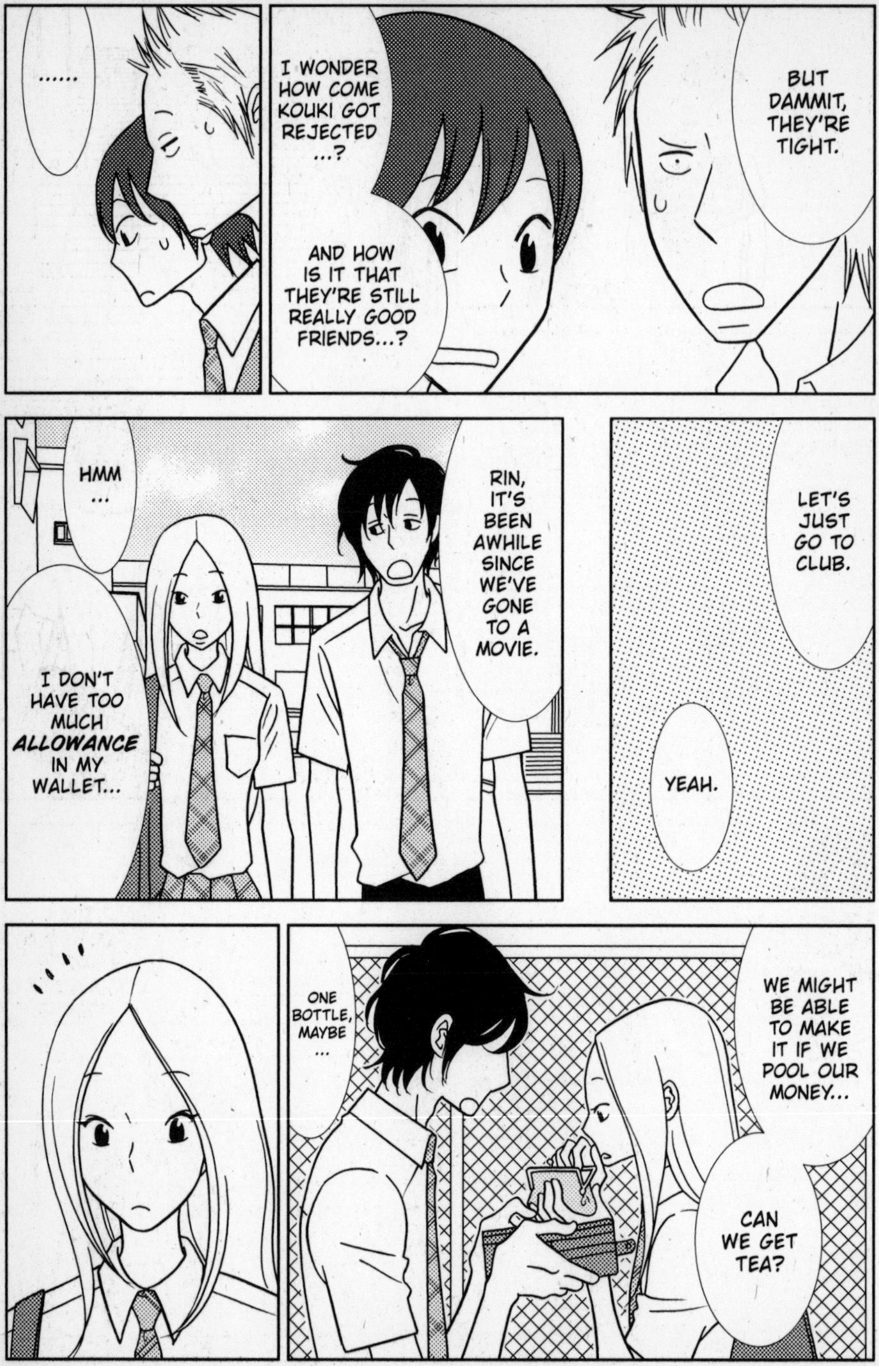
BUT DAMMIT, THEY'RE TIGHT.
I WONDER HOW COME KOUKI GOT REJECTED ...?
AND HOW IS IT THAT THEY'RE STILL REALLY GOOD FRIENDS...?
......
LET'S JUST GO TO CLUB.
YEAH.
RIN, IT'S BEEN AWHILE SINCE WE'VE GONE TO A MOVIE.
HMM ...
I DON'T HAVE TOO MUCH ***ALLOWANCE*** IN MY WALLET...
WE MIGHT BE ABLE TO MAKE IT IF WE POOL OUR MONEY...
CAN WE GET TEA?
ONE BOTTLE, MAYBE ...

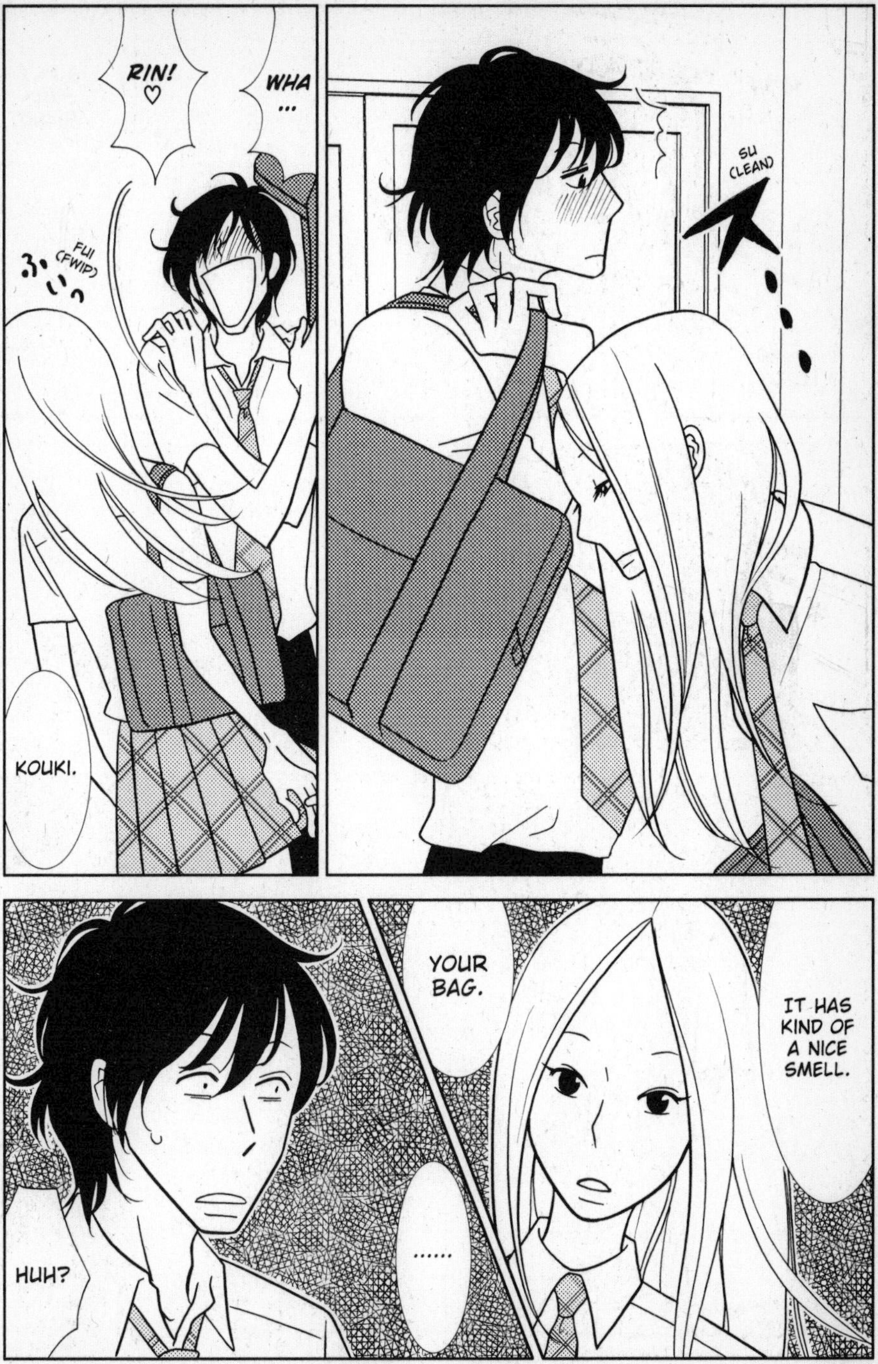
SU (LEAN)
WHA ...
RIN! ♡
ふぃ
FUI (FWIP)
KOUKI.
IT HAS KIND OF A NICE SMELL.
YOUR BAG.
......
HUH?

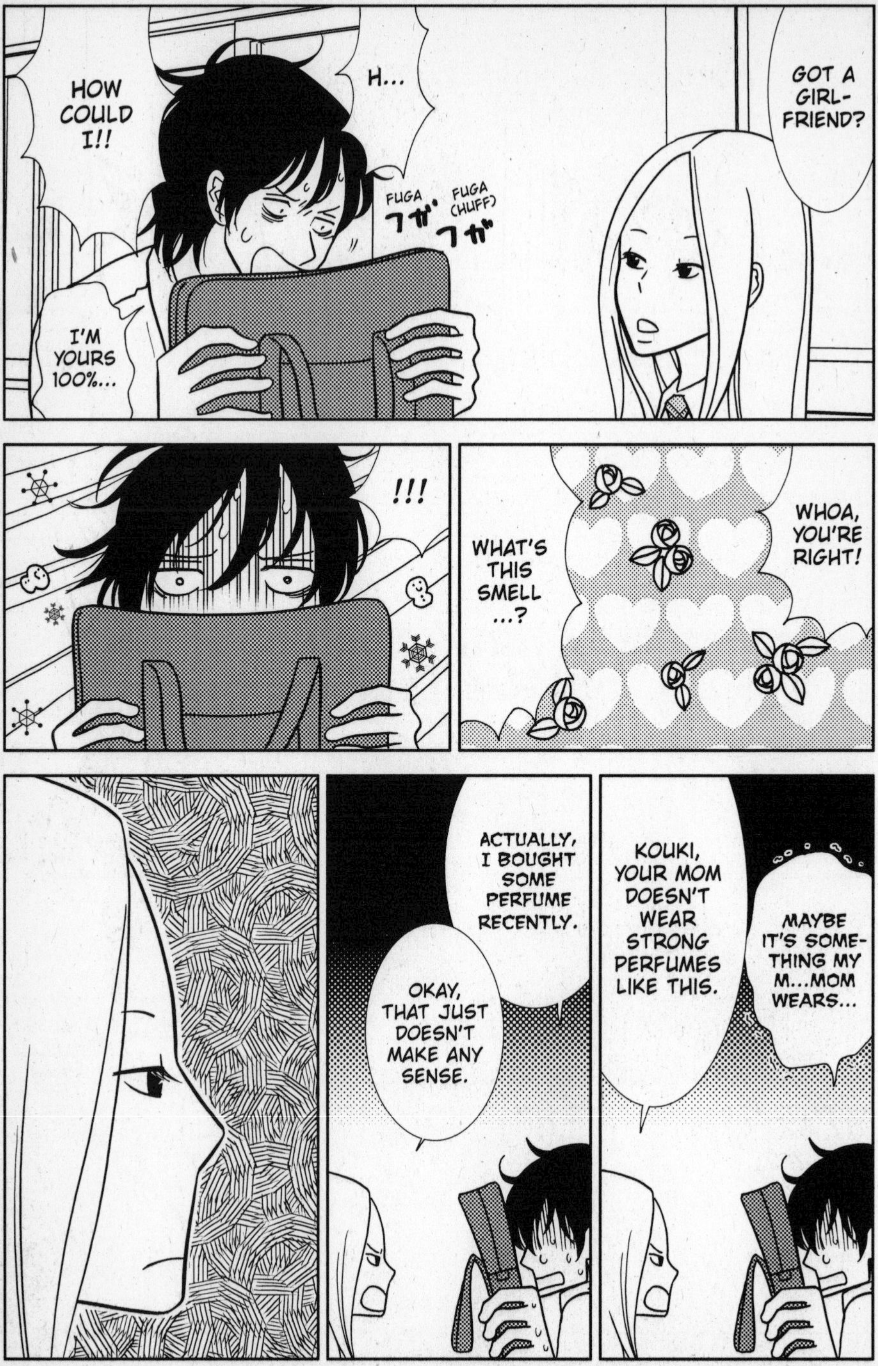
GOT A GIRL-FRIEND?
H...
FUGA フガ FUGA (HUFF) フガ
HOW COULD I!!
I'M YOURS 100%...
WHOA, YOU'RE RIGHT!
WHAT'S THIS SMELL ...?
!!!
MAYBE IT'S SOME-THING MY M...MOM WEARS...
KOUKI, YOUR MOM DOESN'T WEAR STRONG PERFUMES LIKE THIS.
ACTUALLY, I BOUGHT SOME PERFUME RECENTLY.
OKAY, THAT JUST DOESN'T MAKE ANY SENSE.

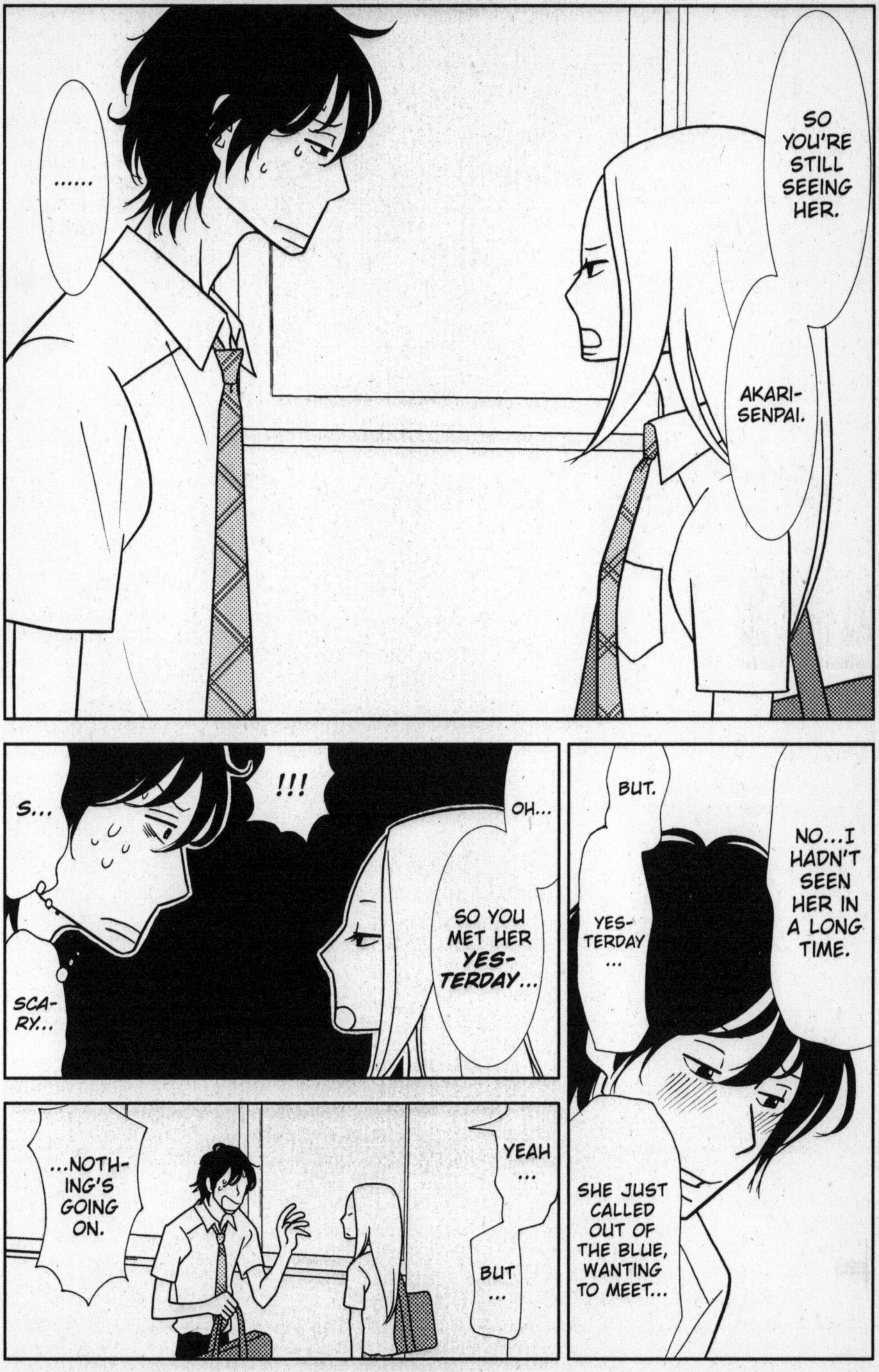
SO YOU'RE STILL SEEING HER.
AKARI-SENPAI.
......
NO...I HADN'T SEEN HER IN A LONG TIME.
BUT.
YES-TERDAY...
SHE JUST CALLED OUT OF THE BLUE, WANTING TO MEET...
OH...
SO YOU MET HER *YES-TERDAY*...
!!!
S...
SCA-RY...
YEAH...
BUT...
...NOTH-ING'S GOING ON.

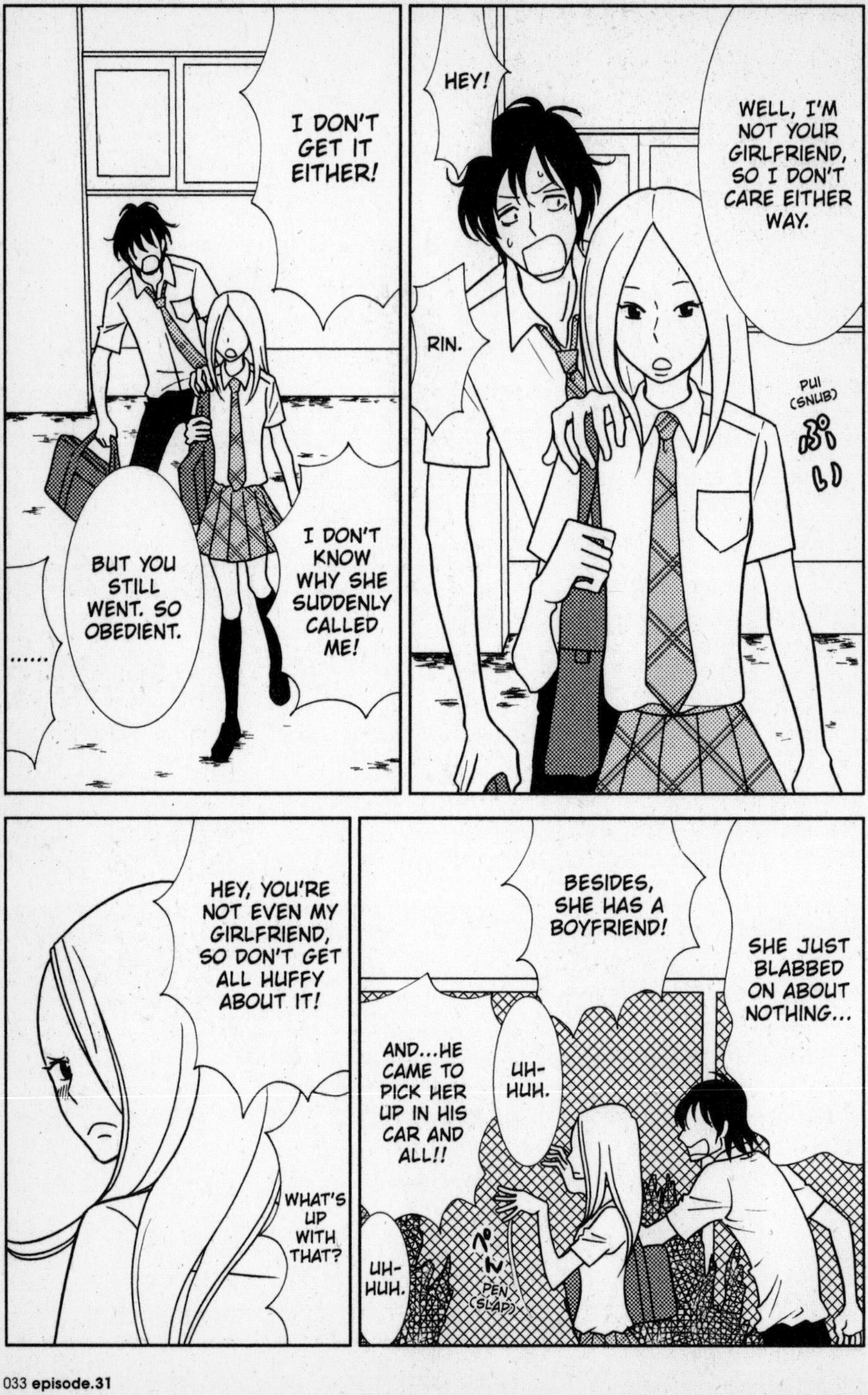
WELL, I'M NOT YOUR GIRLFRIEND, SO I DON'T CARE EITHER WAY.
HEY!
PUI (SNUB)
ぷい
RIN.
I DON'T GET IT EITHER!
I DON'T KNOW WHY SHE SUDDENLY CALLED ME!
BUT YOU STILL WENT. SO OBEDIENT.
......
SHE JUST BLABBED ON ABOUT NOTHING...
BESIDES, SHE HAS A BOYFRIEND!
UH-HUH.
AND...HE CAME TO PICK HER UP IN HIS CAR AND ALL!!
ぺん
PEN (SLAP)
UH-HUH.
HEY, YOU'RE NOT EVEN MY GIRLFRIEND, SO DON'T GET ALL HUFFY ABOUT IT!
WHAT'S UP WITH THAT?

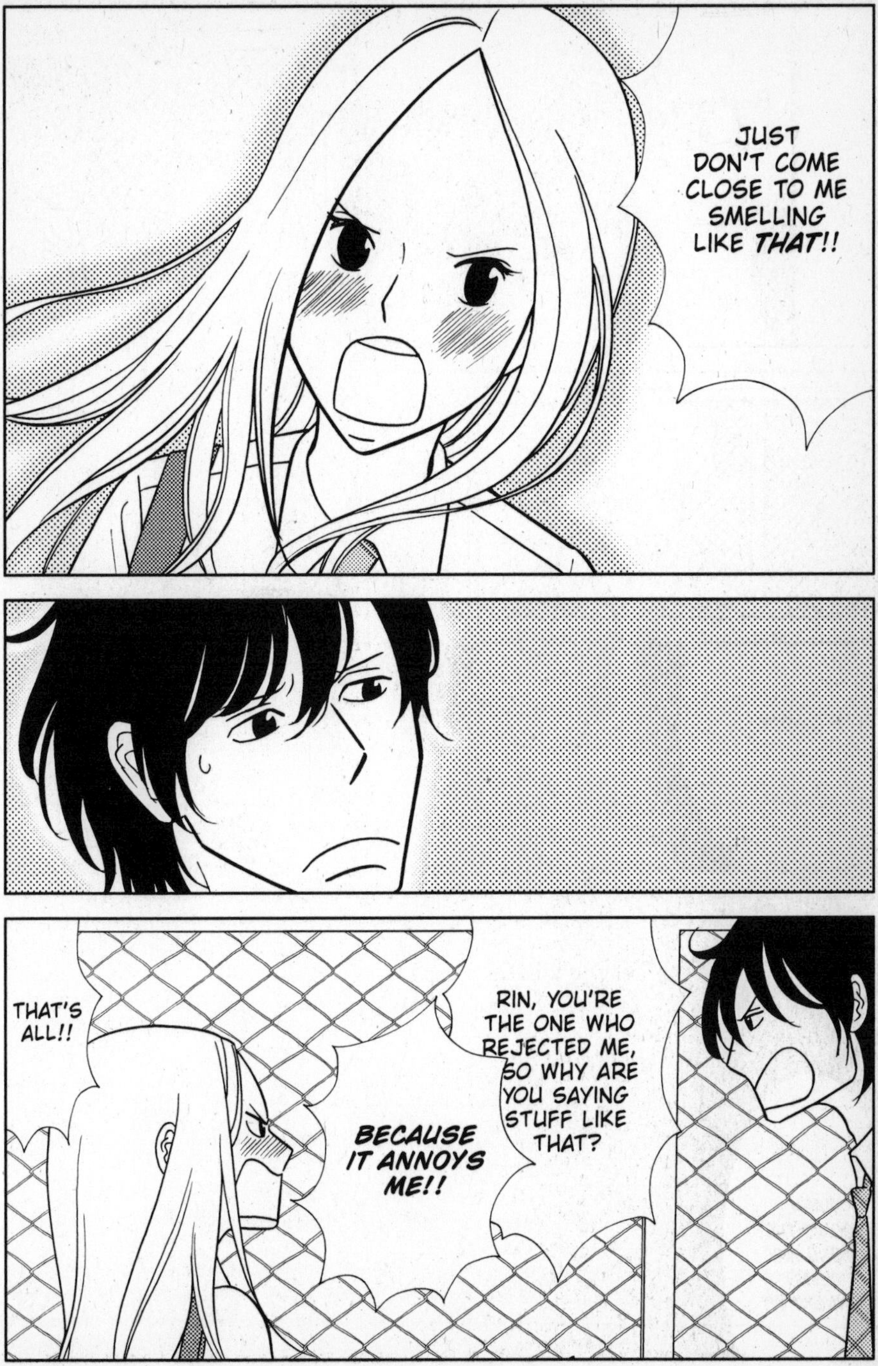
JUST DON'T COME CLOSE TO ME SMELLING LIKE *THAT*!!
RIN, YOU'RE THE ONE WHO REJECTED ME, SO WHY ARE YOU SAYING STUFF LIKE THAT?
BECAUSE IT ANNOYS ME!!
THAT'S ALL!!

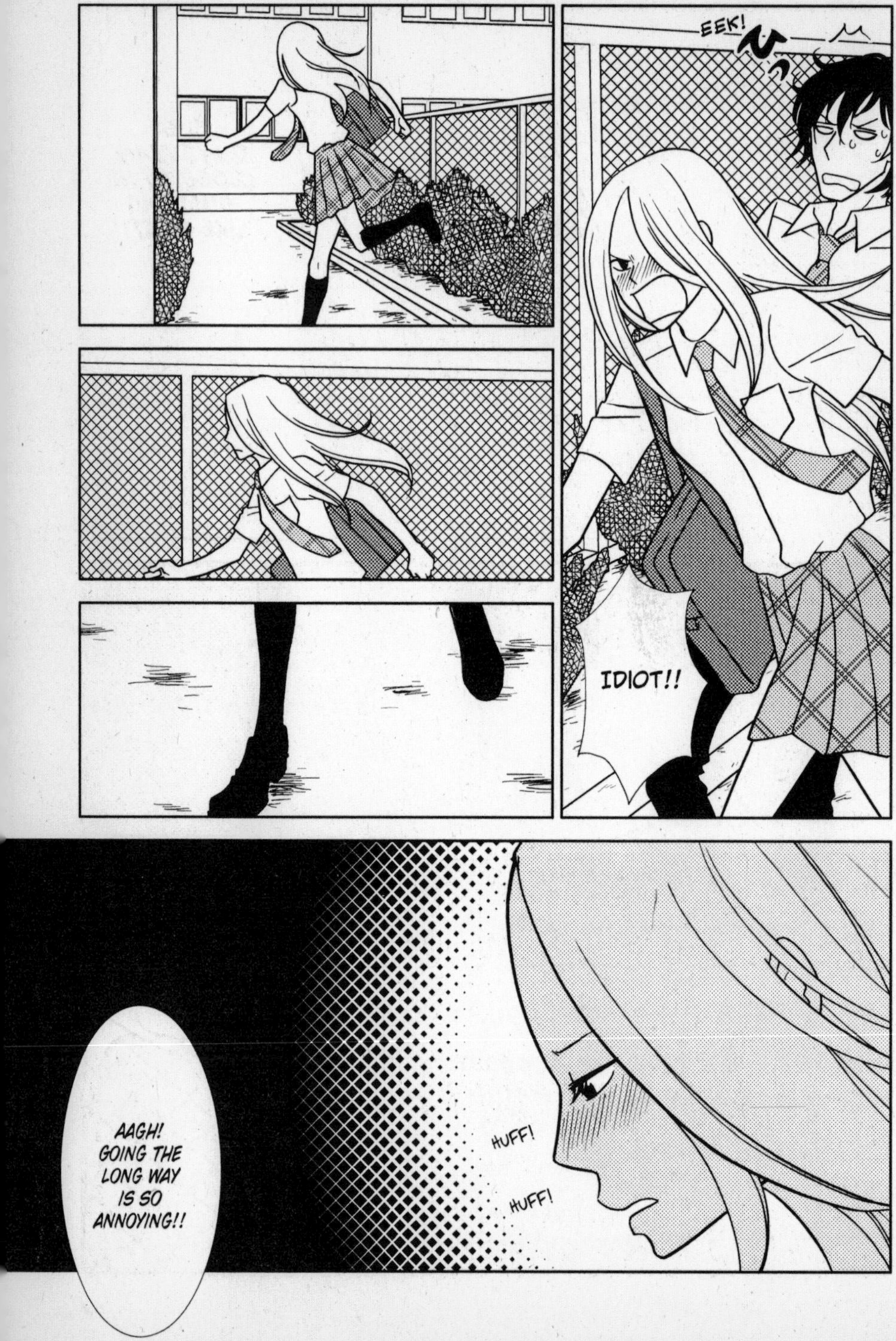
EEK!
IDIOT!!
HUFF!
HUFF!
AAGH! GOING THE LONG WAY IS SO ANNOYING!!

SIGN: MUSASHIBO PUBLIC MIDORI JUNIOR HIGH SCHOOL

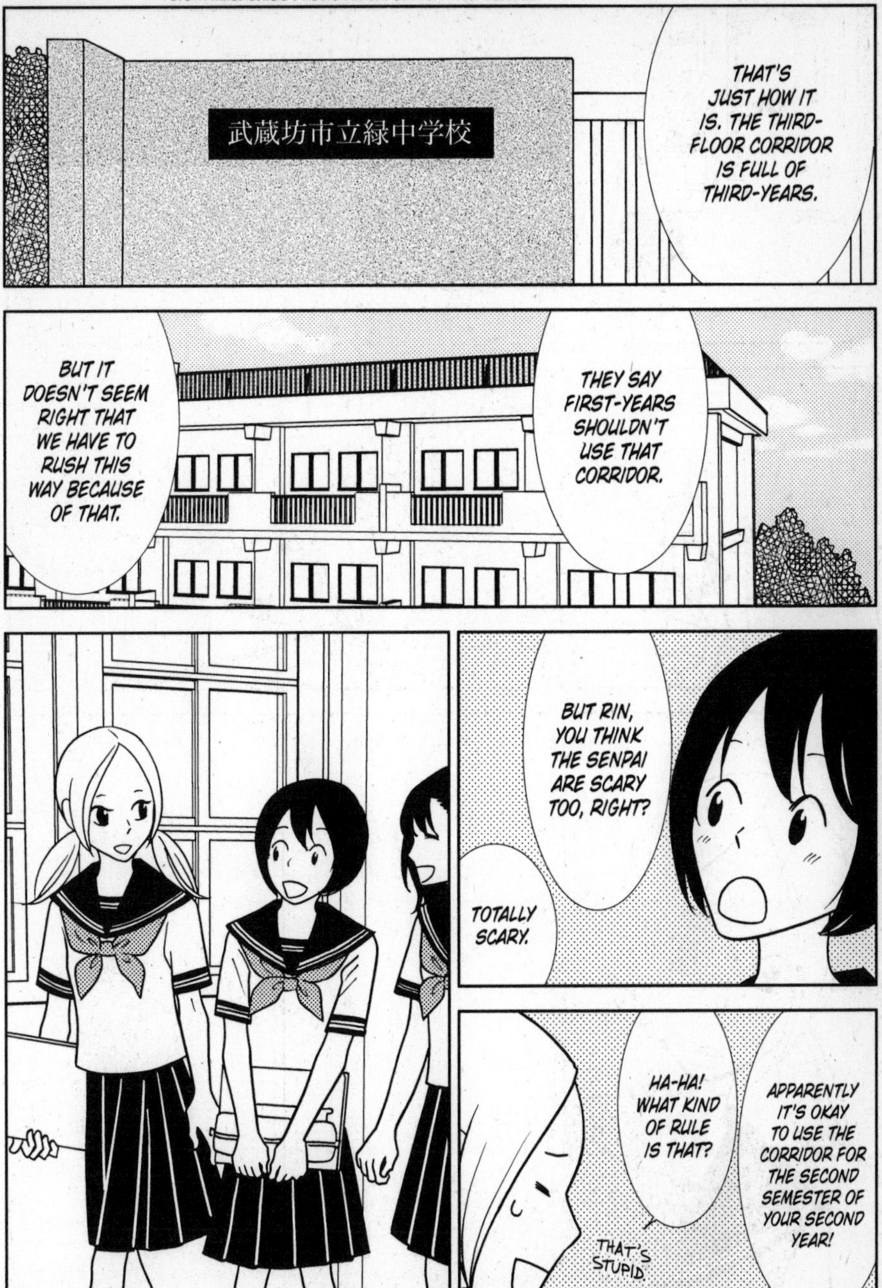
武蔵坊市立緑中学校
THAT'S JUST HOW IT IS. THE THIRD-FLOOR CORRIDOR IS FULL OF THIRD-YEARS.
THEY SAY FIRST-YEARS SHOULDN'T USE THAT CORRIDOR.
BUT IT DOESN'T SEEM RIGHT THAT WE HAVE TO RUSH THIS WAY BECAUSE OF THAT.
BUT RIN, YOU THINK THE SENPAI ARE SCARY TOO, RIGHT?
TOTALLY SCARY.
APPARENTLY IT'S OKAY TO USE THE CORRIDOR FOR THE SECOND SEMESTER OF YOUR SECOND YEAR!
HA-HA! WHAT KIND OF RULE IS THAT?
THAT'S STUPID.

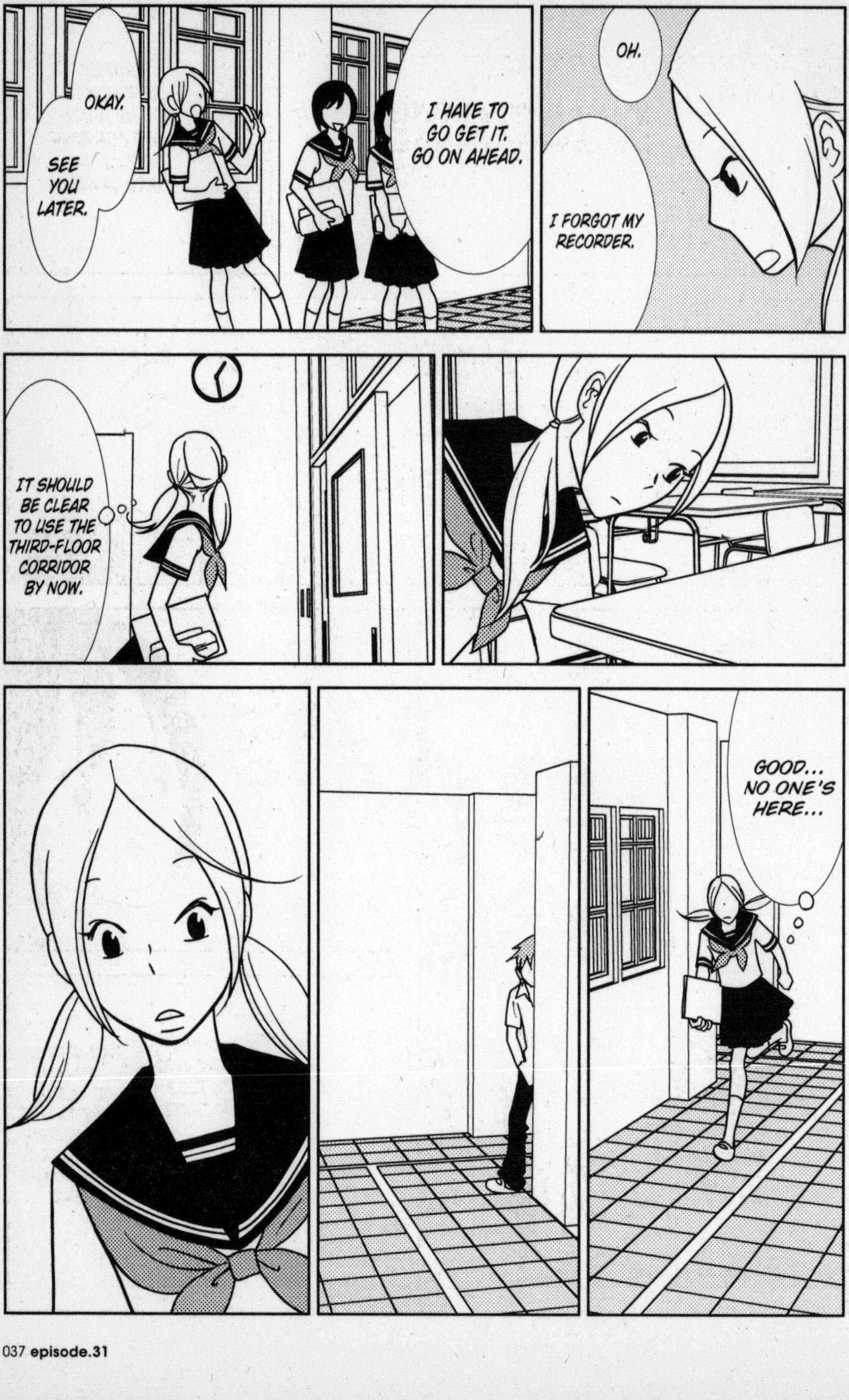
OH.
I FORGOT MY RECORDER.
I HAVE TO GO GET IT. GO ON AHEAD.
OKAY.
SEE YOU LATER.
IT SHOULD BE CLEAR TO USE THE THIRD-FLOOR CORRIDOR BY NOW.
GOOD... NO ONE'S HERE...

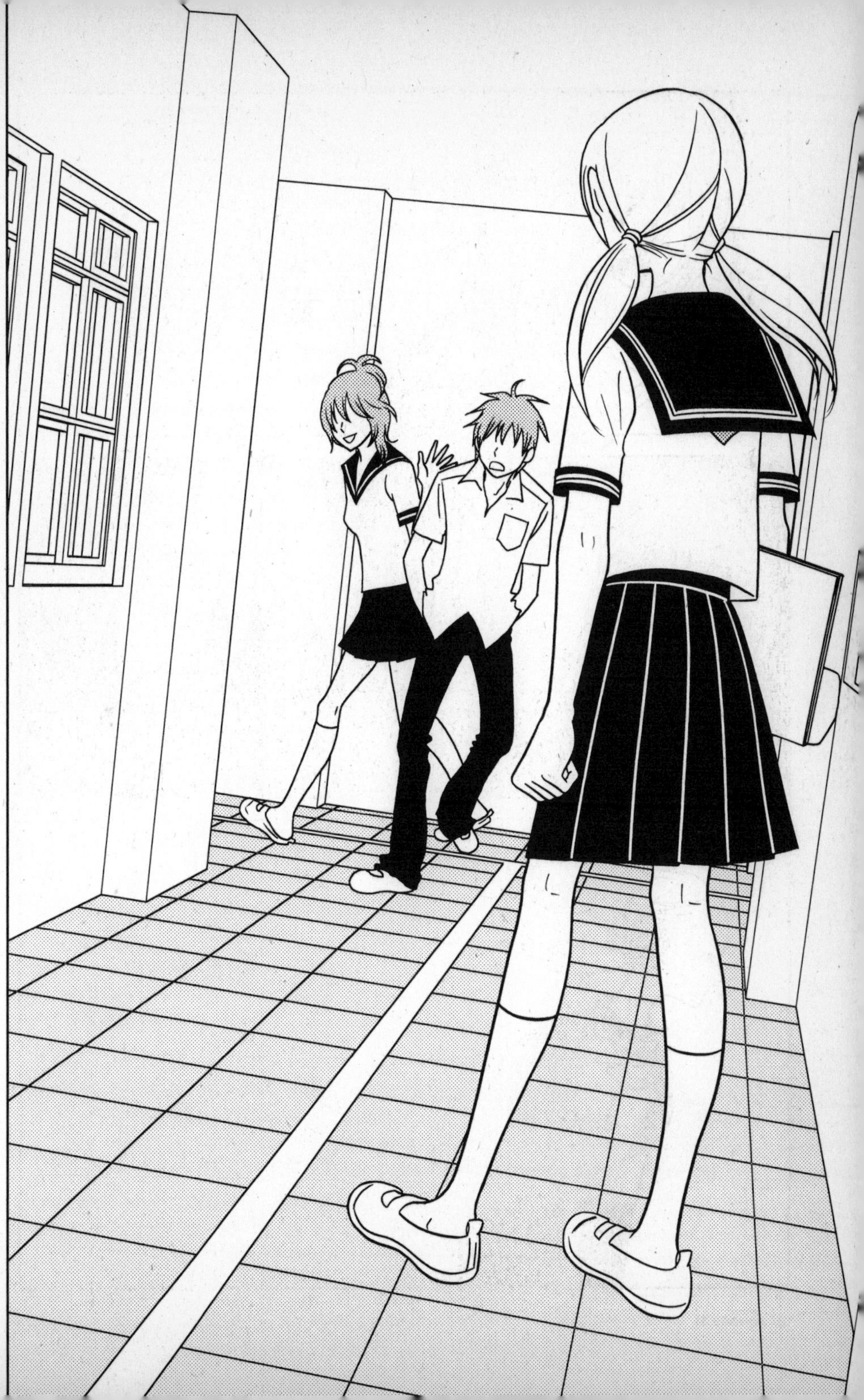

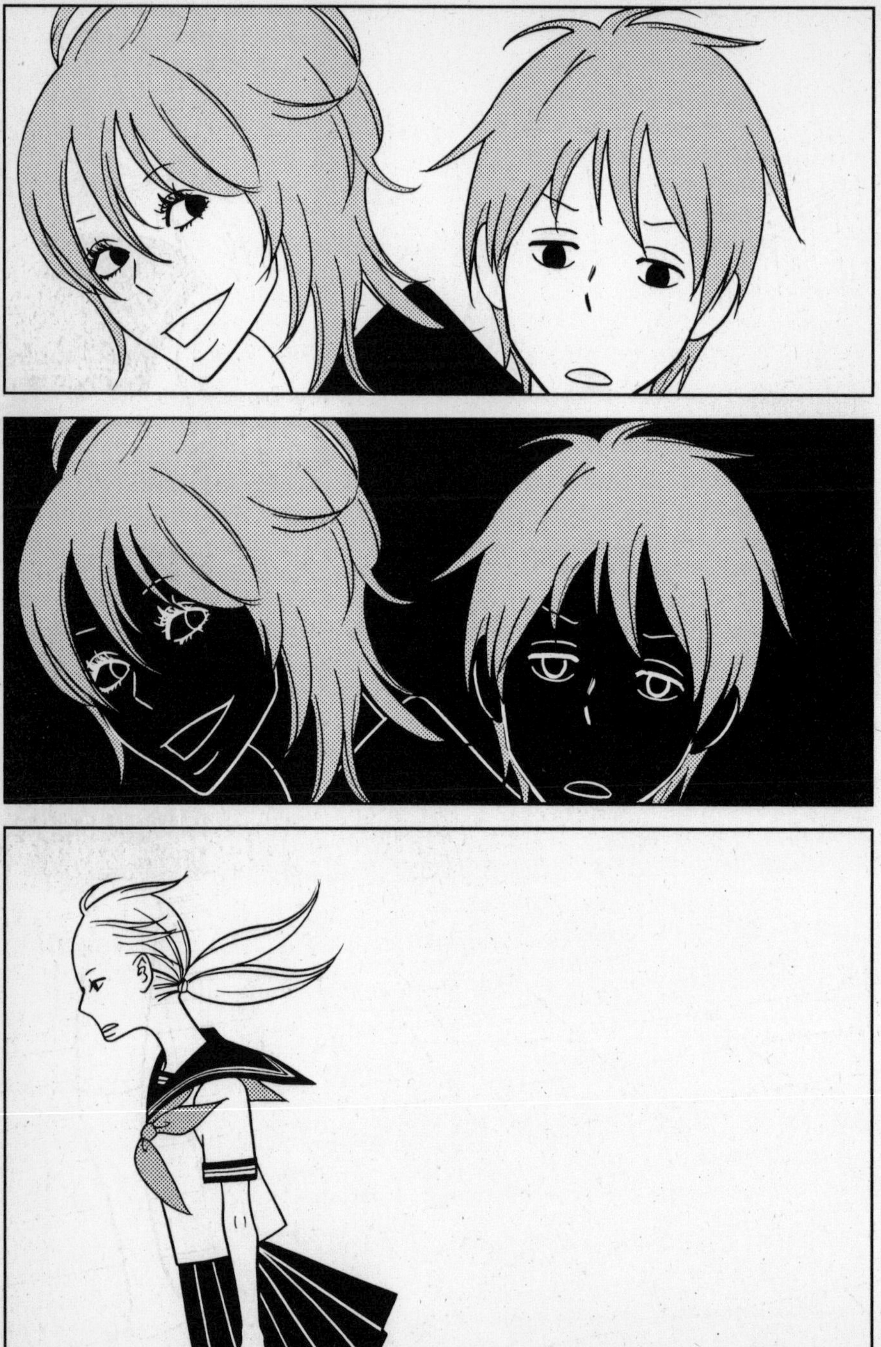

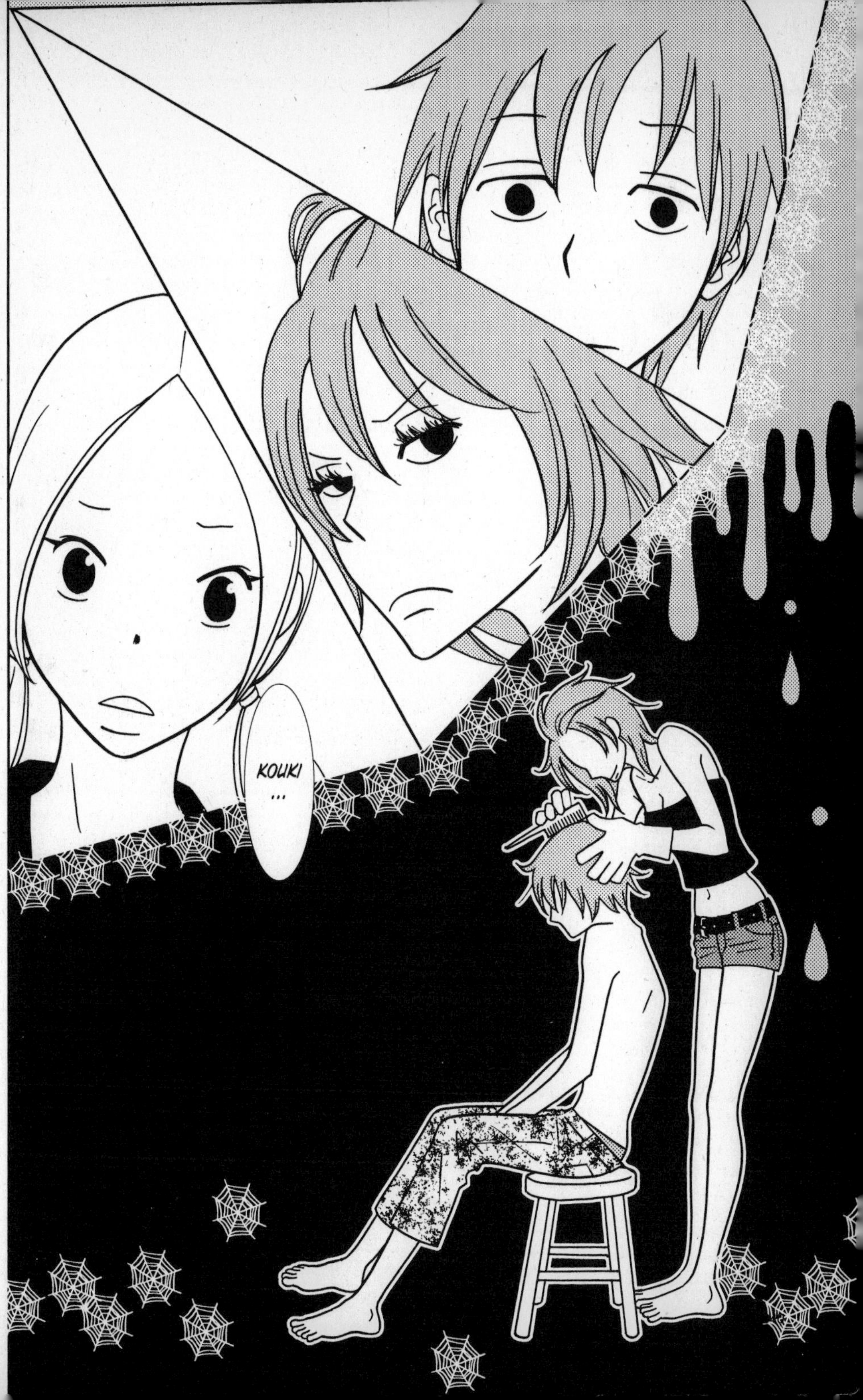
KOUKI ...

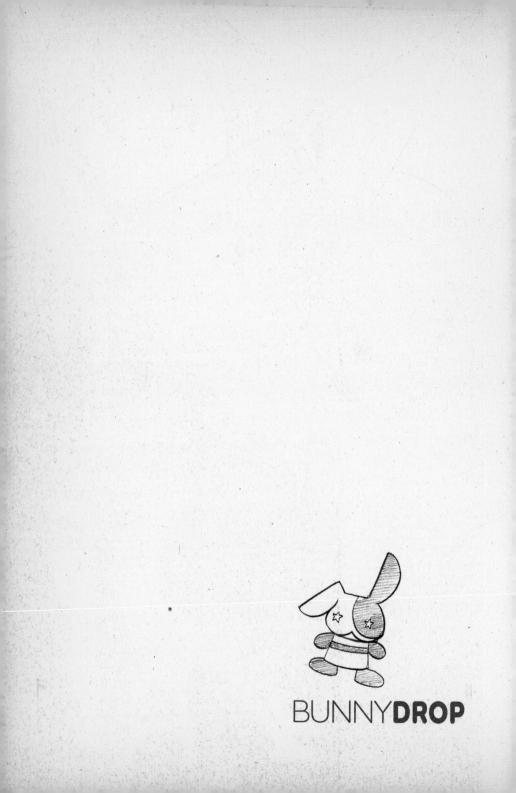

BUNNY**DROP**

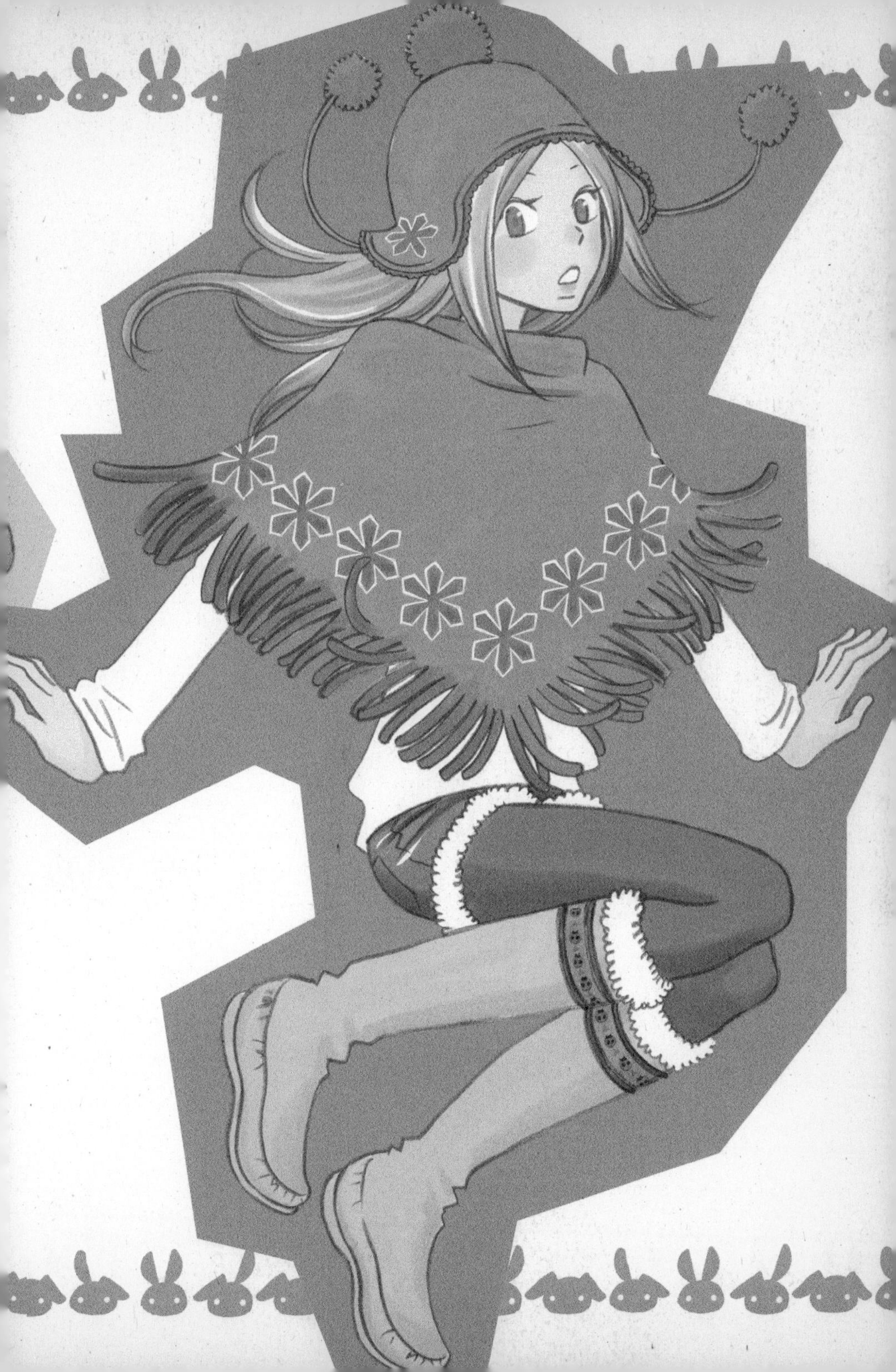

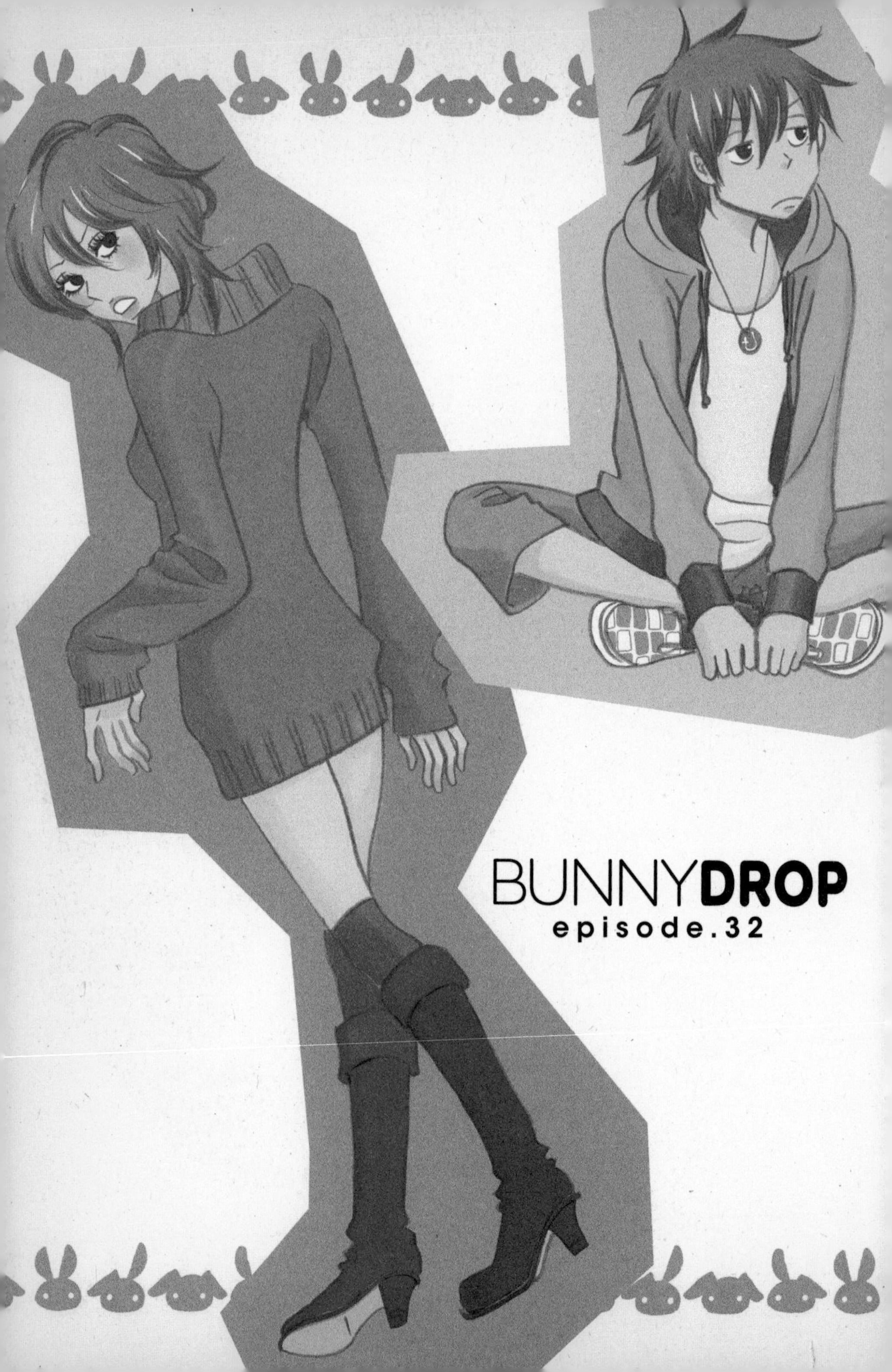

BUNNY**DROP**
episode.32

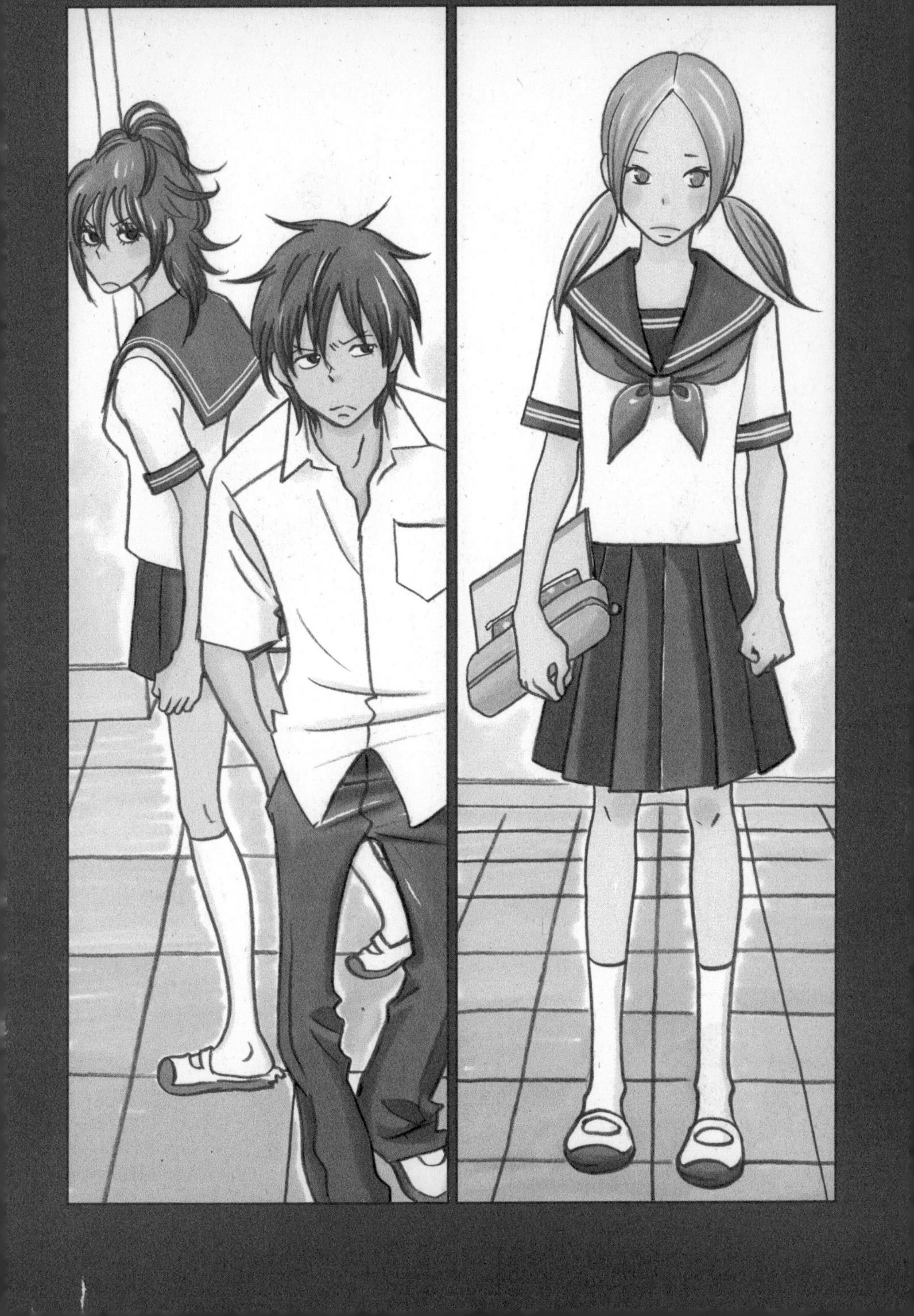

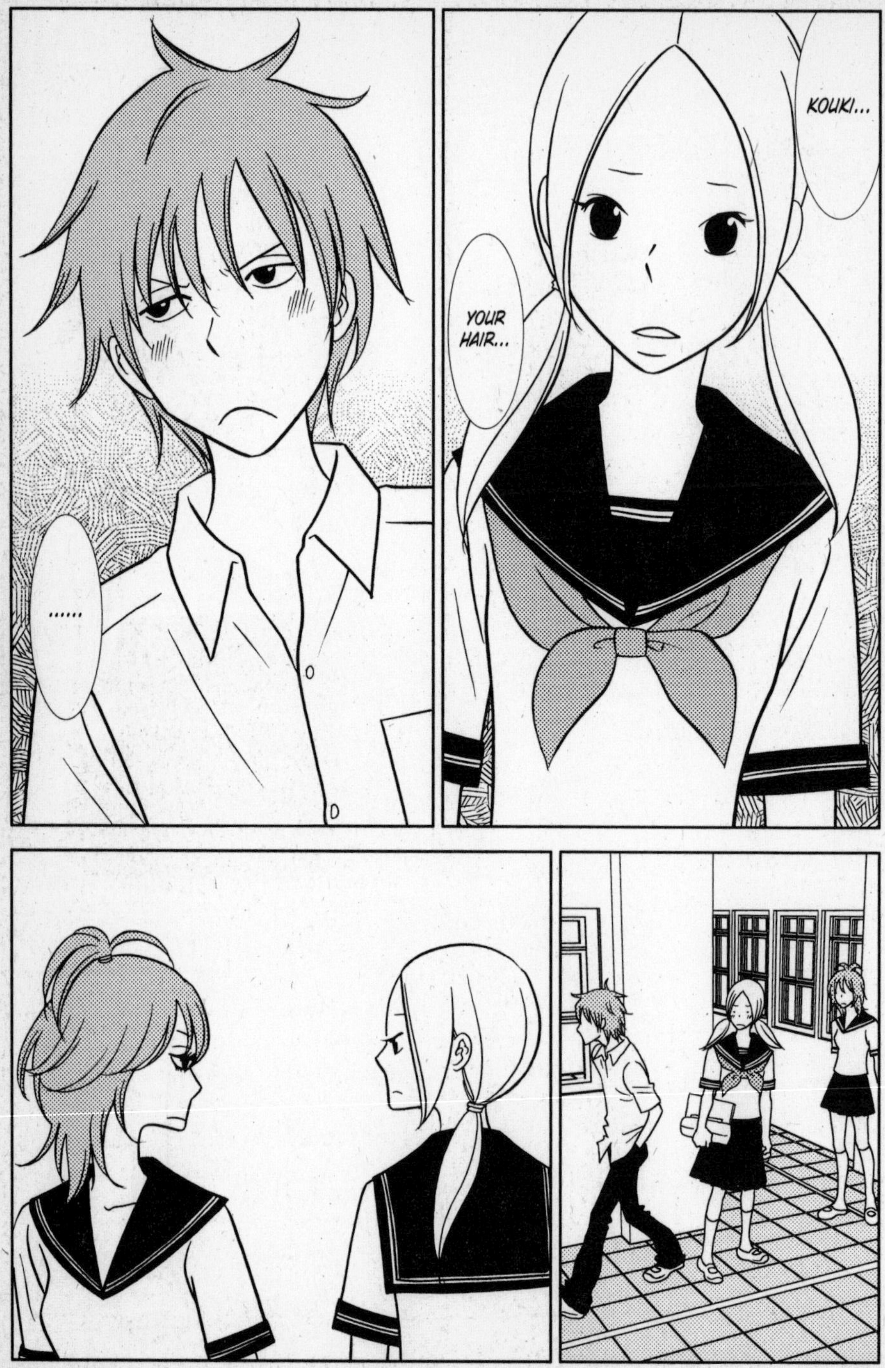
KOUKI...
YOUR HAIR...
......

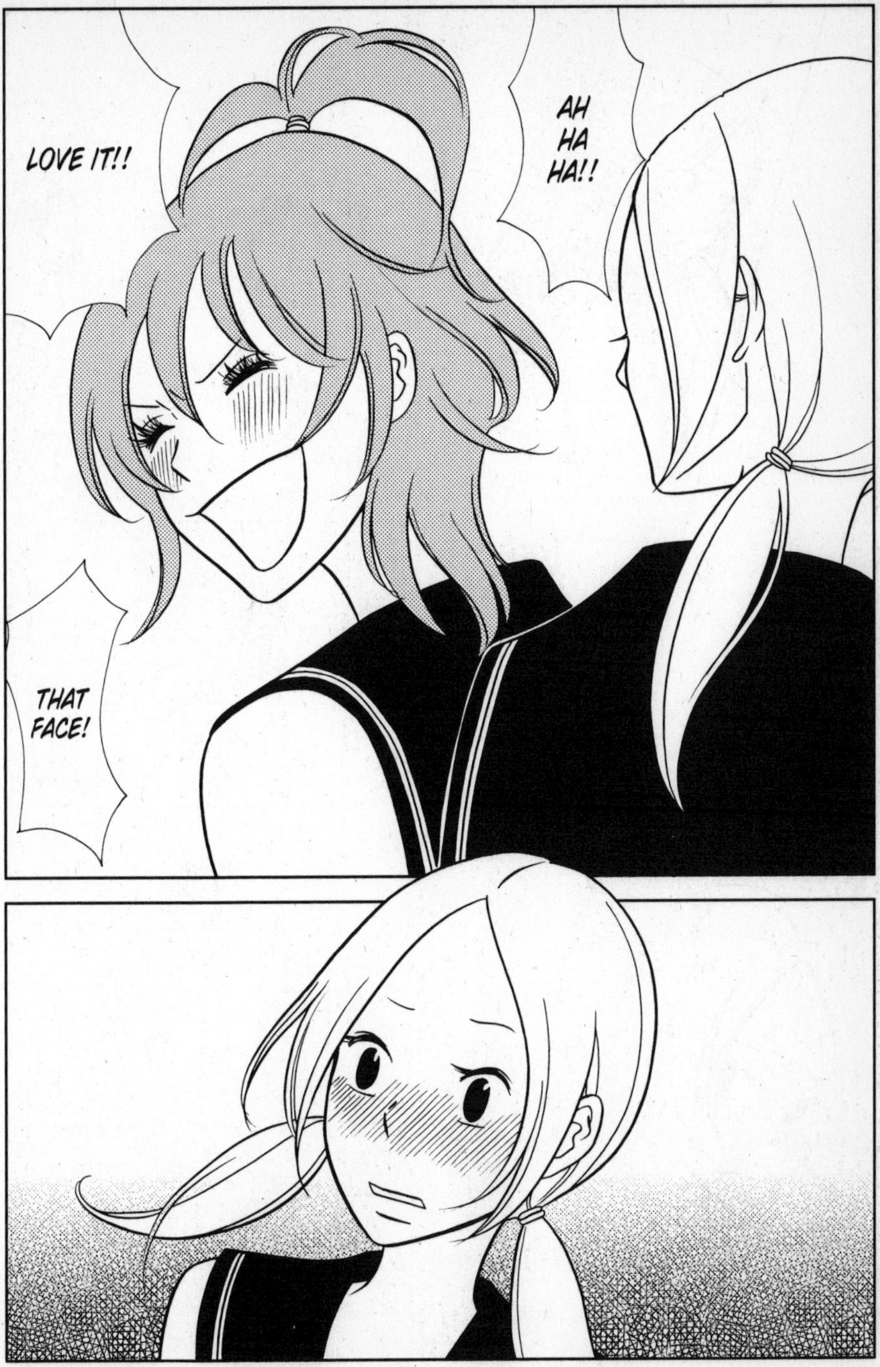
AH HA HA!!
LOVE IT!!
THAT FACE!

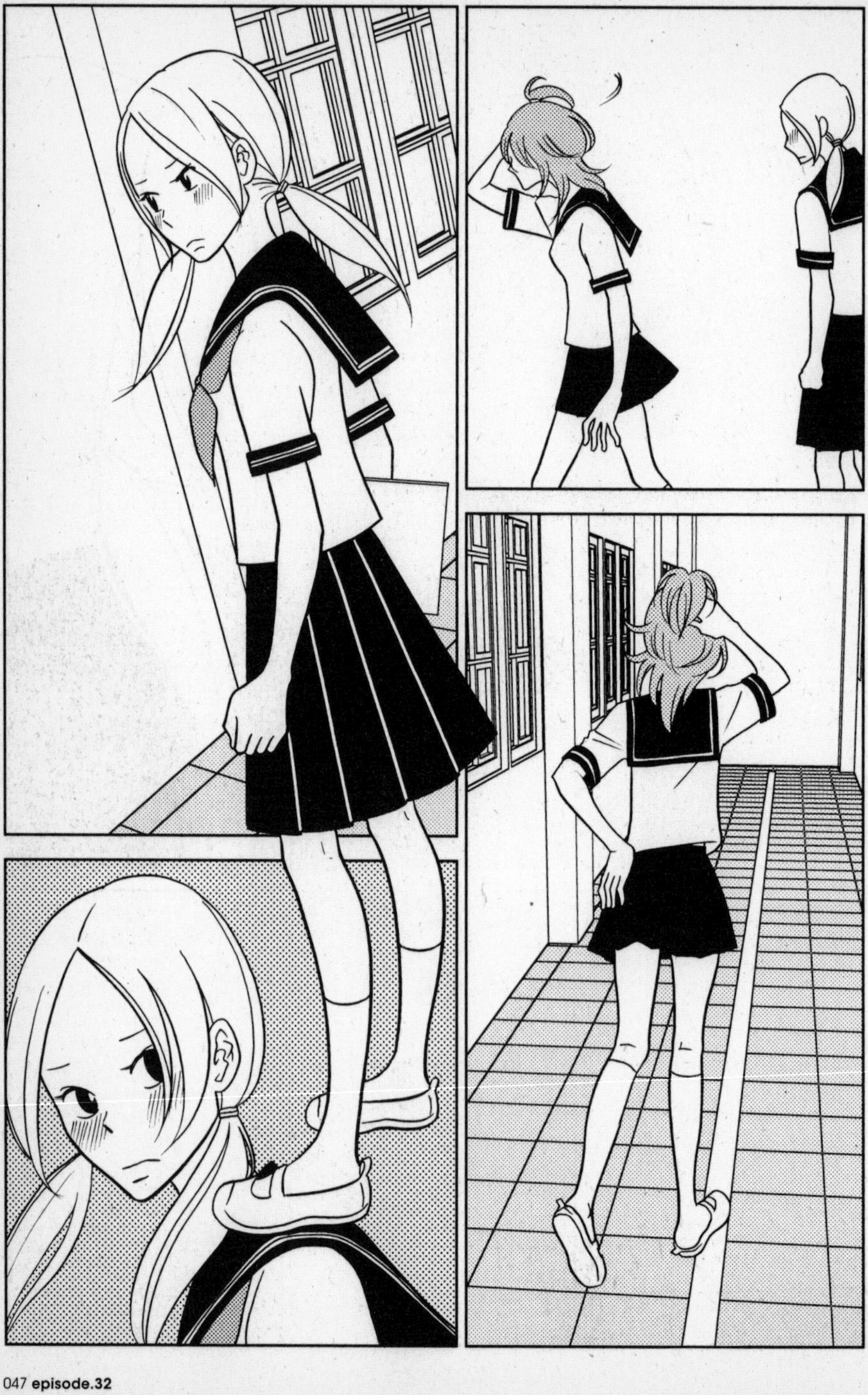

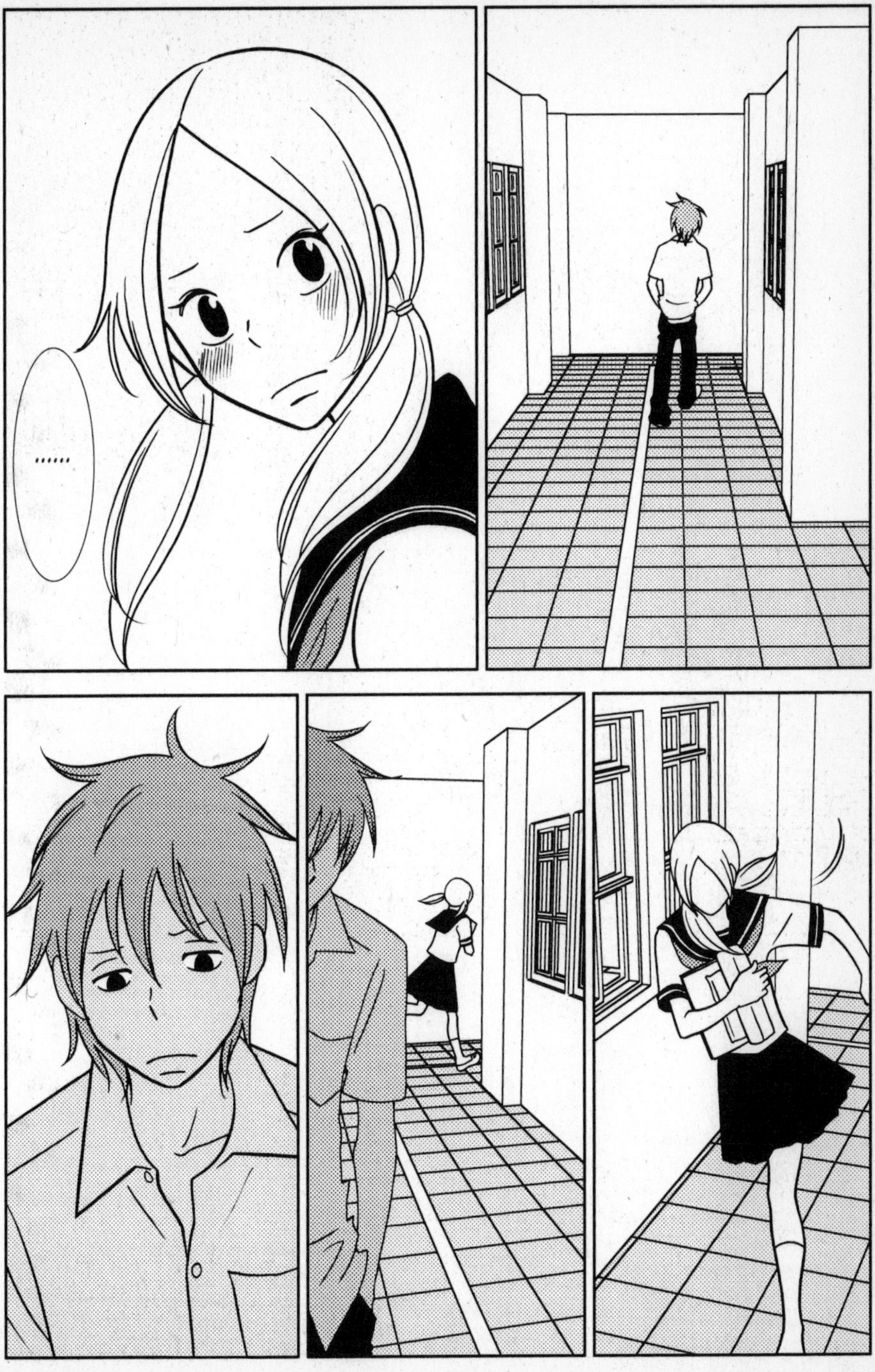
......

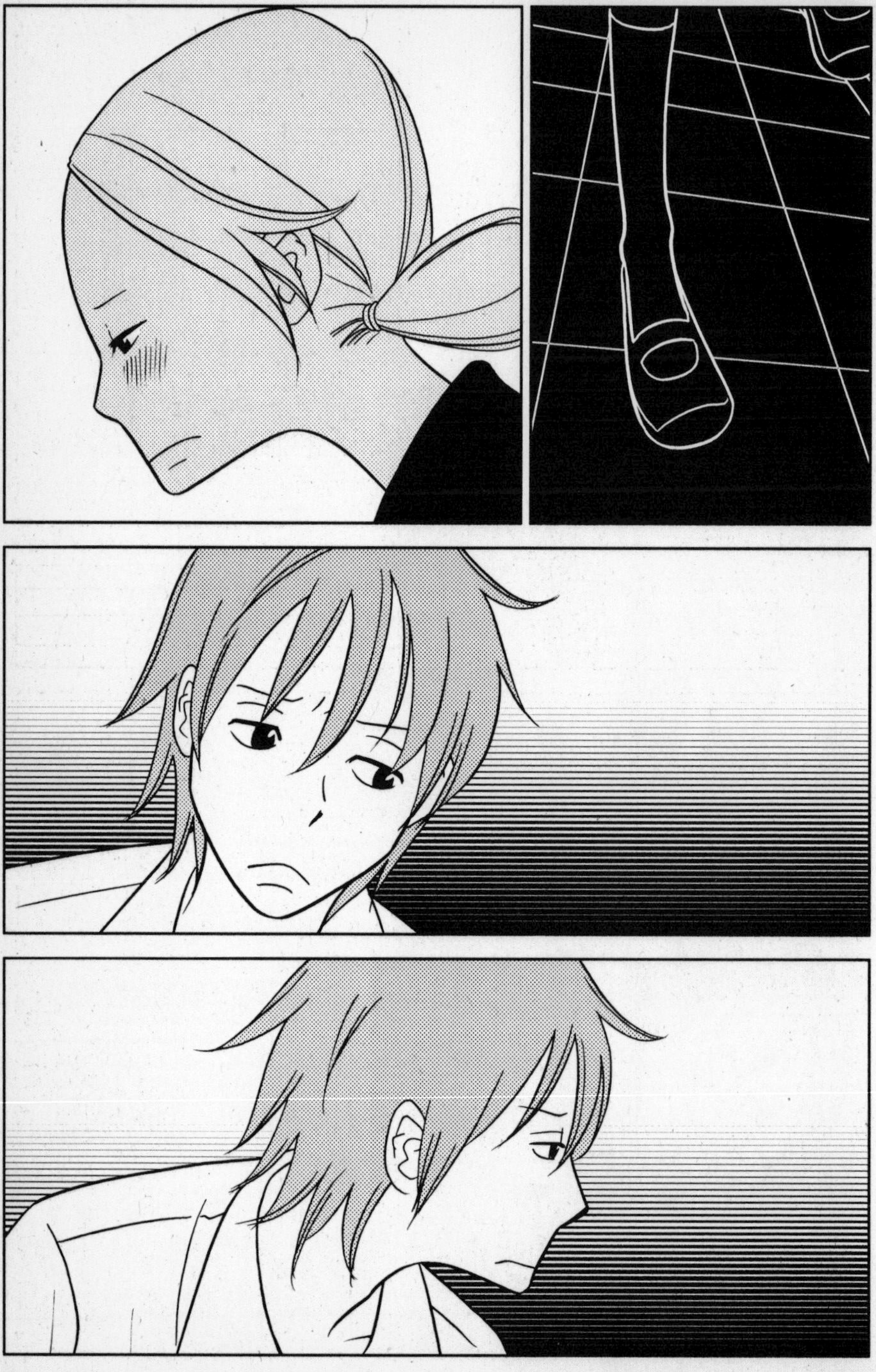

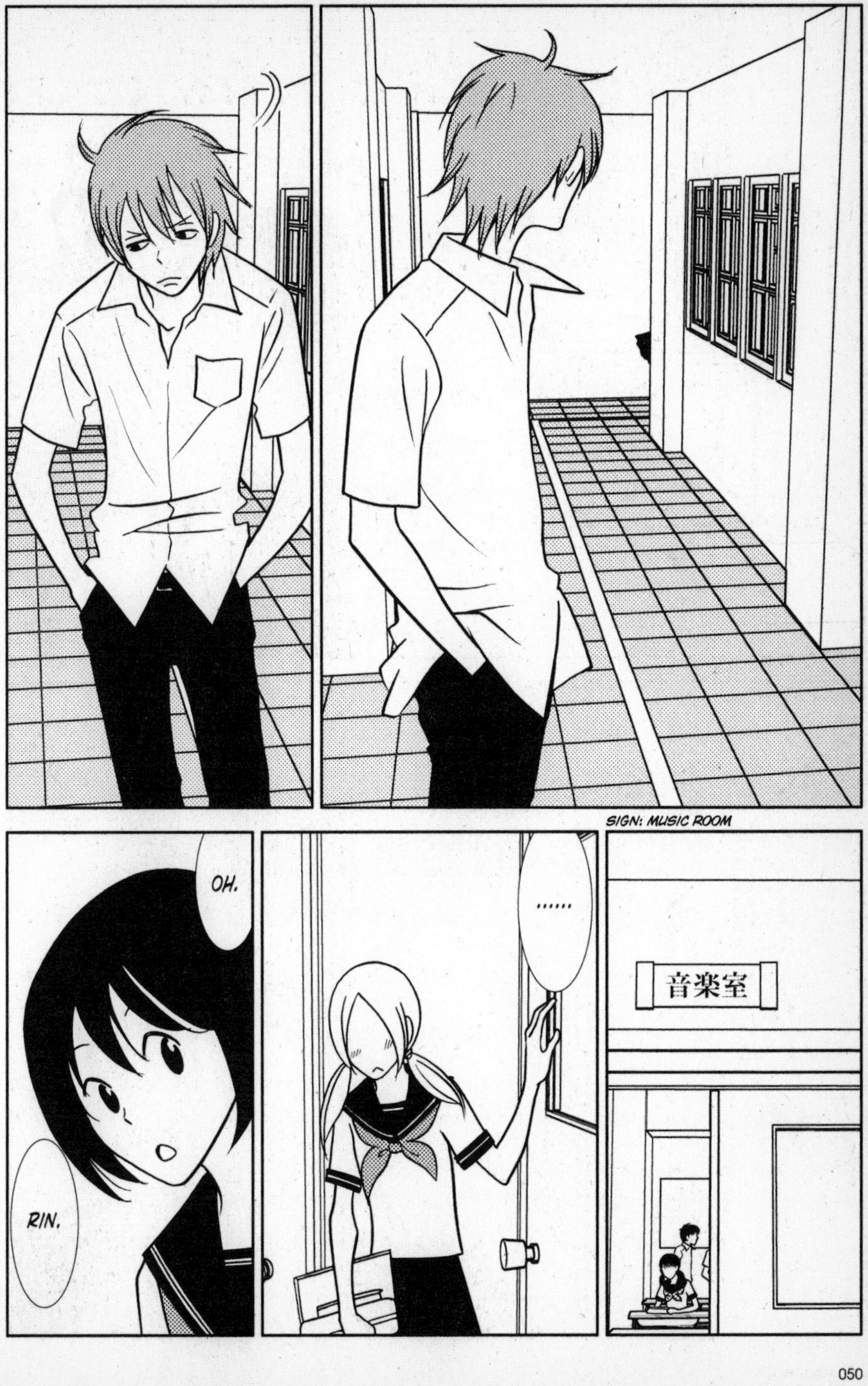
SIGN: MUSIC ROOM
音楽室
......
OH.
RIN.

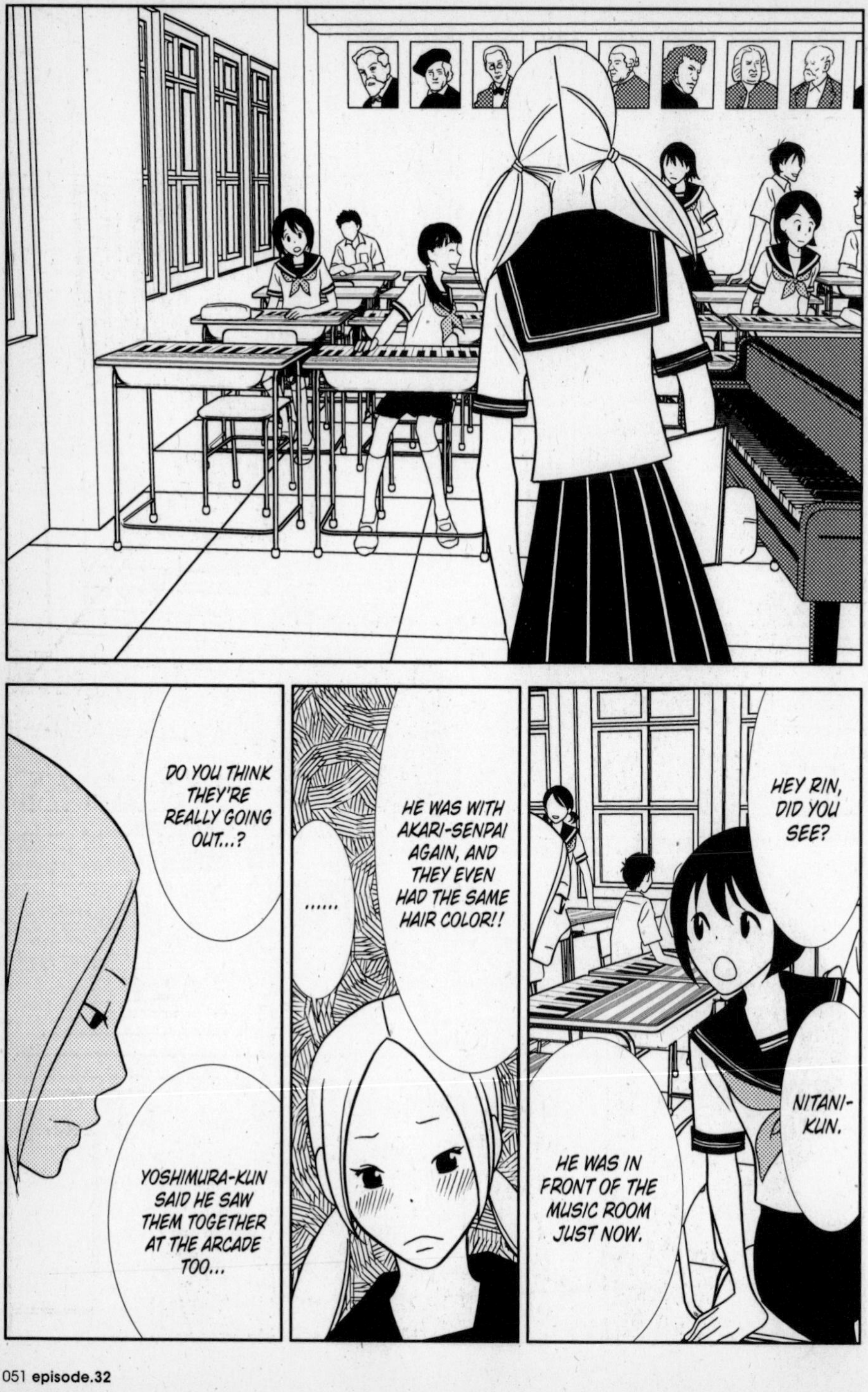
HEY RIN, DID YOU SEE?
NITANI-KUN.
HE WAS IN FRONT OF THE MUSIC ROOM JUST NOW.
HE WAS WITH AKARI-SENPAI AGAIN, AND THEY EVEN HAD THE SAME HAIR COLOR!!
......
DO YOU THINK THEY'RE REALLY GOING OUT...?
YOSHIMURA-KUN SAID HE SAW THEM TOGETHER AT THE ARCADE TOO...

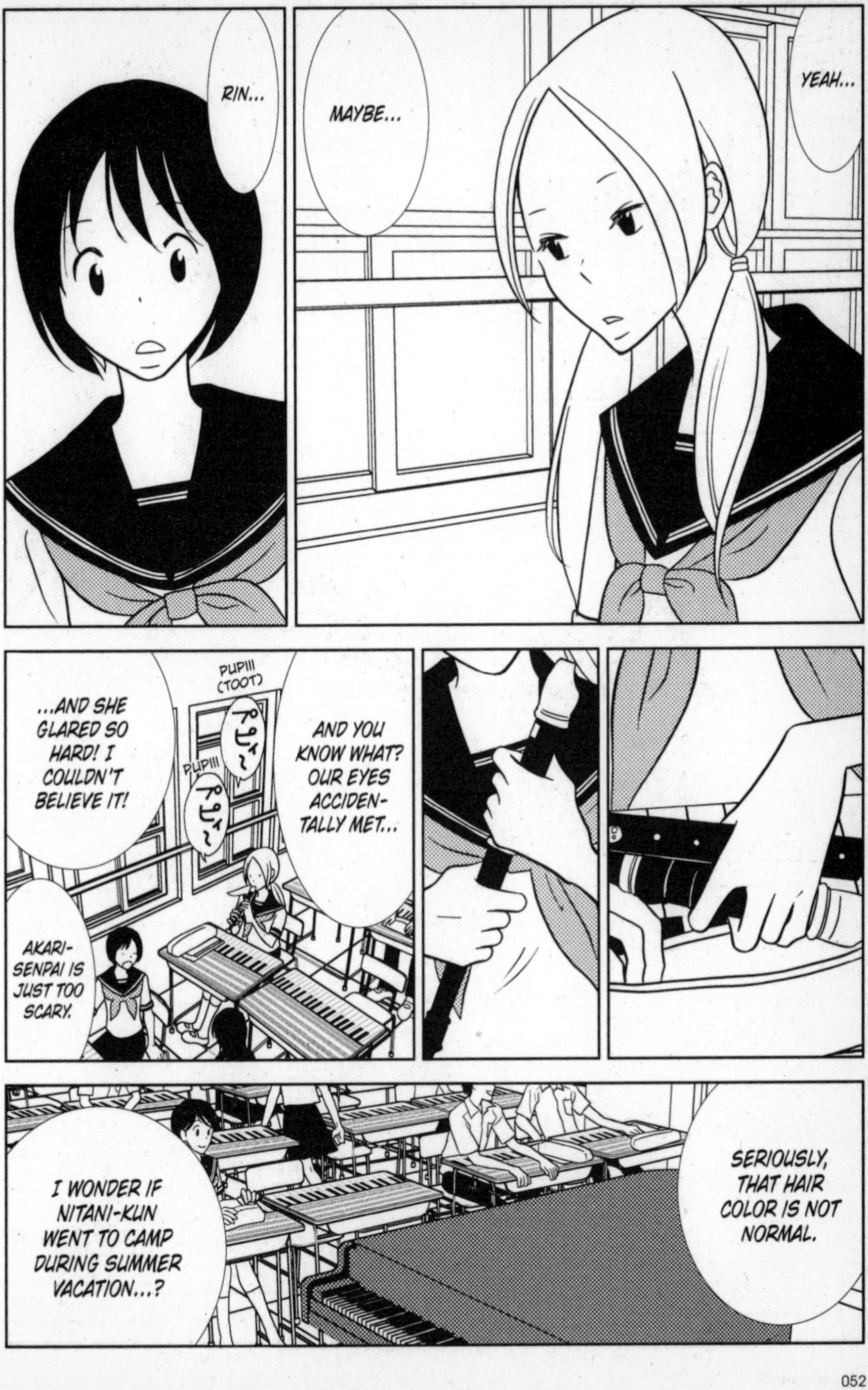
YEAH...
MAYBE...
RIN...
AND YOU KNOW WHAT? OUR EYES ACCIDENTALLY MET...
PUPIII (TOOT)
ピィ〜
...AND SHE GLARED SO HARD! I COULDN'T BELIEVE IT!
PUPIII
ピィ〜
AKARI-SENPAI IS JUST TOO SCARY.
SERIOUSLY, THAT HAIR COLOR IS NOT NORMAL.
I WONDER IF NITANI-KUN WENT TO CAMP DURING SUMMER VACATION...?

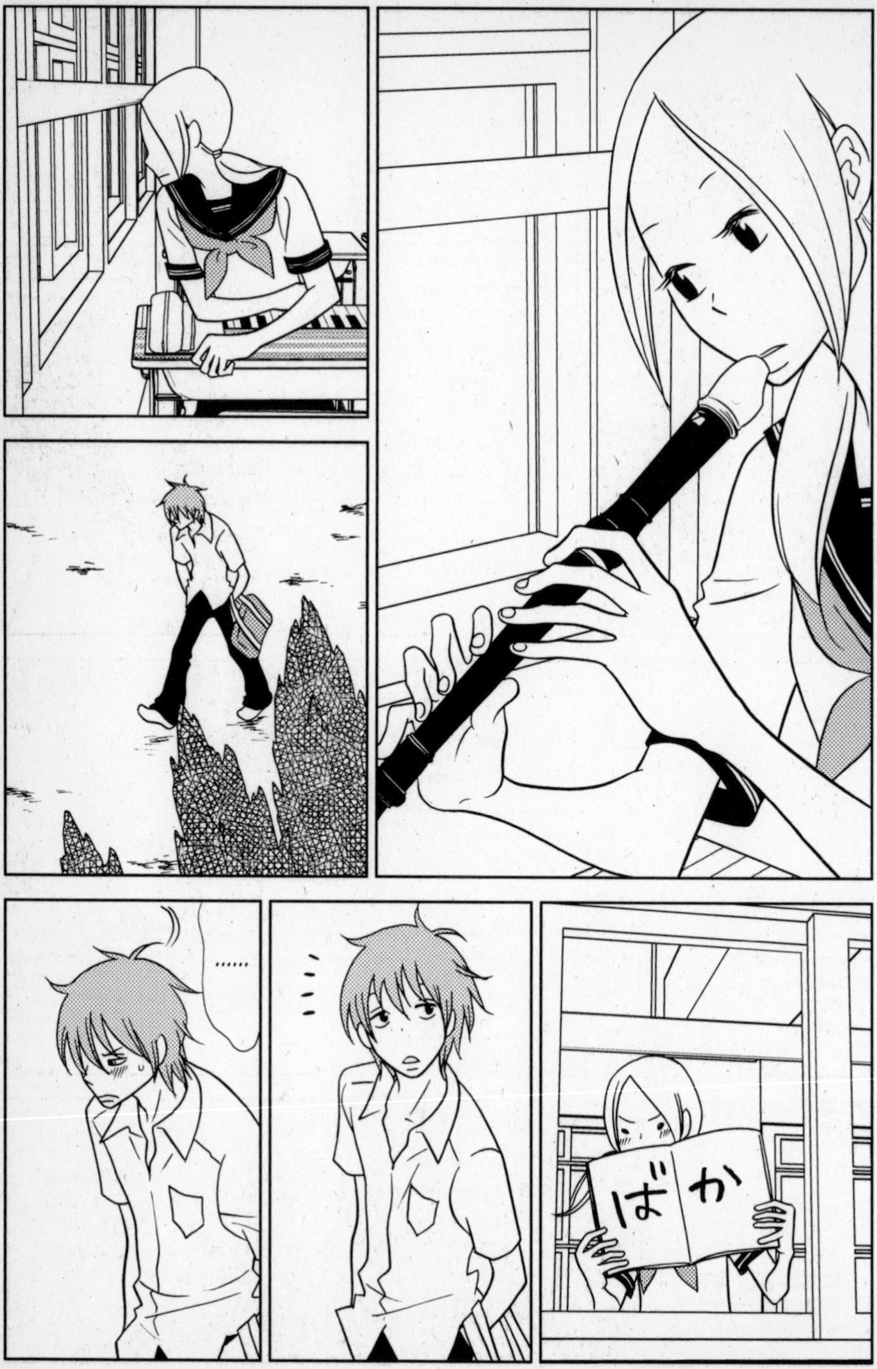
ばか
......

BOOK: IDIOT

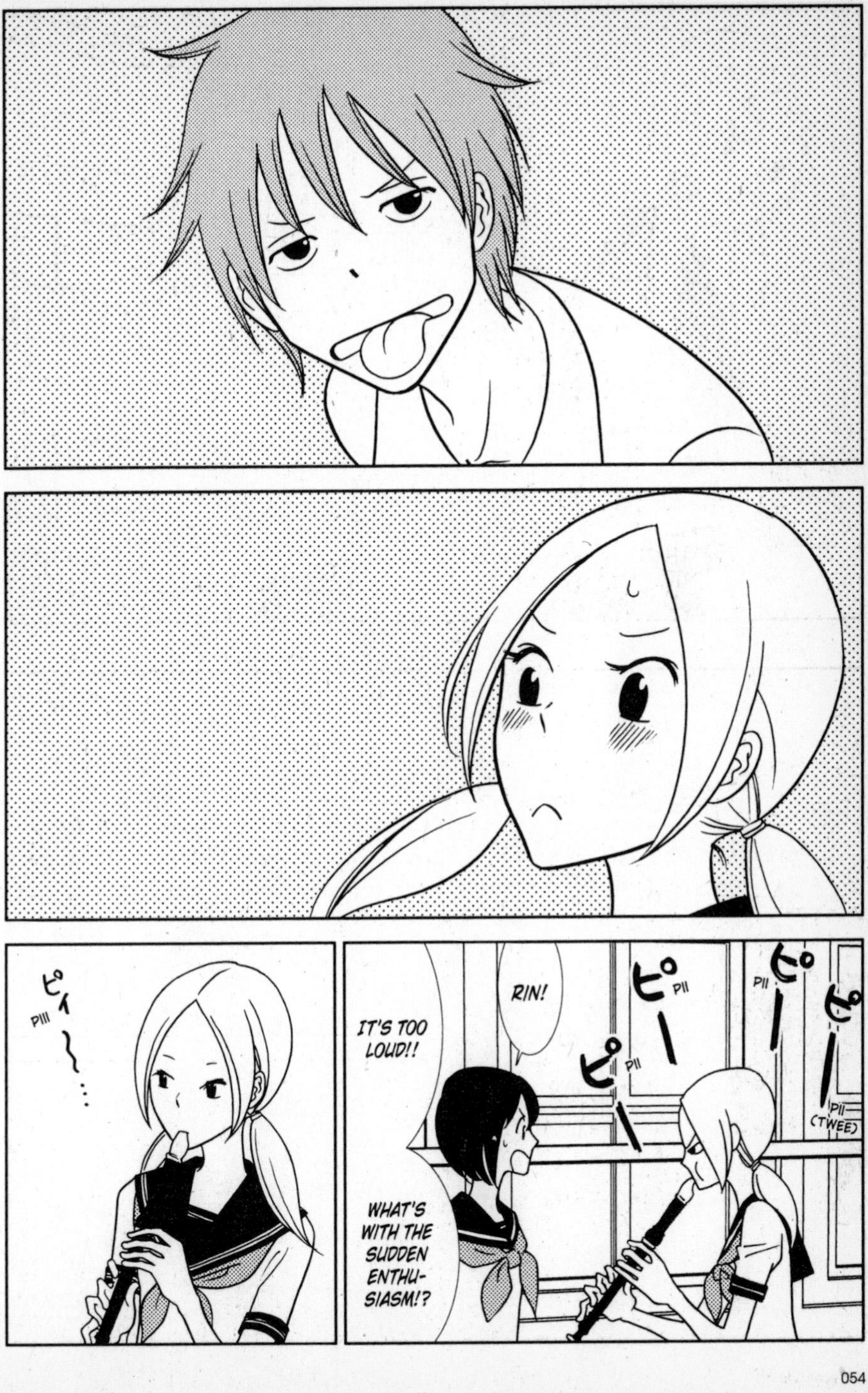

ピー
PII
ピー
PII
(TWEE)
ピー
PII
ピー
PII
RIN!
IT'S TOO LOUD!!
WHAT'S WITH THE SUDDEN ENTHU-SIASM!?
ピイ~…
PIII

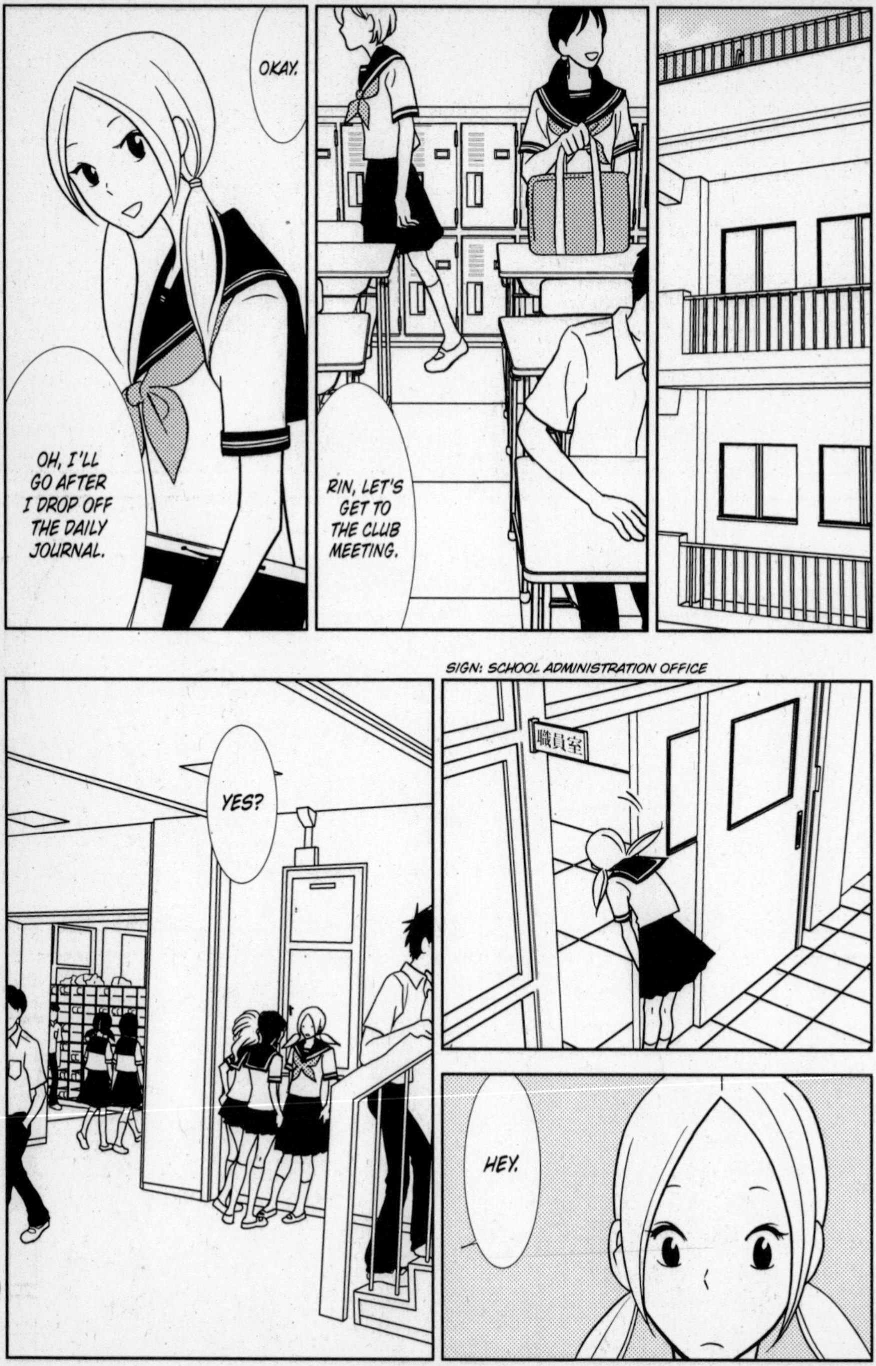
RIN, LET'S GET TO THE CLUB MEETING.
OKAY.
OH, I'LL GO AFTER I DROP OFF THE DAILY JOURNAL.
SIGN: SCHOOL ADMINISTRATION OFFICE
職員室
HEY.
YES?

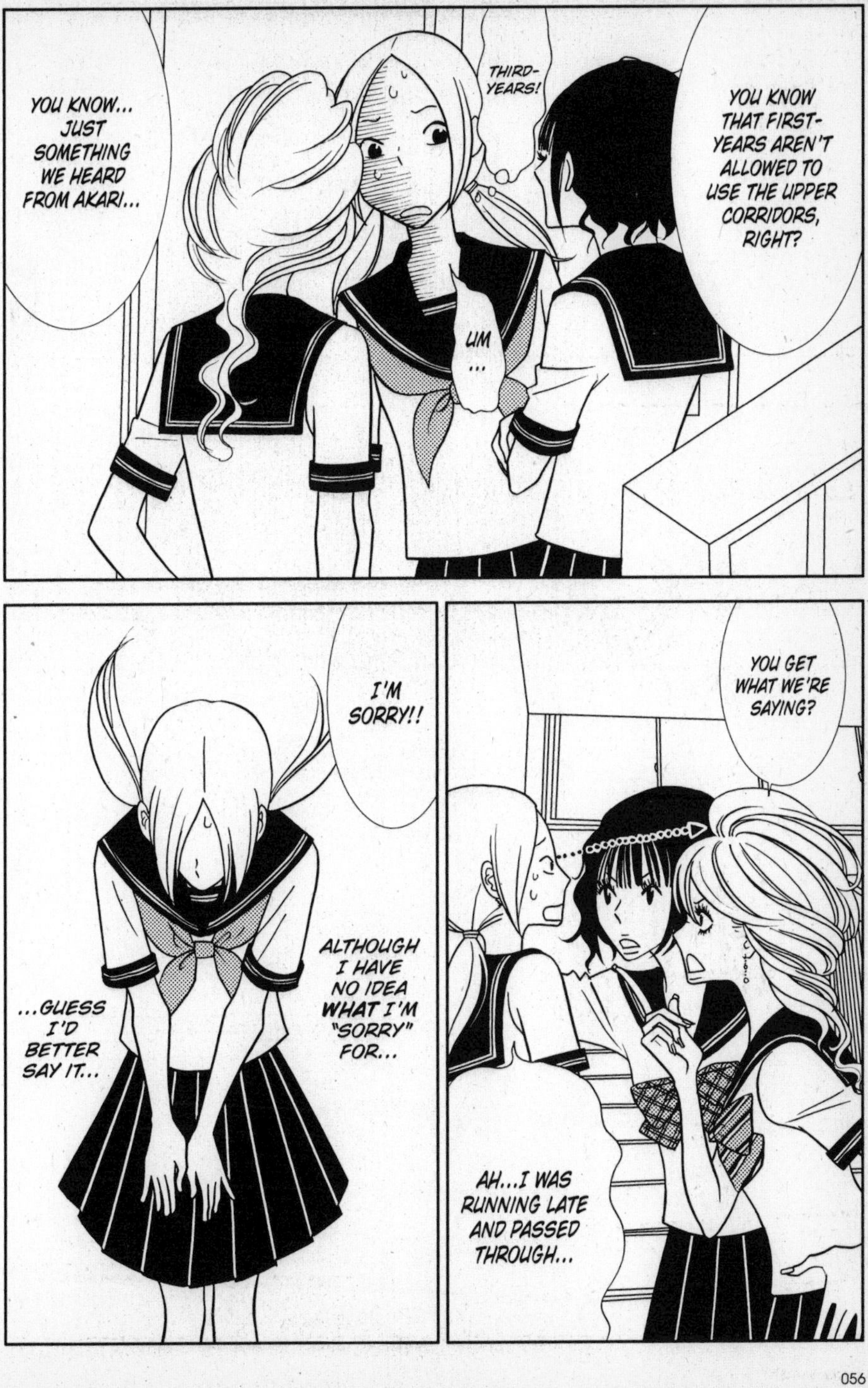
YOU KNOW THAT FIRST-YEARS AREN'T ALLOWED TO USE THE UPPER CORRIDORS, RIGHT?
THIRD-YEARS!
YOU KNOW... JUST SOMETHING WE HEARD FROM AKARI...
UM ...
YOU GET WHAT WE'RE SAYING?
AH...I WAS RUNNING LATE AND PASSED THROUGH...
I'M SORRY!!
ALTHOUGH I HAVE NO IDEA **WHAT I'M** "SORRY" FOR...
...GUESS I'D BETTER SAY IT...

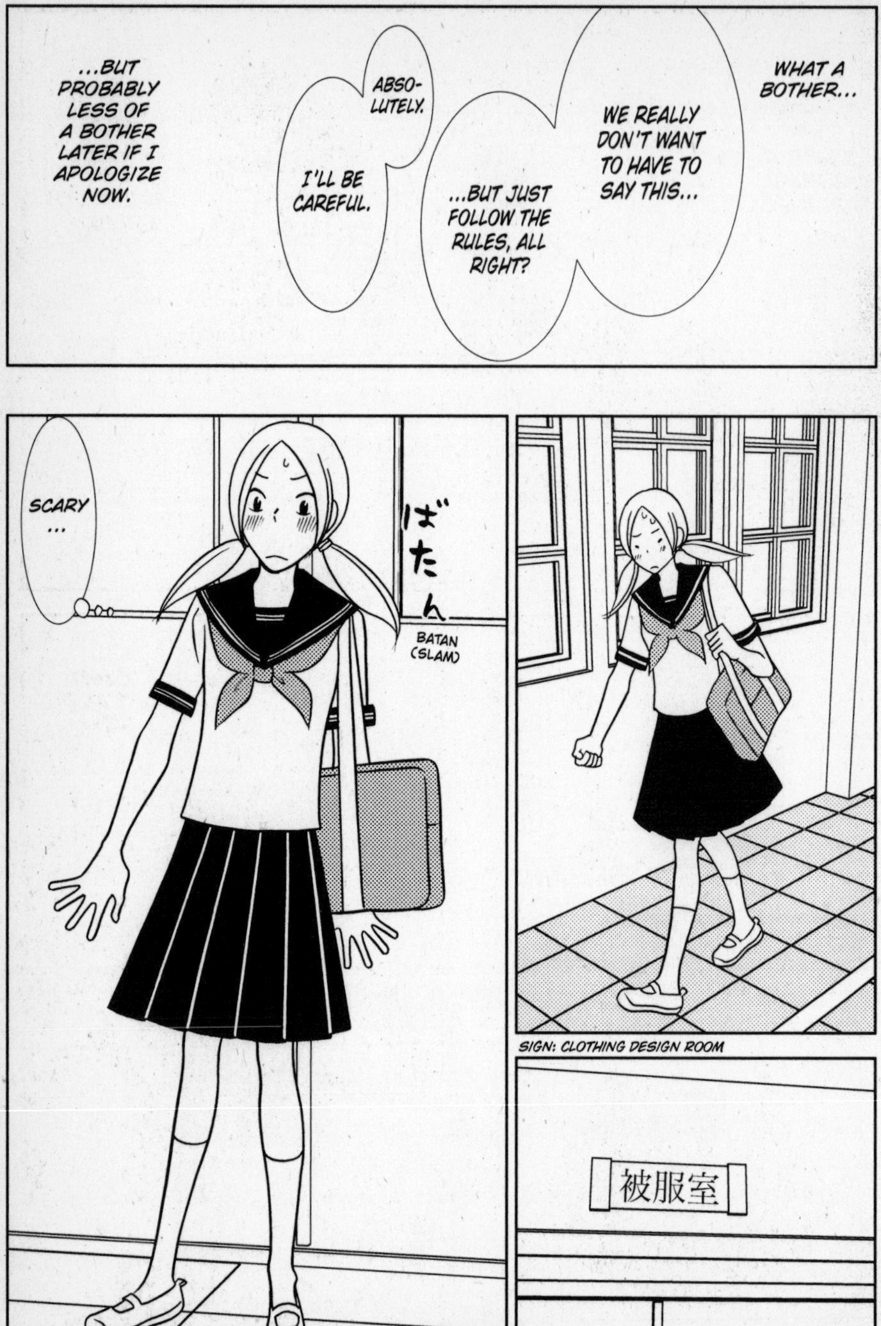
WHAT A BOTHER...
WE REALLY DON'T WANT TO HAVE TO SAY THIS...
...BUT JUST FOLLOW THE RULES, ALL RIGHT?
ABSO-LUTELY.
I'LL BE CAREFUL.
...BUT PROBABLY LESS OF A BOTHER LATER IF I APOLOGIZE NOW.
SIGN: CLOTHING DESIGN ROOM
被服室
ばたん
BATAN (SLAM)
SCARY ...

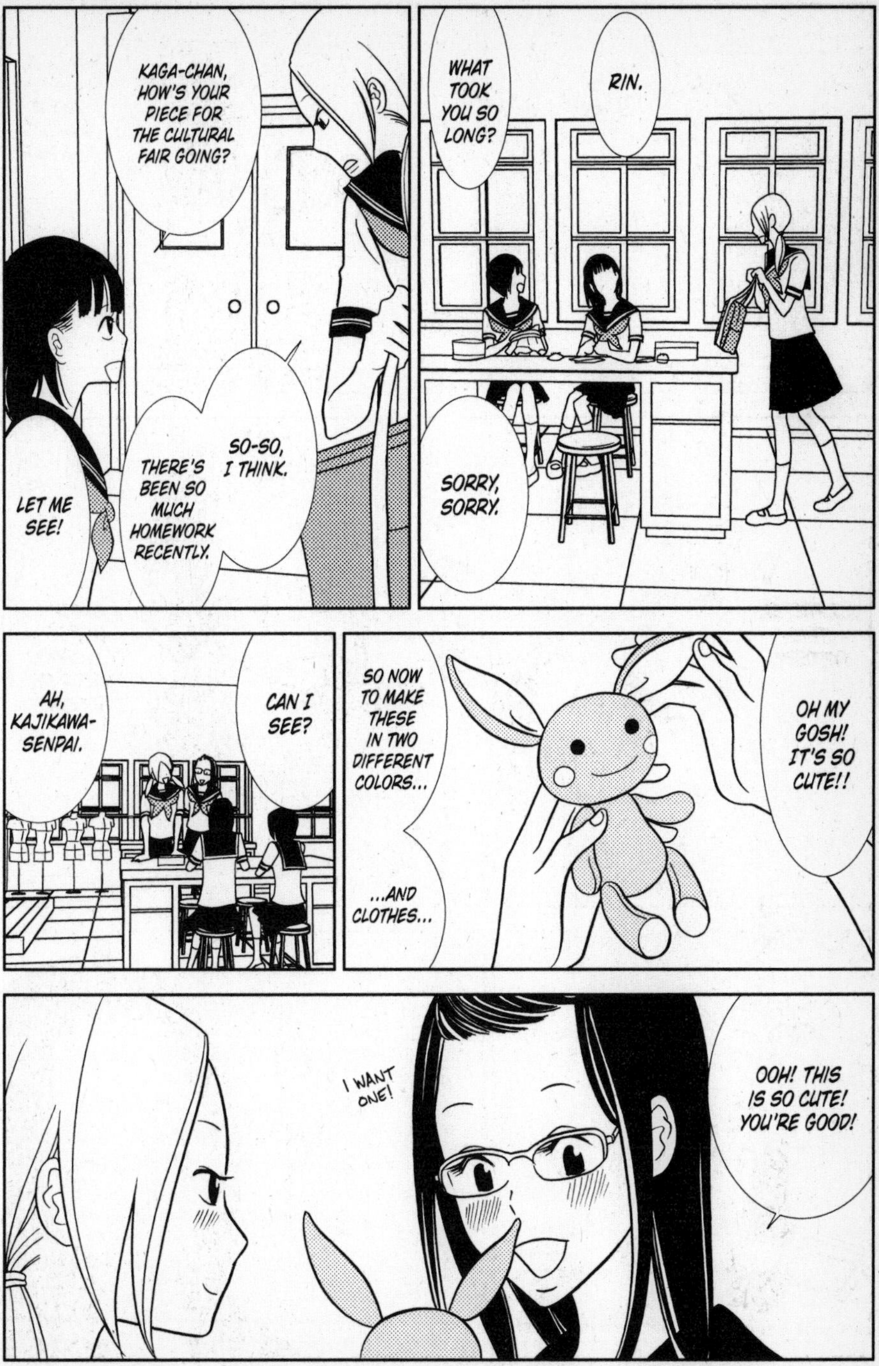
RIN.
WHAT TOOK YOU SO LONG?
SORRY, SORRY.
KAGA-CHAN, HOW'S YOUR PIECE FOR THE CULTURAL FAIR GOING?
SO-SO, I THINK.
THERE'S BEEN SO MUCH HOMEWORK RECENTLY.
LET ME SEE!
OH MY GOSH! IT'S SO CUTE!!
SO NOW TO MAKE THESE IN TWO DIFFERENT COLORS...
...AND CLOTHES...
CAN I SEE?
AH, KAJIKAWA-SENPAI.
OOH! THIS IS SO CUTE! YOU'RE GOOD!
I WANT ONE!

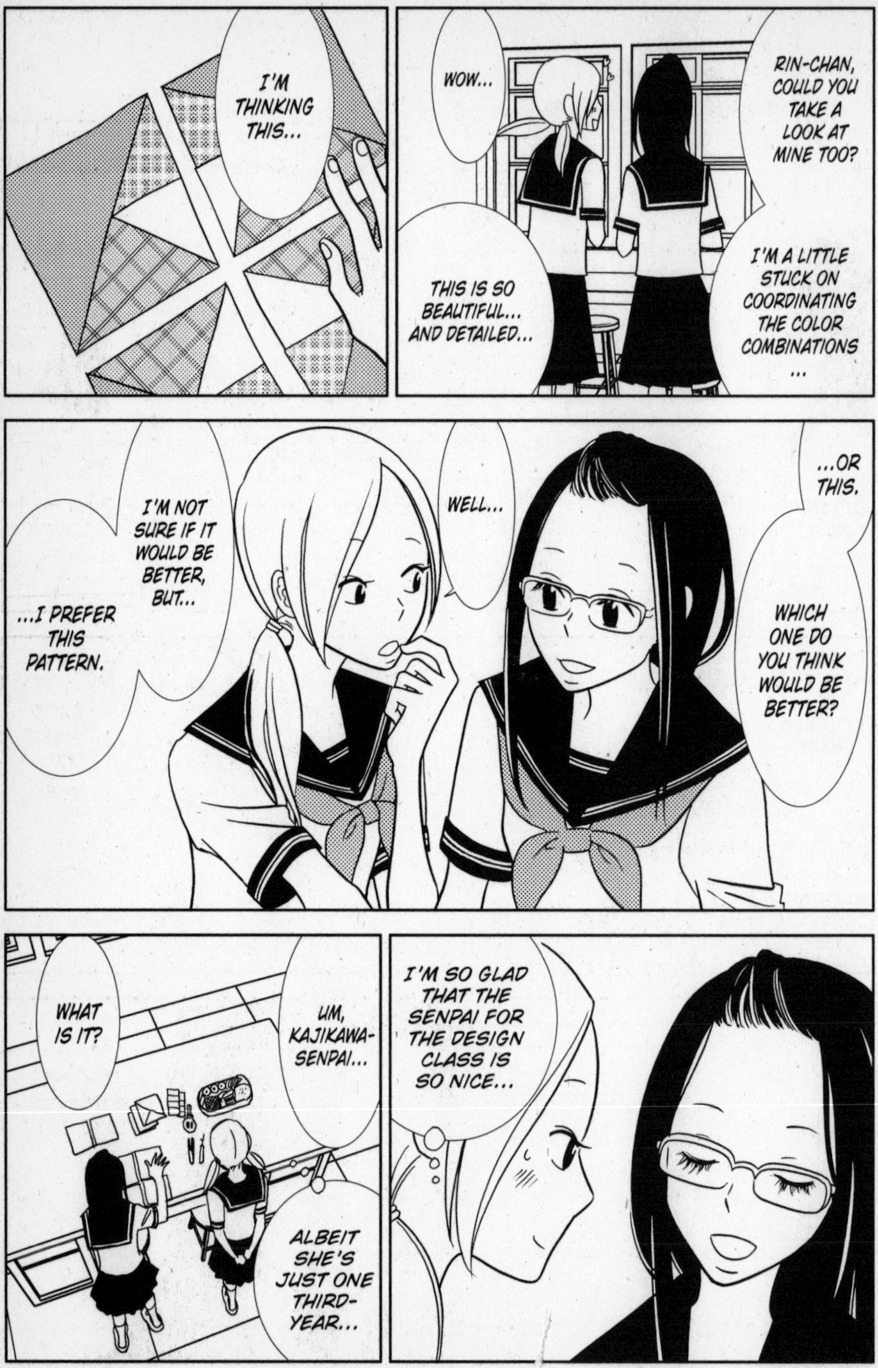
RIN-CHAN, COULD YOU TAKE A LOOK AT MINE TOO?
I'M A LITTLE STUCK ON COORDINATING THE COLOR COMBINATIONS ...
WOW...
THIS IS SO BEAUTIFUL... AND DETAILED...
I'M THINKING THIS...
...OR THIS.
WHICH ONE DO YOU THINK WOULD BE BETTER?
WELL...
I'M NOT SURE IF IT WOULD BE BETTER, BUT...
...I PREFER THIS PATTERN.
I'M SO GLAD THAT THE SENPAI FOR THE DESIGN CLASS IS SO NICE...
UM, KAJIKAWA-SENPAI...
WHAT IS IT?
ALBEIT SHE'S JUST ONE THIRD-YEAR...

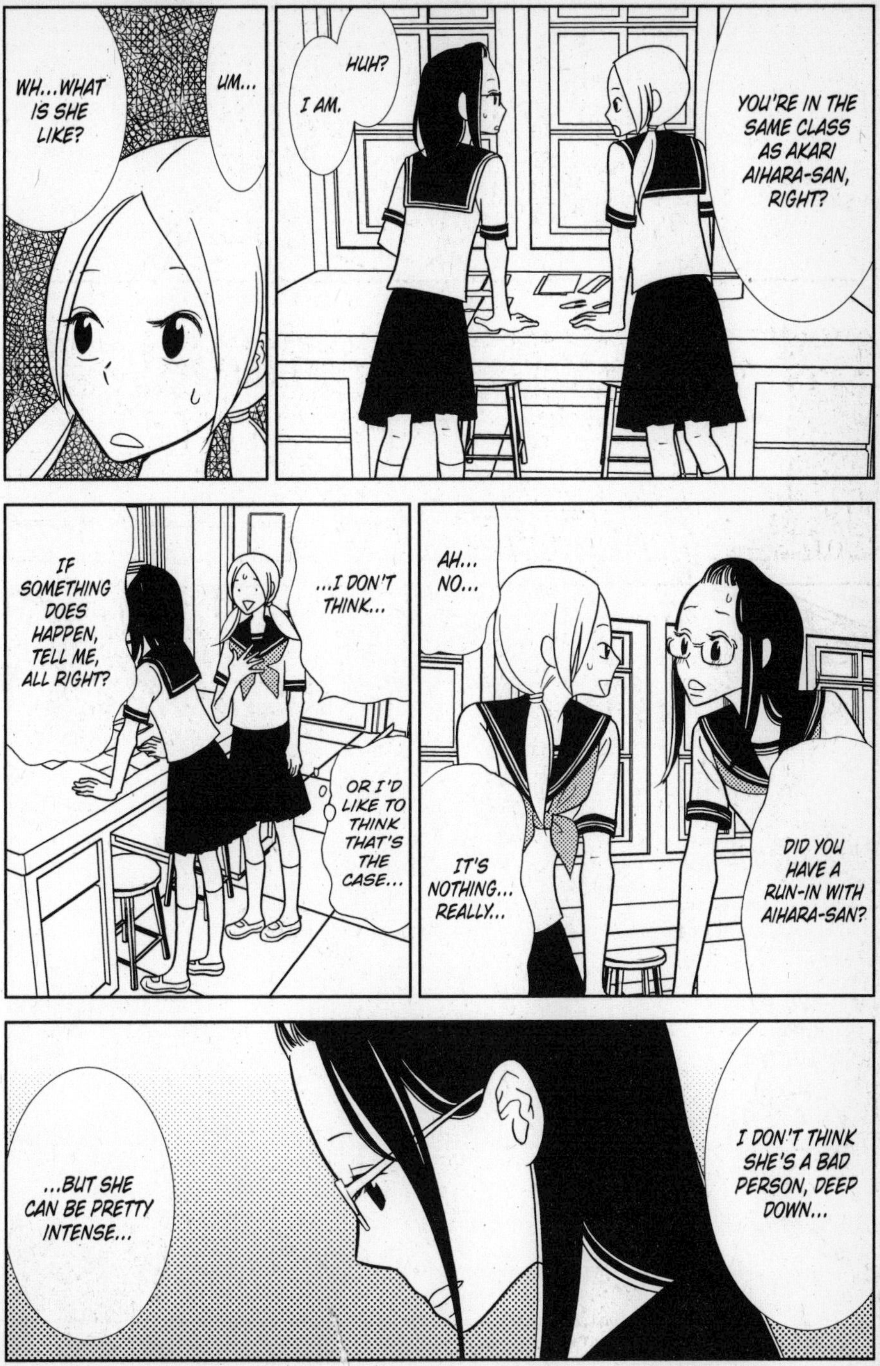
YOU'RE IN THE SAME CLASS AS AKARI AIHARA-SAN, RIGHT?
HUH?
I AM.
UM...
WH...WHAT IS SHE LIKE?
DID YOU HAVE A RUN-IN WITH AIHARA-SAN?
AH... NO...
IT'S NOTHING... REALLY...
...I DON'T THINK...
OR I'D LIKE TO THINK THAT'S THE CASE...
IF SOMETHING DOES HAPPEN, TELL ME, ALL RIGHT?
I DON'T THINK SHE'S A BAD PERSON, DEEP DOWN...
...BUT SHE CAN BE PRETTY INTENSE...

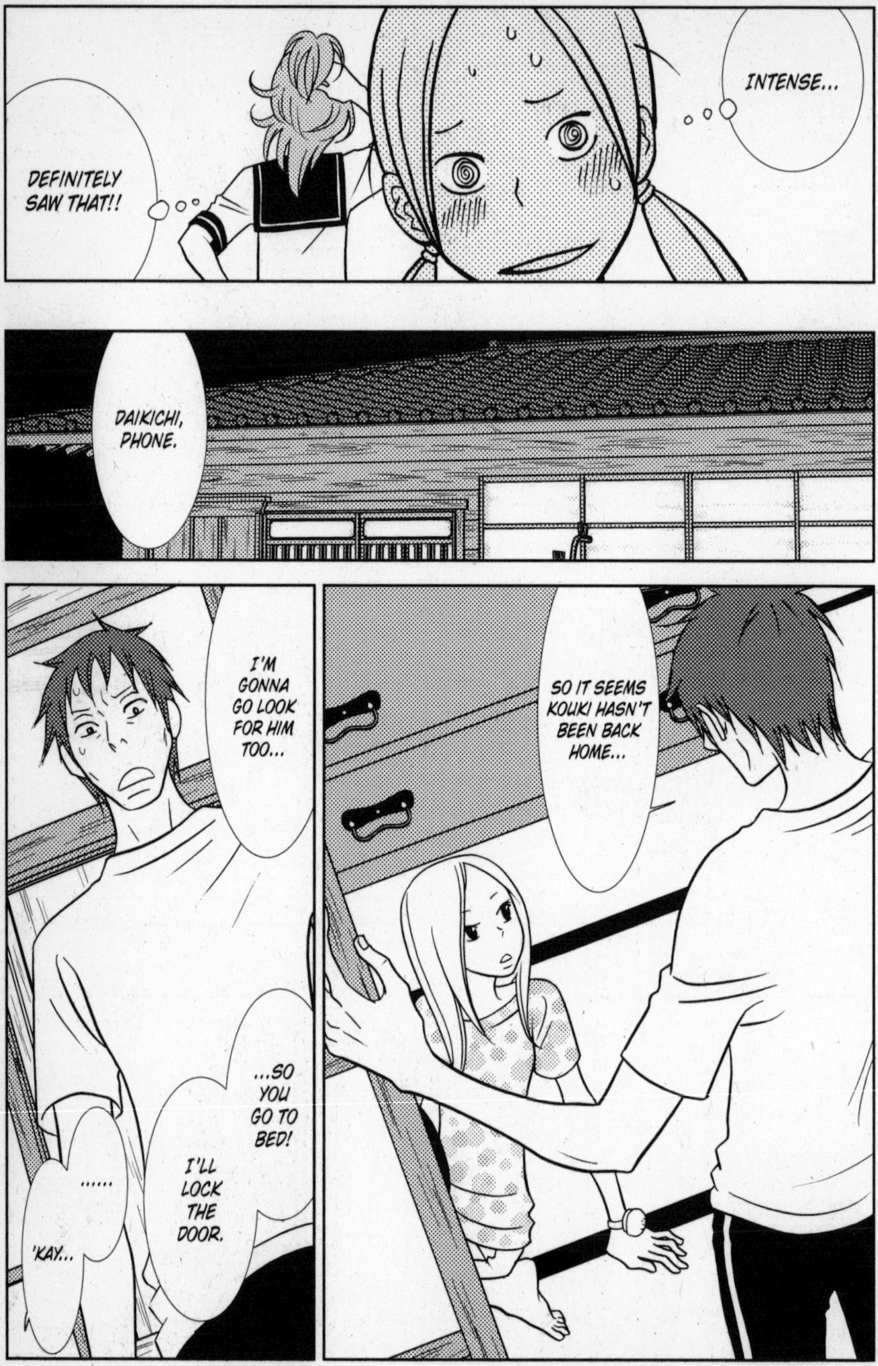
INTENSE...
DEFINITELY SAW THAT!!
DAIKICHI, PHONE.
SO IT SEEMS KOUKI HASN'T BEEN BACK HOME...
I'M GONNA GO LOOK FOR HIM TOO...
...SO YOU GO TO BED!
I'LL LOCK THE DOOR.
......
'KAY...

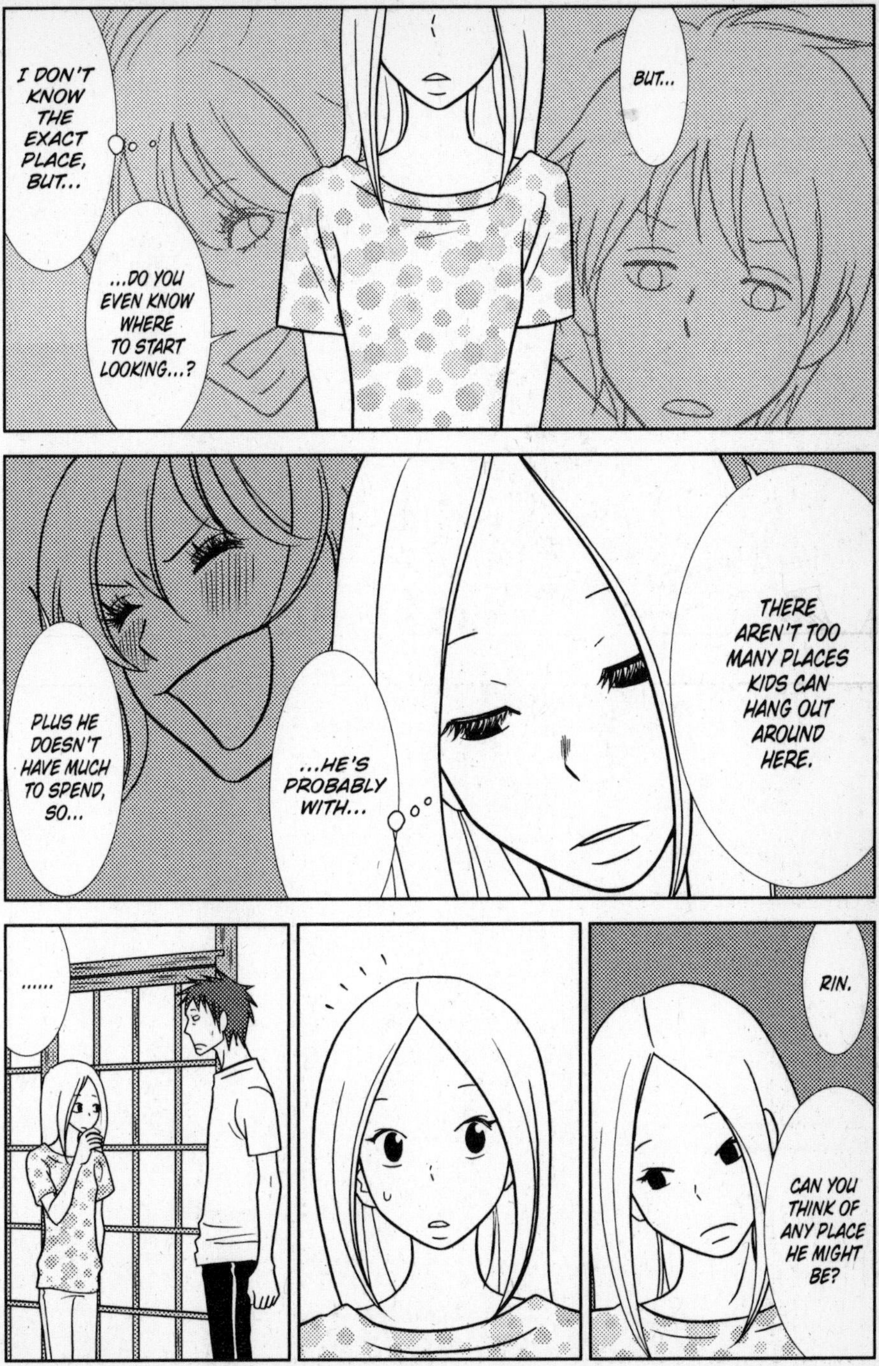
BUT...
I DON'T KNOW THE EXACT PLACE, BUT...
...DO YOU EVEN KNOW WHERE TO START LOOKING...?
THERE AREN'T TOO MANY PLACES KIDS CAN HANG OUT AROUND HERE.
...HE'S PROBABLY WITH...
PLUS HE DOESN'T HAVE MUCH TO SPEND, SO...
RIN.
CAN YOU THINK OF ANY PLACE HE MIGHT BE?
......

THE ARCADE?
SERIOUSLY, GO TO SLEEP, OKAY?
I HAVE THE KEY, SO DON'T OPEN THE DOOR FOR ANYTHING, OKAY?
OKAY.
ガラ
GARA (SLIDE)
OKAY ...
TO (THMP)
トッ
TO
トッ
TO
トッ
TO
トッ
TO
トッ
TO
トッ
TO
トッ
......
ペタ
PETA (PAT)
PETA
ペタ
WHICH AM I MORE WORRIED ABOUT...

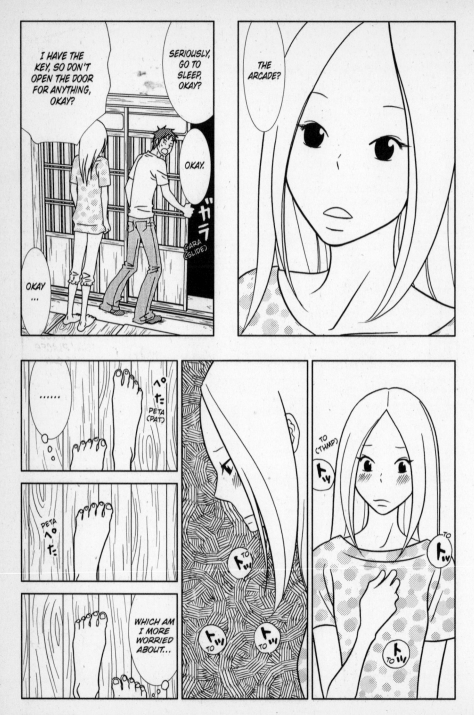

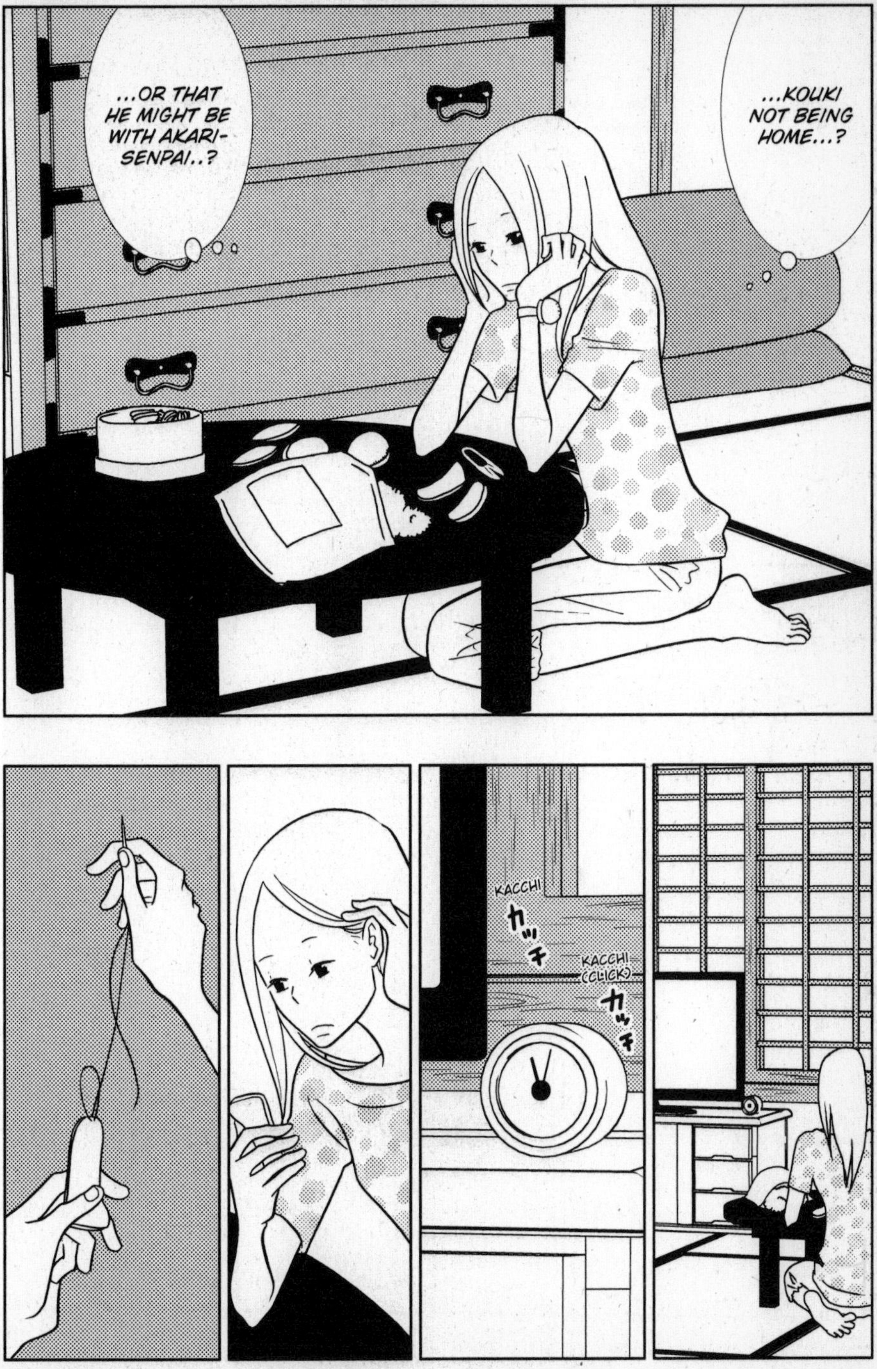
...KOUKI NOT BEING HOME...?
...OR THAT HE MIGHT BE WITH AKARI-SENPAI..?
KACCHI
カッチ
KACCHI (CLICK)
カッチ

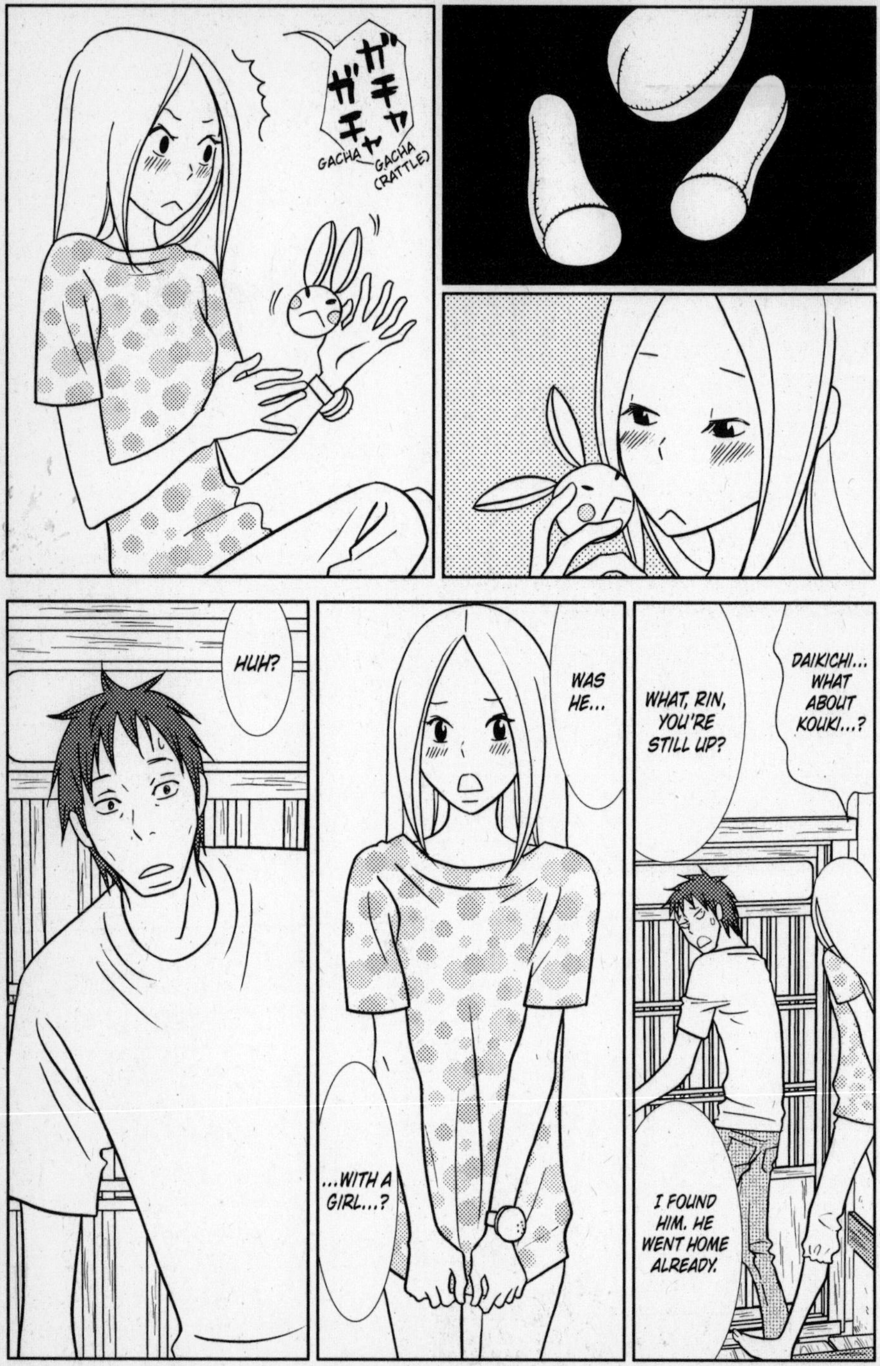
ガチャガチャ
GACHA GACHA (RATTLE)
DAIKICHI... WHAT ABOUT KOUKI...?
WHAT, RIN, YOU'RE STILL UP?
I FOUND HIM. HE WENT HOME ALREADY.
WAS HE...
...WITH A GIRL...?
HUH?

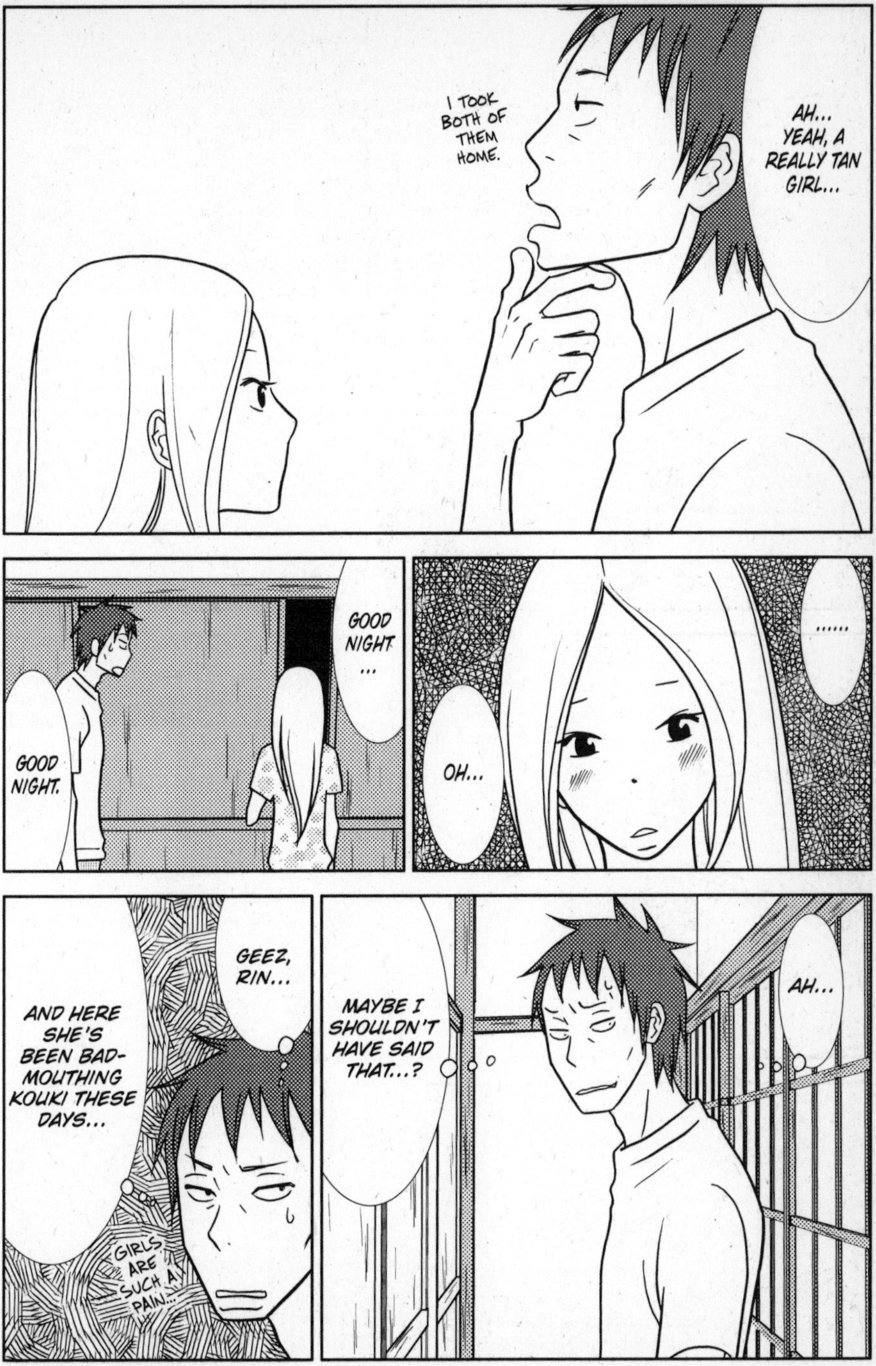
AH... YEAH, A REALLY TAN GIRL...
I TOOK BOTH OF THEM HOME.
......
OH...
GOOD NIGHT...
GOOD NIGHT.
AH...
MAYBE I SHOULDN'T HAVE SAID THAT...?
GEEZ, RIN...
AND HERE SHE'S BEEN BAD-MOUTHING KOUKI THESE DAYS...
GIRLS ARE SUCH A PAIN...

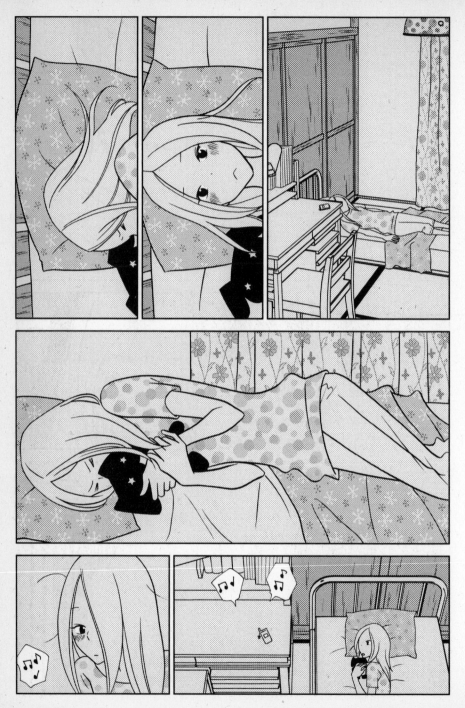

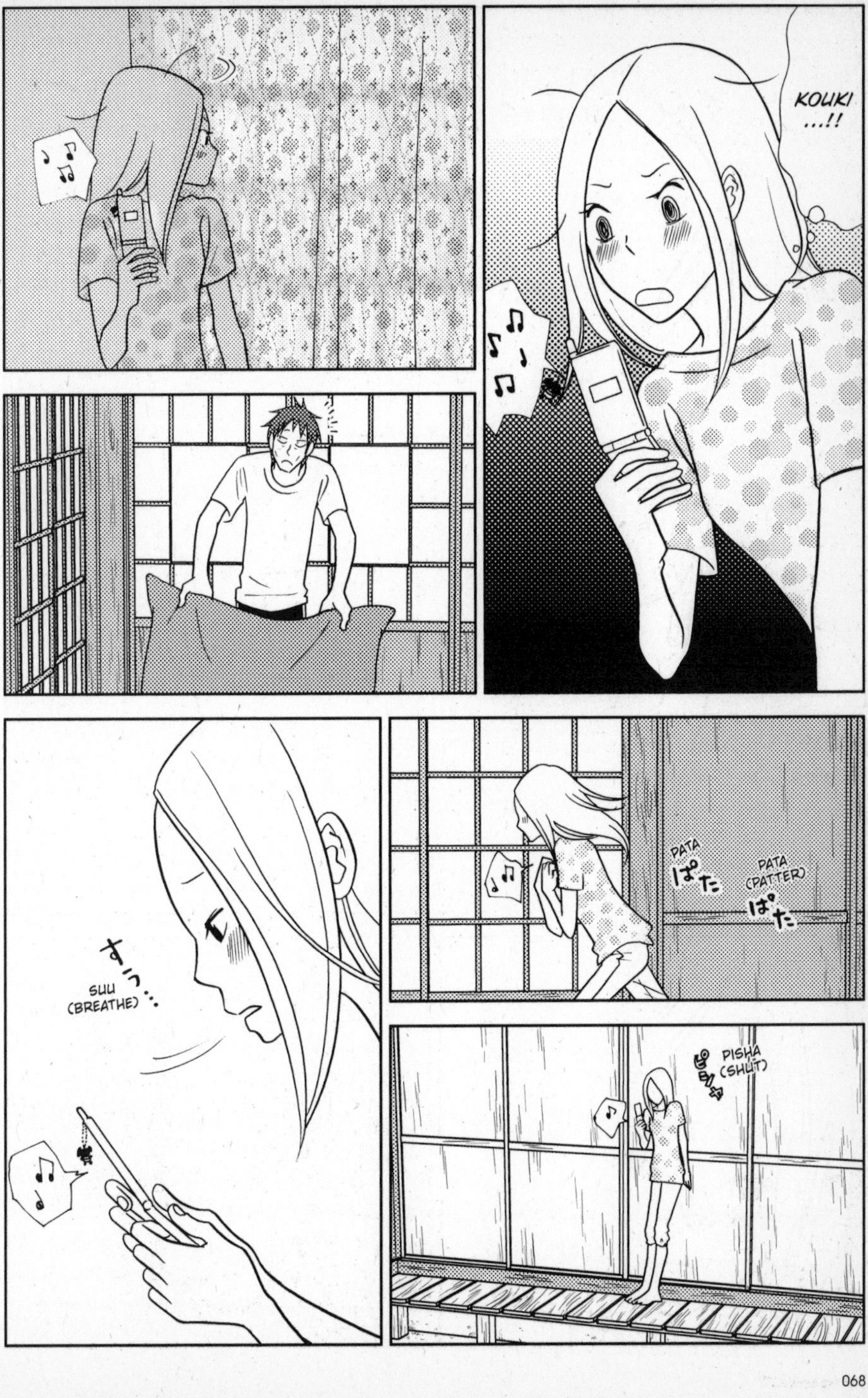
KOUKI ...!!
PATA ぱた
PATA (PATTER) ぱた
ピシャ PISHA (SHUT)
すぅ… SUU (BREATHE)

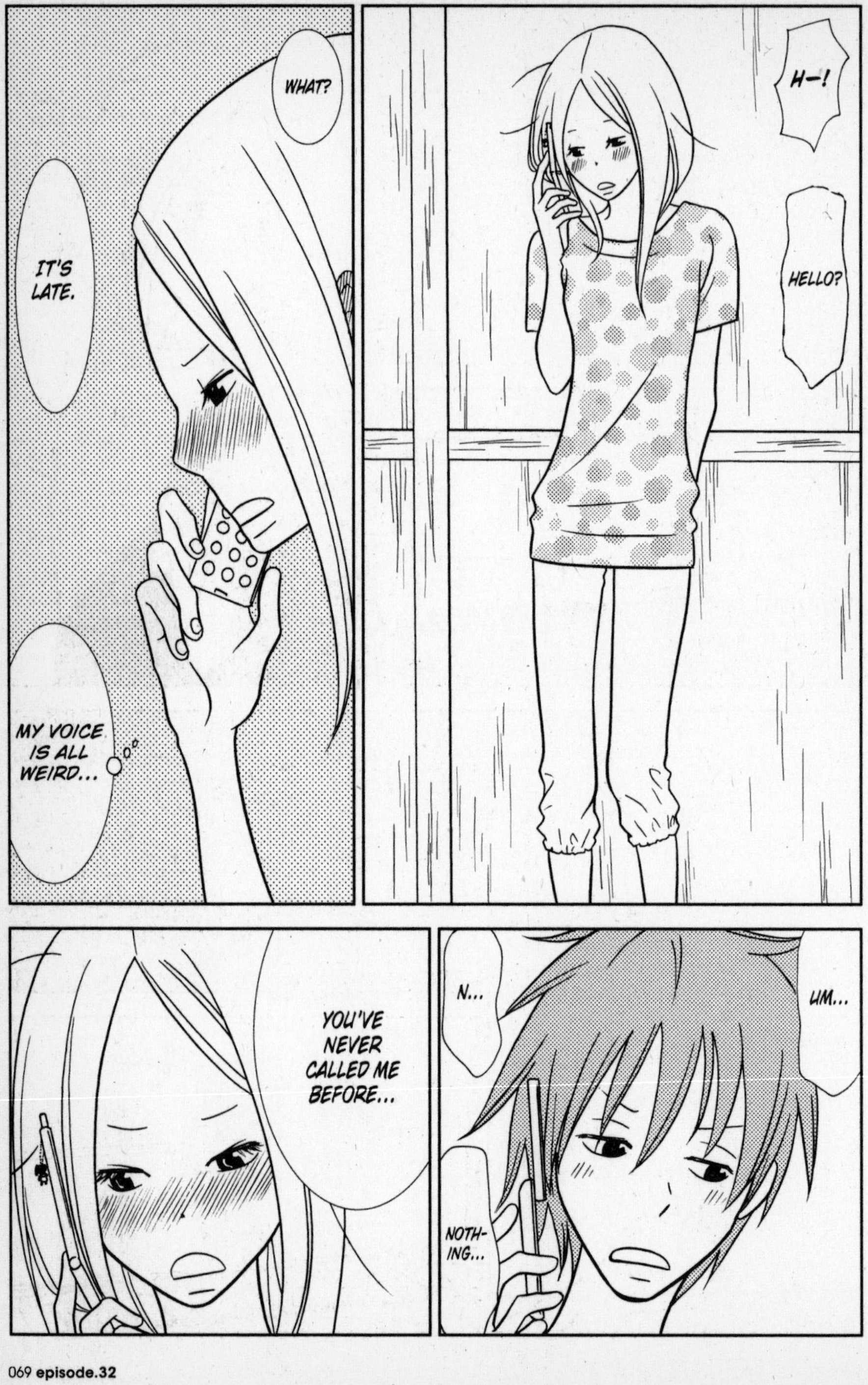
H–!
HELLO?
WHAT?
IT'S LATE.
MY VOICE IS ALL WEIRD...
UM...
N...
NOTH-ING...
YOU'VE NEVER CALLED ME BEFORE...

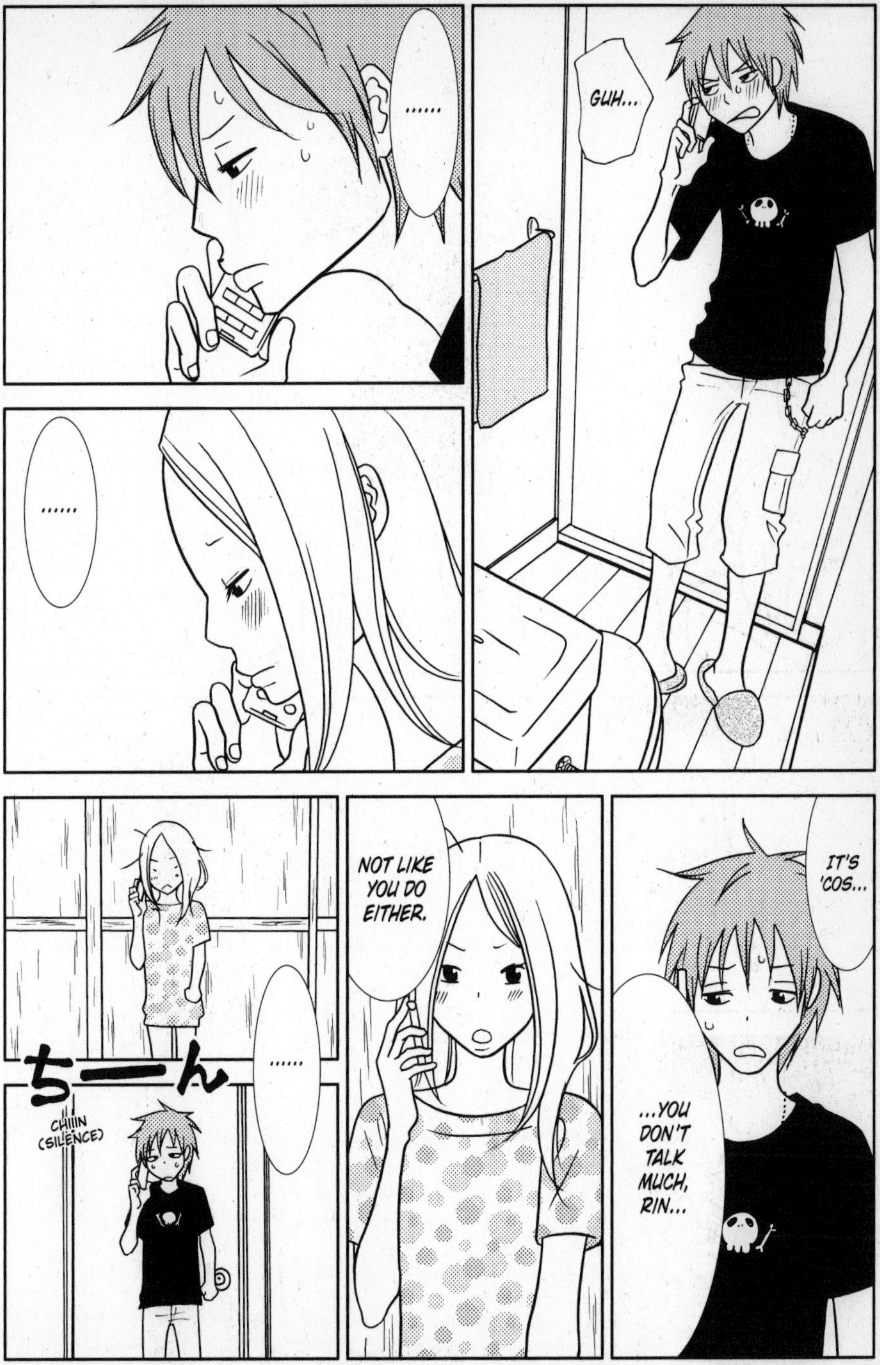
GUH...
......
......
IT'S 'COS...
...YOU DON'T TALK MUCH, RIN...
NOT LIKE YOU DO EITHER.
......
ちーん
CHIIIN (SILENCE)

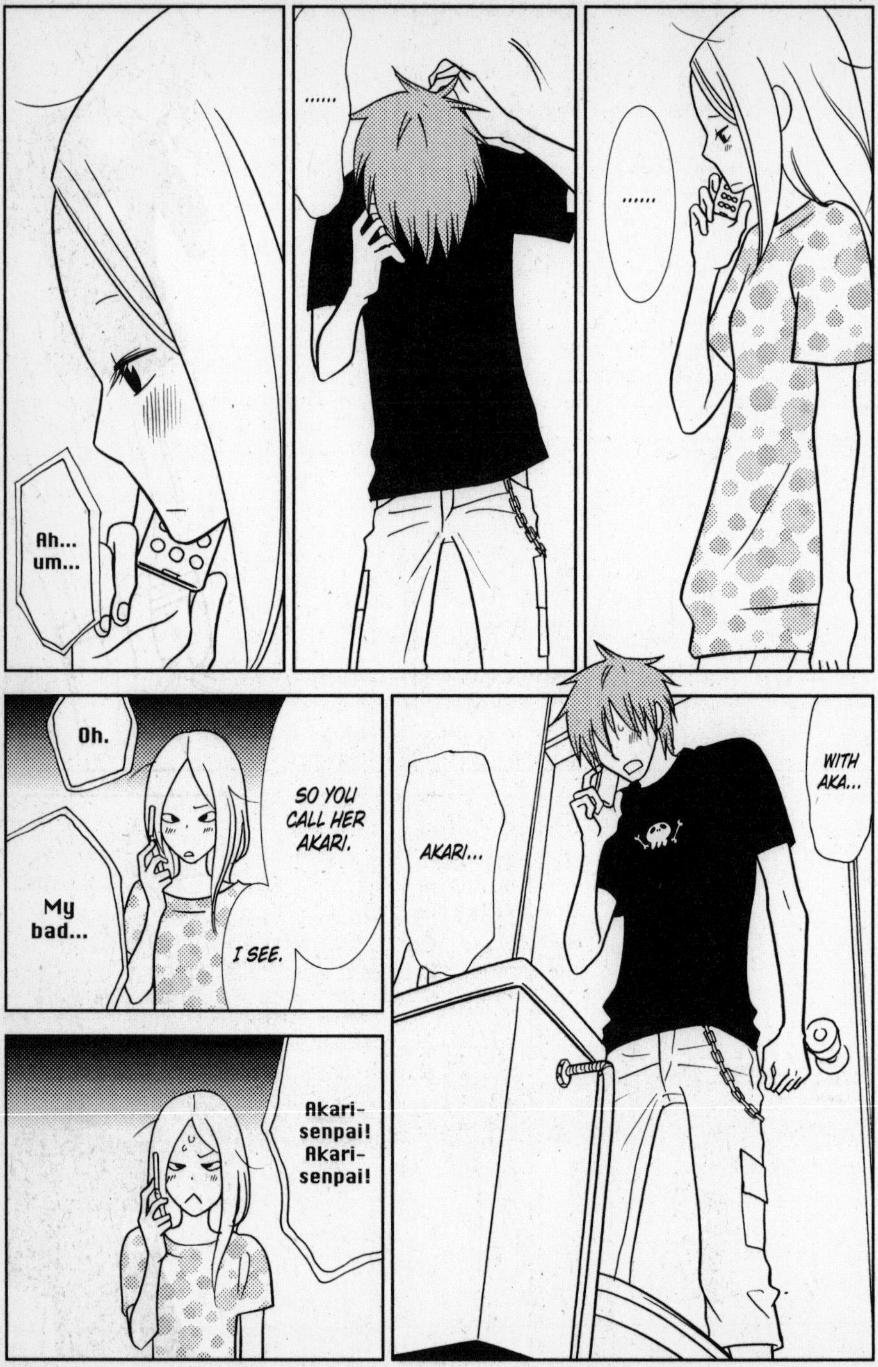
……
……
Ah... um...
WITH AKA...
AKARI...
SO YOU CALL HER AKARI.
Oh.
I SEE.
My bad...
Akari-senpai! Akari-senpai!

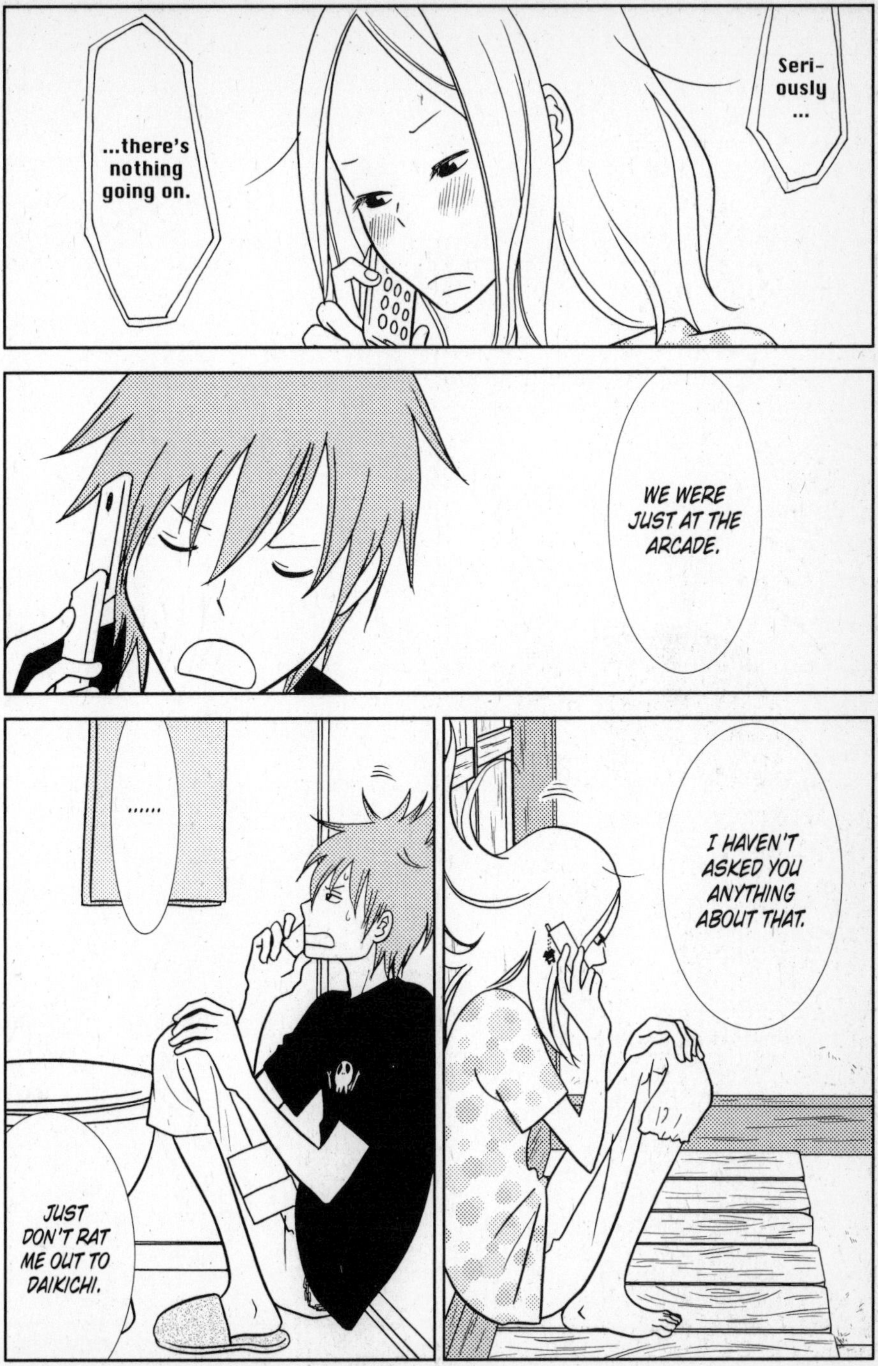
Seri-
ously
...
...there's nothing going on.
WE WERE JUST AT THE ARCADE.
I HAVEN'T ASKED YOU ANYTHING ABOUT THAT.
......
JUST DON'T RAT ME OUT TO DAIKICHI.

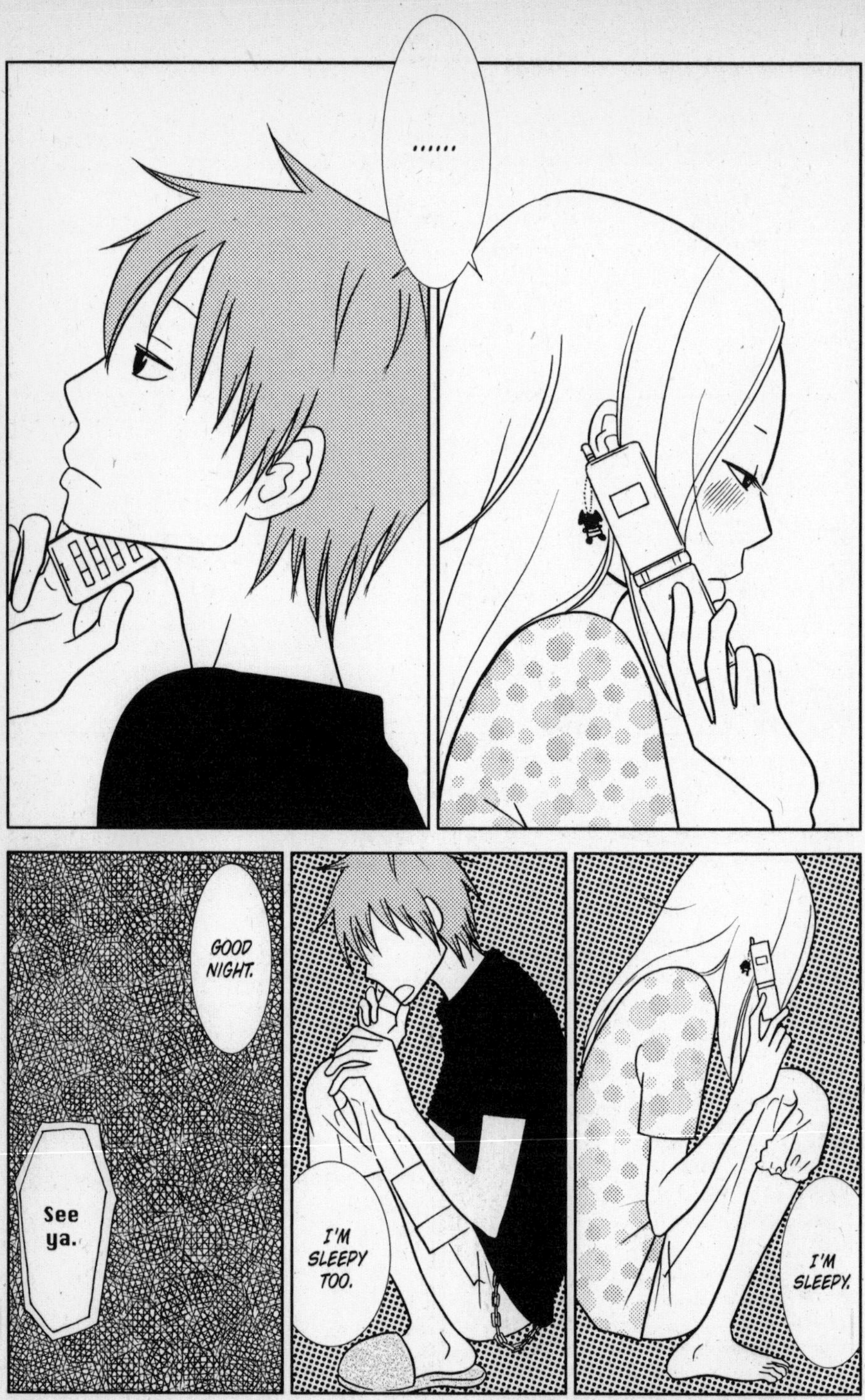
......
I'M SLEEPY.
I'M SLEEPY TOO.
GOOD NIGHT.
See ya.

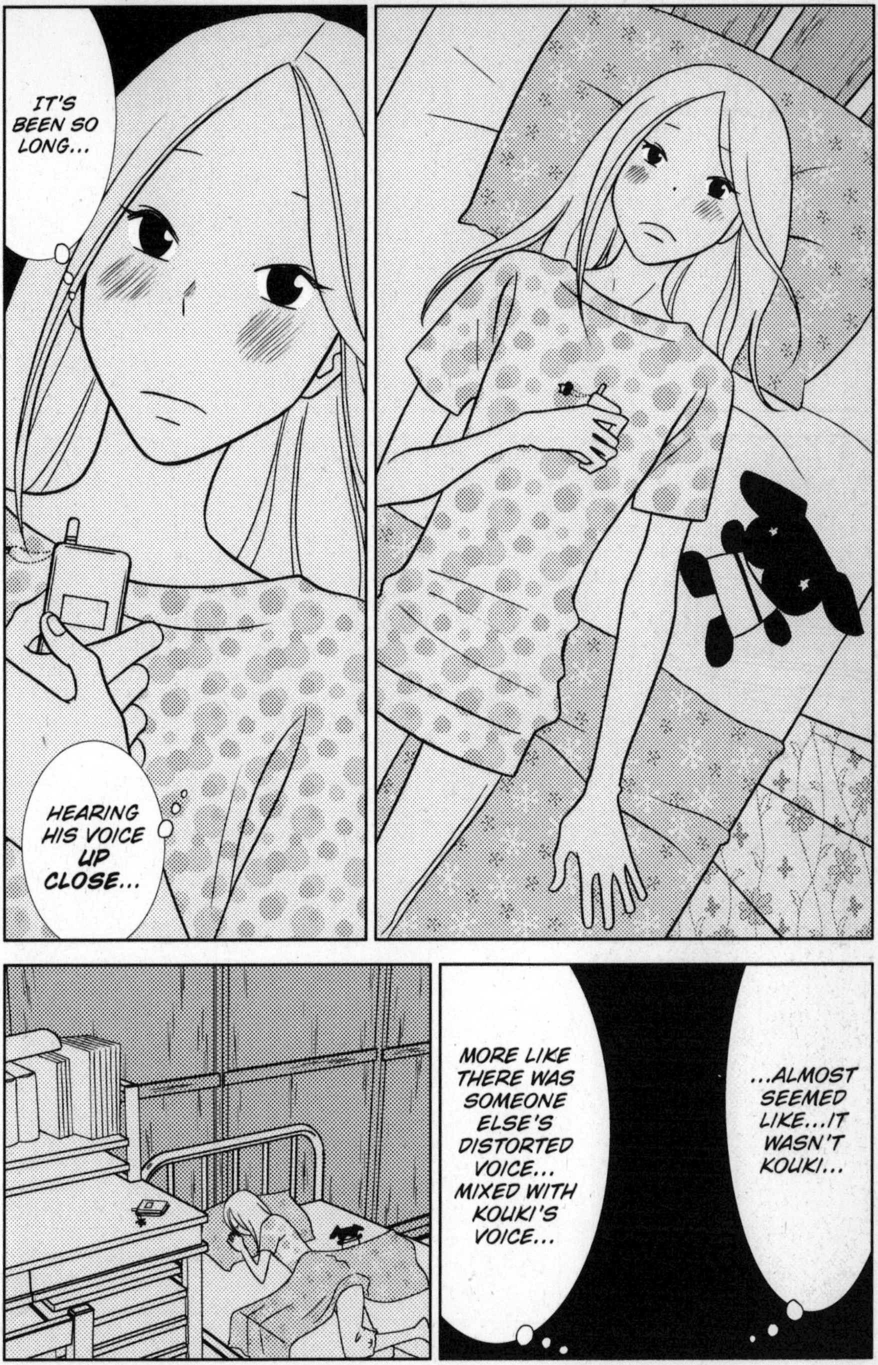
IT'S BEEN SO LONG...
HEARING HIS VOICE UP CLOSE...
...ALMOST SEEMED LIKE...IT WASN'T KOUKI...
MORE LIKE THERE WAS SOMEONE ELSE'S DISTORTED VOICE... MIXED WITH KOUKI'S VOICE...

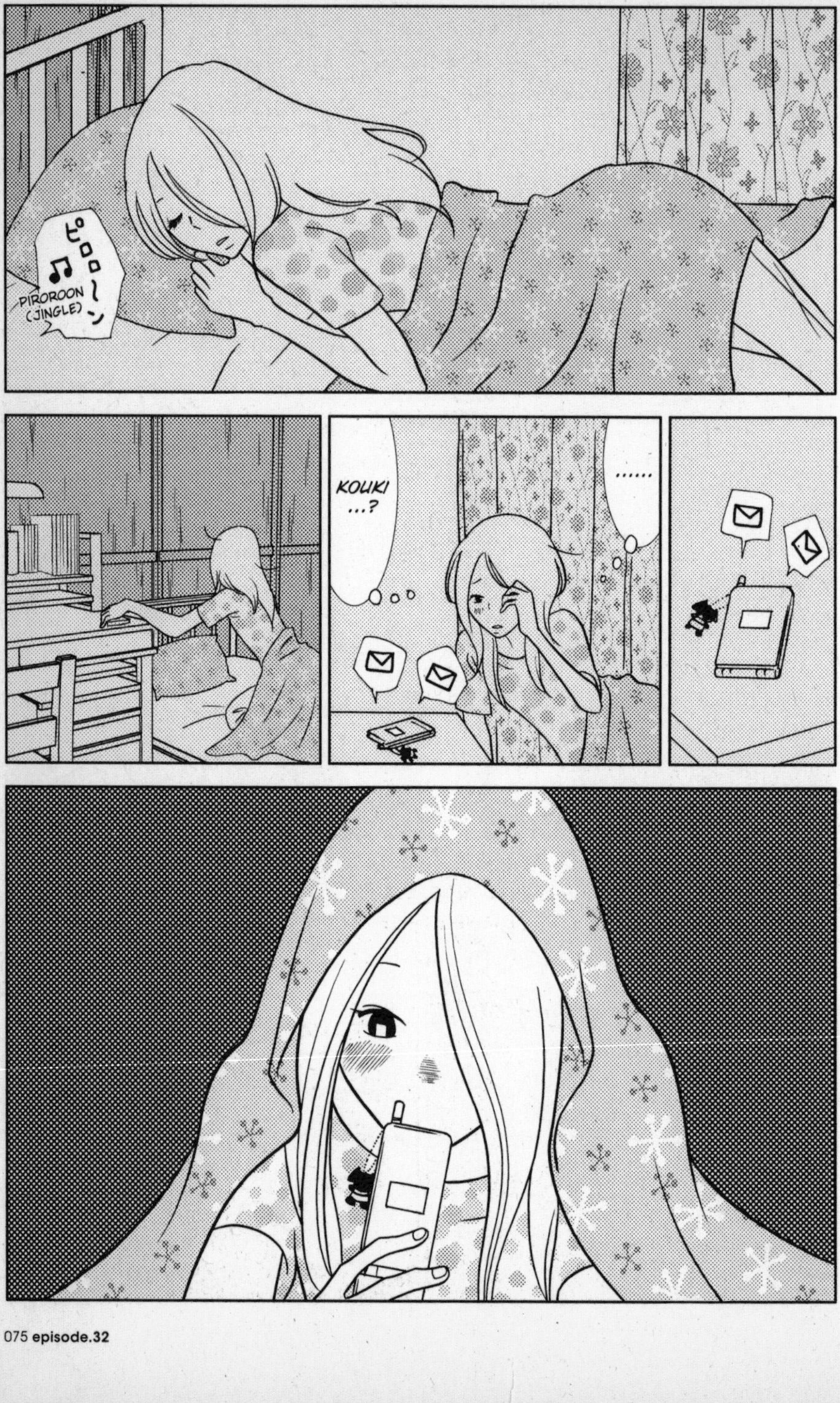
ピロローン
PIROROON (JINGLE)
......
KOUKI ...?

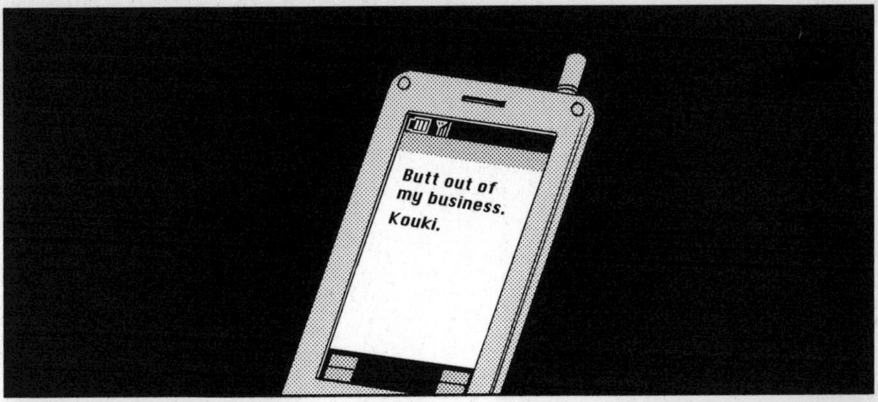
Butt out of
my business.
Kouki.
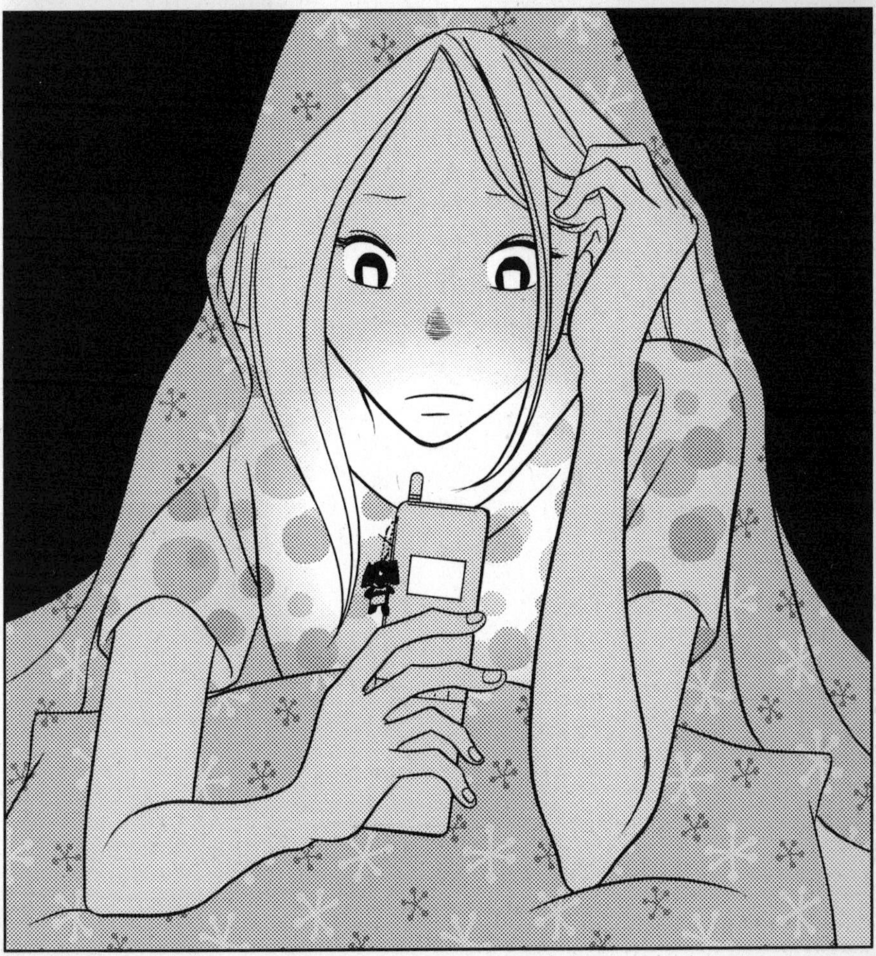

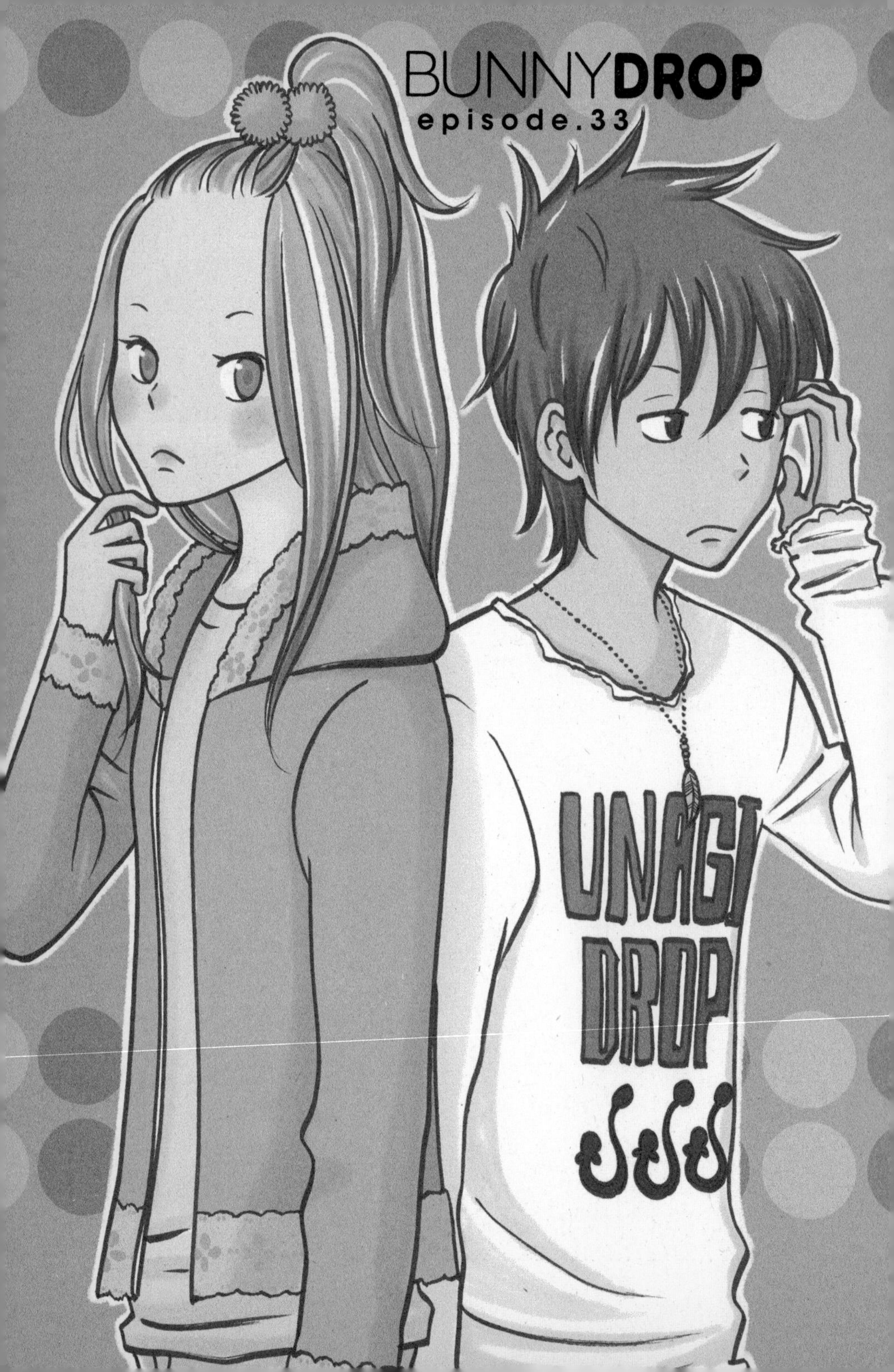
BUNNYDROP
episode.33
UNAGI
DROP

BUNNY**DROP**

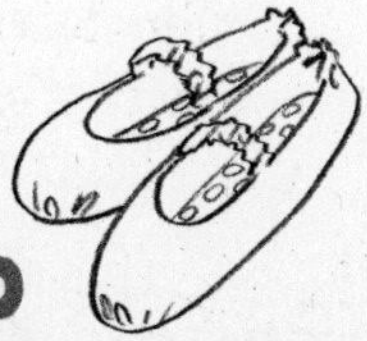

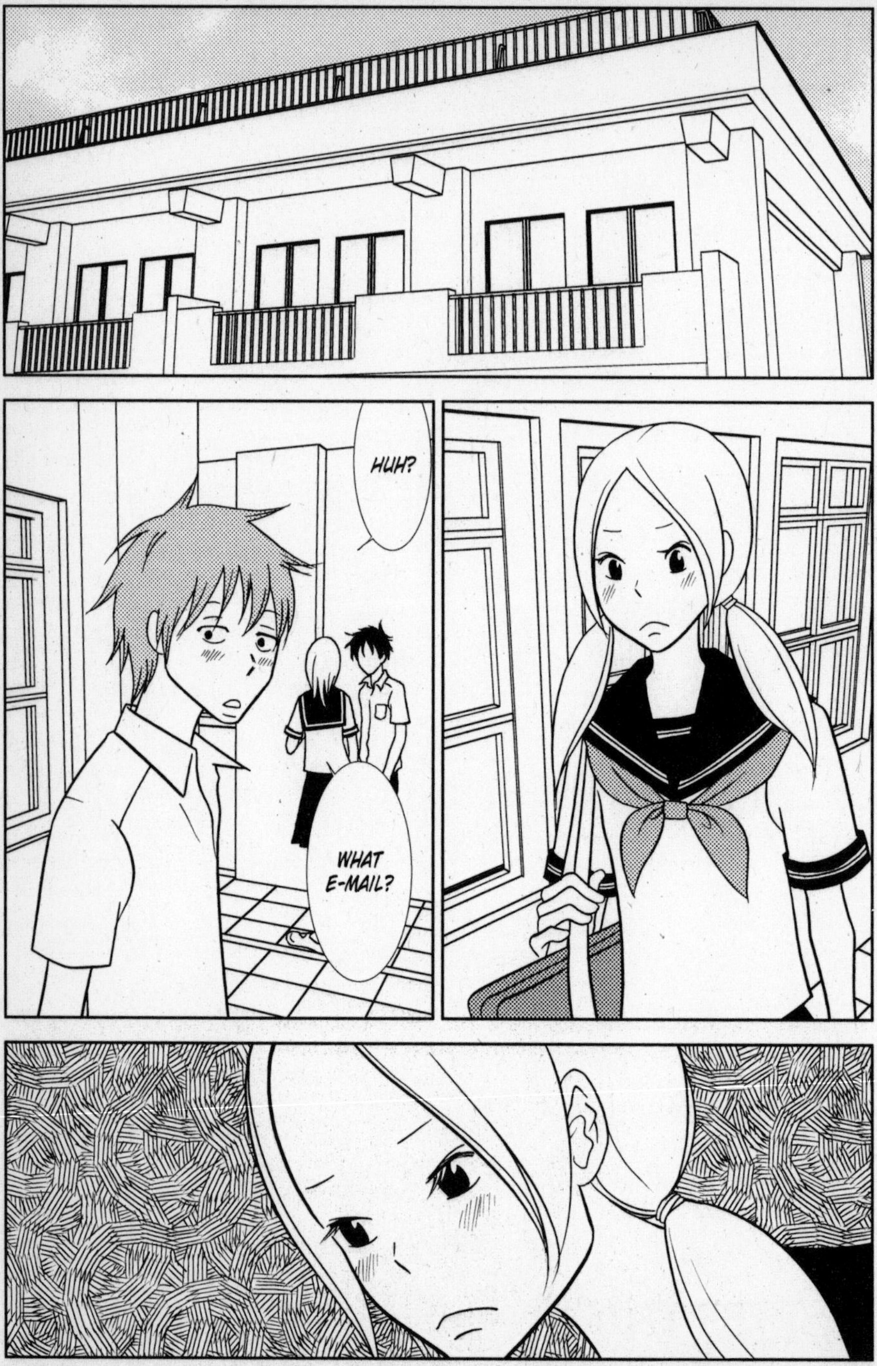
HUH?
WHAT E-MAIL?

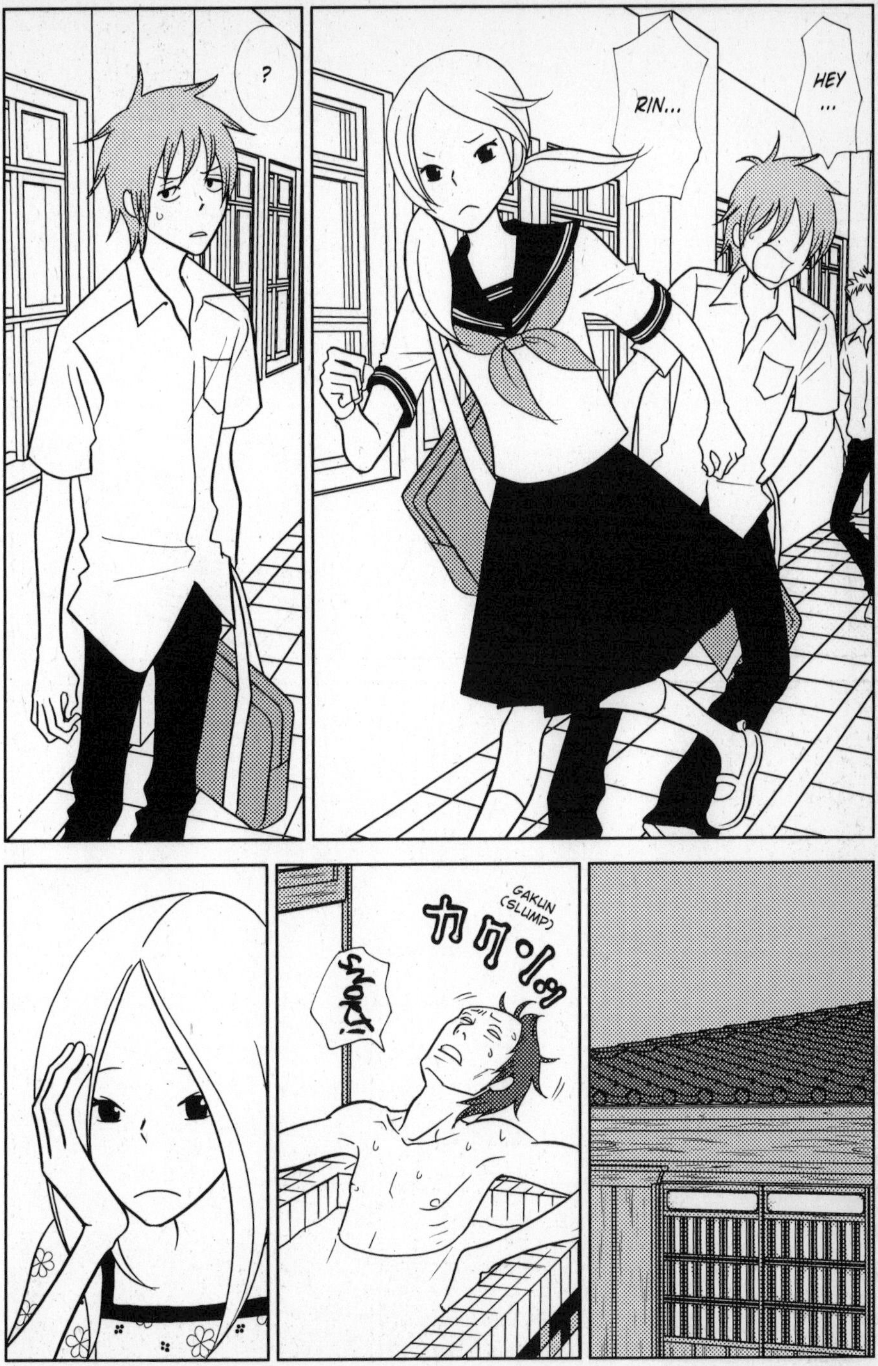
HEY ...
RIN...
?
GAKUN (SLUMP)
SNORT!

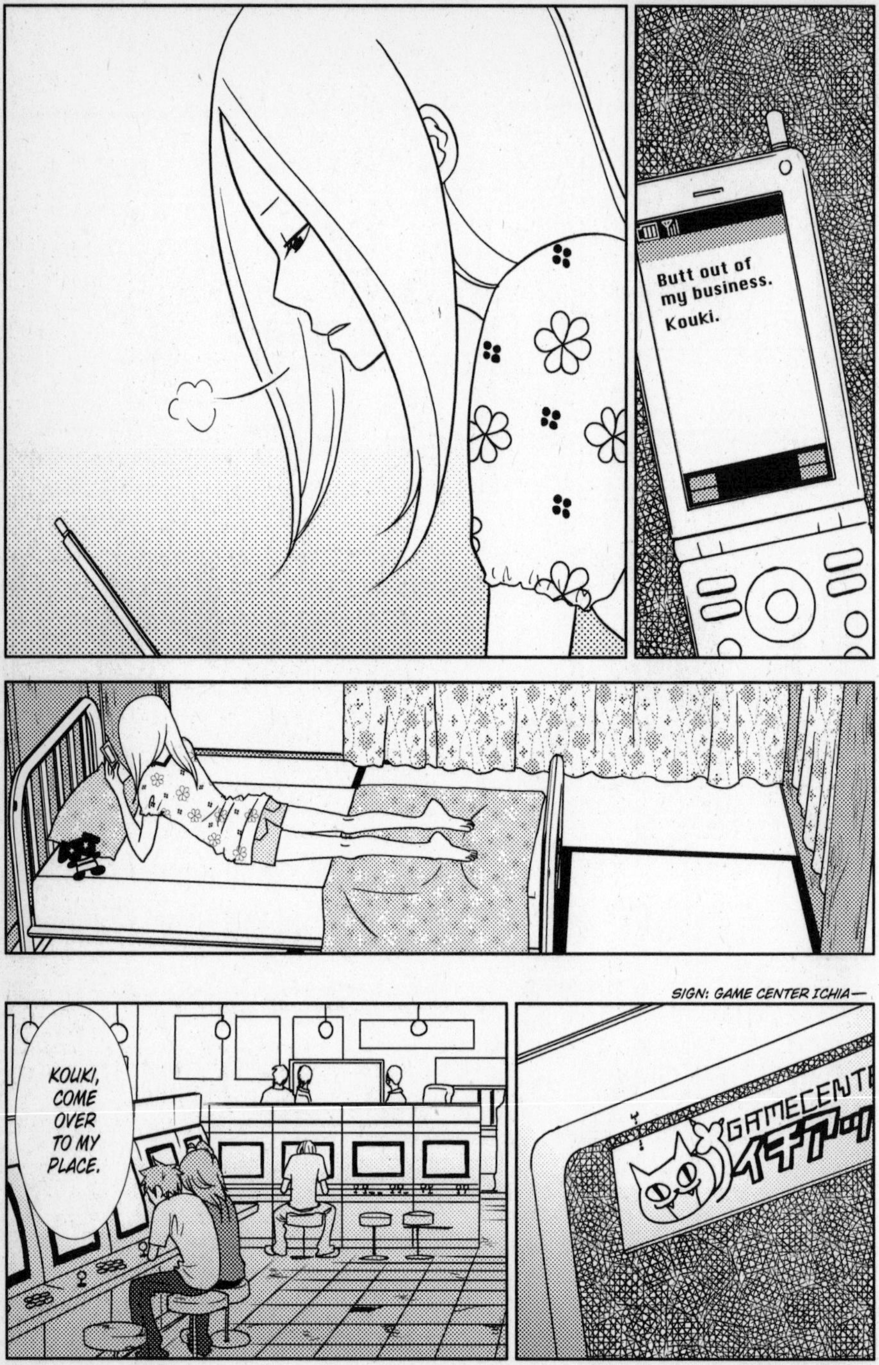
Butt out of my business. Kouki.
SIGN: GAME CENTER ICHIA—
KOUKI, COME OVER TO MY PLACE.

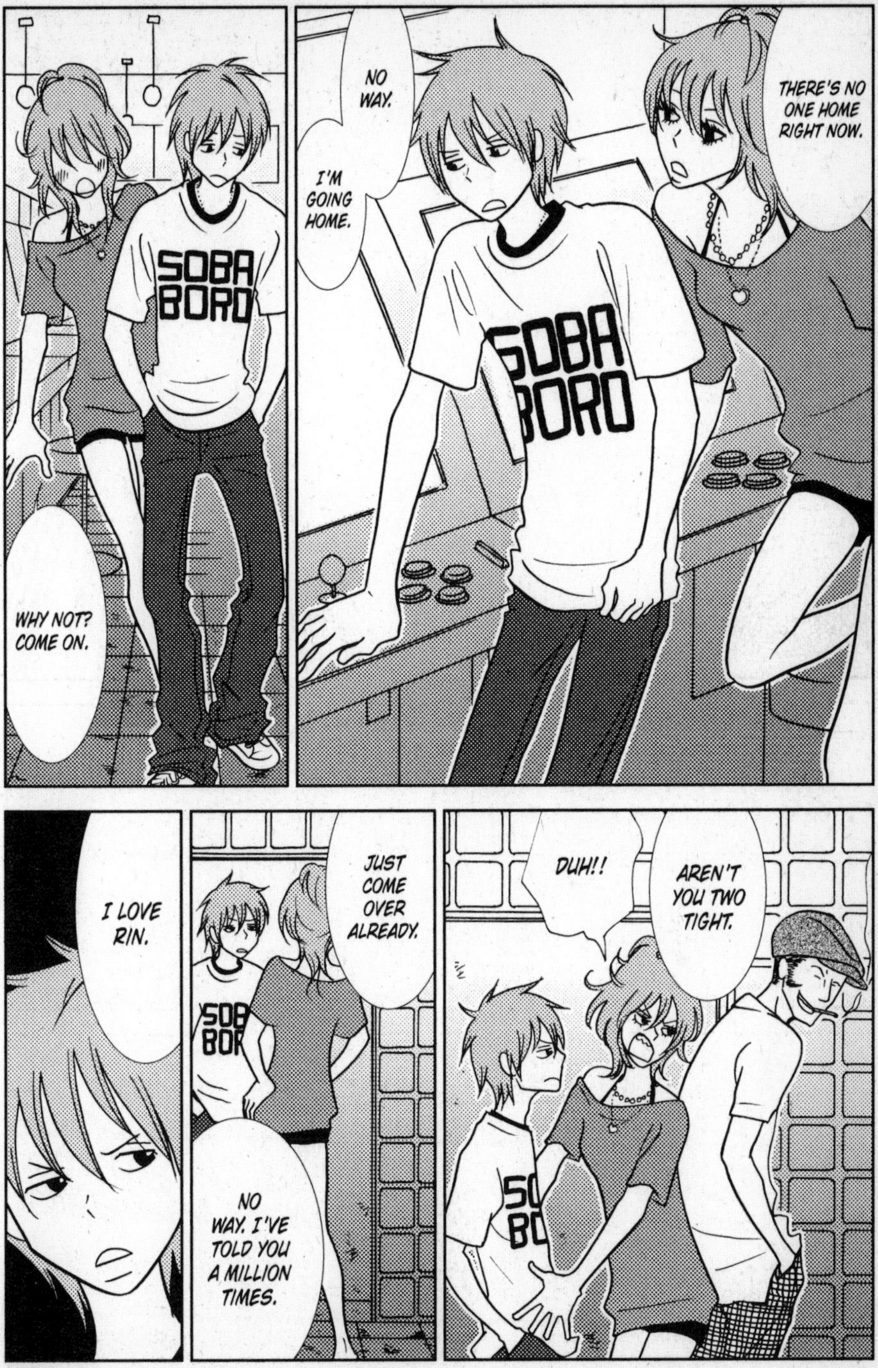
THERE'S NO ONE HOME RIGHT NOW.
NO WAY.
I'M GOING HOME.
WHY NOT? COME ON.
AREN'T YOU TWO TIGHT.
DUH!!
JUST COME OVER ALREADY.
NO WAY. I'VE TOLD YOU A MILLION TIMES.
I LOVE RIN.

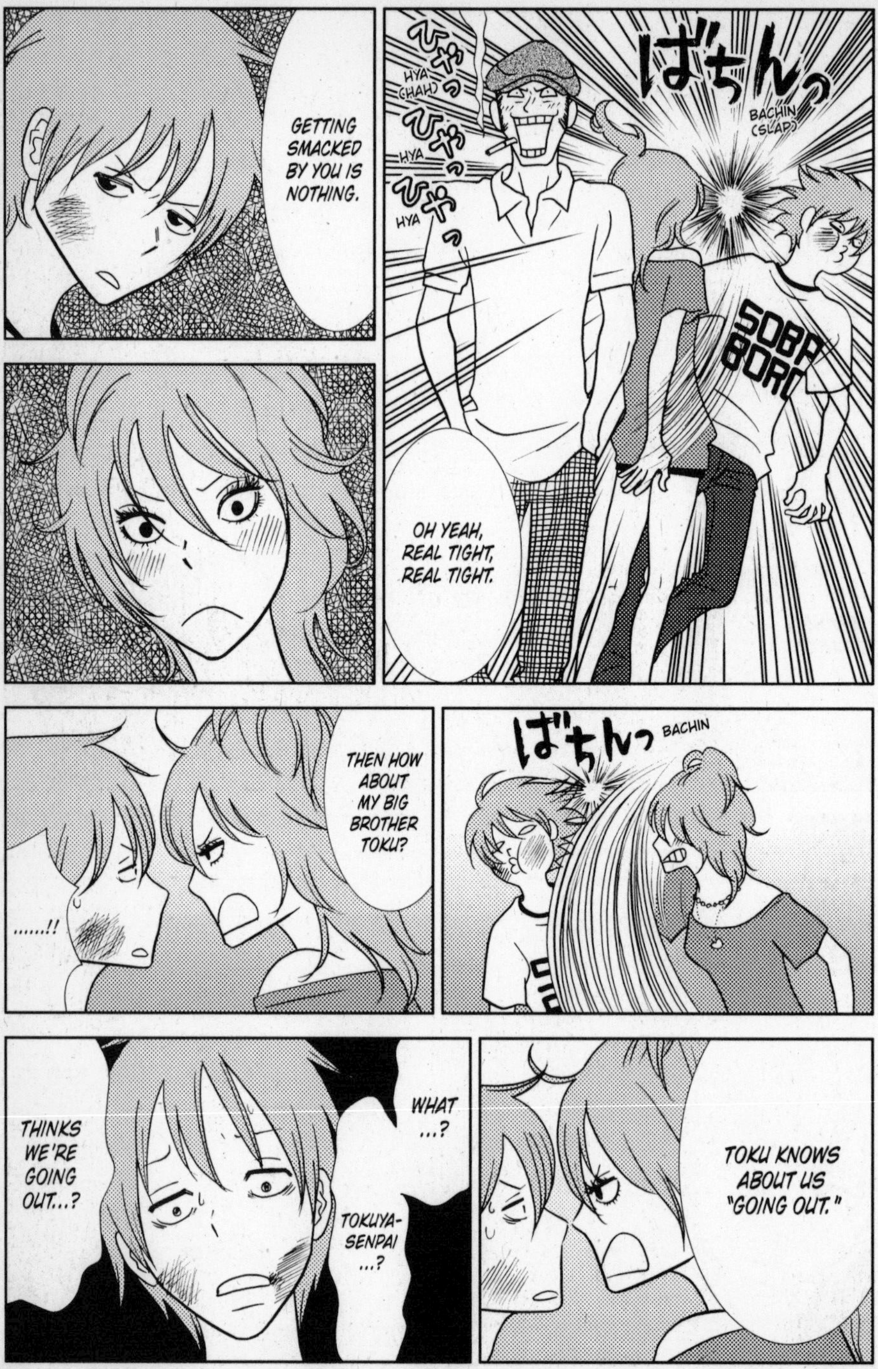
ばちんっ
BACHIN (SLAP)
ひゃっ
HYA (HAH)
ひゃっ
HYA
ひゃっ
HYA
OH YEAH, REAL TIGHT, REAL TIGHT.
GETTING SMACKED BY YOU IS NOTHING.
ばちんっ
BACHIN
THEN HOW ABOUT MY BIG BROTHER TOKU?
......!!
TOKU KNOWS ABOUT US "GOING OUT."
WHAT ...?
TOKUYA-SENPAI ...?
THINKS WE'RE GOING OUT...?

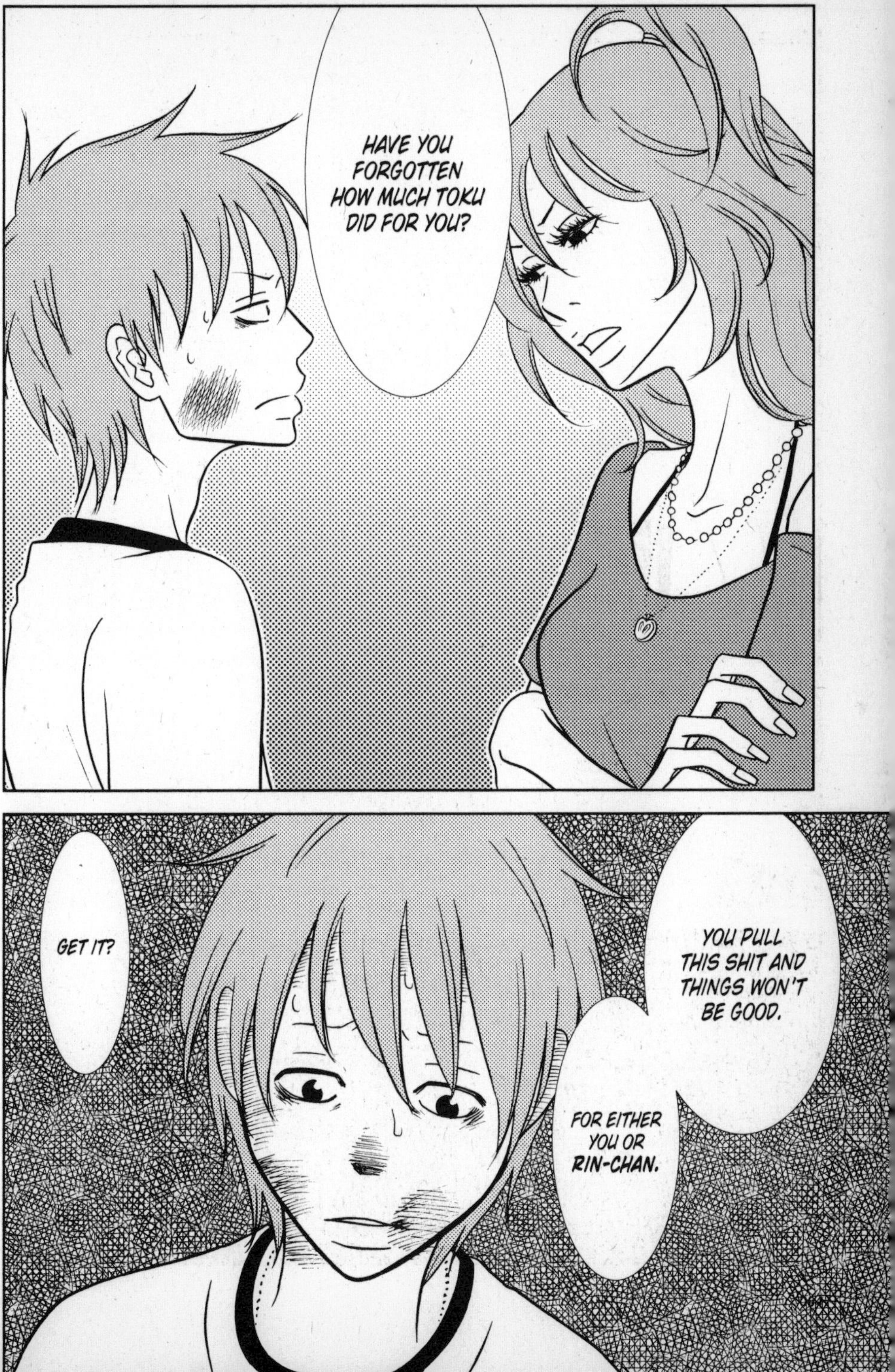
HAVE YOU FORGOTTEN HOW MUCH TOKU DID FOR YOU?
YOU PULL THIS SHIT AND THINGS WON'T BE GOOD.
FOR EITHER YOU OR RIN-CHAN.
GET IT?

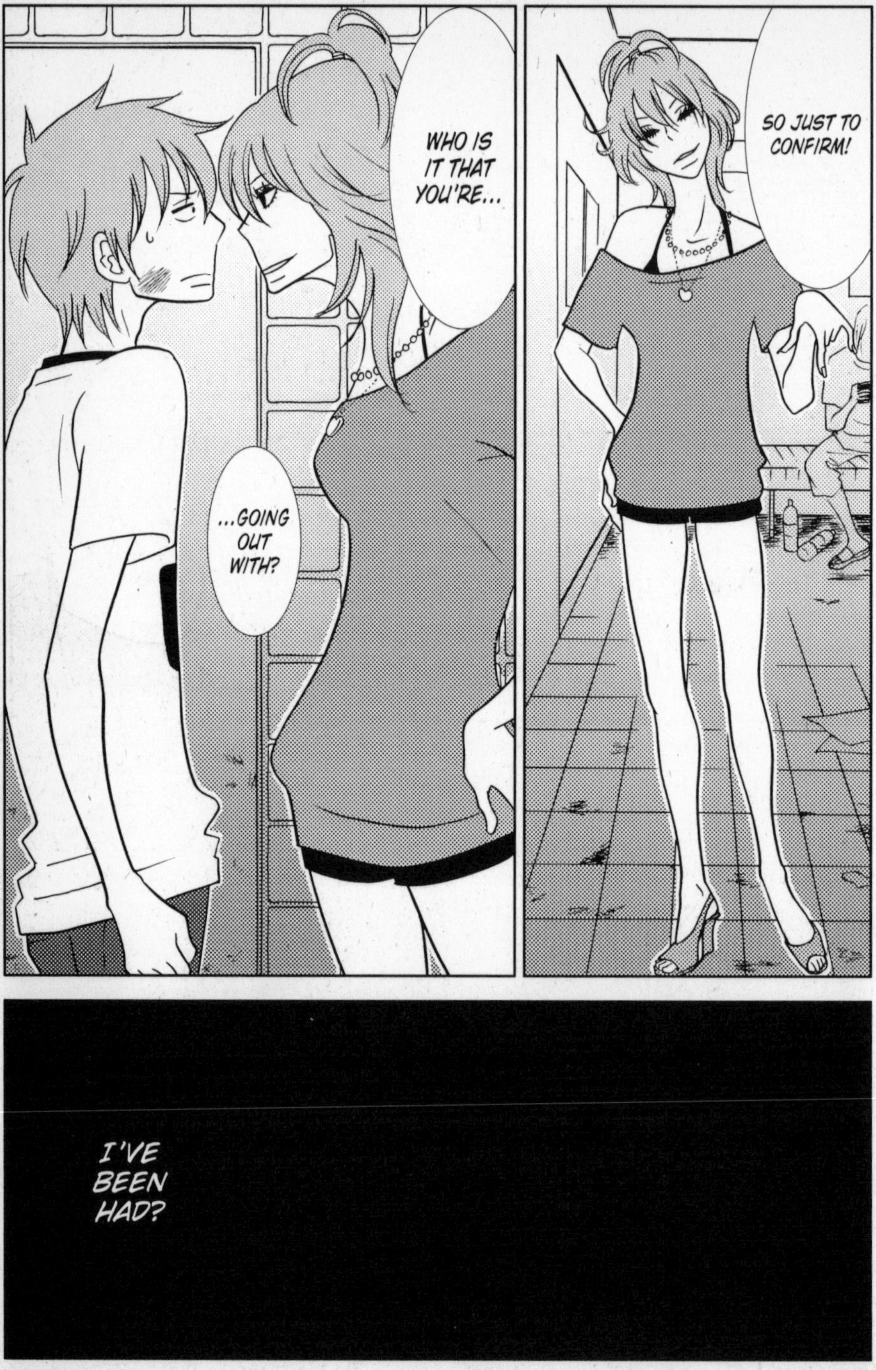
SO JUST TO CONFIRM!
WHO IS IT THAT YOU'RE...
...GOING OUT WITH?
I'VE BEEN HAD?

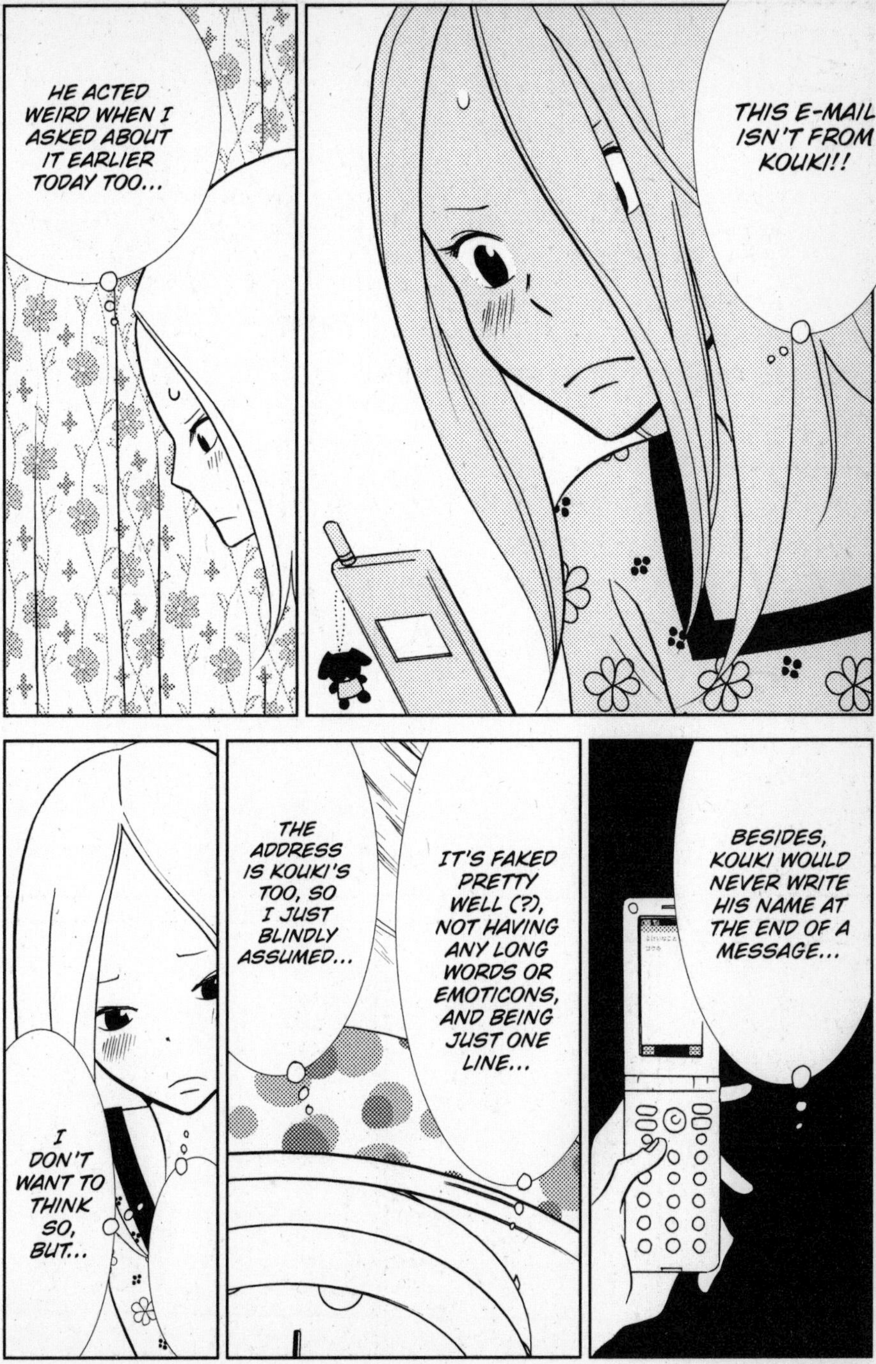
THIS E-MAIL ISN'T FROM KOUKI!!
HE ACTED WEIRD WHEN I ASKED ABOUT IT EARLIER TODAY TOO...
BESIDES, KOUKI WOULD NEVER WRITE HIS NAME AT THE END OF A MESSAGE...
IT'S FAKED PRETTY WELL (?), NOT HAVING ANY LONG WORDS OR EMOTICONS, AND BEING JUST ONE LINE...
THE ADDRESS IS KOUKI'S TOO, SO I JUST BLINDLY ASSUMED...
I DON'T WANT TO THINK SO, BUT...

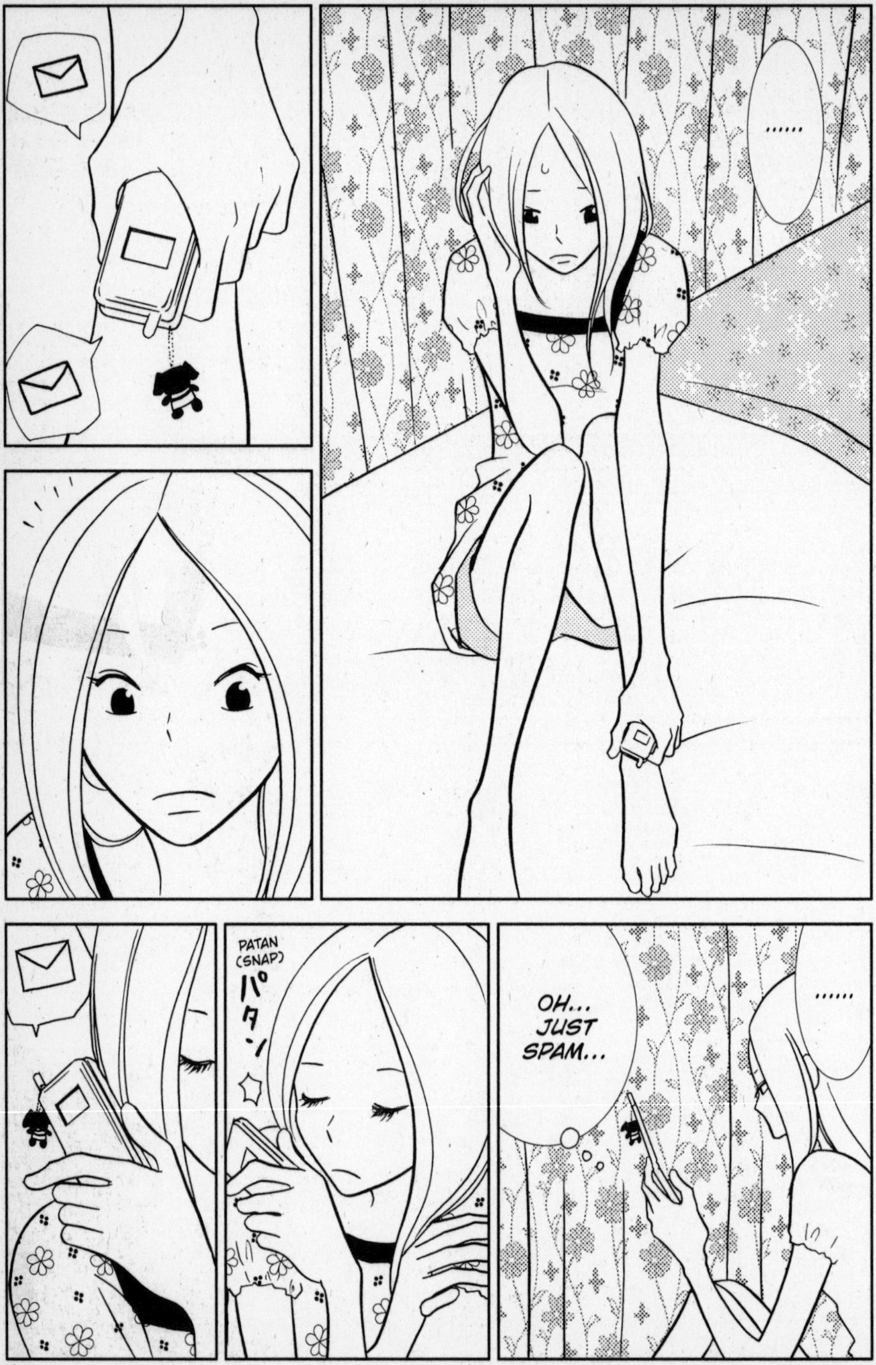

......
......
OH... JUST SPAM...
PATAN (SNAP)
パタン

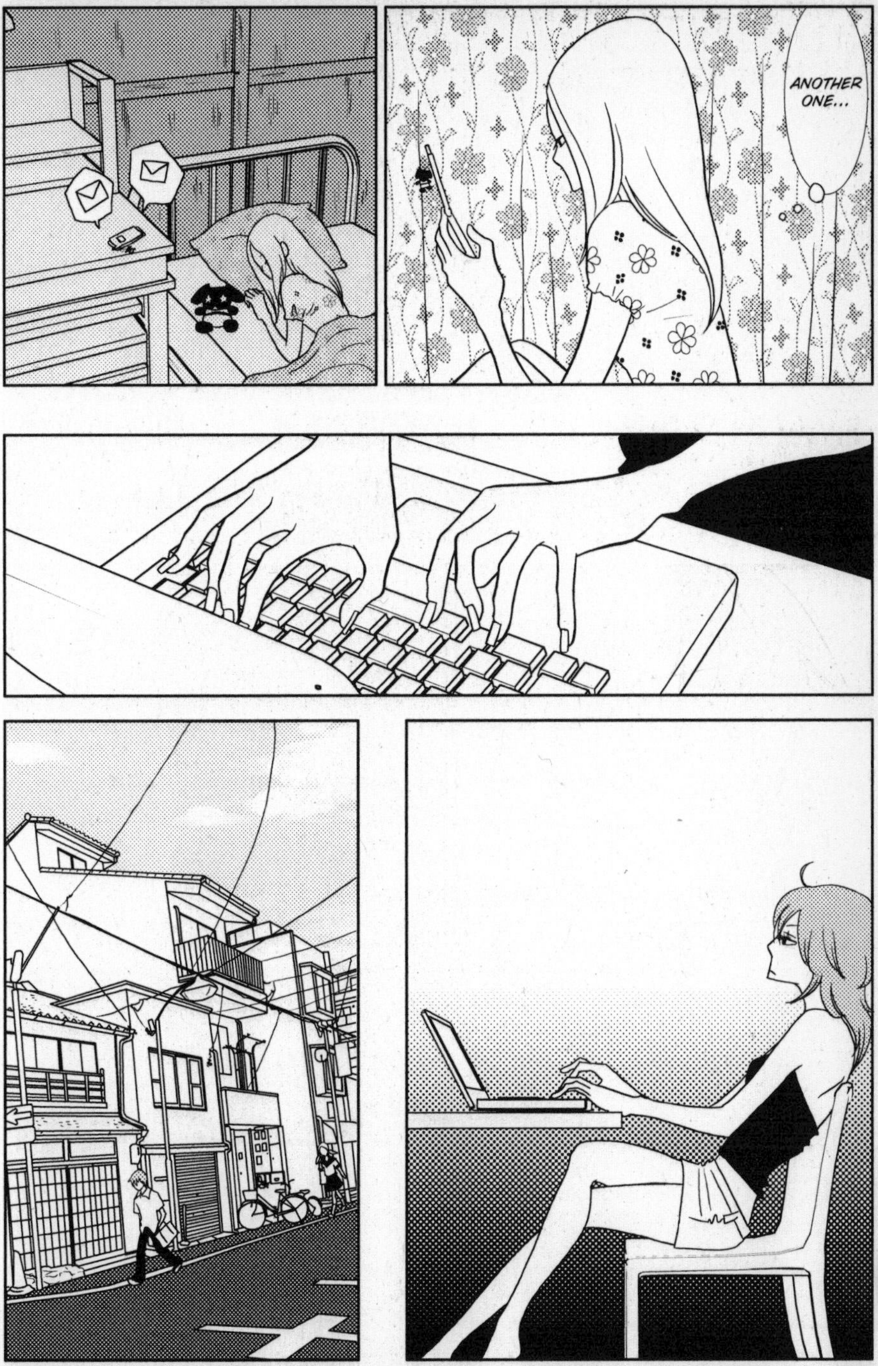
ANOTHER ONE...

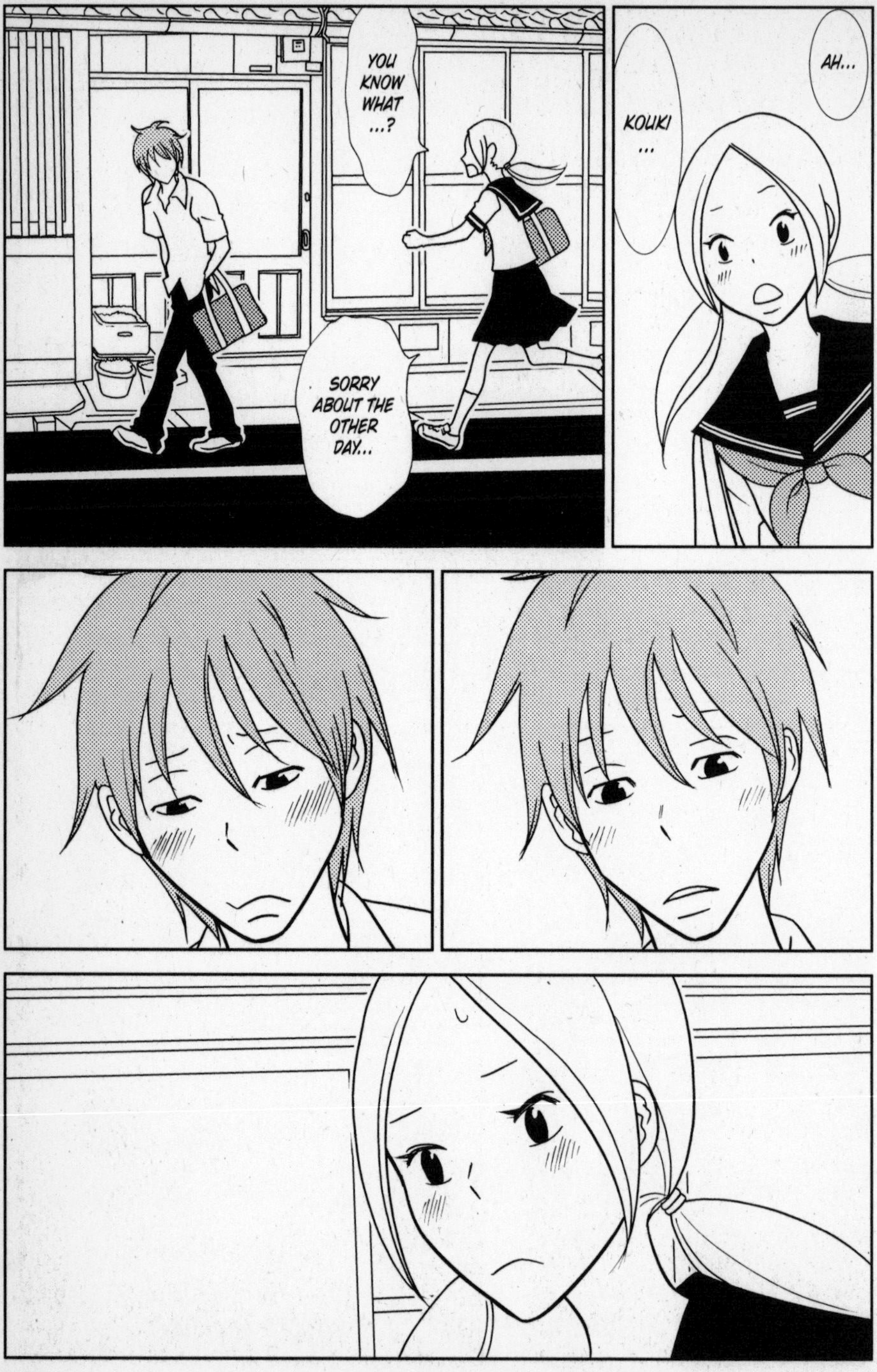
AH...
KOUKI...
YOU KNOW WHAT ...?
SORRY ABOUT THE OTHER DAY...

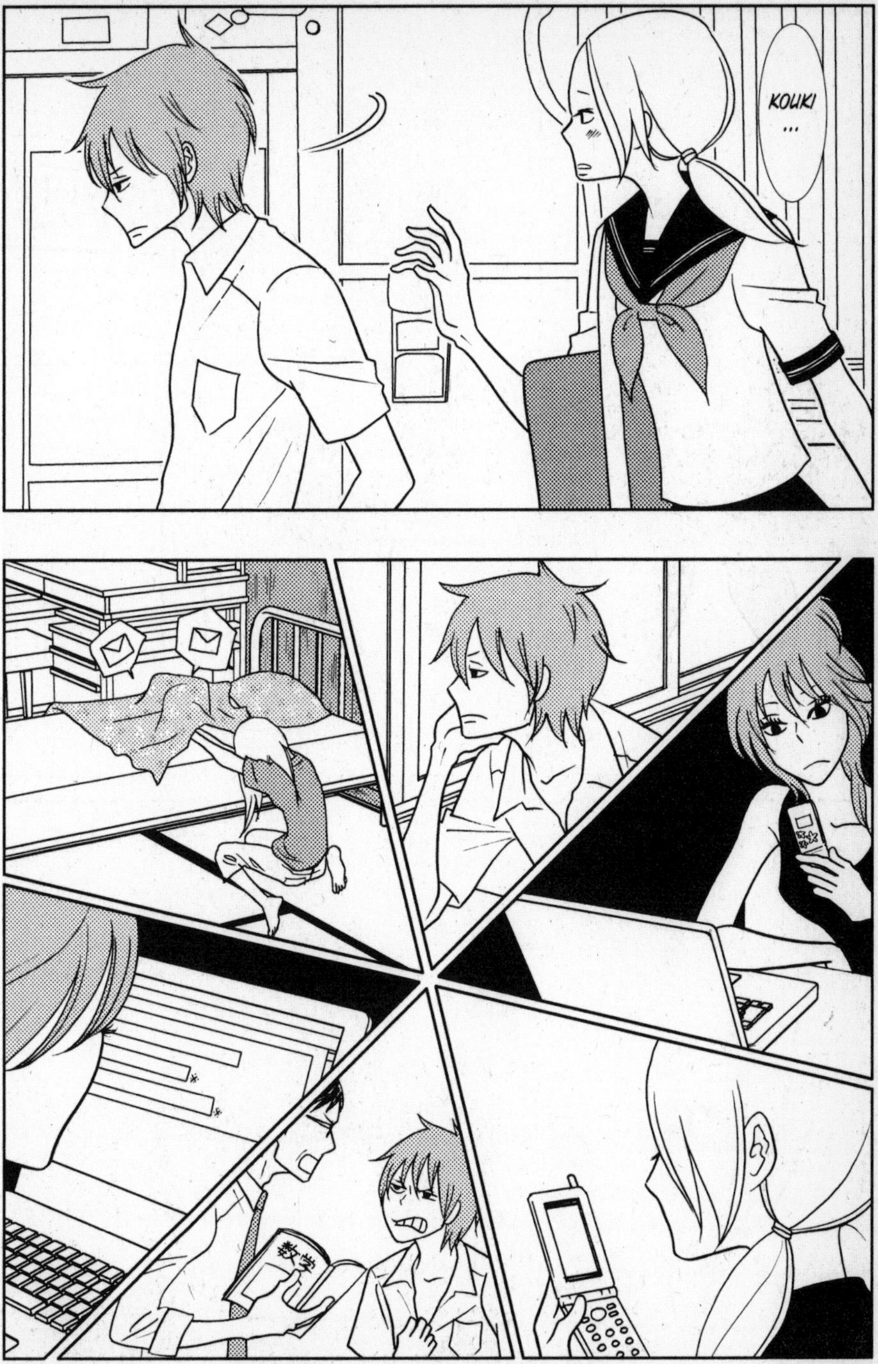
KOUKI ...
数学

BOOK: MATH

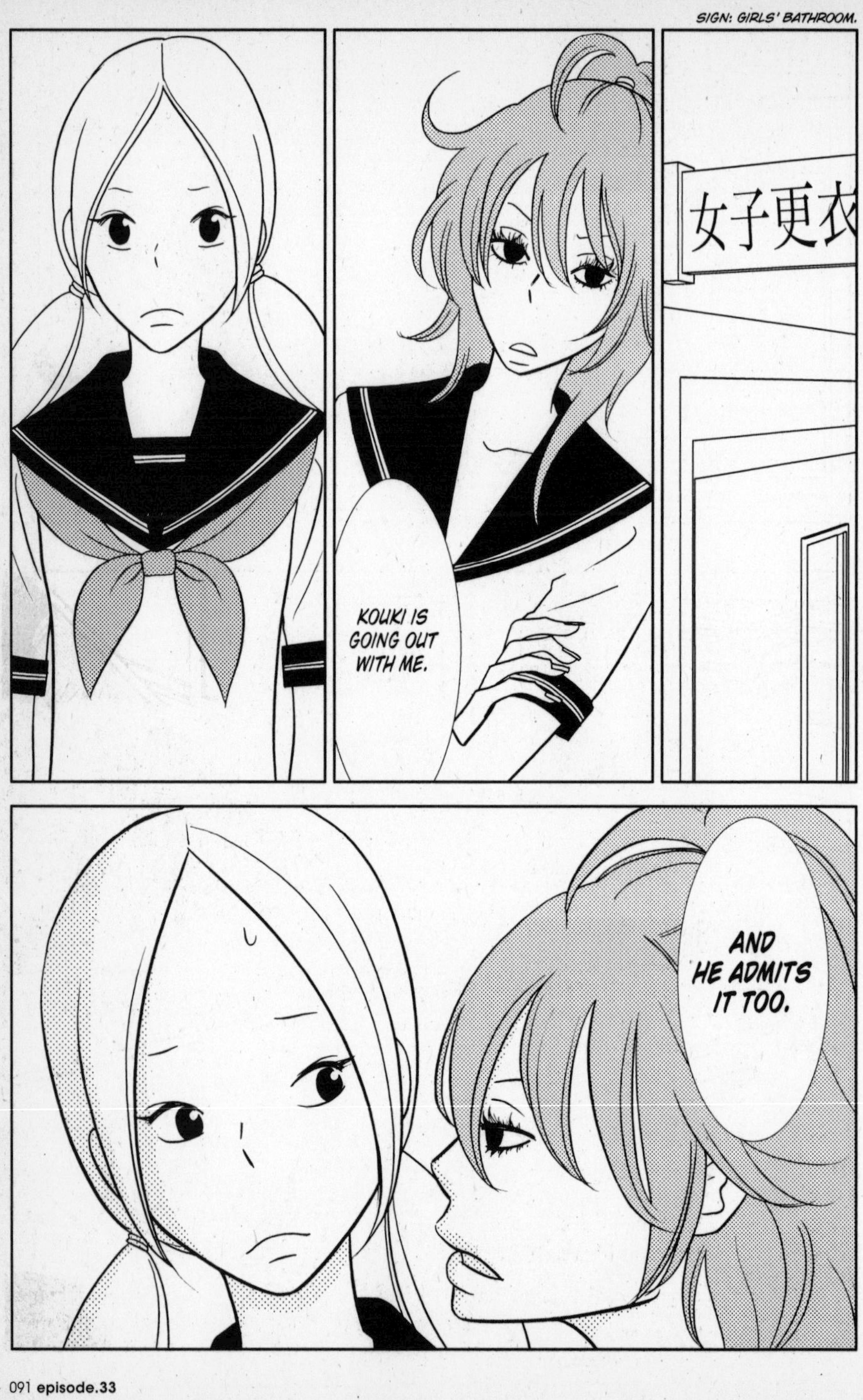
SIGN: GIRLS' BATHROOM.
女子更衣
KOUKI IS GOING OUT WITH ME.
AND HE ADMITS IT TOO.

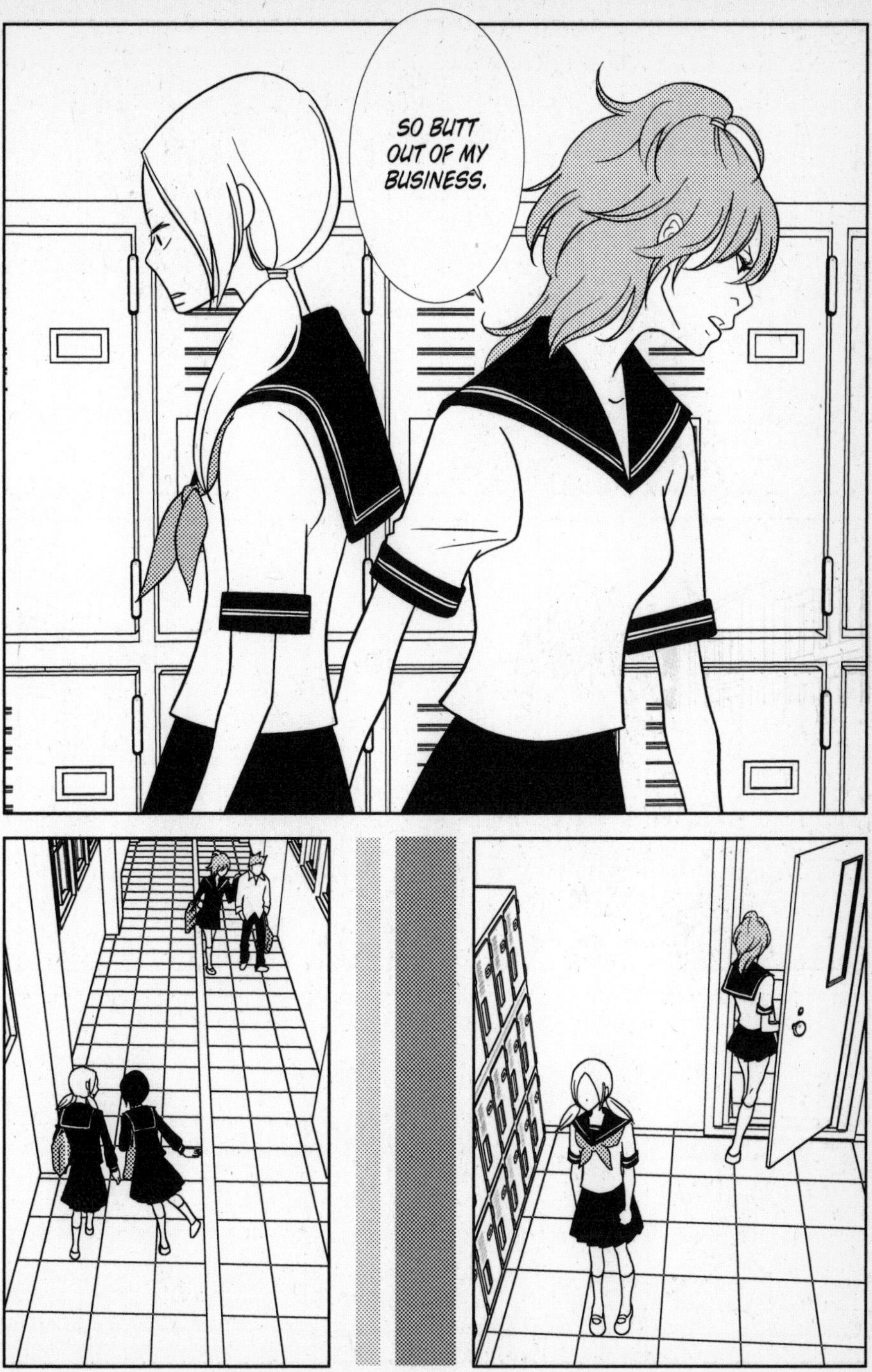
SO BUTT OUT OF MY BUSINESS.

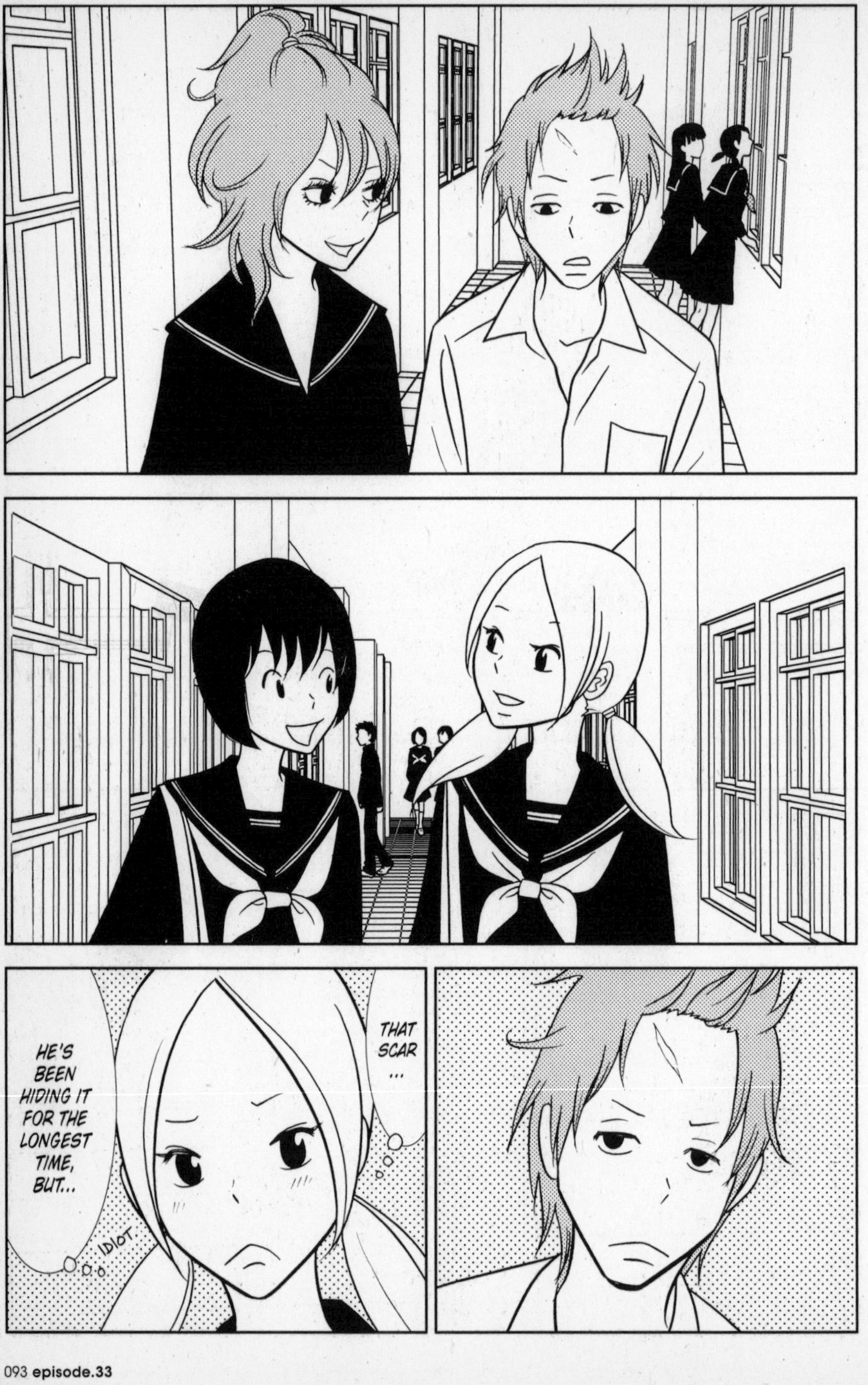
THAT SCAR ...
HE'S BEEN HIDING IT FOR THE LONGEST TIME, BUT...
IDIOT

YOU HAVE MAIL.
YOU HAVE MAIL.

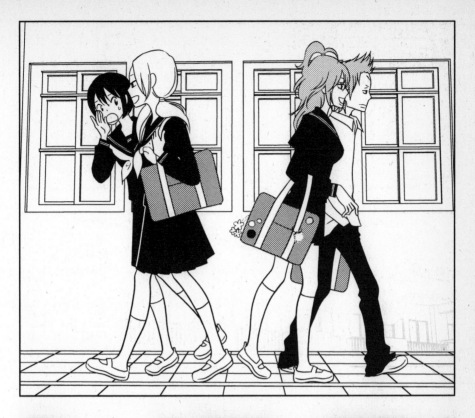

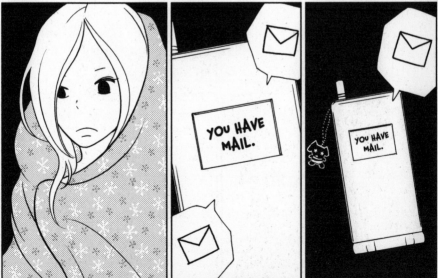

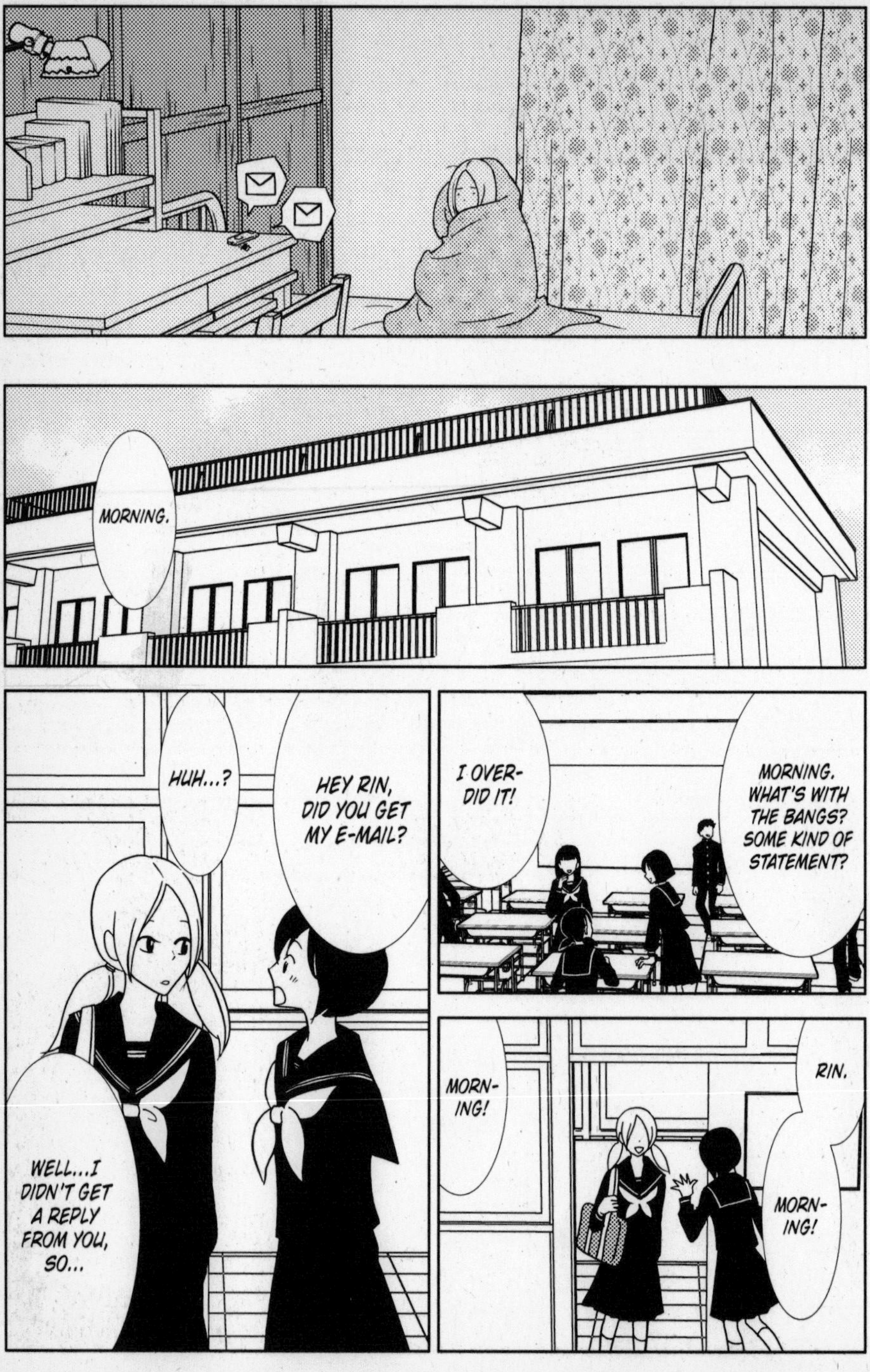
MORNING.
MORNING. WHAT'S WITH THE BANGS? SOME KIND OF STATEMENT?
I OVER-DID IT!
RIN.
MORN-ING!
MORN-ING!
HEY RIN, DID YOU GET MY E-MAIL?
HUH...?
WELL...I DIDN'T GET A REPLY FROM YOU, SO...

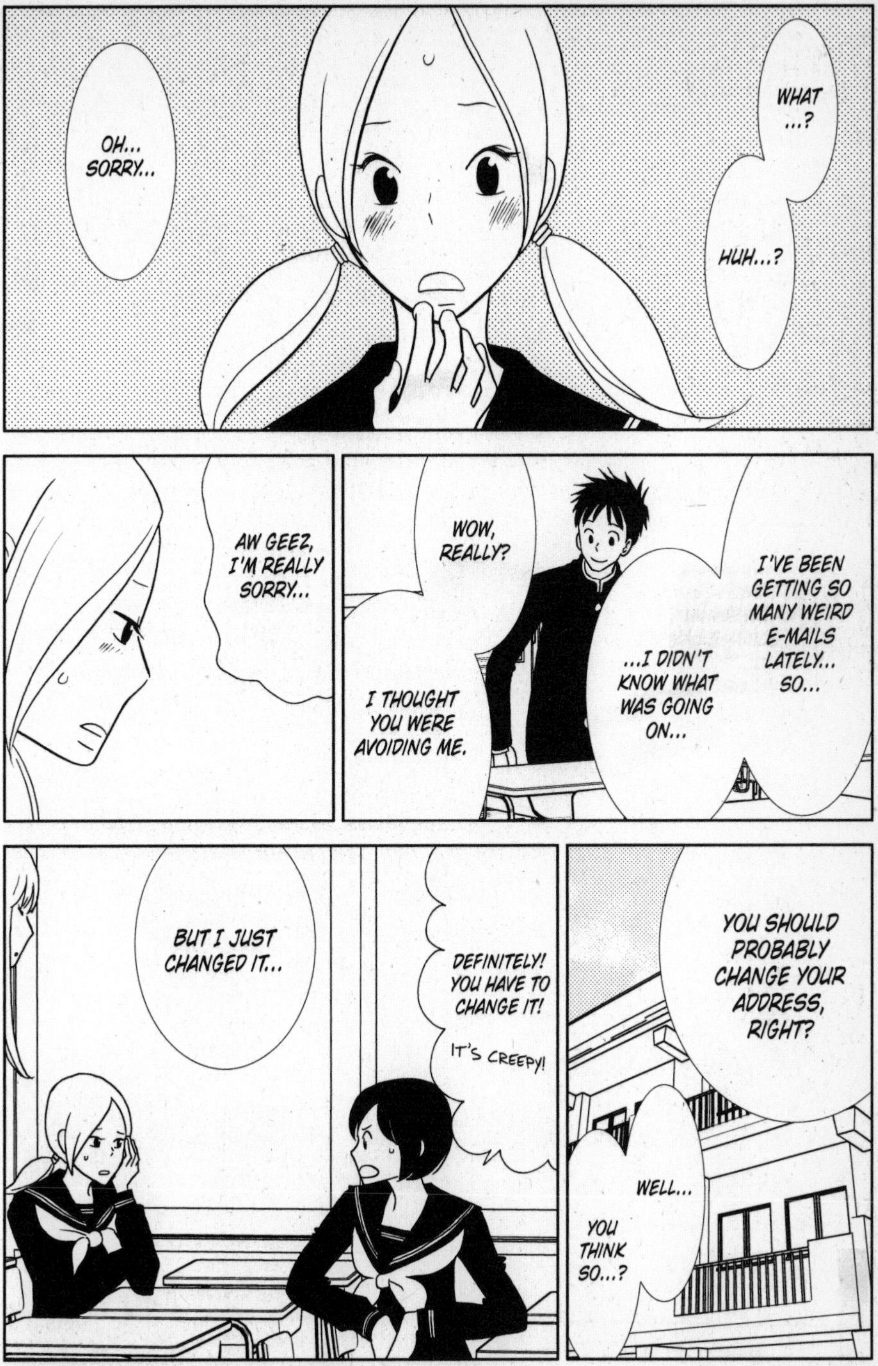
WHAT ...?
HUH...?
OH... SORRY...
I'VE BEEN GETTING SO MANY WEIRD E-MAILS LATELY... SO...
...I DIDN'T KNOW WHAT WAS GOING ON...
WOW, REALLY?
I THOUGHT YOU WERE AVOIDING ME.
AW GEEZ, I'M REALLY SORRY...
YOU SHOULD PROBABLY CHANGE YOUR ADDRESS, RIGHT?
WELL...
YOU THINK SO...?
DEFINITELY! YOU HAVE TO CHANGE IT!
IT'S CREEPY!
BUT I JUST CHANGED IT...

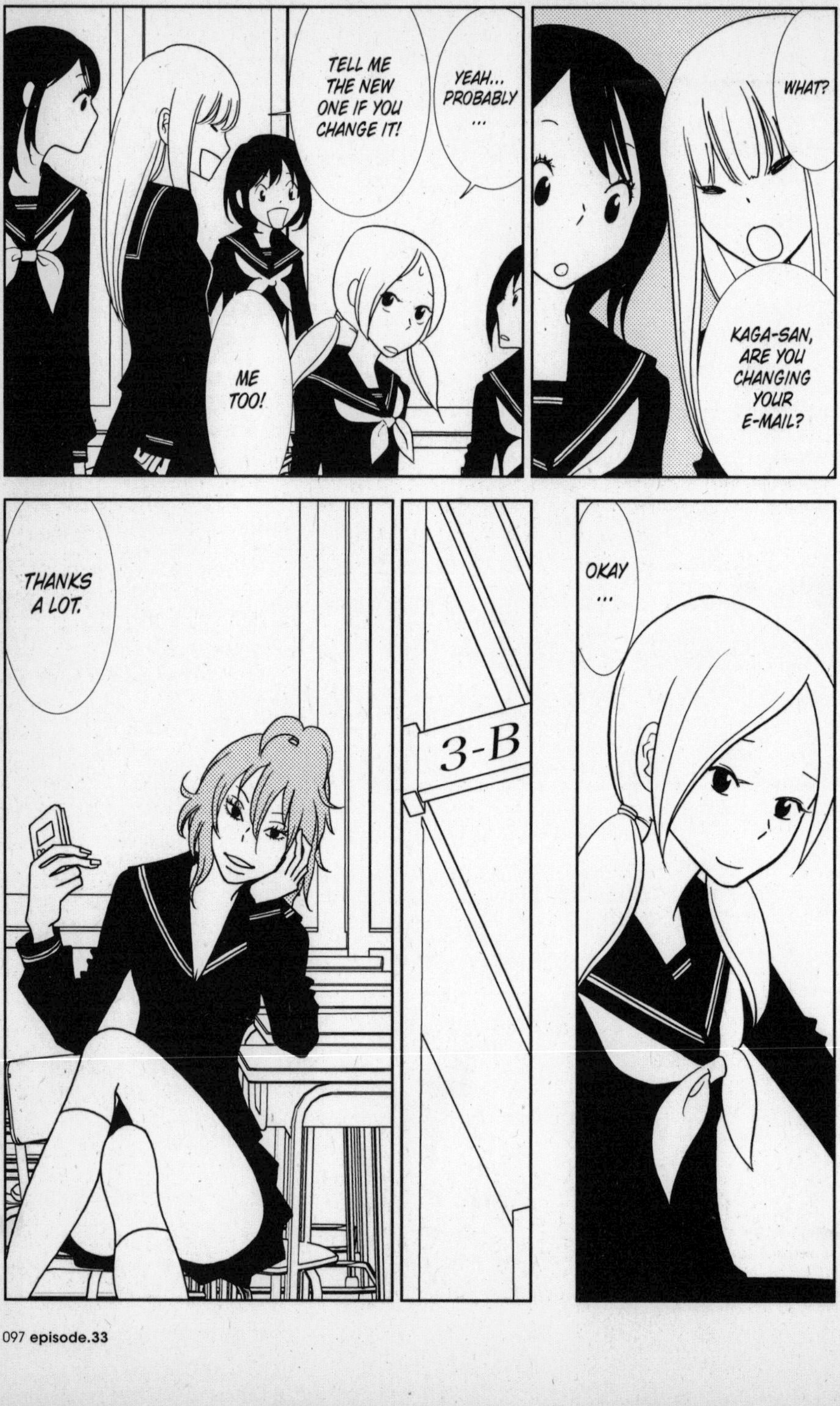
WHAT?
KAGA-SAN, ARE YOU CHANGING YOUR E-MAIL?
YEAH... PROBABLY ...
TELL ME THE NEW ONE IF YOU CHANGE IT!
ME TOO!
OKAY ...
3-B
THANKS A LOT.

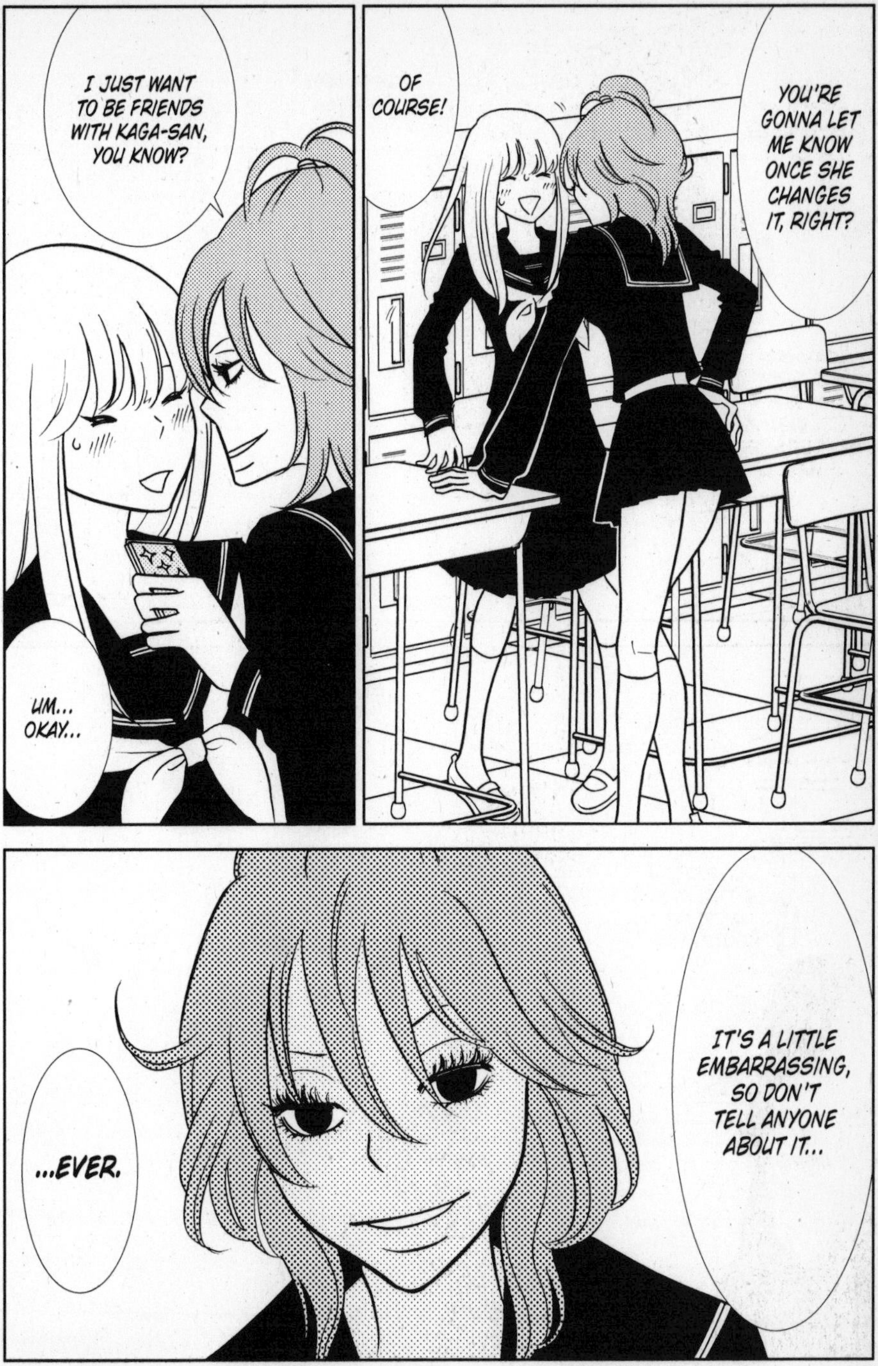
YOU'RE GONNA LET ME KNOW ONCE SHE CHANGES IT, RIGHT?
OF COURSE!
I JUST WANT TO BE FRIENDS WITH KAGA-SAN, YOU KNOW?
UM... OKAY...
IT'S A LITTLE EMBARRASSING, SO DON'T TELL ANYONE ABOUT IT...
...EVER.

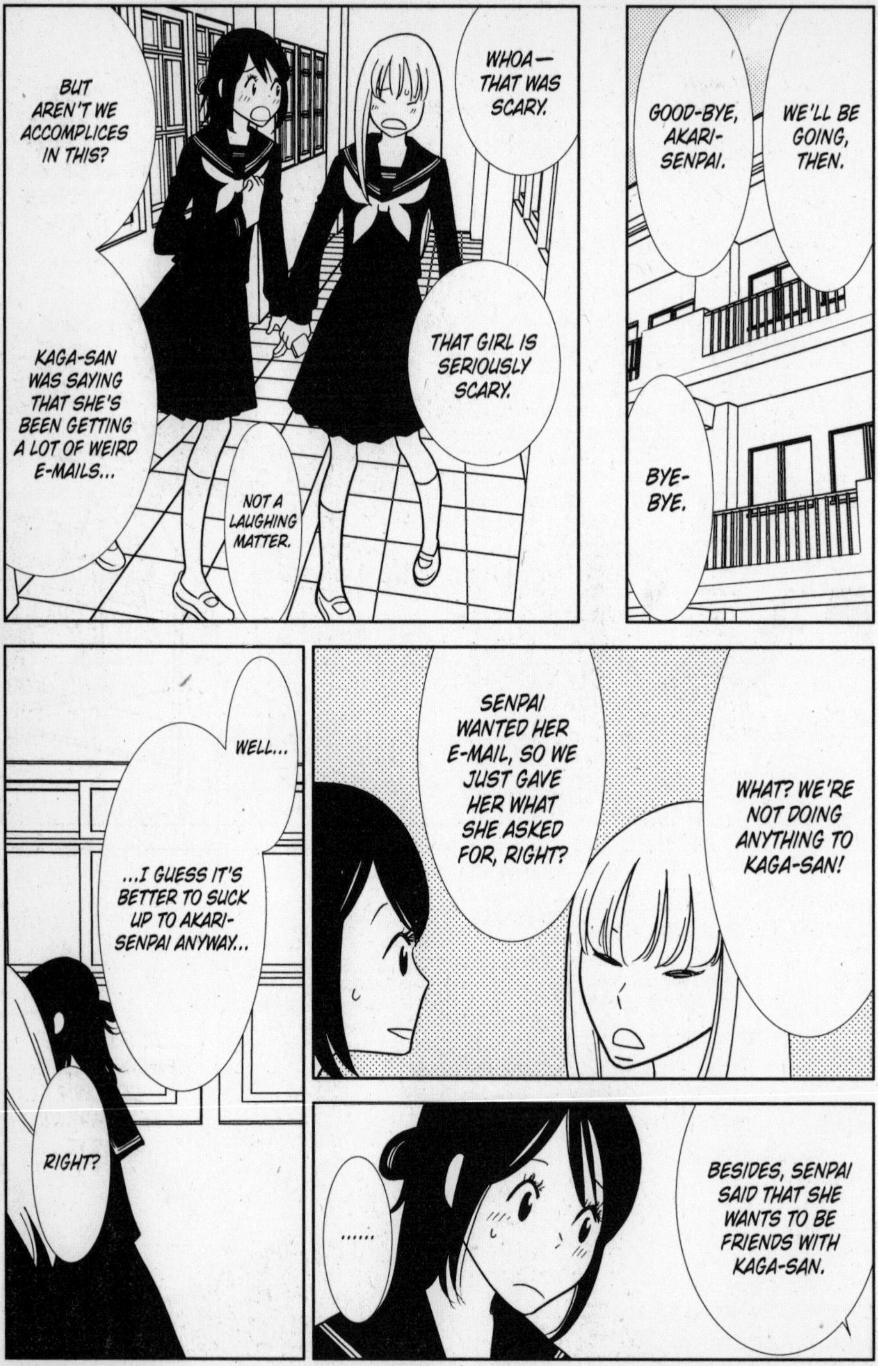
WE'LL BE GOING, THEN.
GOOD-BYE, AKARI-SENPAI.
BYE-BYE.
WHOA—THAT WAS SCARY.
BUT AREN'T WE ACCOMPLICES IN THIS?
THAT GIRL IS SERIOUSLY SCARY.
KAGA-SAN WAS SAYING THAT SHE'S BEEN GETTING A LOT OF WEIRD E-MAILS...
NOT A LAUGHING MATTER.
WHAT? WE'RE NOT DOING ANYTHING TO KAGA-SAN!
SENPAI WANTED HER E-MAIL, SO WE JUST GAVE HER WHAT SHE ASKED FOR, RIGHT?
BESIDES, SENPAI SAID THAT SHE WANTS TO BE FRIENDS WITH KAGA-SAN.
......
WELL...
...I GUESS IT'S BETTER TO SUCK UP TO AKARI-SENPAI ANYWAY...
RIGHT?

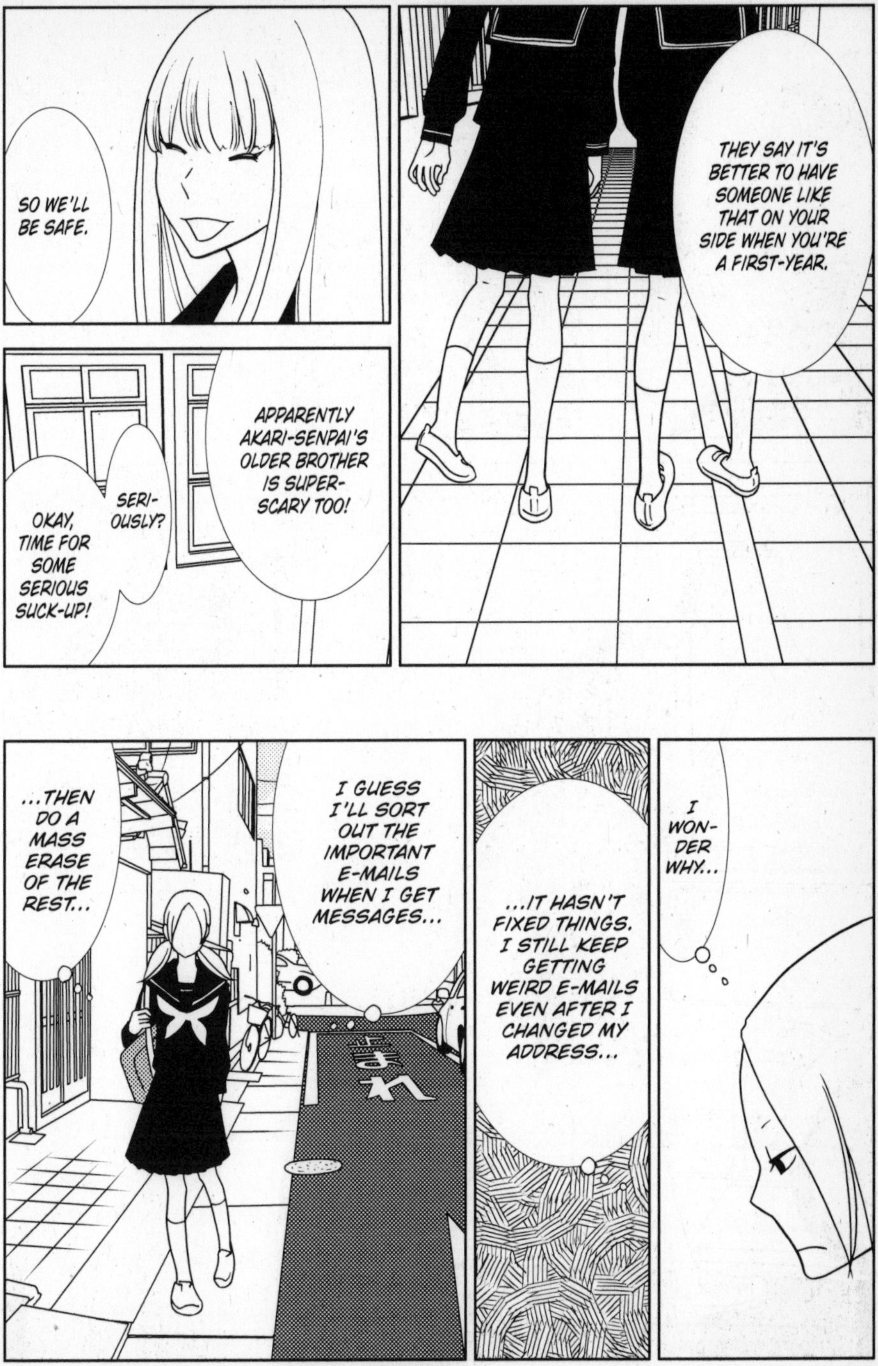
THEY SAY IT'S BETTER TO HAVE SOMEONE LIKE THAT ON YOUR SIDE WHEN YOU'RE A FIRST-YEAR.
SO WE'LL BE SAFE.
APPARENTLY AKARI-SENPAI'S OLDER BROTHER IS SUPER-SCARY TOO!
SERI-OUSLY?
OKAY, TIME FOR SOME SERIOUS SUCK-UP!
I WON-DER WHY...
...IT HASN'T FIXED THINGS. I STILL KEEP GETTING WEIRD E-MAILS EVEN AFTER I CHANGED MY ADDRESS...
I GUESS I'LL SORT OUT THE IMPORTANT E-MAILS WHEN I GET MESSAGES...
...THEN DO A MASS ERASE OF THE REST...

STREET: STOP

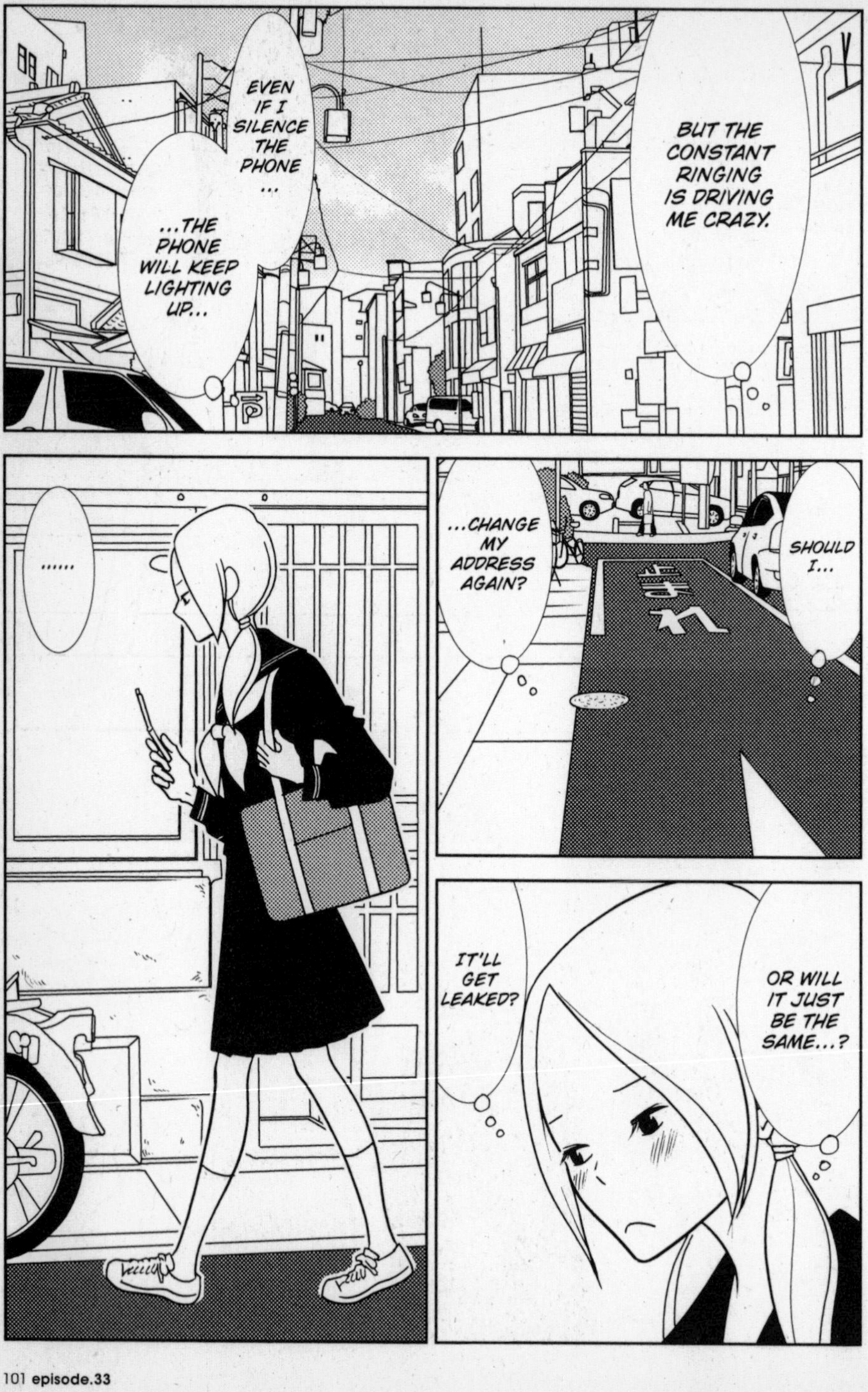
BUT THE CONSTANT RINGING IS DRIVING ME CRAZY.
EVEN IF I SILENCE THE PHONE ...
...THE PHONE WILL KEEP LIGHTING UP...
SHOULD I...
...CHANGE MY ADDRESS AGAIN?
OR WILL IT JUST BE THE SAME...?
IT'LL GET LEAKED?
......

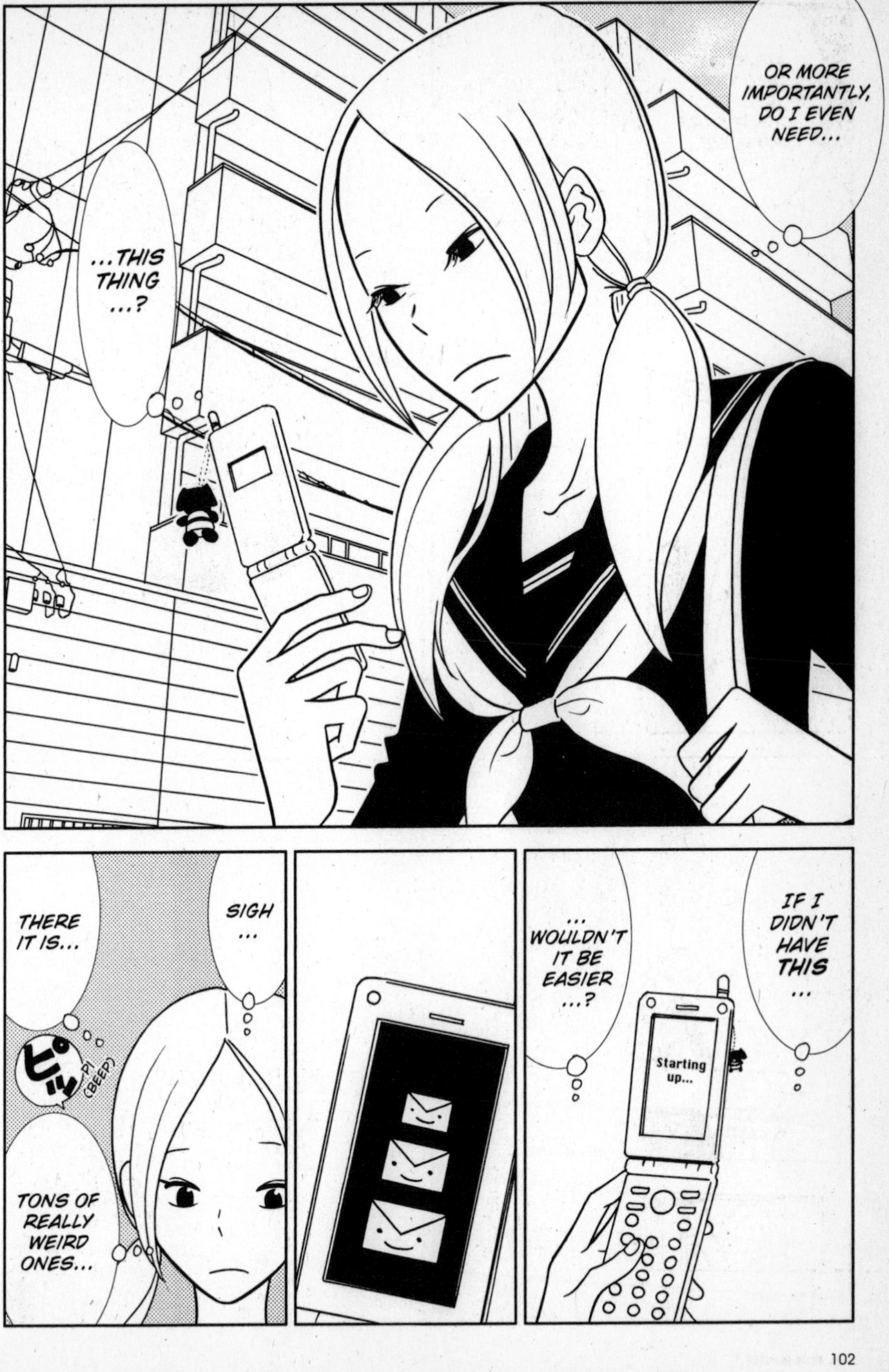

OR MORE IMPORTANTLY, DO I EVEN NEED...
...THIS THING...?
IF I DIDN'T HAVE THIS...
...WOULDN'T IT BE EASIER...?
Starting up...
SIGH...
THERE IT IS...
ピッ
PI (BEEP)
TONS OF REALLY WEIRD ONES...

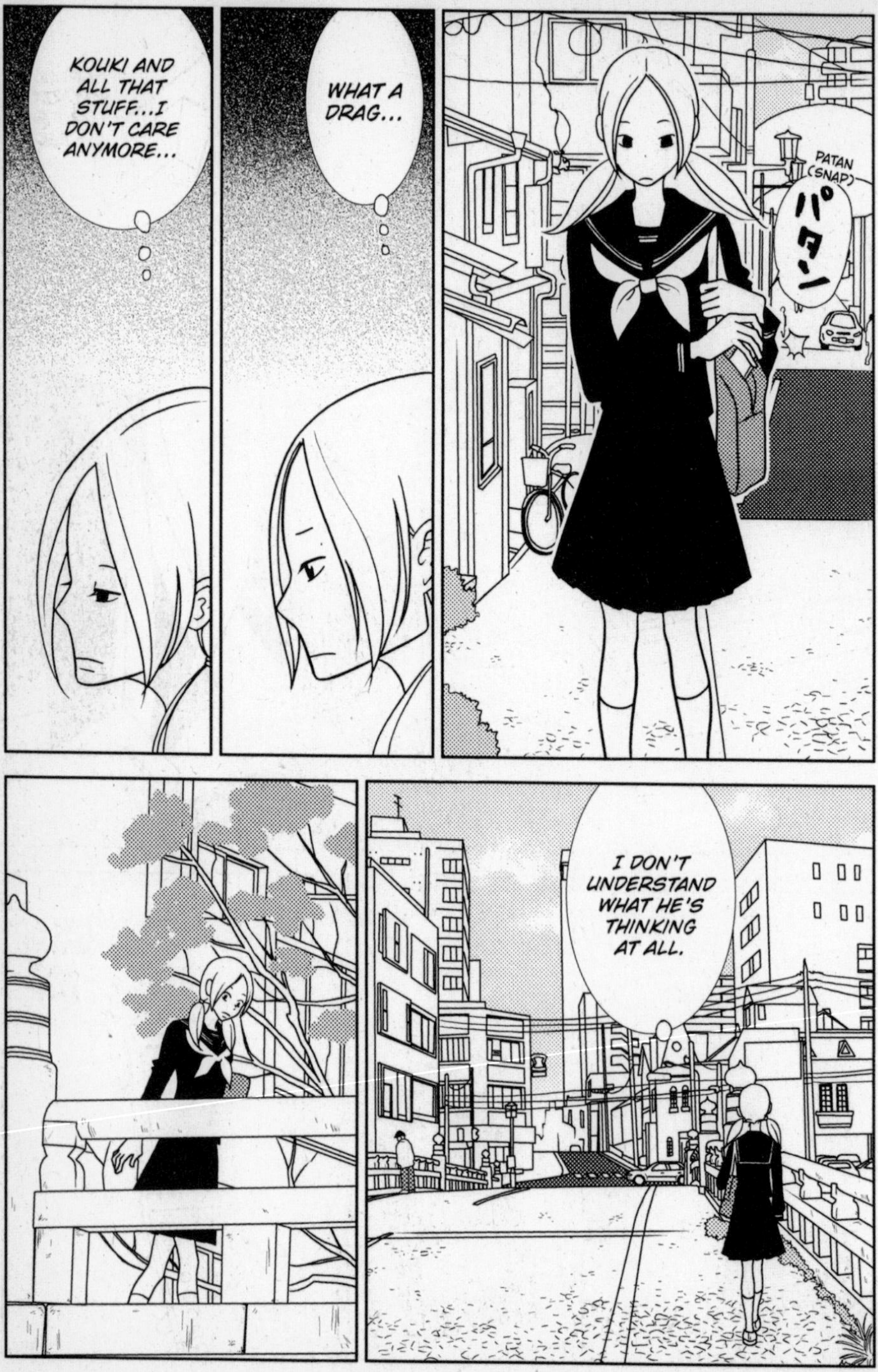
PATAN (SNAP)
パタン
WHAT A DRAG...
KOUKI AND ALL THAT STUFF...I DON'T CARE ANYMORE...
I DON'T UNDERSTAND WHAT HE'S THINKING AT ALL.

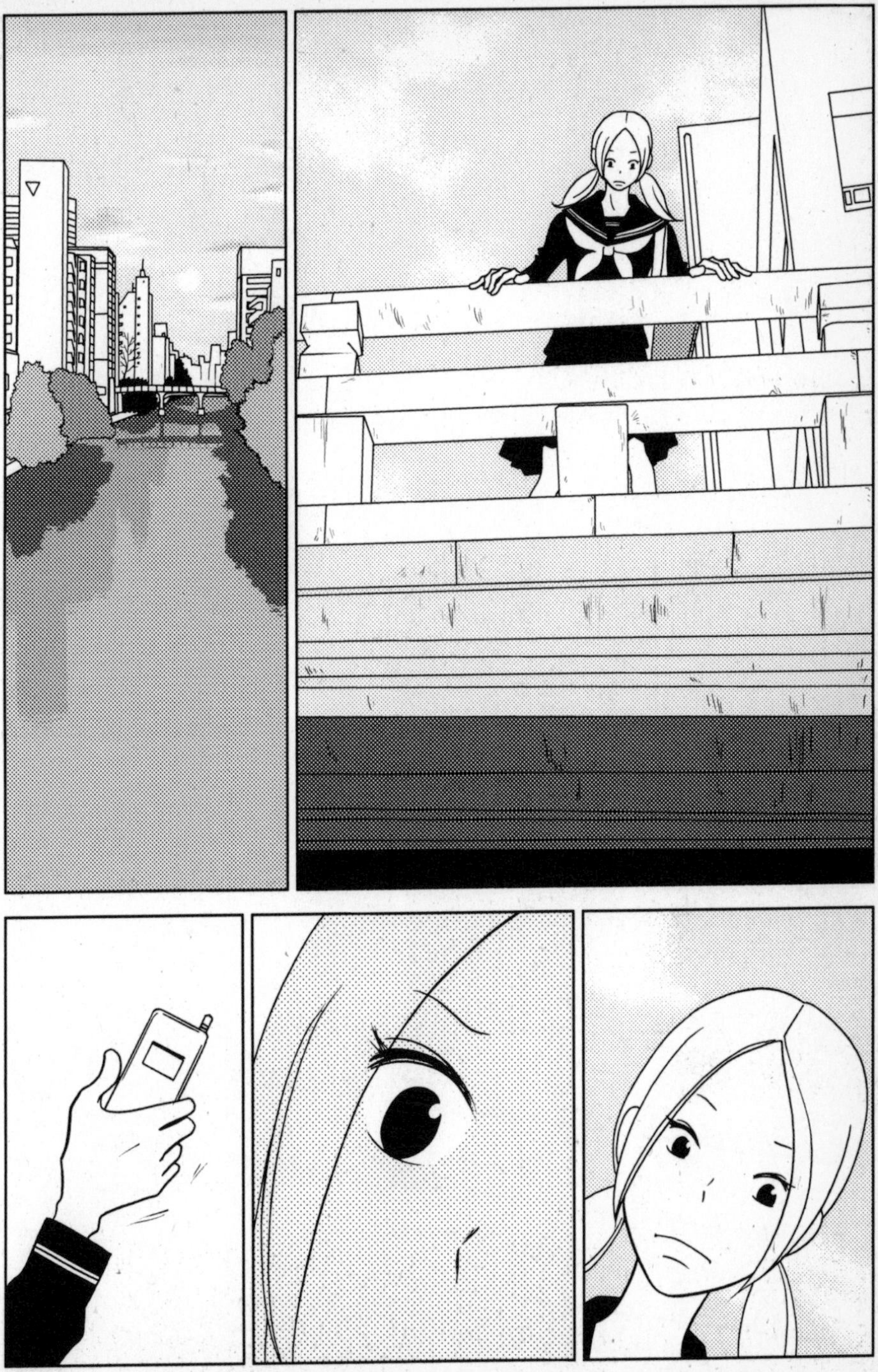

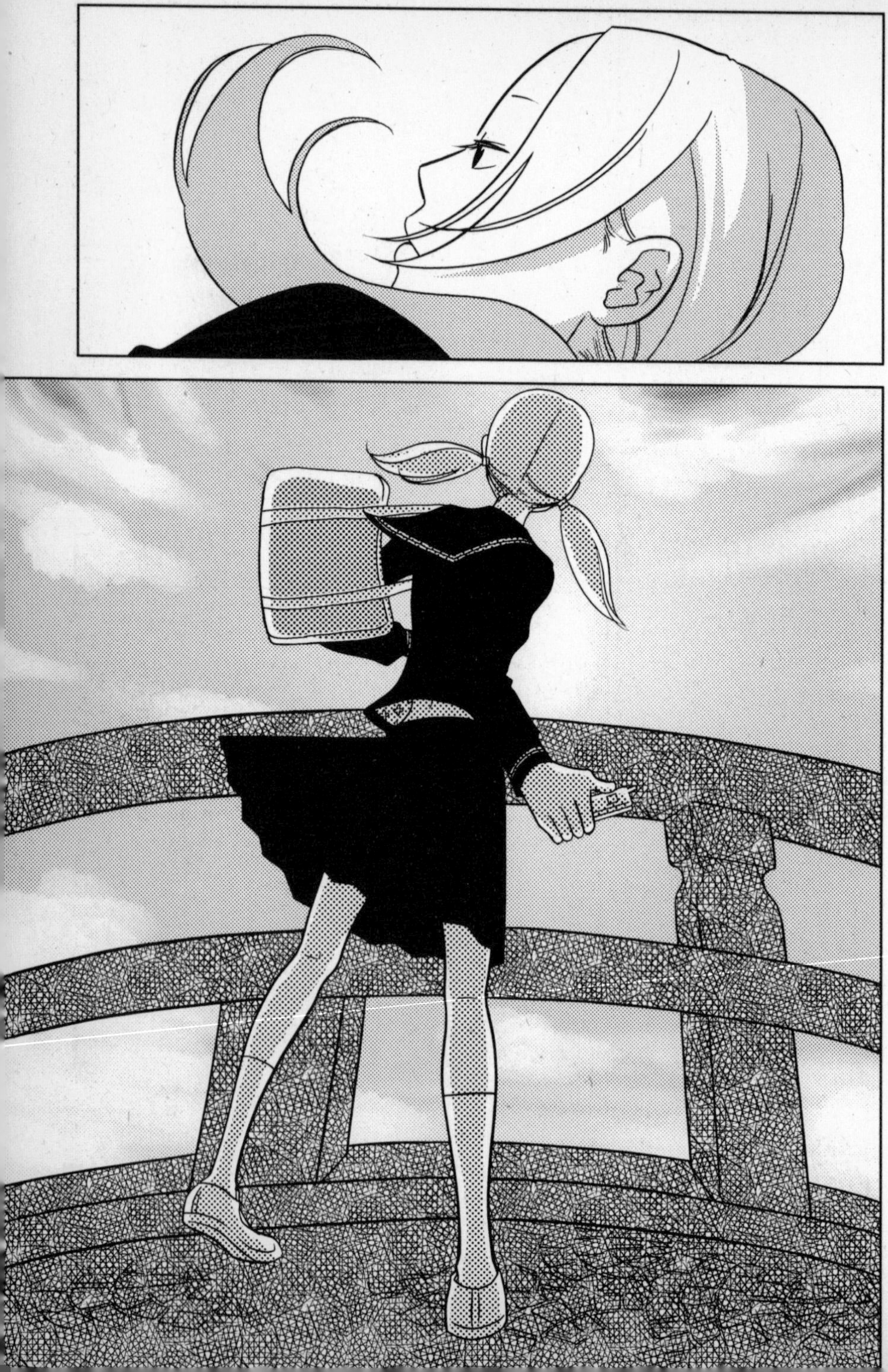

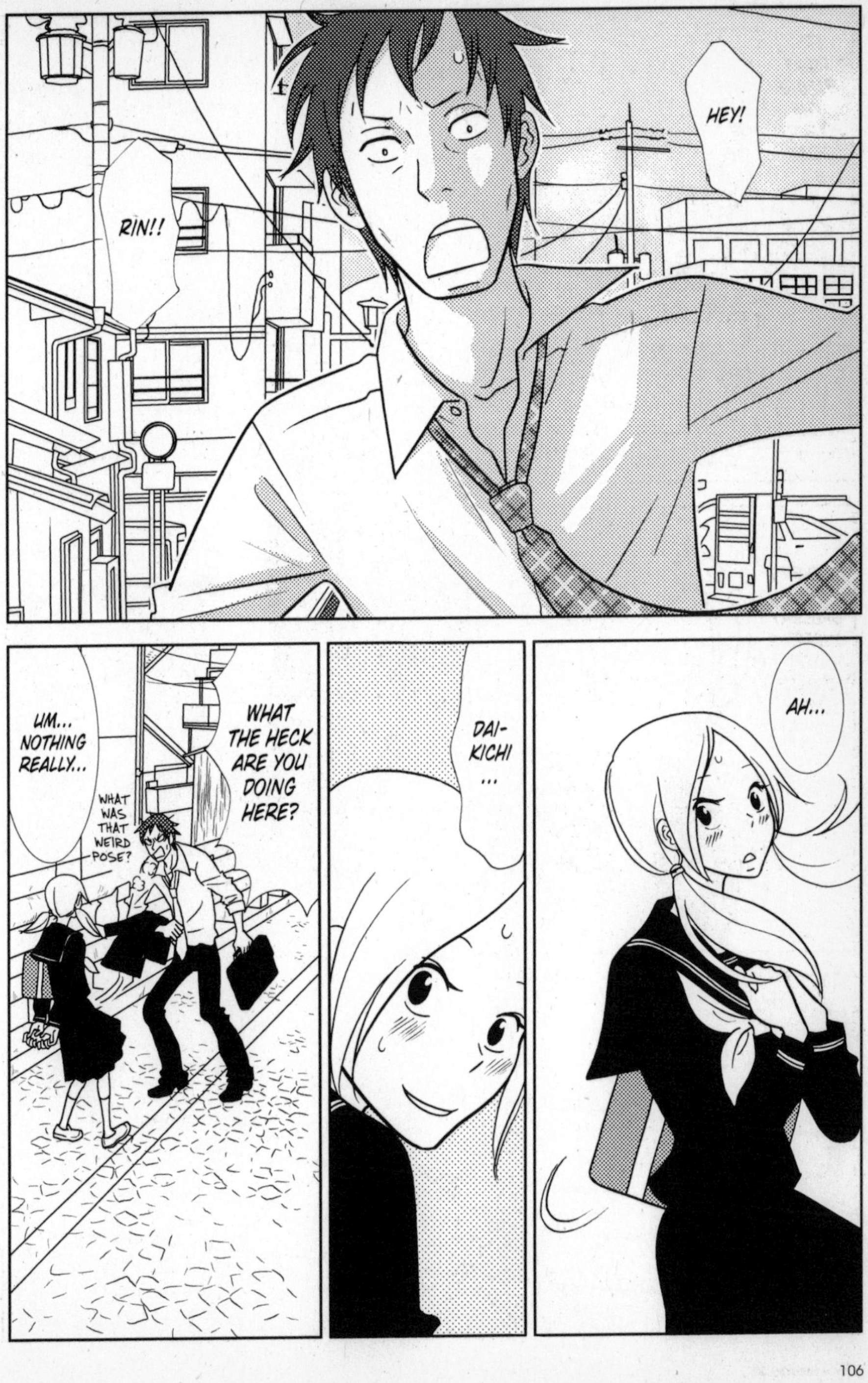
HEY!
RIN!!
AH...
DAI-KICHI ...
WHAT THE HECK ARE YOU DOING HERE?
WHAT WAS THAT WEIRD POSE?
UM... NOTHING REALLY...

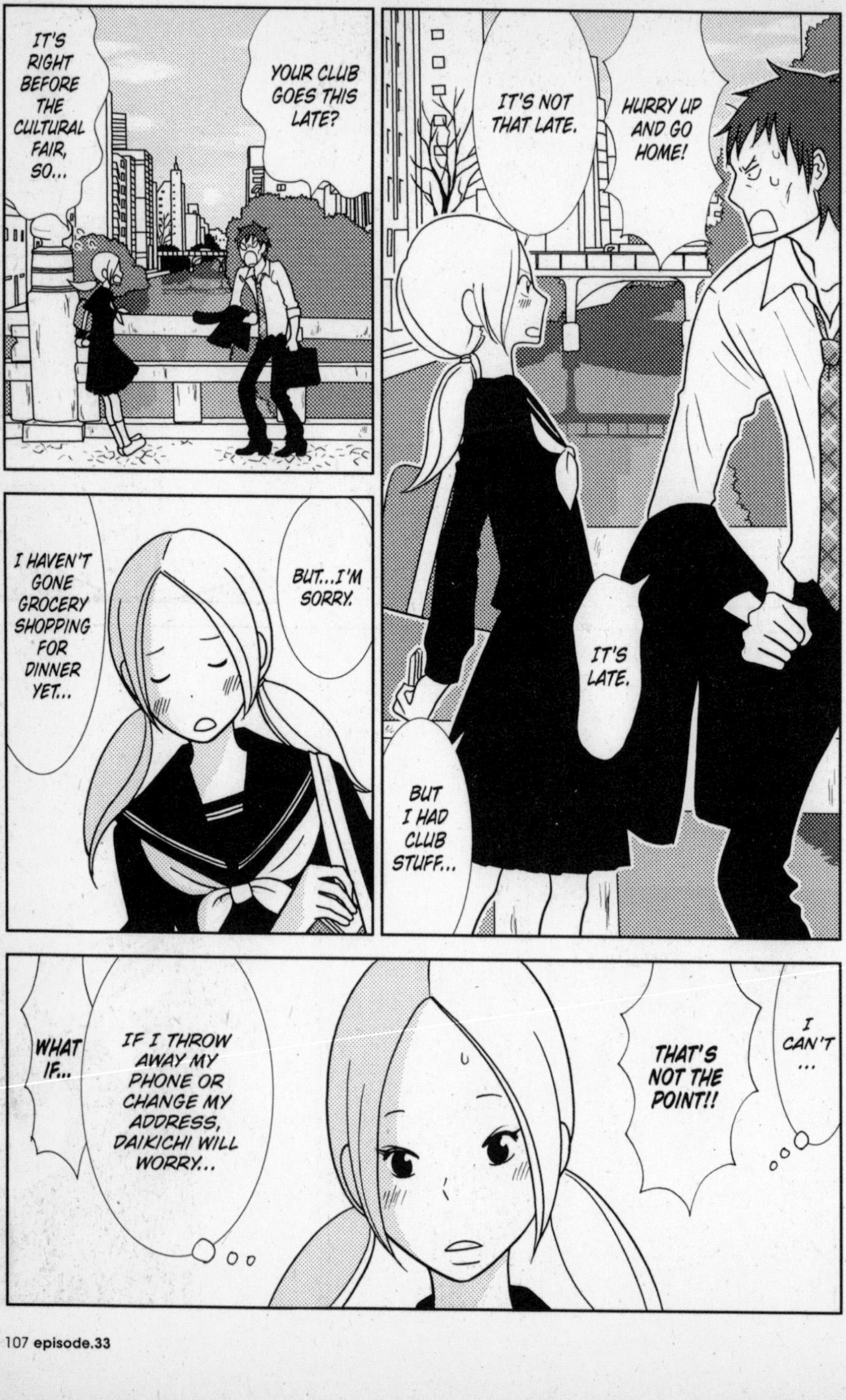
HURRY UP AND GO HOME!
IT'S NOT THAT LATE.
IT'S LATE.
BUT I HAD CLUB STUFF...
YOUR CLUB GOES THIS LATE?
IT'S RIGHT BEFORE THE CULTURAL FAIR, SO...
BUT...I'M SORRY.
I HAVEN'T GONE GROCERY SHOPPING FOR DINNER YET...
I CAN'T...
THAT'S NOT THE POINT!!
IF I THROW AWAY MY PHONE OR CHANGE MY ADDRESS, DAIKICHI WILL WORRY...
WHAT IF...

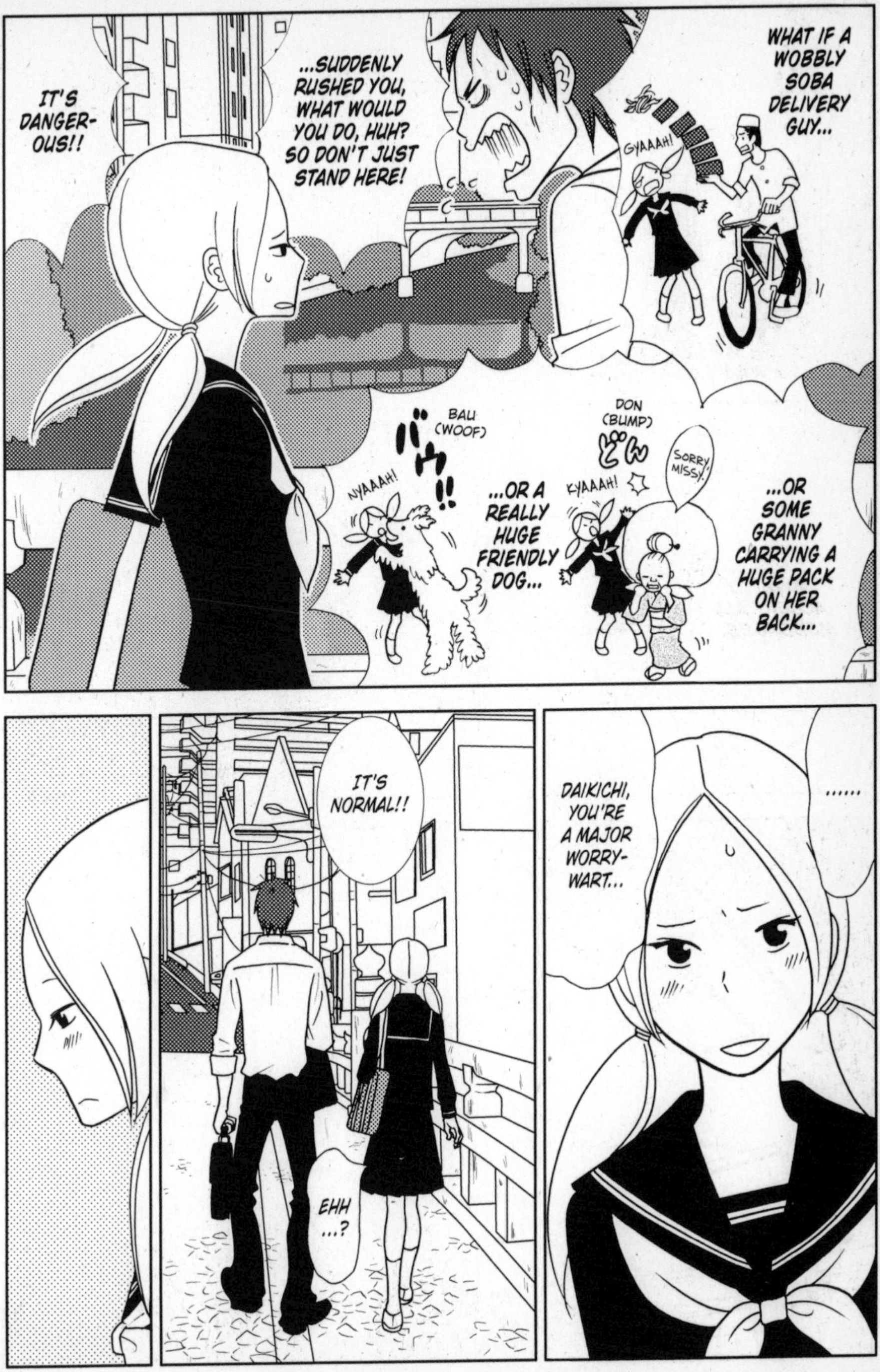
WHAT IF A WOBBLY SOBA DELIVERY GUY...
GYAAAH!
...SUDDENLY RUSHED YOU, WHAT WOULD YOU DO, HUH? SO DON'T JUST STAND HERE!
IT'S DANGER-OUS!!
...OR SOME GRANNY CARRYING A HUGE PACK ON HER BACK...
SORRY, MISSY.
DON (BUMP)
どん
KYAAAH!
...OR A REALLY HUGE FRIENDLY DOG...
BAU (WOOF)
バウ!!
NYAAAH!
......
DAIKICHI, YOU'RE A MAJOR WORRY-WART...
IT'S NORMAL!!
EHH ...?

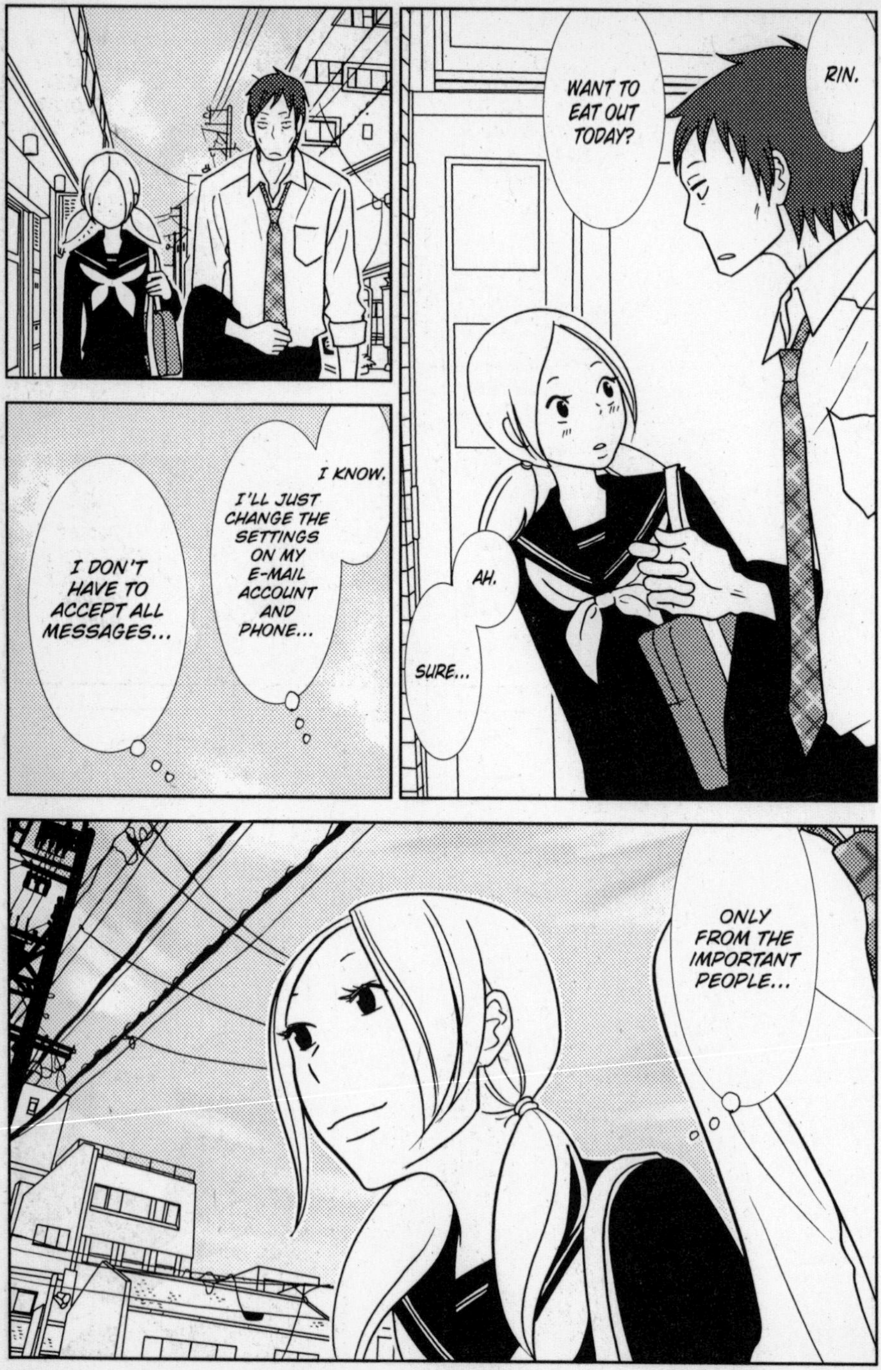
RIN.
WANT TO EAT OUT TODAY?
AH.
SURE...
I KNOW.
I'LL JUST CHANGE THE SETTINGS ON MY E-MAIL ACCOUNT AND PHONE...
I DON'T HAVE TO ACCEPT ALL MESSAGES...
ONLY FROM THE IMPORTANT PEOPLE...

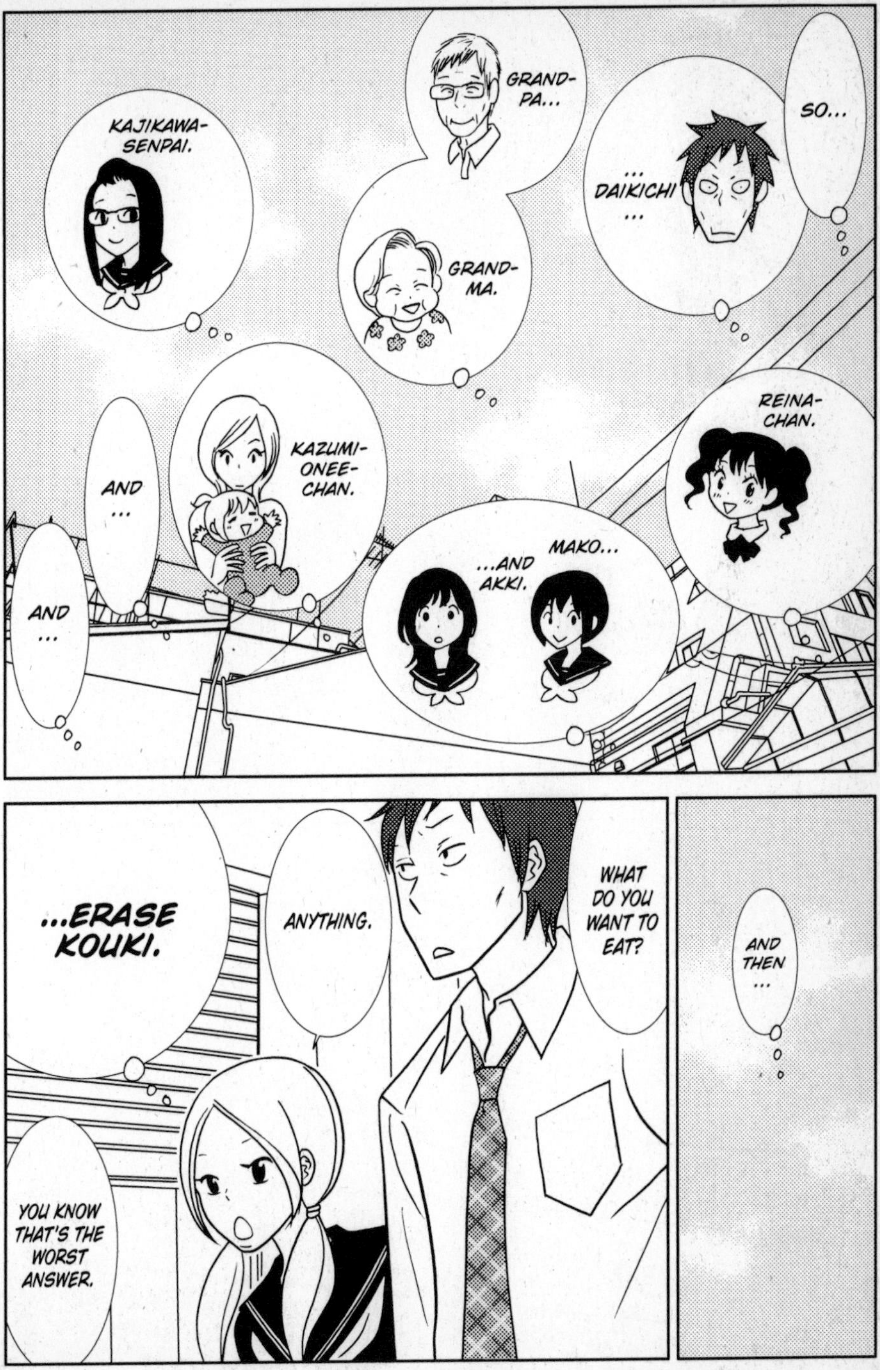
SO...
...DAIKICHI...
GRAND-PA...
GRAND-MA.
KAJIKAWA-SENPAI.
REINA-CHAN.
MAKO...
...AND AKKI.
KAZUMI-ONEE-CHAN.
AND...
AND...
AND THEN...
WHAT DO YOU WANT TO EAT?
ANYTHING.
...ERASE KOUKI.
YOU KNOW THAT'S THE WORST ANSWER.

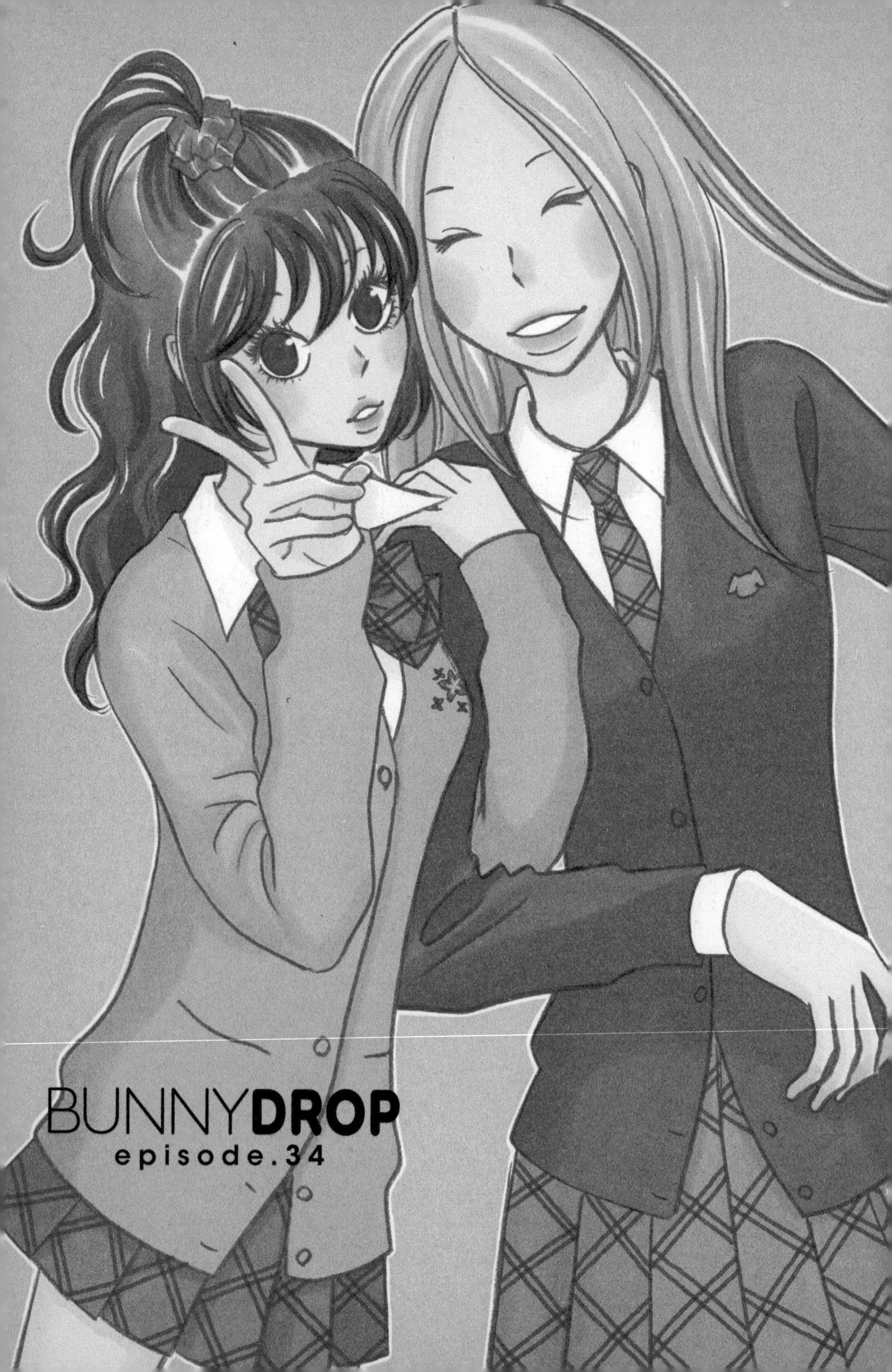
BUNNY DROP
episode.34

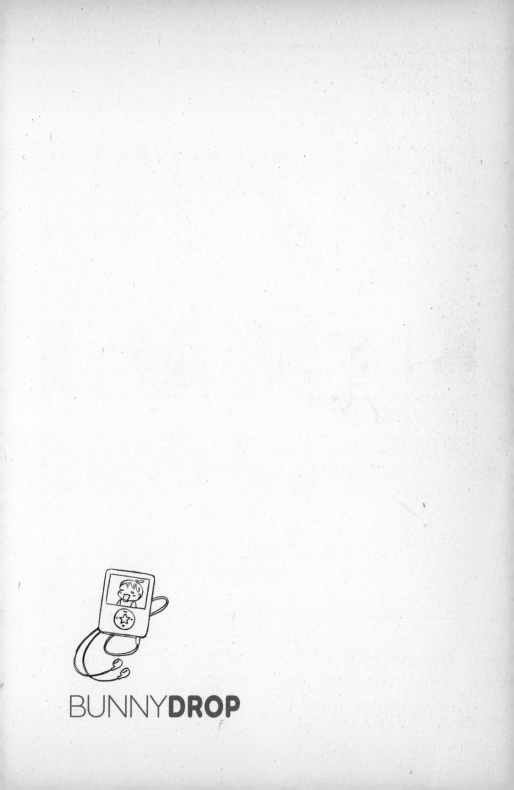

BUNNY**DROP**

BOARD: MINI FESTIVAL - [TWENTY TALLIES] / SHEEP CAFE - [EIGHT TALLIES]

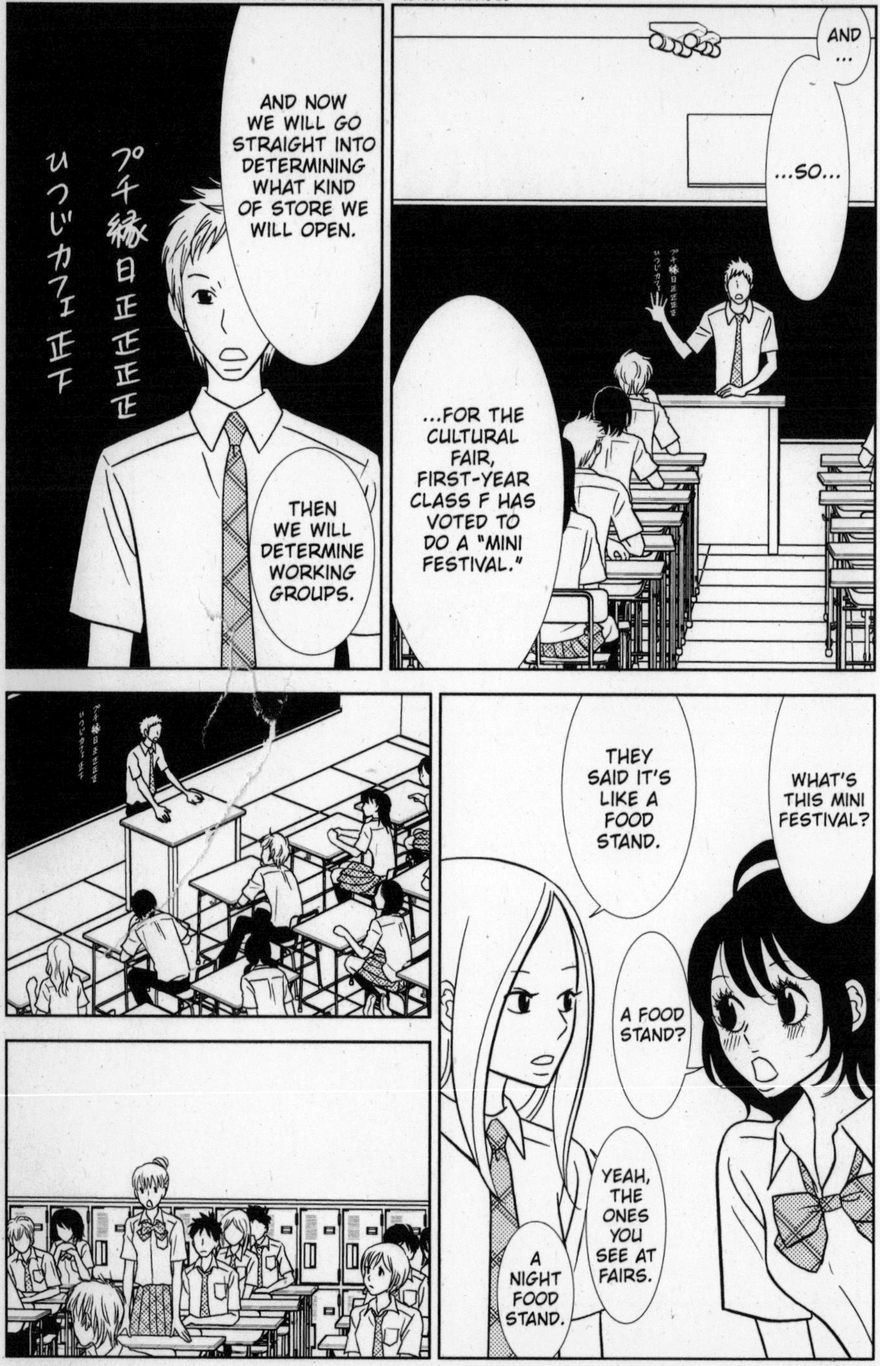
AND ...
...SO...
...FOR THE CULTURAL FAIR, FIRST-YEAR CLASS F HAS VOTED TO DO A "MINI FESTIVAL."
プチ縁日正正正正
ひつじカフェ正下
AND NOW WE WILL GO STRAIGHT INTO DETERMINING WHAT KIND OF STORE WE WILL OPEN.
THEN WE WILL DETERMINE WORKING GROUPS.
WHAT'S THIS MINI FESTIVAL?
THEY SAID IT'S LIKE A FOOD STAND.
A FOOD STAND?
YEAH, THE ONES YOU SEE AT FAIRS.
A NIGHT FOOD STAND.

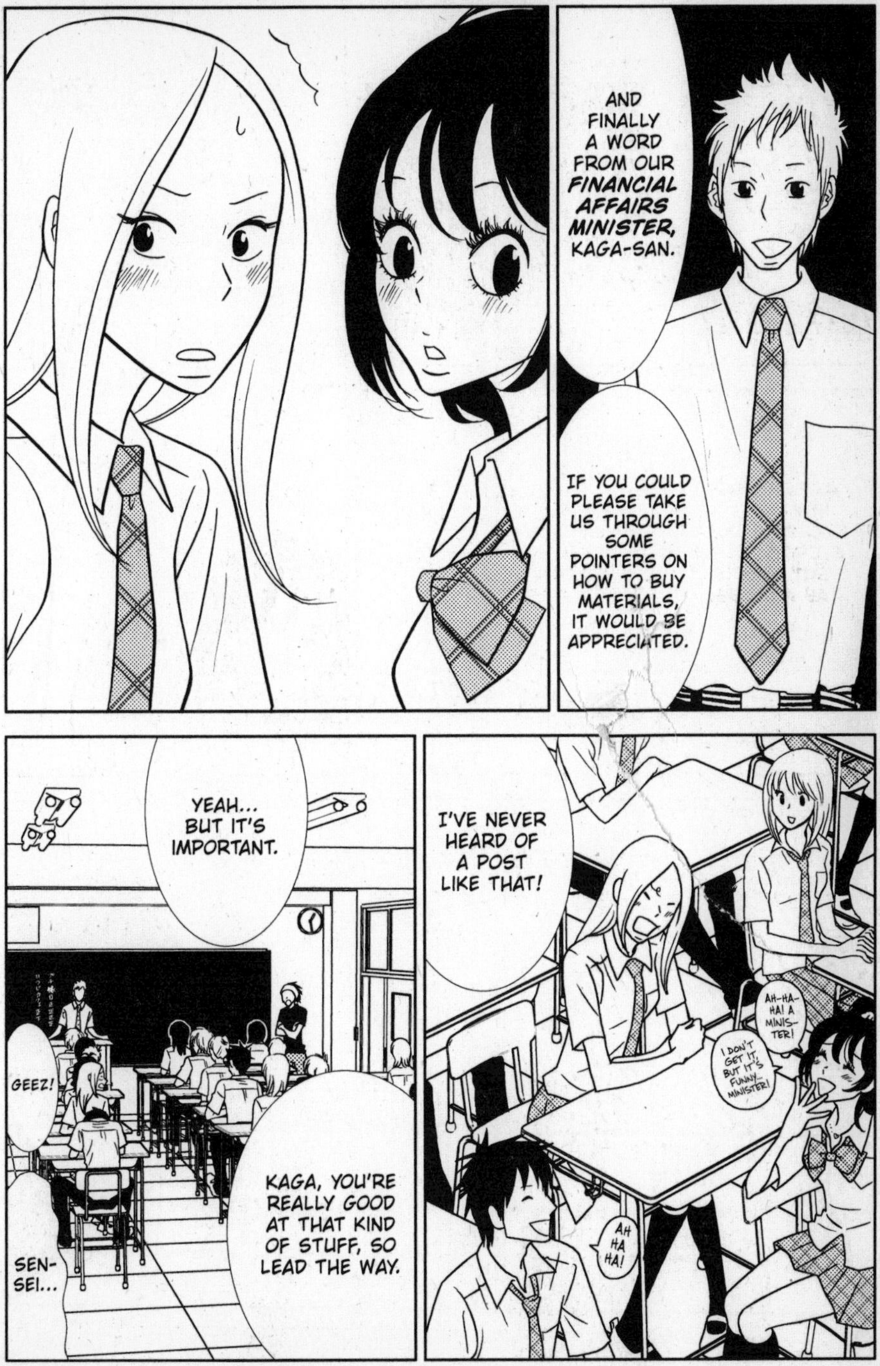
AND FINALLY A WORD FROM OUR *FINANCIAL AFFAIRS MINISTER*, KAGA-SAN.
IF YOU COULD PLEASE TAKE US THROUGH SOME POINTERS ON HOW TO BUY MATERIALS, IT WOULD BE APPRECIATED.
I'VE NEVER HEARD OF A POST LIKE THAT!
AH-HA-HA! A MINISTER!
I DON'T GET IT, BUT IT'S FUNNY... MINISTER!
AH HA HA!
YEAH... BUT IT'S IMPORTANT.
KAGA, YOU'RE REALLY GOOD AT THAT KIND OF STUFF, SO LEAD THE WAY.
GEEZ!
SENSEI...

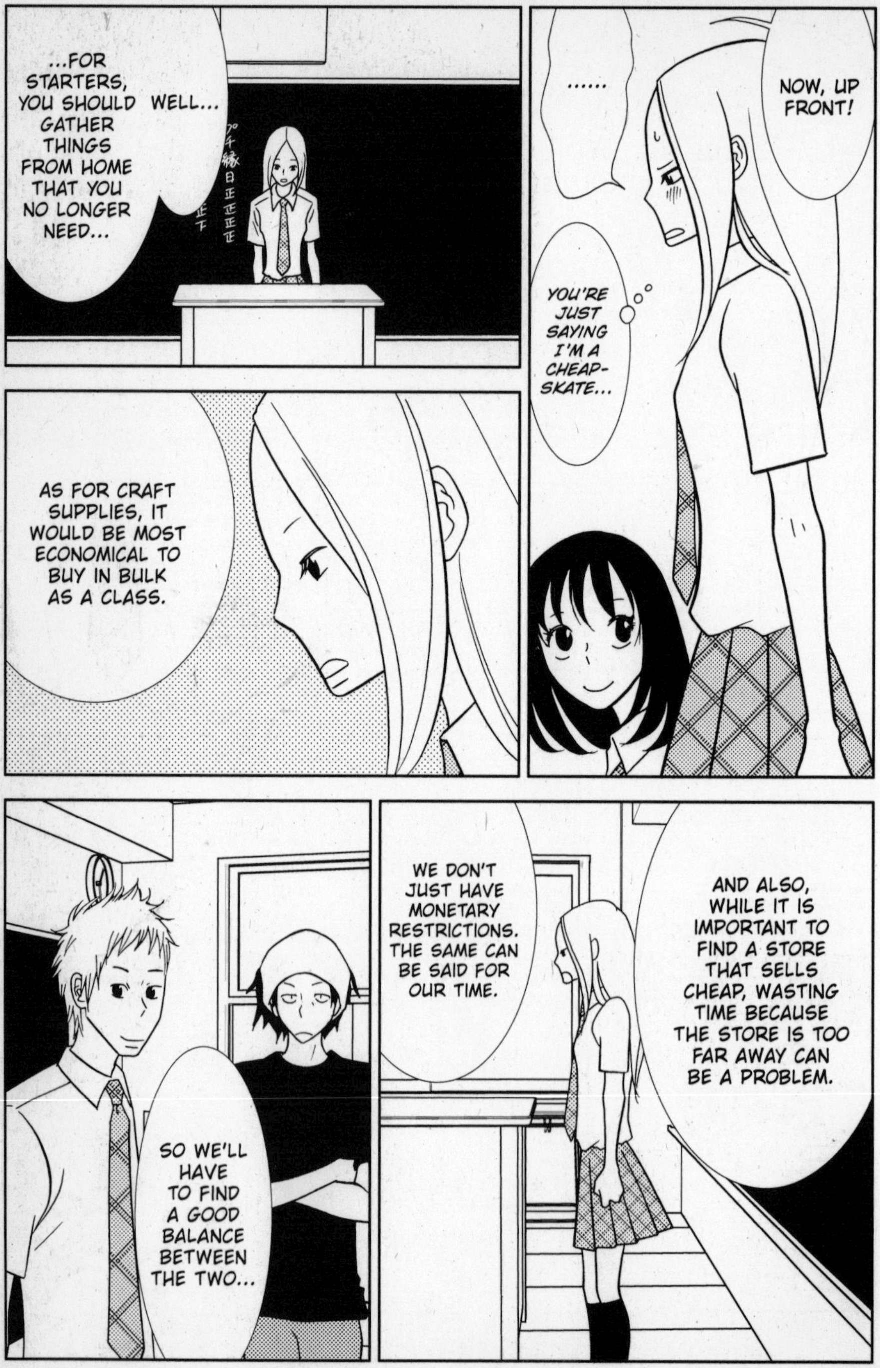
NOW, UP FRONT!
......
YOU'RE JUST SAYING I'M A CHEAPSKATE...
WELL...
...FOR STARTERS, YOU SHOULD GATHER THINGS FROM HOME THAT YOU NO LONGER NEED...
AS FOR CRAFT SUPPLIES, IT WOULD BE MOST ECONOMICAL TO BUY IN BULK AS A CLASS.
AND ALSO, WHILE IT IS IMPORTANT TO FIND A STORE THAT SELLS CHEAP, WASTING TIME BECAUSE THE STORE IS TOO FAR AWAY CAN BE A PROBLEM.
WE DON'T JUST HAVE MONETARY RESTRICTIONS. THE SAME CAN BE SAID FOR OUR TIME.
SO WE'LL HAVE TO FIND A GOOD BALANCE BETWEEN THE TWO...

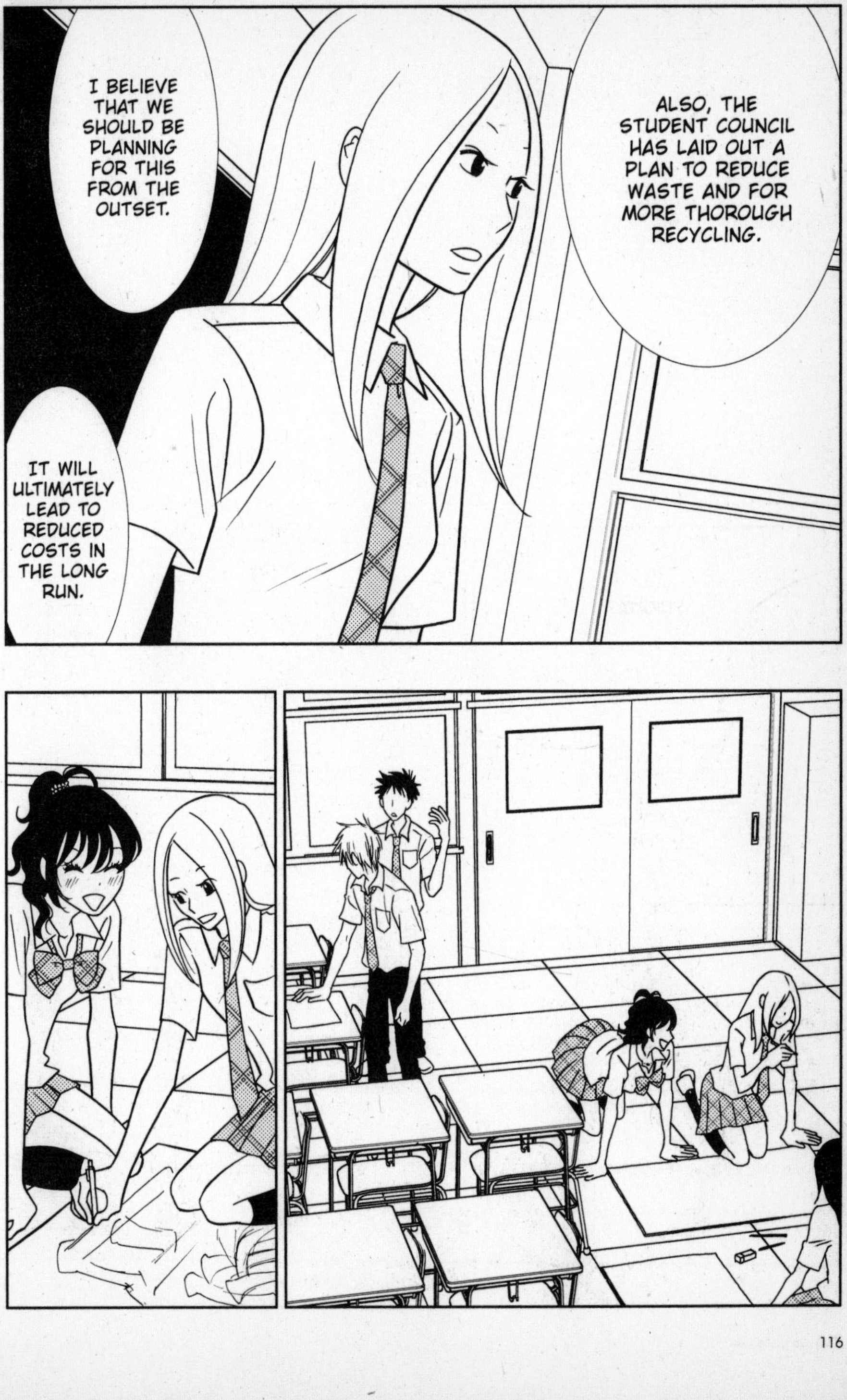
ALSO, THE STUDENT COUNCIL HAS LAID OUT A PLAN TO REDUCE WASTE AND FOR MORE THOROUGH RECYCLING.
I BELIEVE THAT WE SHOULD BE PLANNING FOR THIS FROM THE OUTSET.
IT WILL ULTIMATELY LEAD TO REDUCED COSTS IN THE LONG RUN.

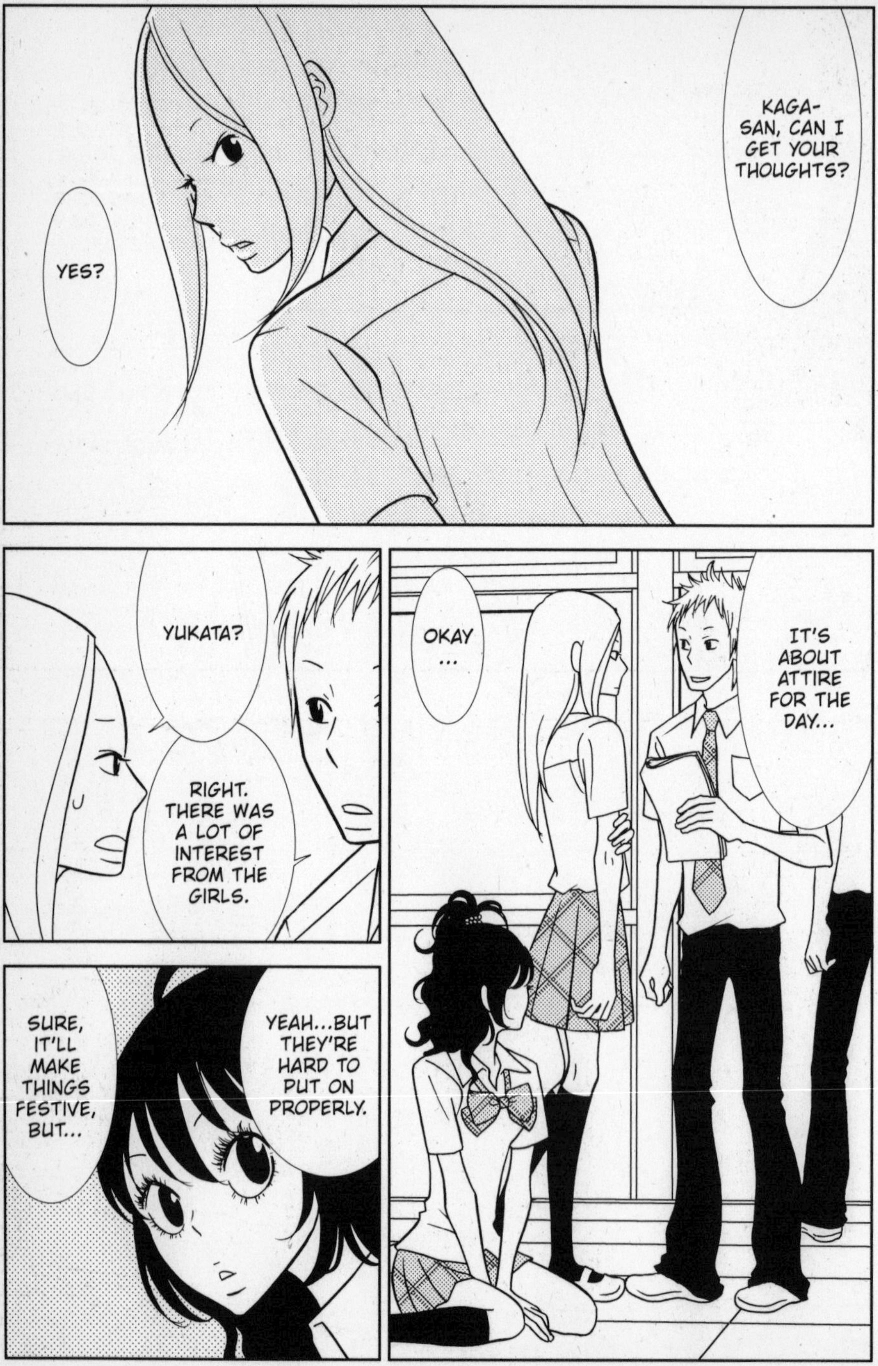
KAGA-SAN, CAN I GET YOUR THOUGHTS?
YES?
IT'S ABOUT ATTIRE FOR THE DAY...
OKAY ...
YUKATA?
RIGHT. THERE WAS A LOT OF INTEREST FROM THE GIRLS.
YEAH...BUT THEY'RE HARD TO PUT ON PROPERLY.
SURE, IT'LL MAKE THINGS FESTIVE, BUT...

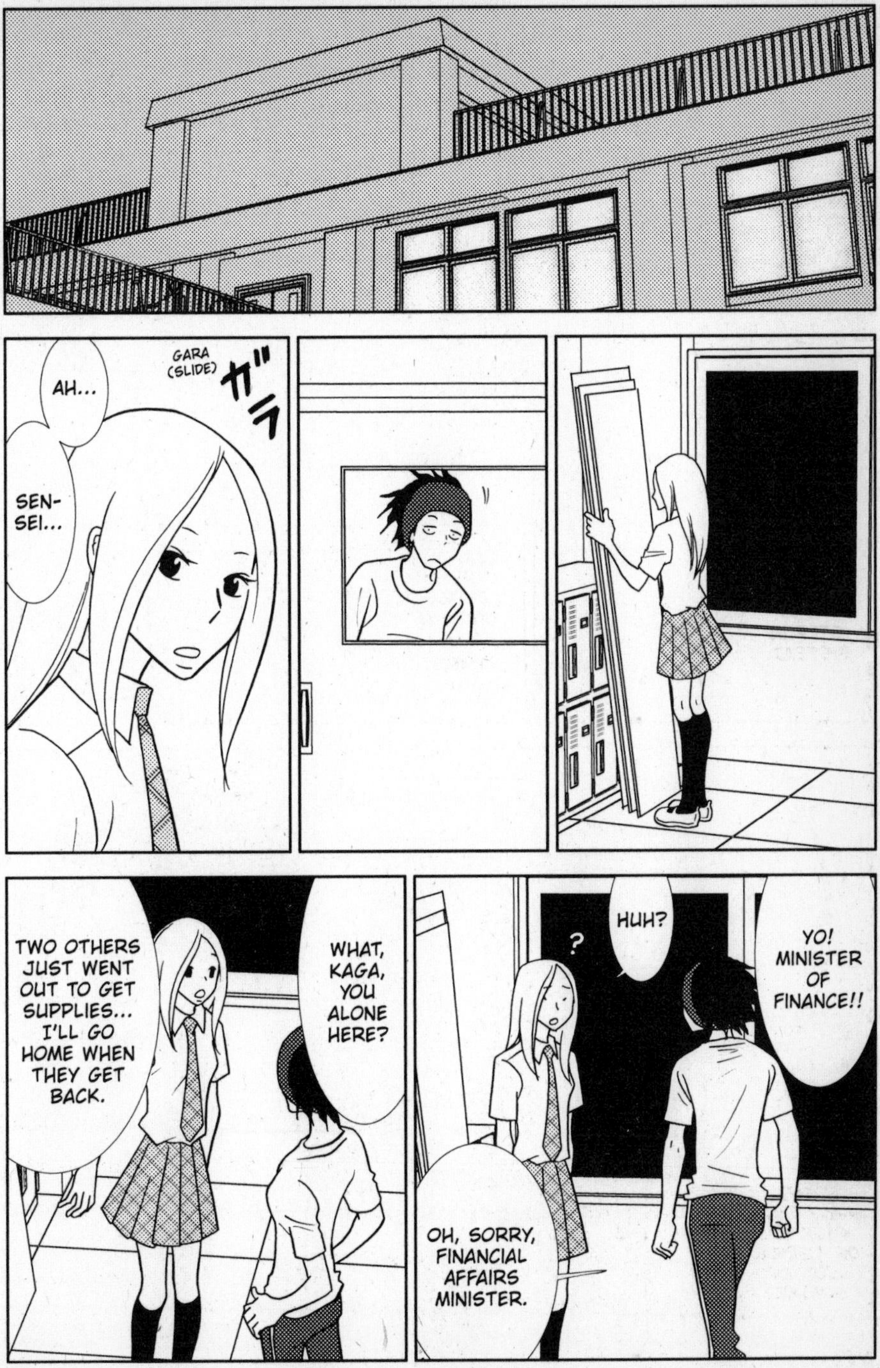
GARA (SLIDE)
ガラ
AH...
SENSEI...
YO! MINISTER OF FINANCE!!
HUH?
?
OH, SORRY, FINANCIAL AFFAIRS MINISTER.
WHAT, KAGA, YOU ALONE HERE?
TWO OTHERS JUST WENT OUT TO GET SUPPLIES... I'LL GO HOME WHEN THEY GET BACK.

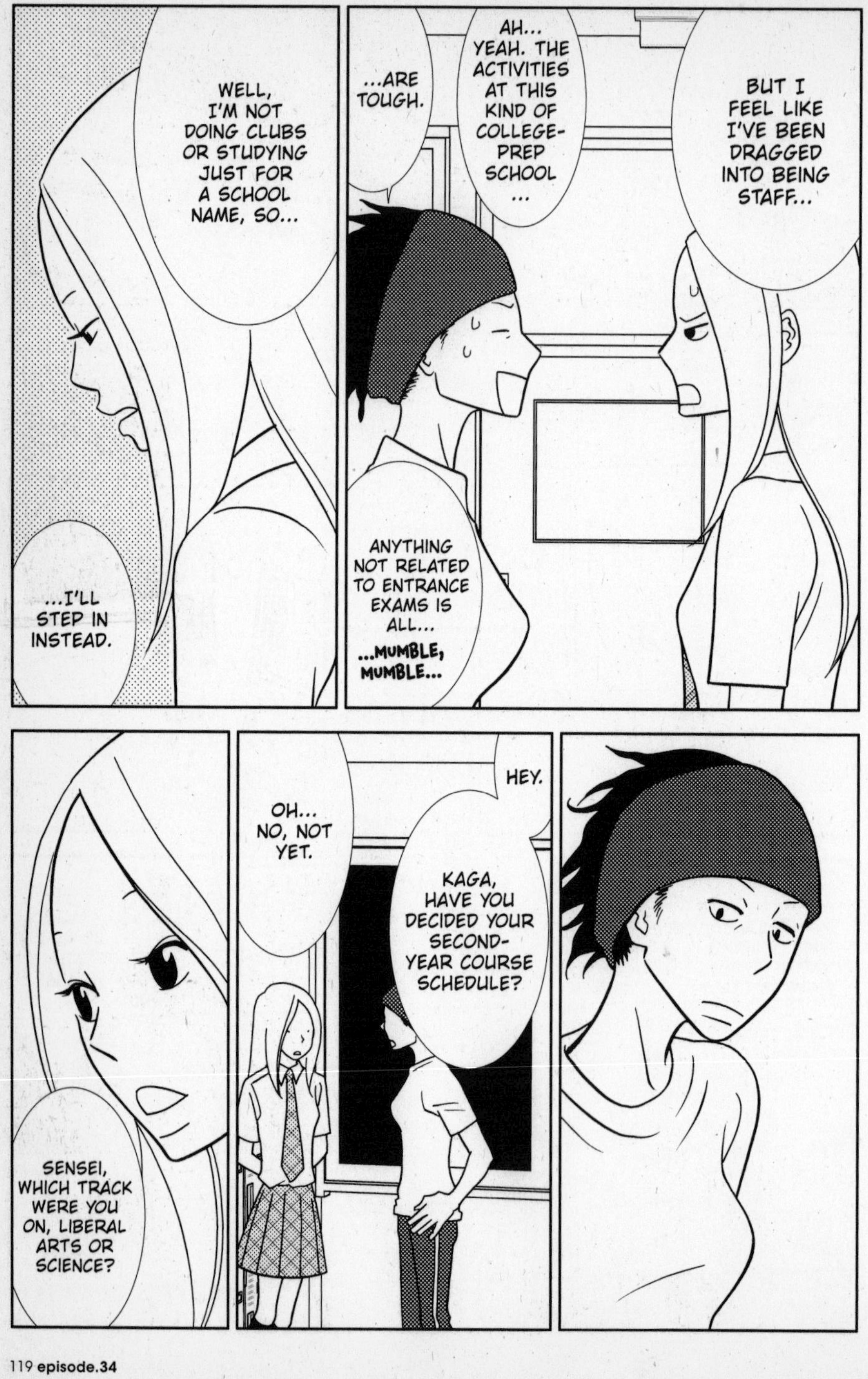
BUT I FEEL LIKE I'VE BEEN DRAGGED INTO BEING STAFF...
AH... YEAH. THE ACTIVITIES AT THIS KIND OF COLLEGE-PREP SCHOOL ...
...ARE TOUGH.
ANYTHING NOT RELATED TO ENTRANCE EXAMS IS ALL... ...MUMBLE, MUMBLE...
WELL, I'M NOT DOING CLUBS OR STUDYING JUST FOR A SCHOOL NAME, SO...
...I'LL STEP IN INSTEAD.
HEY.
KAGA, HAVE YOU DECIDED YOUR SECOND-YEAR COURSE SCHEDULE?
OH... NO, NOT YET.
SENSEI, WHICH TRACK WERE YOU ON, LIBERAL ARTS OR SCIENCE?

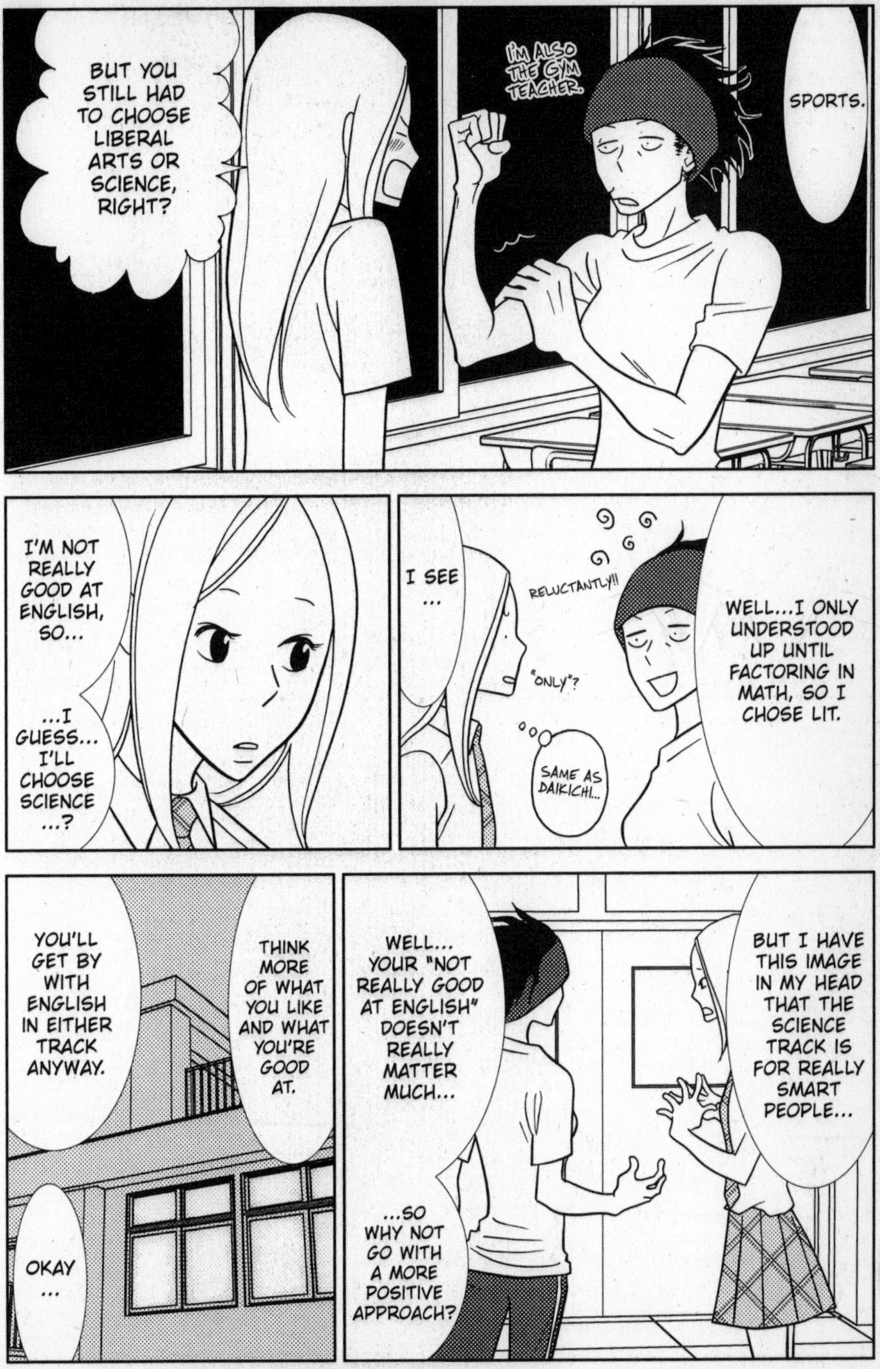

SPORTS.
I'M ALSO THE GYM TEACHER.
BUT YOU STILL HAD TO CHOOSE LIBERAL ARTS OR SCIENCE, RIGHT?
WELL...I ONLY UNDERSTOOD UP UNTIL FACTORING IN MATH, SO I CHOSE LIT.
RELUCTANTLY!!
I SEE ...
"ONLY"?
SAME AS DAIKICHI...
I'M NOT REALLY GOOD AT ENGLISH, SO...
...I GUESS... I'LL CHOOSE SCIENCE ...?
BUT I HAVE THIS IMAGE IN MY HEAD THAT THE SCIENCE TRACK IS FOR REALLY SMART PEOPLE...
WELL... YOUR "NOT REALLY GOOD AT ENGLISH" DOESN'T REALLY MATTER MUCH...
...SO WHY NOT GO WITH A MORE POSITIVE APPROACH?
THINK MORE OF WHAT YOU LIKE AND WHAT YOU'RE GOOD AT.
YOU'LL GET BY WITH ENGLISH IN EITHER TRACK ANYWAY.
OKAY ...

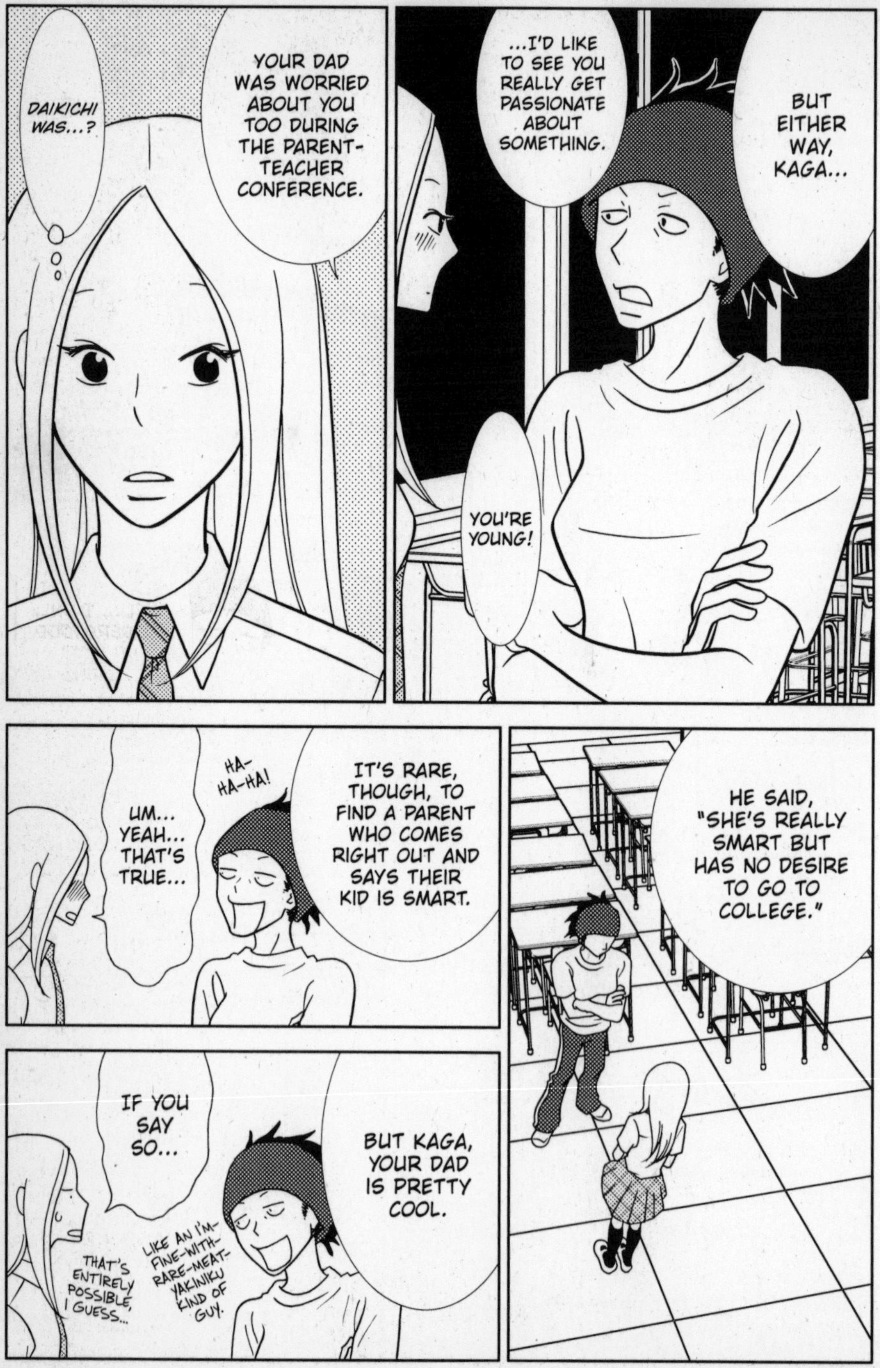
BUT EITHER WAY, KAGA...
...I'D LIKE TO SEE YOU REALLY GET PASSIONATE ABOUT SOMETHING.
YOU'RE YOUNG!
YOUR DAD WAS WORRIED ABOUT YOU TOO DURING THE PARENT-TEACHER CONFERENCE.
DAIKICHI WAS...?
HE SAID, "SHE'S REALLY SMART BUT HAS NO DESIRE TO GO TO COLLEGE."
IT'S RARE, THOUGH, TO FIND A PARENT WHO COMES RIGHT OUT AND SAYS THEIR KID IS SMART.
HA-HA-HA!
UM... YEAH... THAT'S TRUE...
BUT KAGA, YOUR DAD IS PRETTY COOL.
LIKE AN I'M-FINE-WITH-RARE-MEAT-YAKINIKU KIND OF GUY.
IF YOU SAY SO...
THAT'S ENTIRELY POSSIBLE, I GUESS...

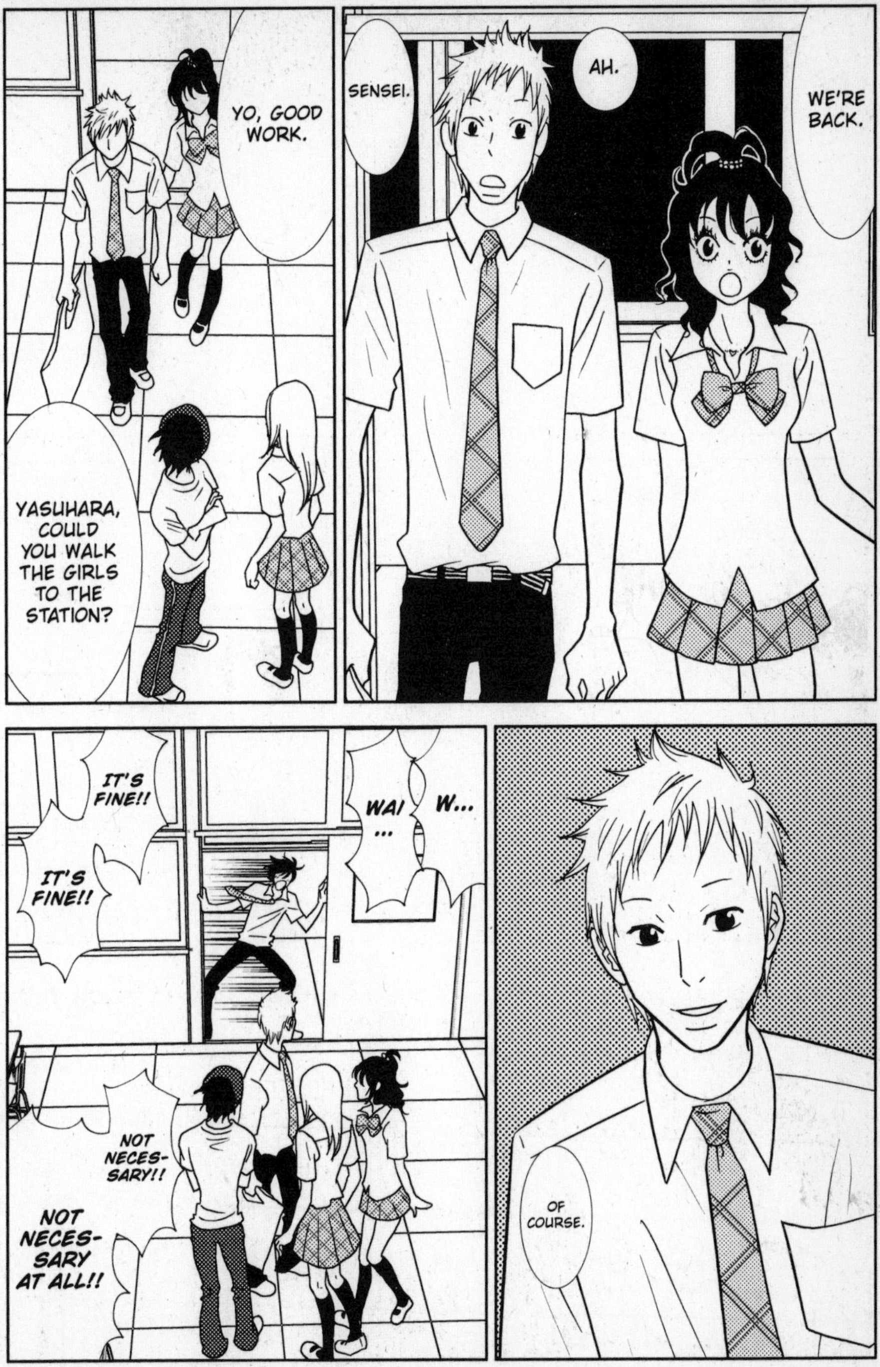
WE'RE BACK.
AH.
SENSEI.
YO, GOOD WORK.
YASUHARA, COULD YOU WALK THE GIRLS TO THE STATION?
OF COURSE.
W...
WAI ...
IT'S FINE!!
IT'S FINE!!
NOT NECES-SARY!!
NOT NECES-SARY AT ALL!!

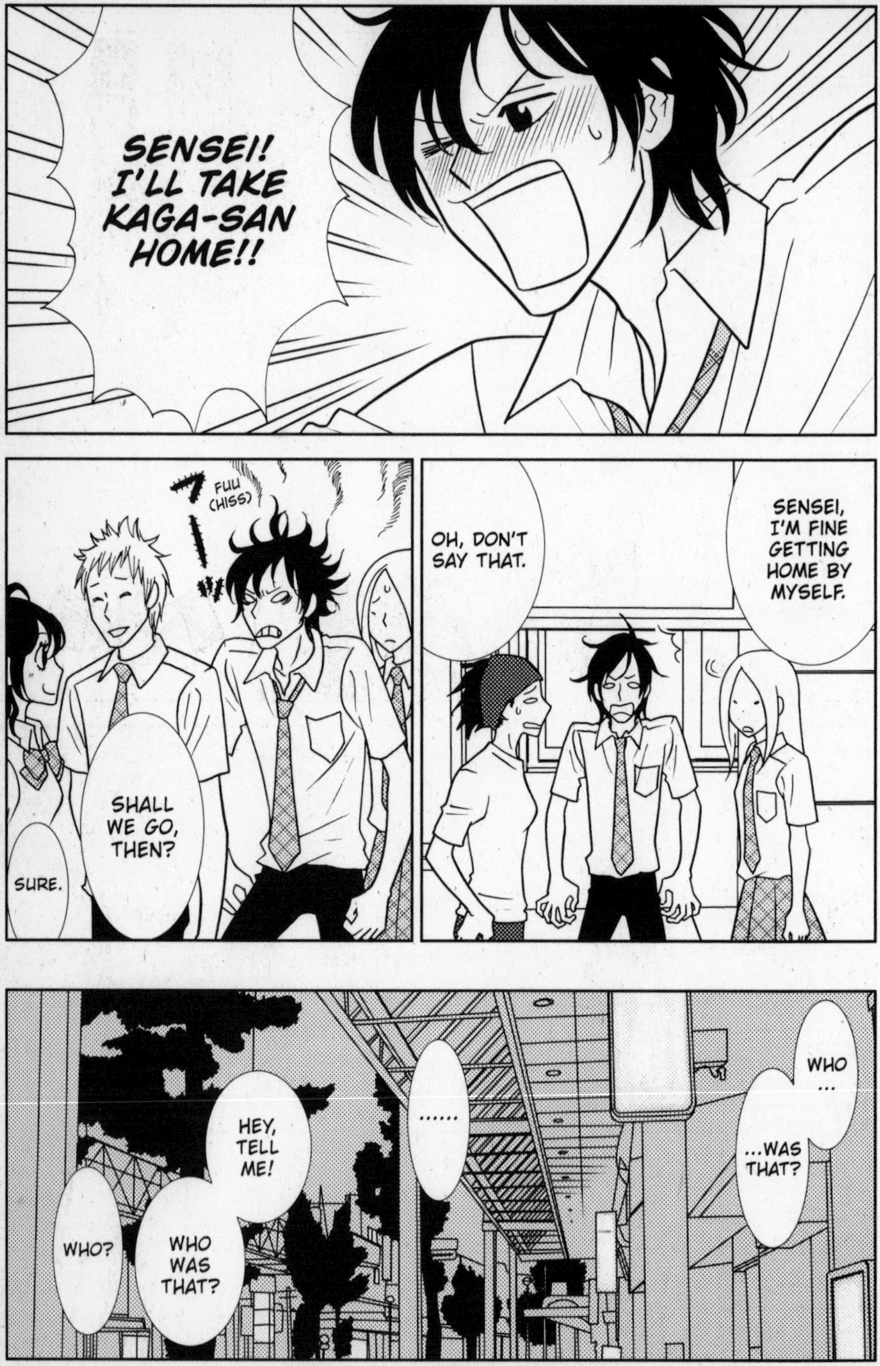
SENSEI! I'LL TAKE KAGA-SAN HOME!!
SENSEI, I'M FINE GETTING HOME BY MYSELF.
OH, DON'T SAY THAT.
FUU (HISS)
SHALL WE GO, THEN?
SURE.
WHO ...
...WAS THAT?
......
HEY, TELL ME!
WHO WAS THAT?
WHO?

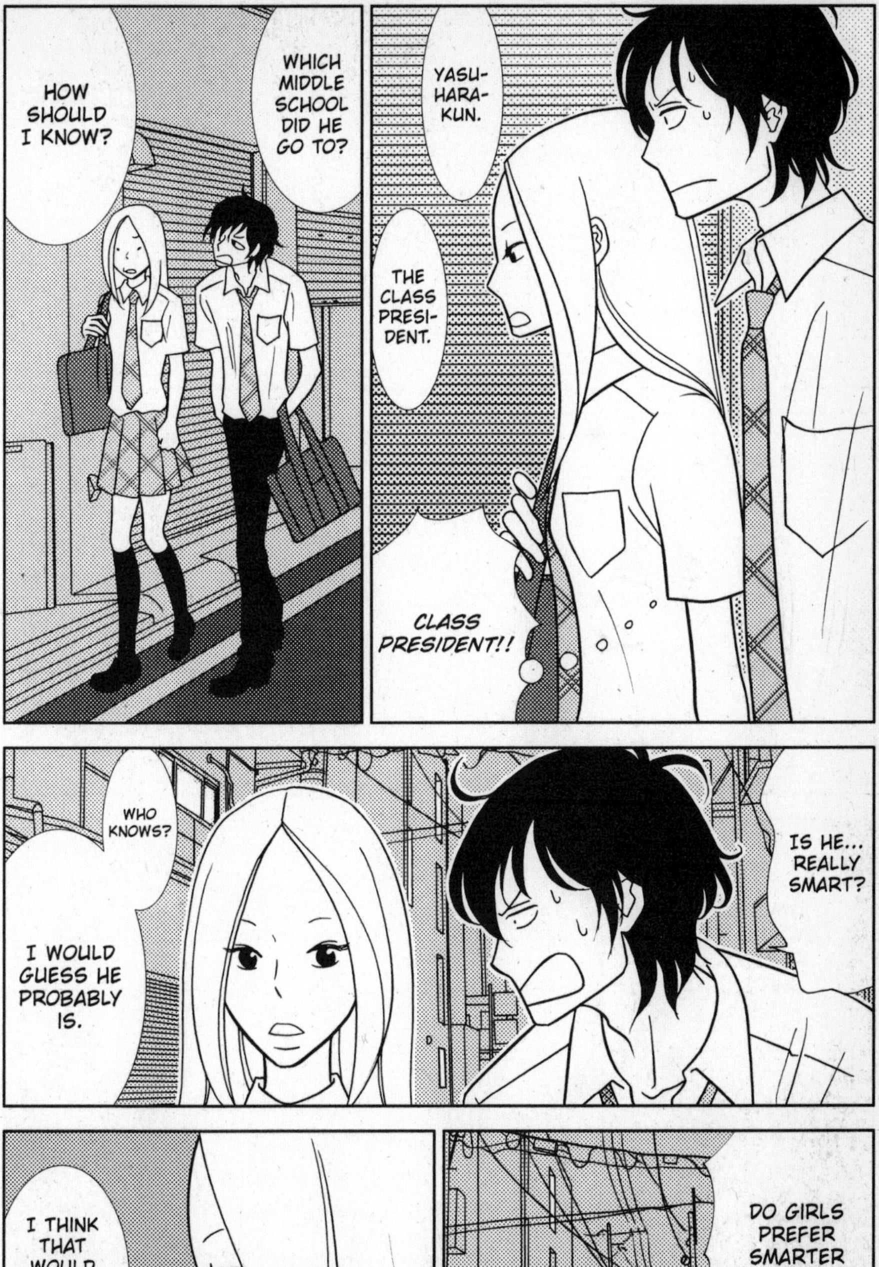
YASU-HARA-KUN.
THE CLASS PRESIDENT.
CLASS PRESIDENT!!
WHICH MIDDLE SCHOOL DID HE GO TO?
HOW SHOULD I KNOW?
IS HE... REALLY SMART?
WHO KNOWS?
I WOULD GUESS HE PROBABLY IS.
DO GIRLS PREFER SMARTER GUYS?
I THINK THAT WOULD DEPEND ON THE PERSON.

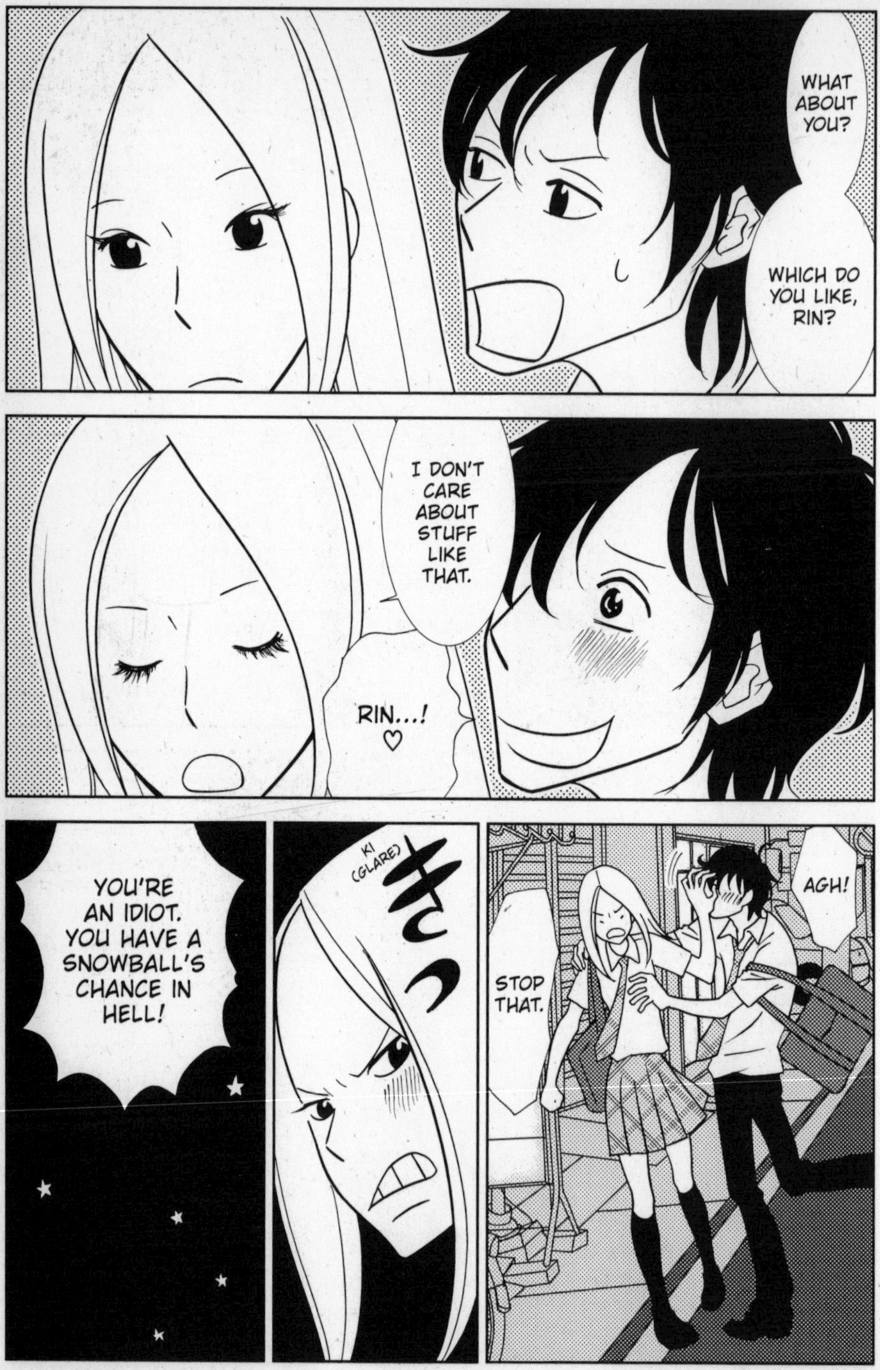
WHAT ABOUT YOU?
WHICH DO YOU LIKE, RIN?
I DON'T CARE ABOUT STUFF LIKE THAT.
RIN...! ♡
AGH!
STOP THAT.
きっ
KI (GLARE)
YOU'RE AN IDIOT. YOU HAVE A SNOWBALL'S CHANCE IN HELL!

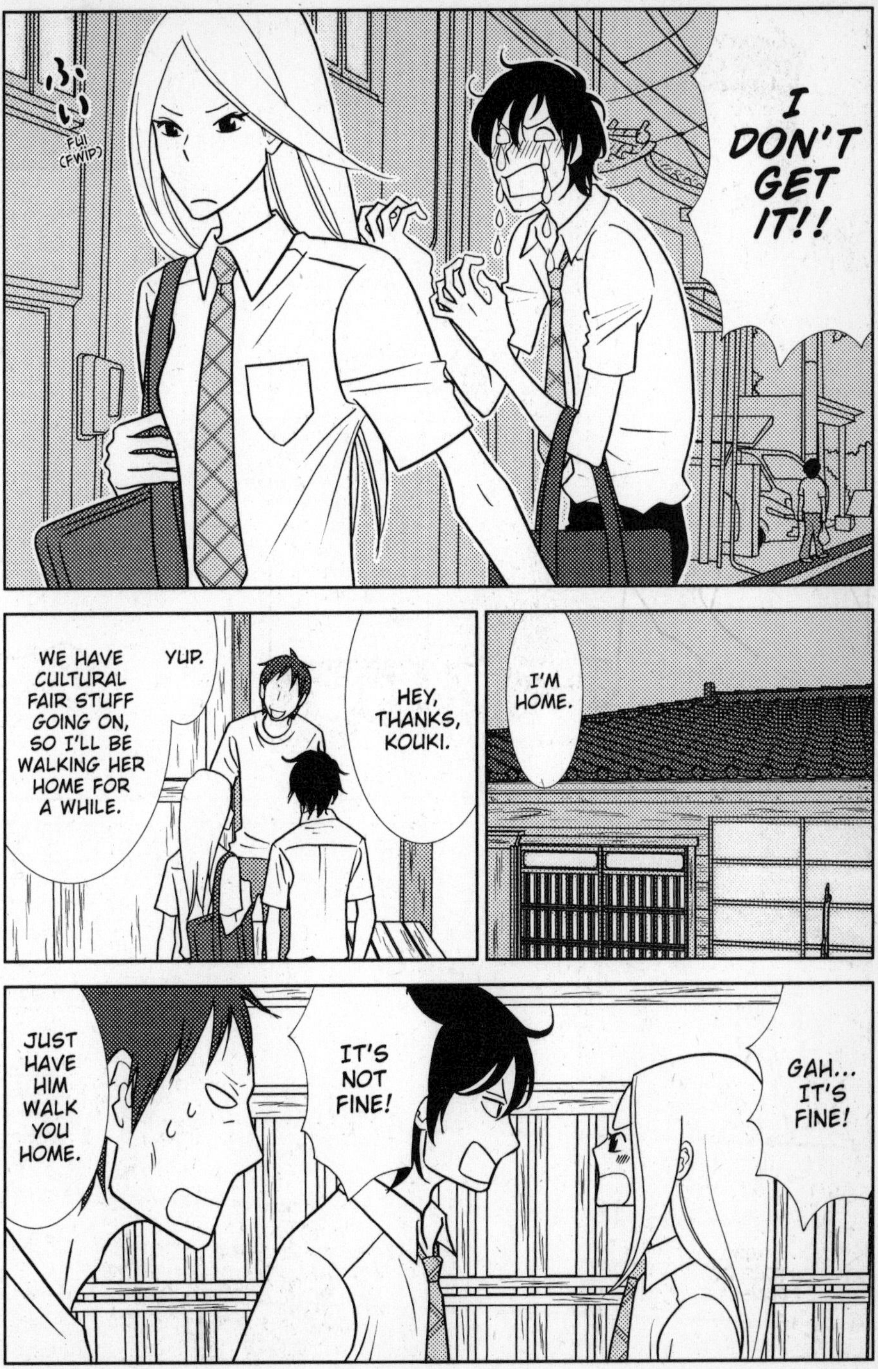
I DON'T GET IT!!
ふい
FUI (FWIP)
I'M HOME.
HEY, THANKS, KOUKI.
YUP.
WE HAVE CULTURAL FAIR STUFF GOING ON, SO I'LL BE WALKING HER HOME FOR A WHILE.
GAH... IT'S FINE!
IT'S NOT FINE!
JUST HAVE HIM WALK YOU HOME.

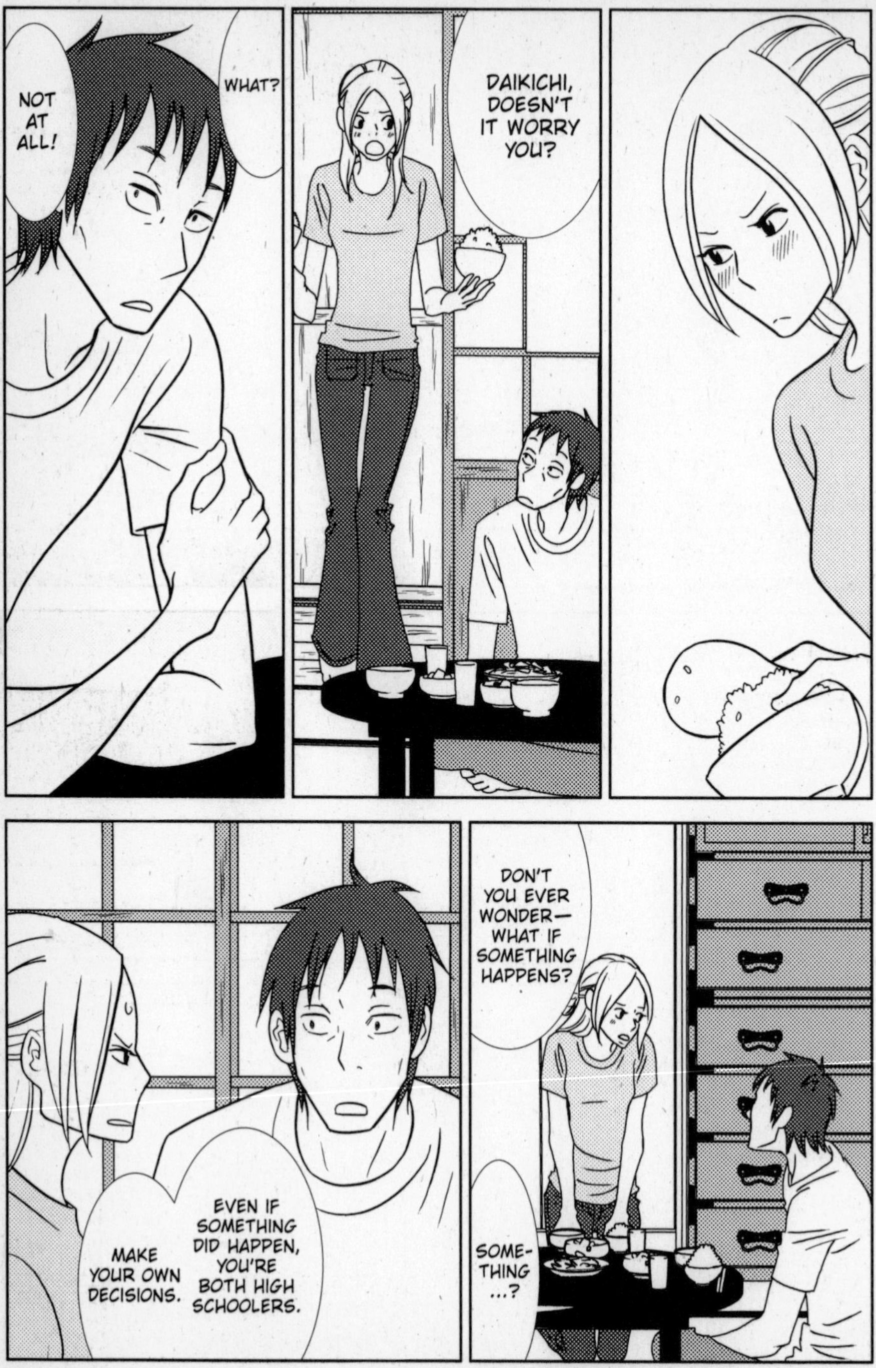
DAIKICHI, DOESN'T IT WORRY YOU?
WHAT?
NOT AT ALL!
DON'T YOU EVER WONDER—WHAT IF SOMETHING HAPPENS?
SOMETHING...?
EVEN IF SOMETHING DID HAPPEN, YOU'RE BOTH HIGH SCHOOLERS.
MAKE YOUR OWN DECISIONS.

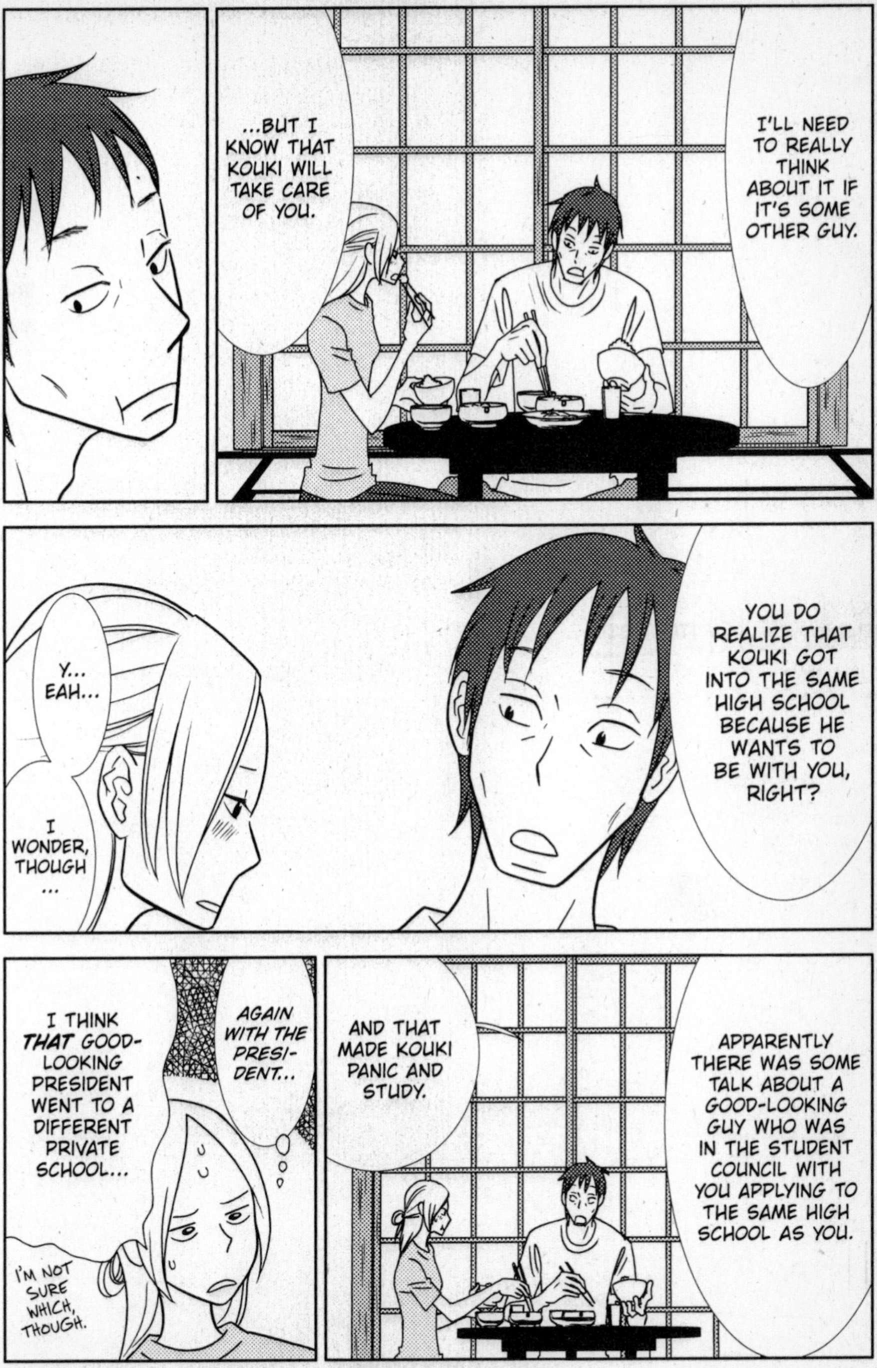
I'LL NEED TO REALLY THINK ABOUT IT IF IT'S SOME OTHER GUY.
...BUT I KNOW THAT KOUKI WILL TAKE CARE OF YOU.
YOU DO REALIZE THAT KOUKI GOT INTO THE SAME HIGH SCHOOL BECAUSE HE WANTS TO BE WITH YOU, RIGHT?
Y... EAH...
I WONDER, THOUGH ...
APPARENTLY THERE WAS SOME TALK ABOUT A GOOD-LOOKING GUY WHO WAS IN THE STUDENT COUNCIL WITH YOU APPLYING TO THE SAME HIGH SCHOOL AS YOU.
AND THAT MADE KOUKI PANIC AND STUDY.
AGAIN WITH THE PRESI- DENT...
I THINK *THAT* GOOD-LOOKING PRESIDENT WENT TO A DIFFERENT PRIVATE SCHOOL...
I'M NOT SURE WHICH, THOUGH.

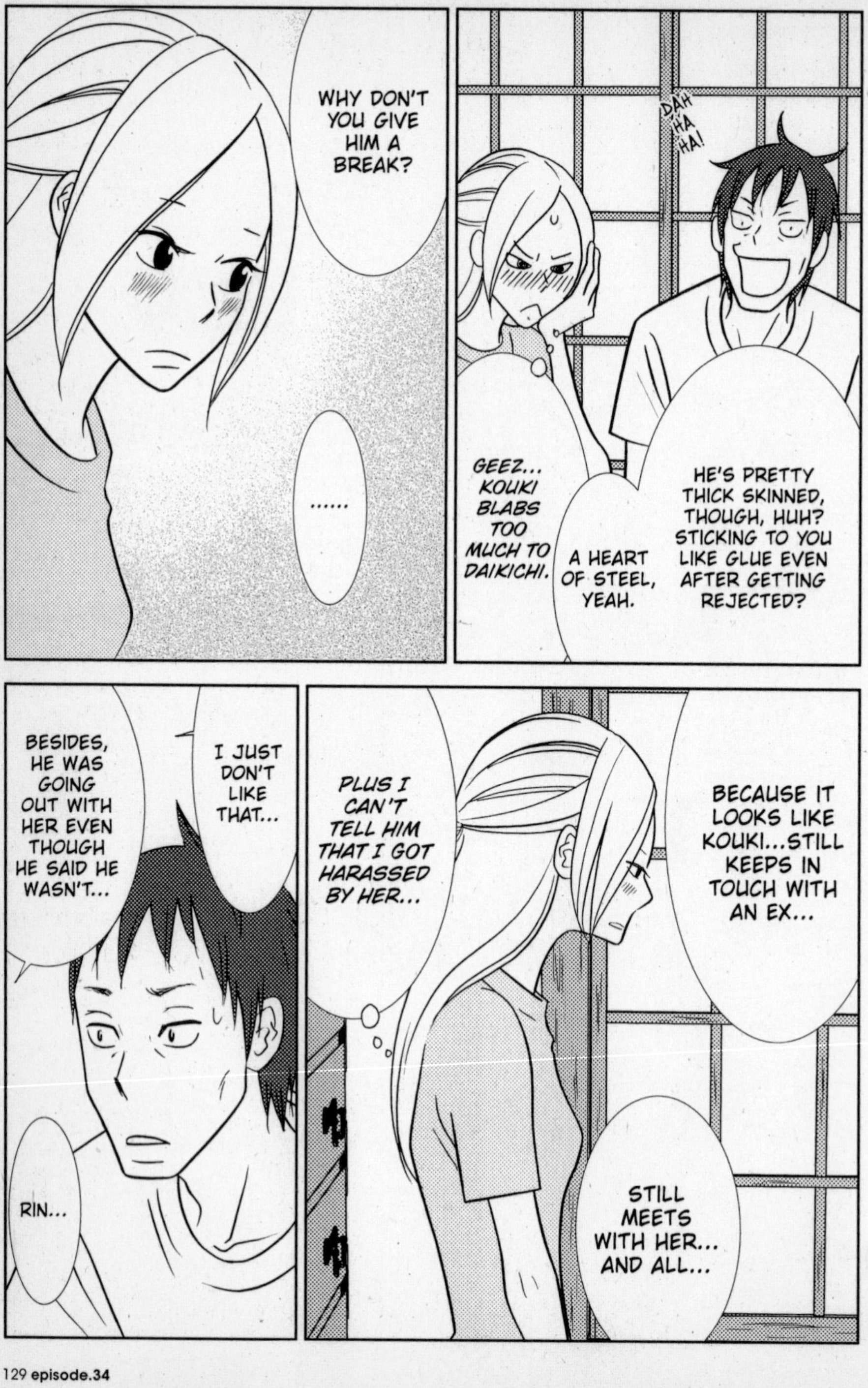
DAH HA HA!
HE'S PRETTY THICK SKINNED, THOUGH, HUH? STICKING TO YOU LIKE GLUE EVEN AFTER GETTING REJECTED?
A HEART OF STEEL, YEAH.
GEEZ... KOUKI BLABS TOO MUCH TO DAIKICHI.
WHY DON'T YOU GIVE HIM A BREAK?
......
BECAUSE IT LOOKS LIKE KOUKI...STILL KEEPS IN TOUCH WITH AN EX...
PLUS I CAN'T TELL HIM THAT I GOT HARASSED BY HER...
STILL MEETS WITH HER... AND ALL...
I JUST DON'T LIKE THAT...
BESIDES, HE WAS GOING OUT WITH HER EVEN THOUGH HE SAID HE WASN'T...
RIN...

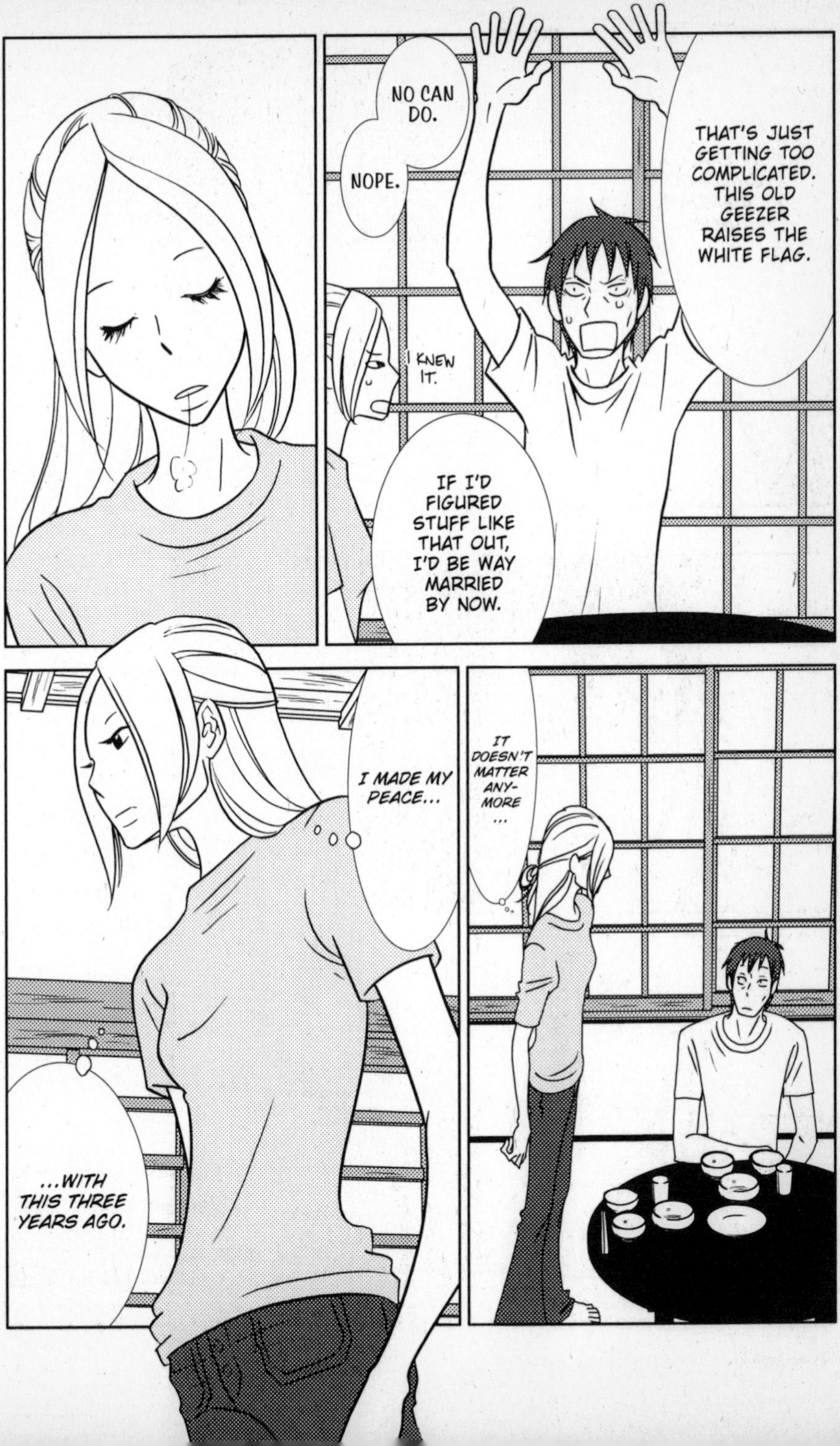
THAT'S JUST GETTING TOO COMPLICATED. THIS OLD GEEZER RAISES THE WHITE FLAG.
NO CAN DO.
NOPE.
I KNEW IT.
IF I'D FIGURED STUFF LIKE THAT OUT, I'D BE WAY MARRIED BY NOW.
IT DOESN'T MATTER ANYMORE...
I MADE MY PEACE...
...WITH THIS THREE YEARS AGO.

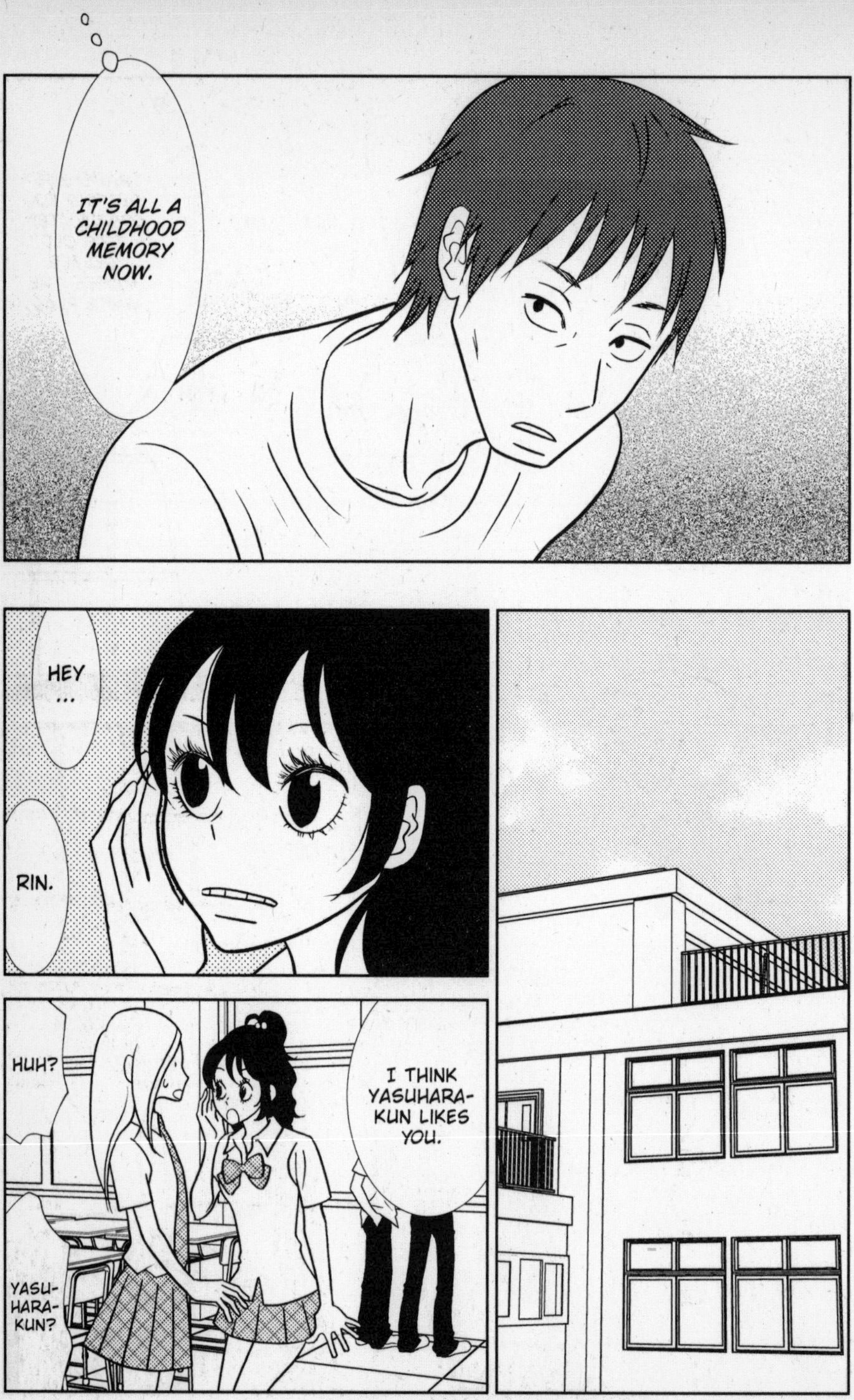
IT'S ALL A CHILDHOOD MEMORY NOW.
HEY ...
RIN.
I THINK YASUHARA-KUN LIKES YOU.
HUH?
YASU-HARA-KUN?

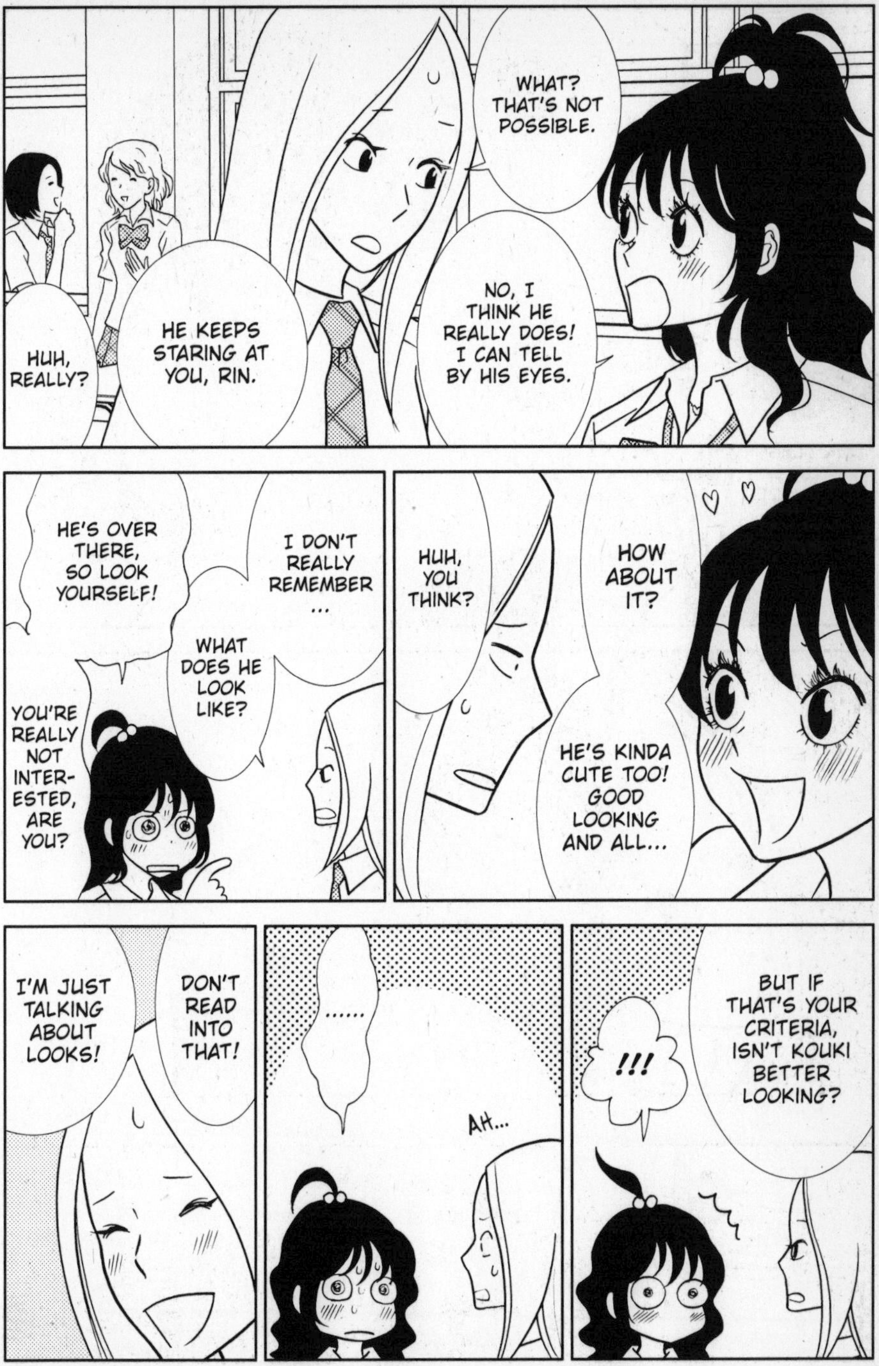

WHAT? THAT'S NOT POSSIBLE.
NO, I THINK HE REALLY DOES! I CAN TELL BY HIS EYES.
HE KEEPS STARING AT YOU, RIN.
HUH, REALLY?
HOW ABOUT IT?
HUH, YOU THINK?
HE'S KINDA CUTE TOO! GOOD LOOKING AND ALL...
I DON'T REALLY REMEMBER ...
HE'S OVER THERE, SO LOOK YOURSELF!
WHAT DOES HE LOOK LIKE?
YOU'RE REALLY NOT INTER-ESTED, ARE YOU?
BUT IF THAT'S YOUR CRITERIA, ISN'T KOUKI BETTER LOOKING?
!!!
......
AH...
DON'T READ INTO THAT!
I'M JUST TALKING ABOUT LOOKS!

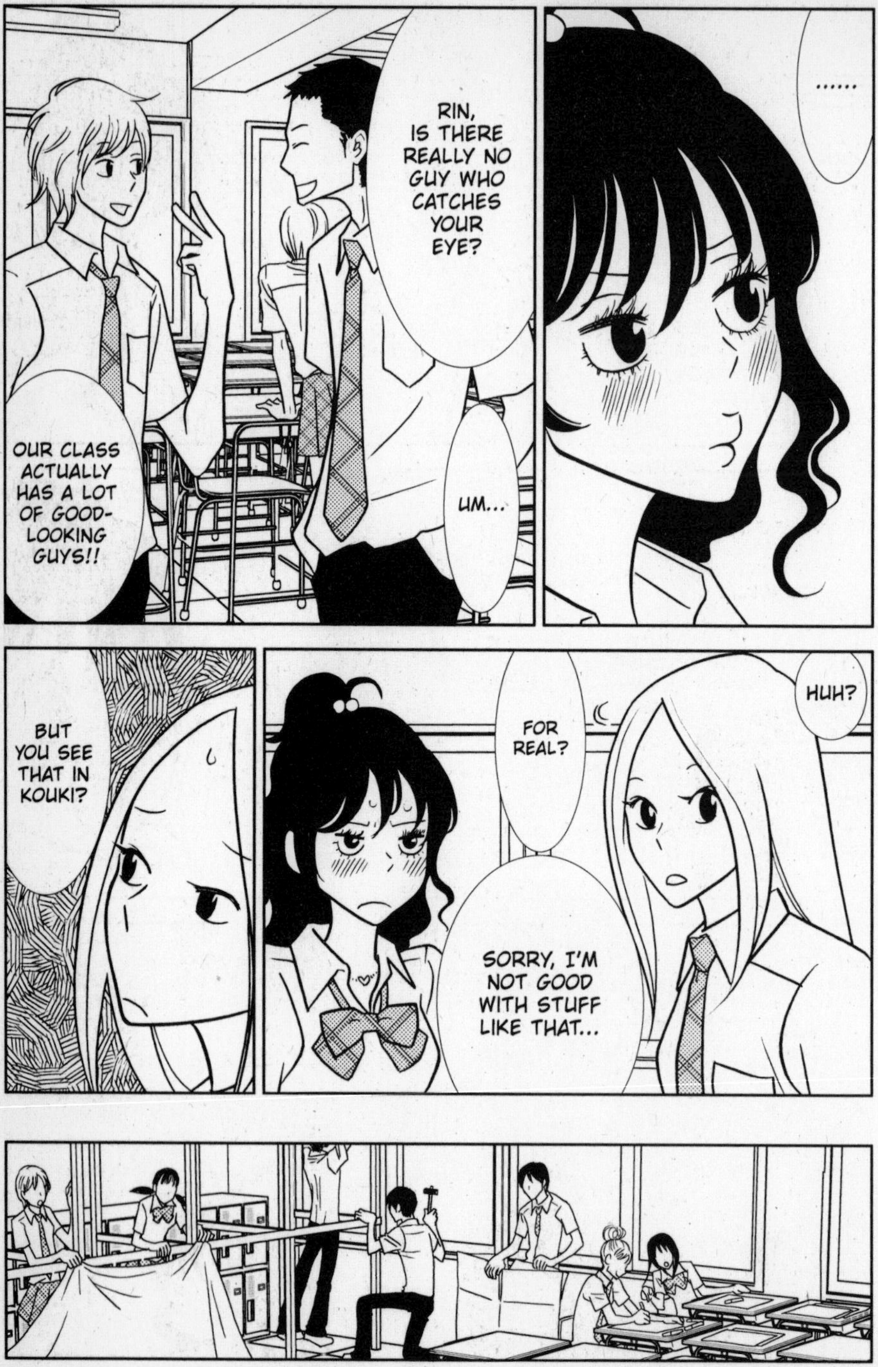
......
RIN, IS THERE REALLY NO GUY WHO CATCHES YOUR EYE?
UM...
OUR CLASS ACTUALLY HAS A LOT OF GOOD-LOOKING GUYS!!
HUH?
FOR REAL?
SORRY, I'M NOT GOOD WITH STUFF LIKE THAT...
BUT YOU SEE THAT IN KOUKI?

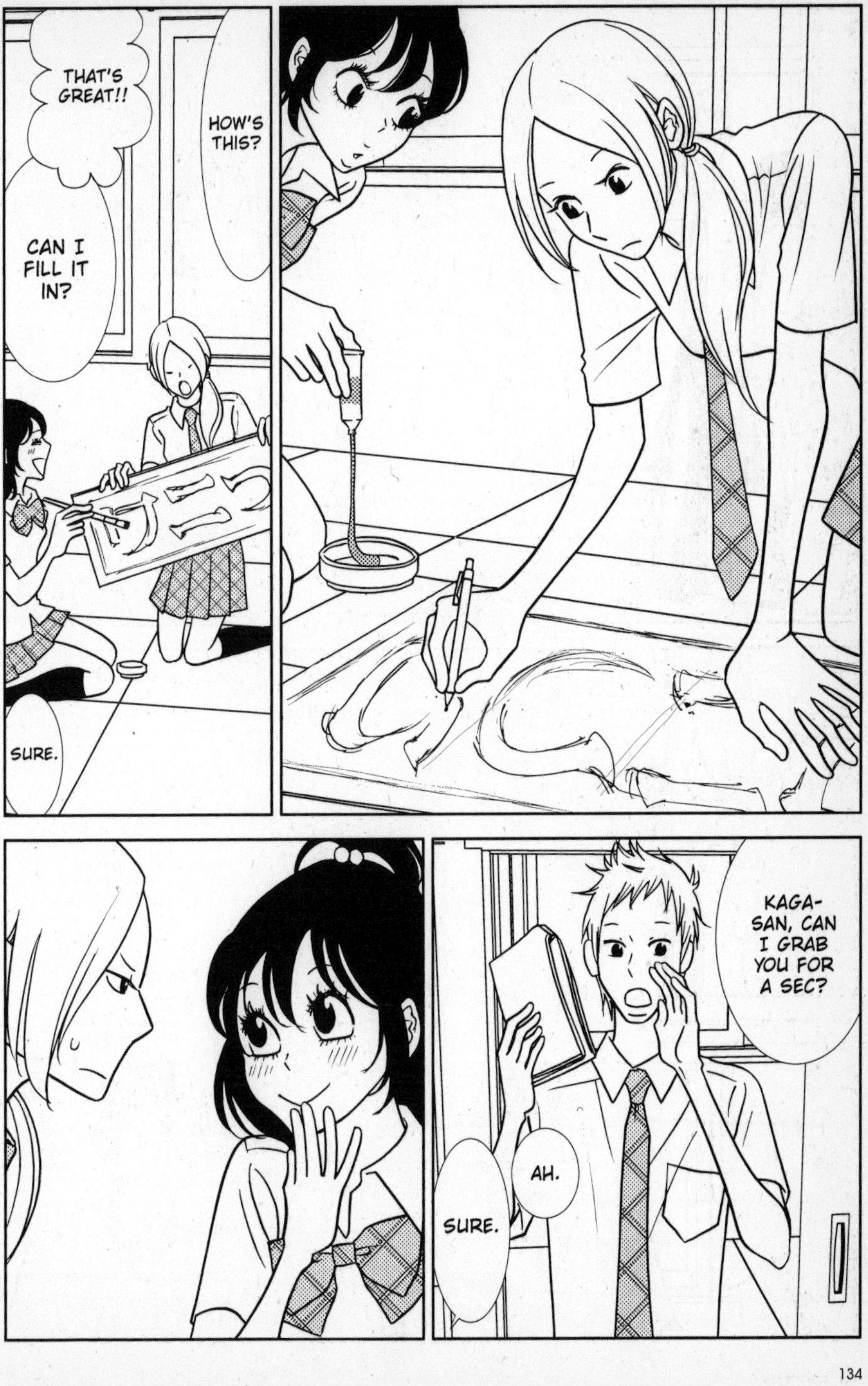
HOW'S THIS?
THAT'S GREAT!!
CAN I FILL IT IN?
SURE.
KAGA-SAN, CAN I GRAB YOU FOR A SEC?
AH.
SURE.

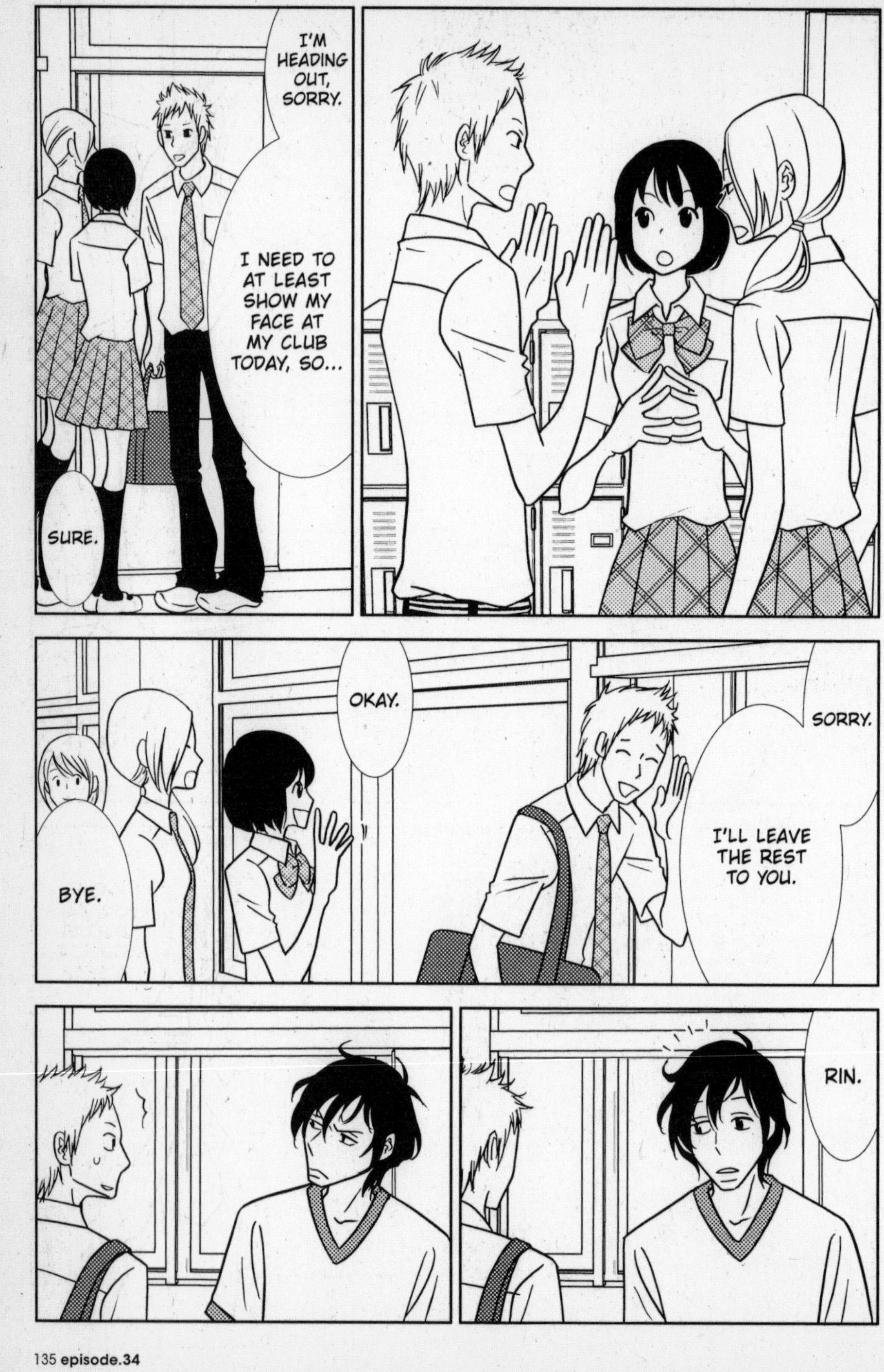
I'M HEADING OUT, SORRY.
I NEED TO AT LEAST SHOW MY FACE AT MY CLUB TODAY, SO...
SURE.
SORRY.
I'LL LEAVE THE REST TO YOU.
OKAY.
BYE.
RIN.

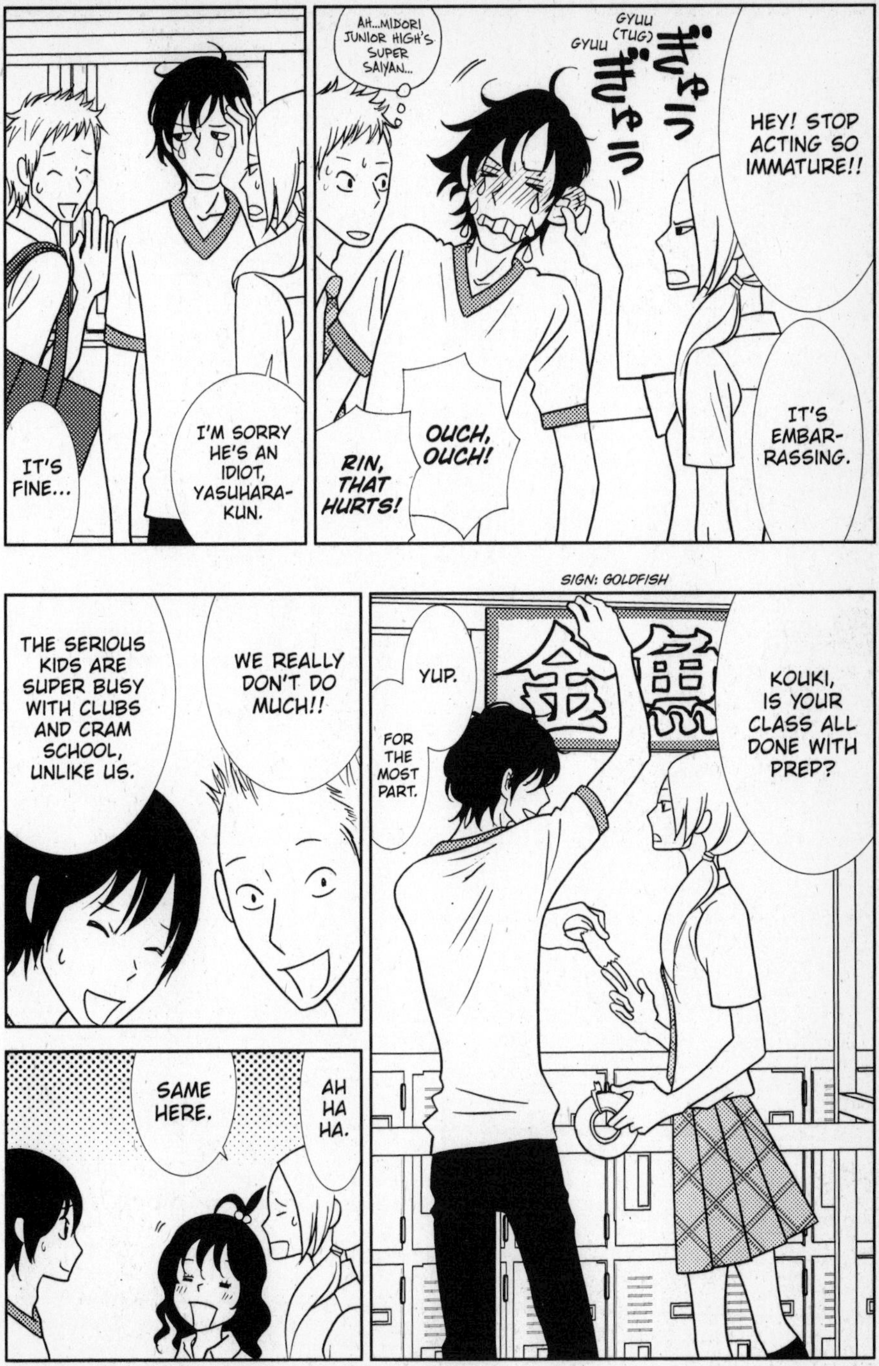
GYUU (TUG) GYUU
ぎゅう ぎゅう
HEY! STOP ACTING SO IMMATURE!!
IT'S EMBARRASSING.
AH...MIDORI JUNIOR HIGH'S SUPER SAIYAN...
OUCH, OUCH!
RIN, THAT HURTS!
I'M SORRY HE'S AN IDIOT, YASUHARA-KUN.
IT'S FINE...
SIGN: GOLDFISH
金魚
KOUKI, IS YOUR CLASS ALL DONE WITH PREP?
YUP.
FOR THE MOST PART.
WE REALLY DON'T DO MUCH!!
THE SERIOUS KIDS ARE SUPER BUSY WITH CLUBS AND CRAM SCHOOL, UNLIKE US.
AH HA HA.
SAME HERE.

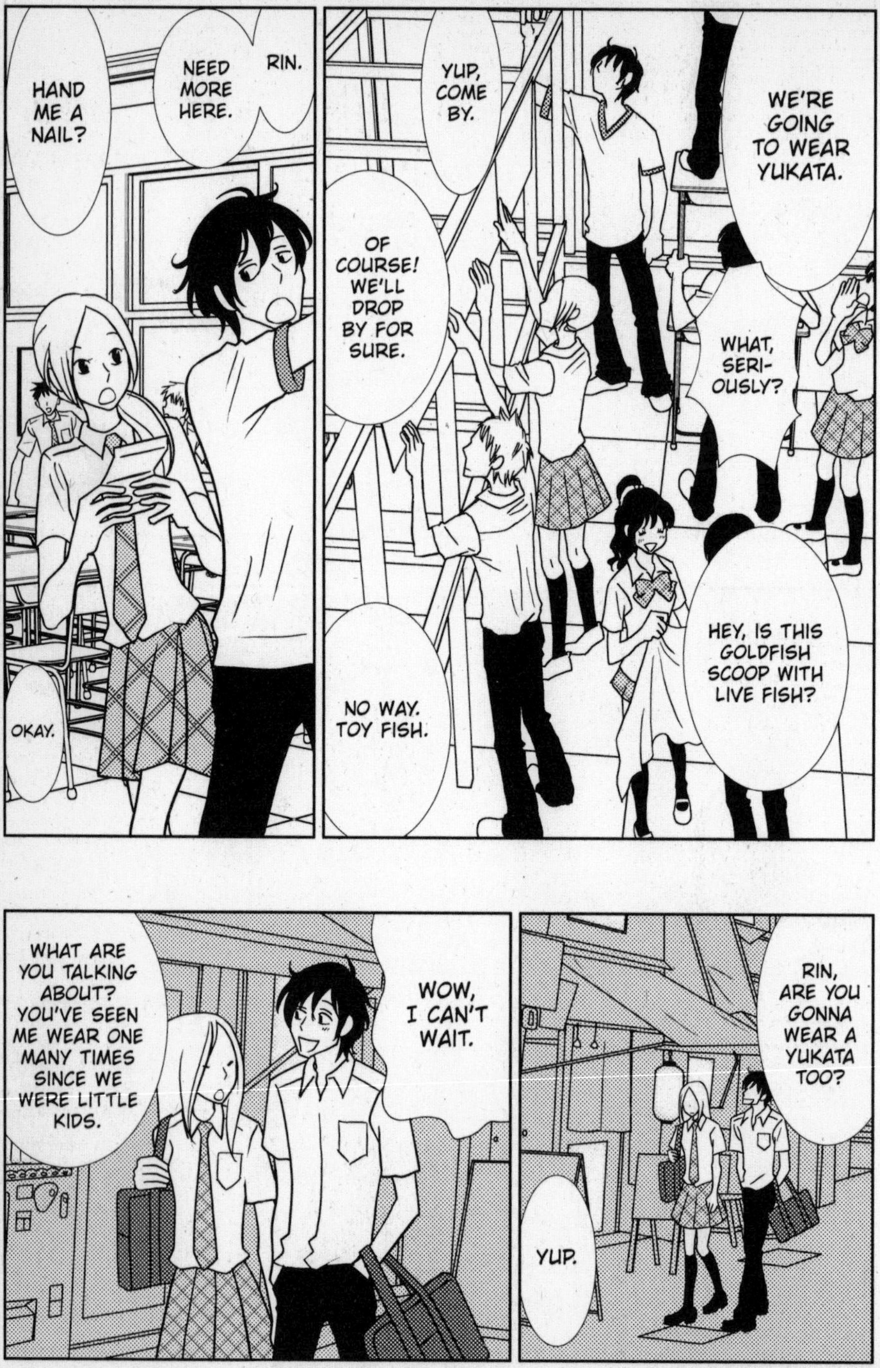
WE'RE GOING TO WEAR YUKATA.
YUP, COME BY.
WHAT, SERIOUSLY?
OF COURSE! WE'LL DROP BY FOR SURE.
HEY, IS THIS GOLDFISH SCOOP WITH LIVE FISH?
NO WAY. TOY FISH.
RIN.
NEED MORE HERE.
HAND ME A NAIL?
OKAY.
RIN, ARE YOU GONNA WEAR A YUKATA TOO?
YUP.
WOW, I CAN'T WAIT.
WHAT ARE YOU TALKING ABOUT? YOU'VE SEEN ME WEAR ONE MANY TIMES SINCE WE WERE LITTLE KIDS.

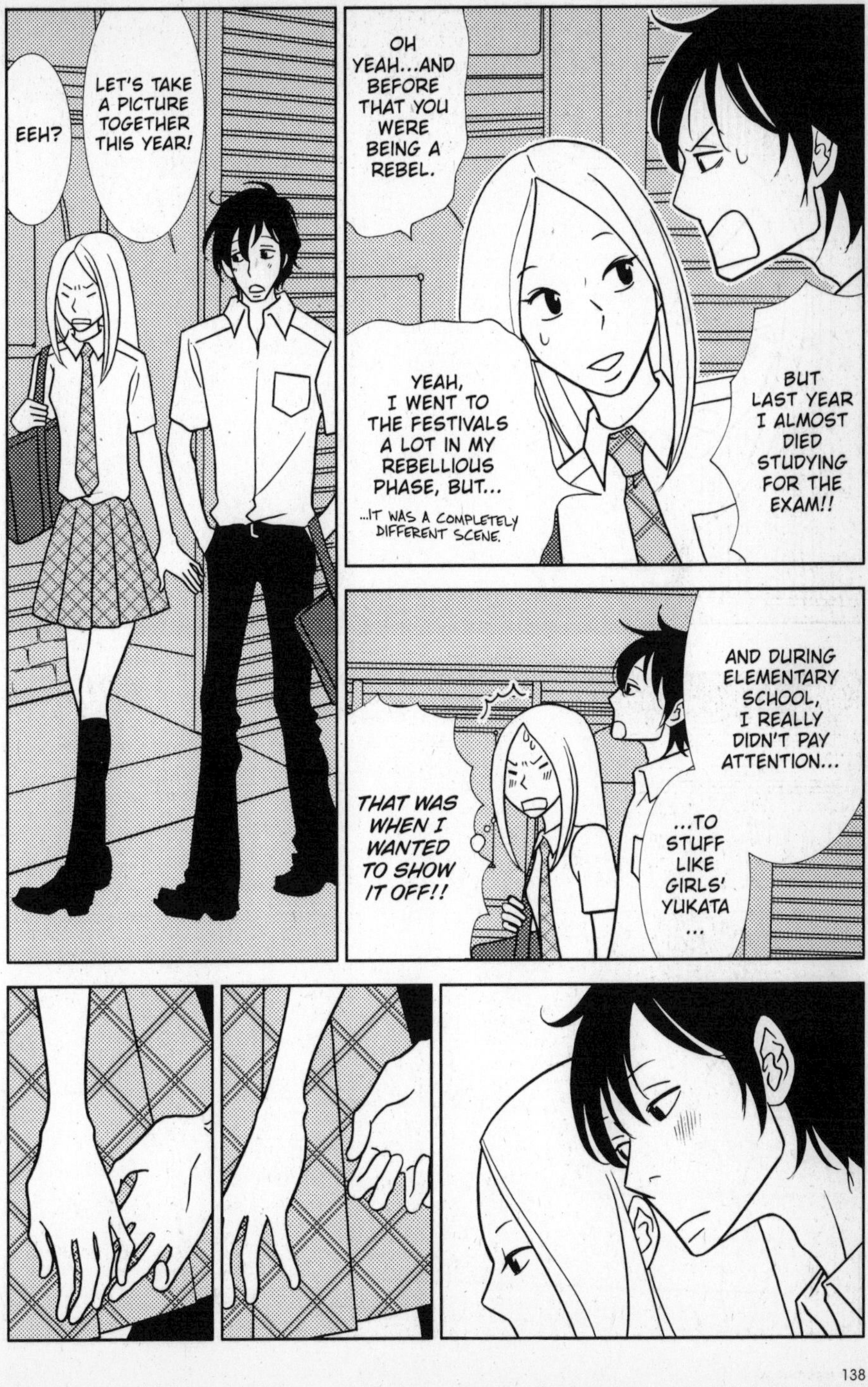
BUT LAST YEAR I ALMOST DIED STUDYING FOR THE EXAM!!
OH YEAH...AND BEFORE THAT YOU WERE BEING A REBEL.
YEAH, I WENT TO THE FESTIVALS A LOT IN MY REBELLIOUS PHASE, BUT...
...IT WAS A COMPLETELY DIFFERENT SCENE.
AND DURING ELEMENTARY SCHOOL, I REALLY DIDN'T PAY ATTENTION...
...TO STUFF LIKE GIRLS' YUKATA...
THAT WAS WHEN I WANTED TO SHOW IT OFF!!
LET'S TAKE A PICTURE TOGETHER THIS YEAR!
EEH?

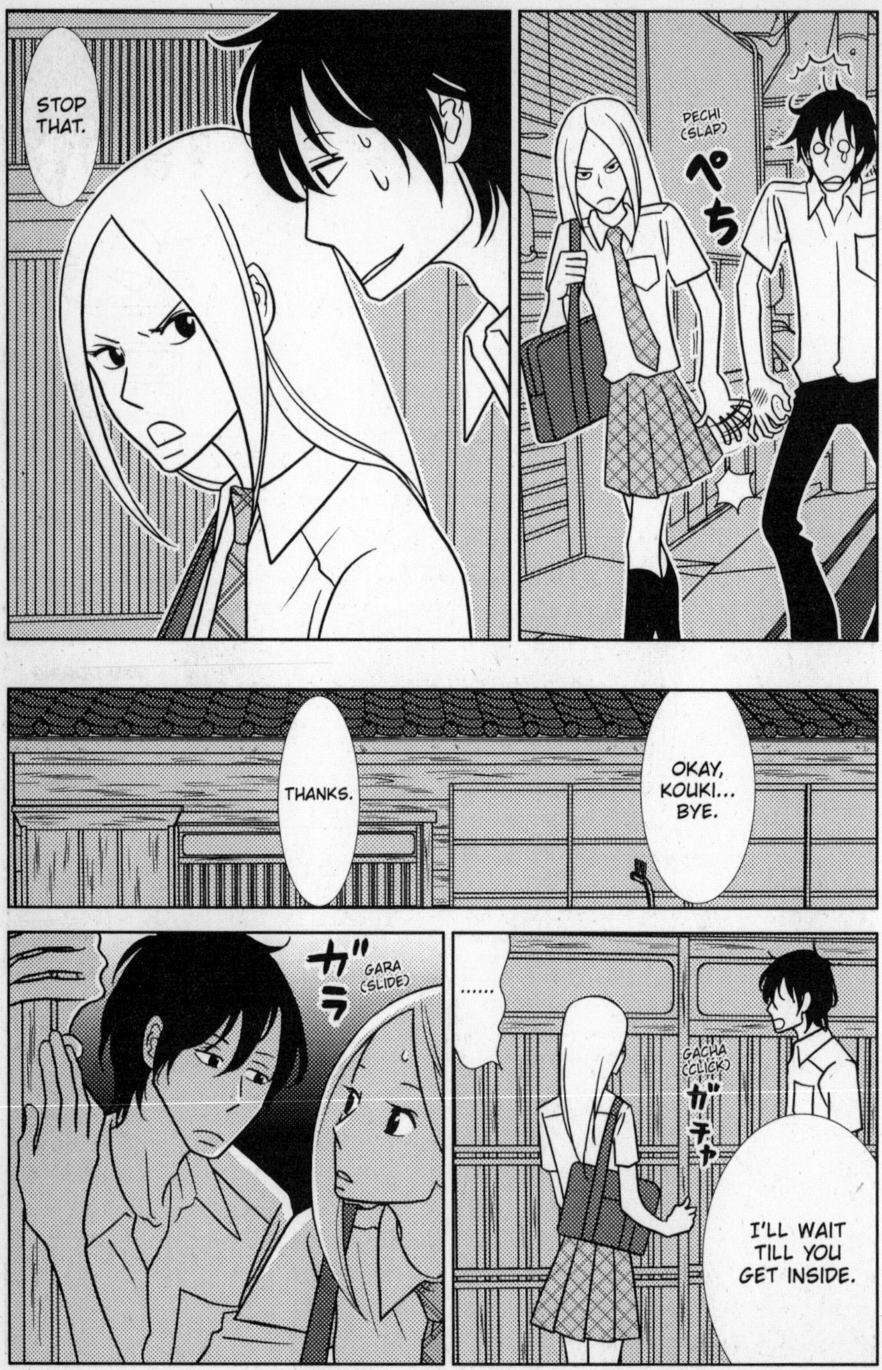
PECHI (SLAP)
ぺち
STOP THAT.
OKAY, KOUKI... BYE.
THANKS.
......
GACHA (CLICK)
ガチャ
I'LL WAIT TILL YOU GET INSIDE.
ガラ
GARA (SLIDE)

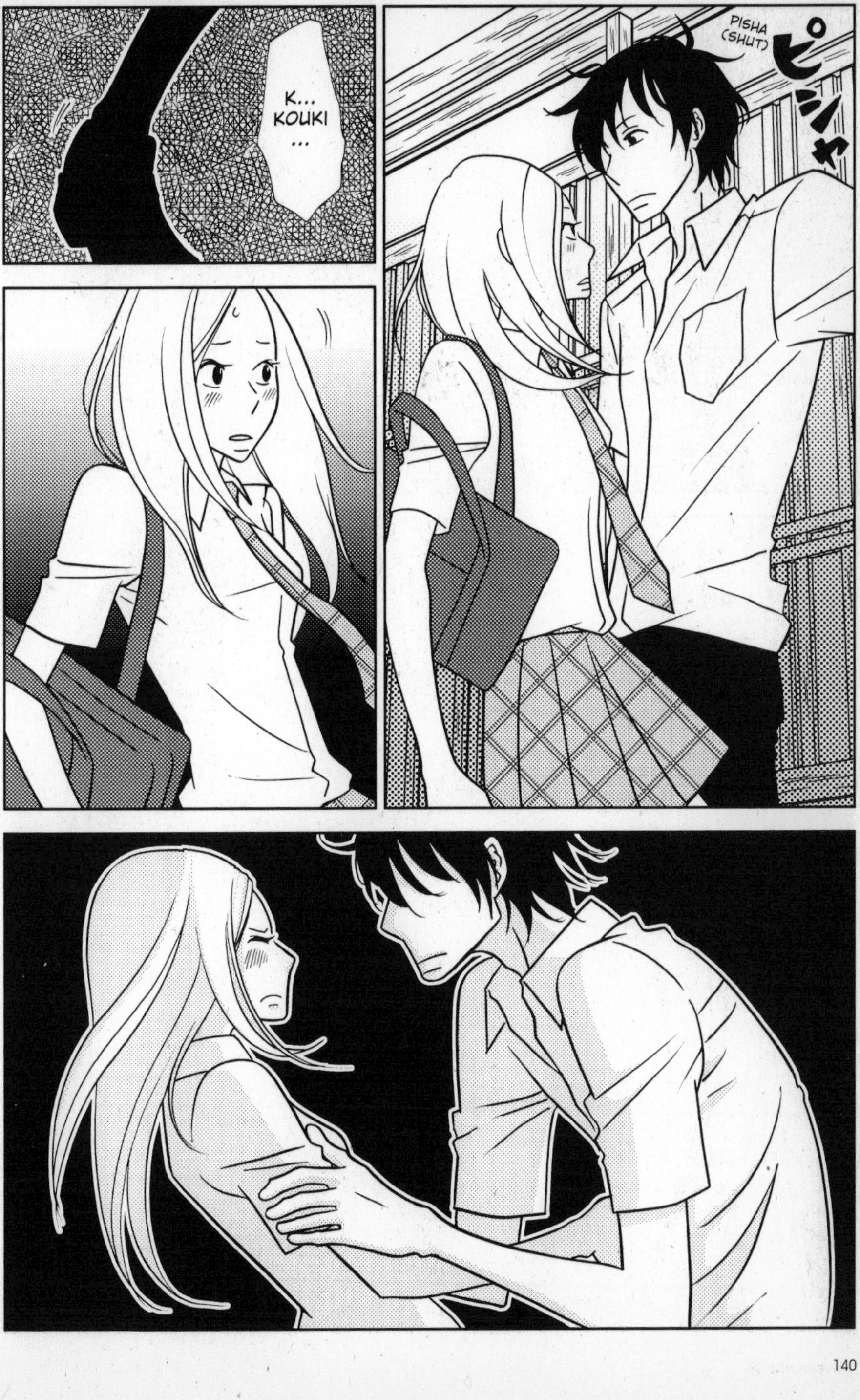
ピシャ
PISHA (SHUT)
K... KOUKI ...

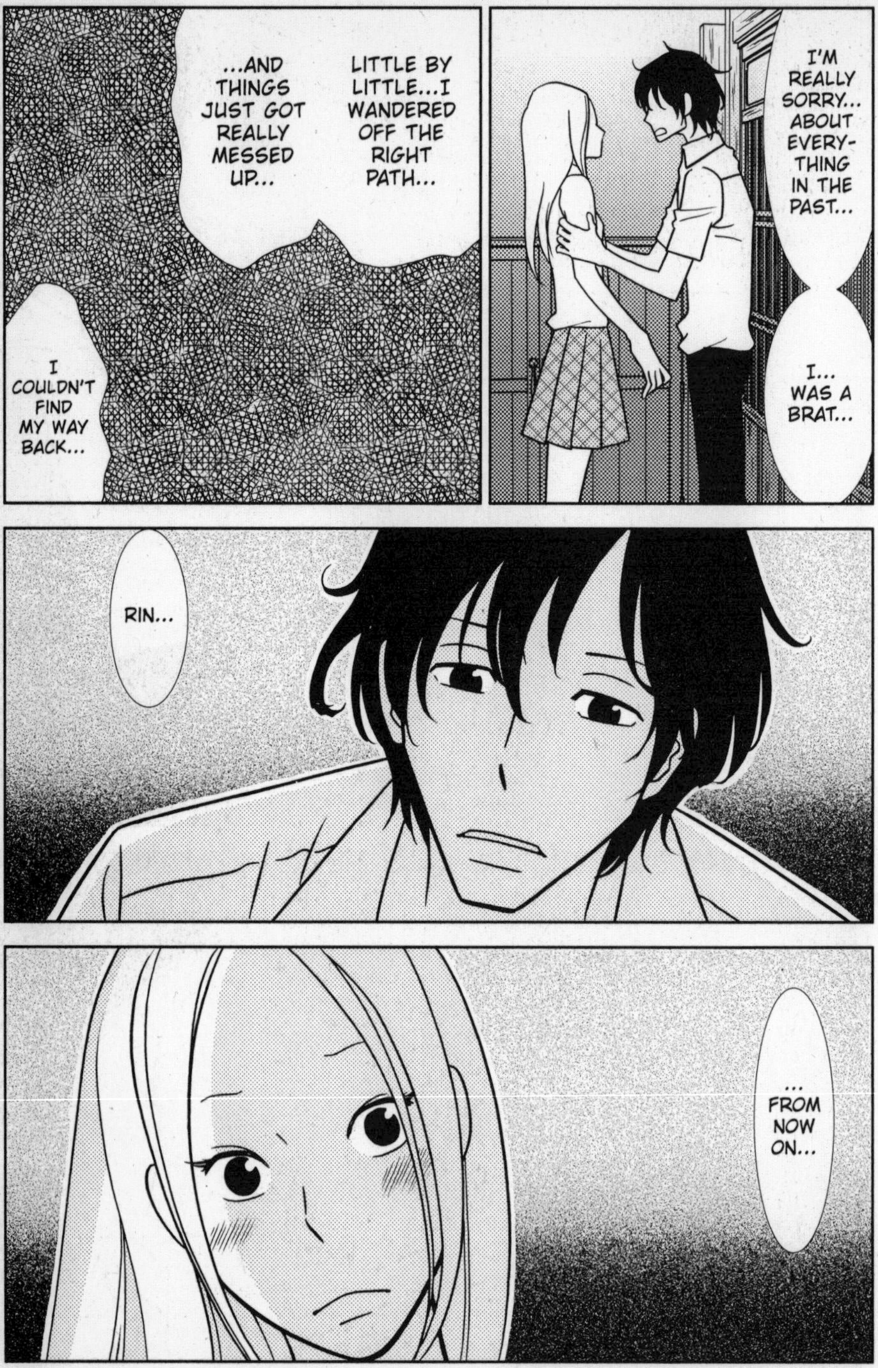
I'M REALLY SORRY... ABOUT EVERY-THING IN THE PAST...
I... WAS A BRAT...
LITTLE BY LITTLE...I WANDERED OFF THE RIGHT PATH...
...AND THINGS JUST GOT REALLY MESSED UP...
I COULDN'T FIND MY WAY BACK...
RIN...
...FROM NOW ON...

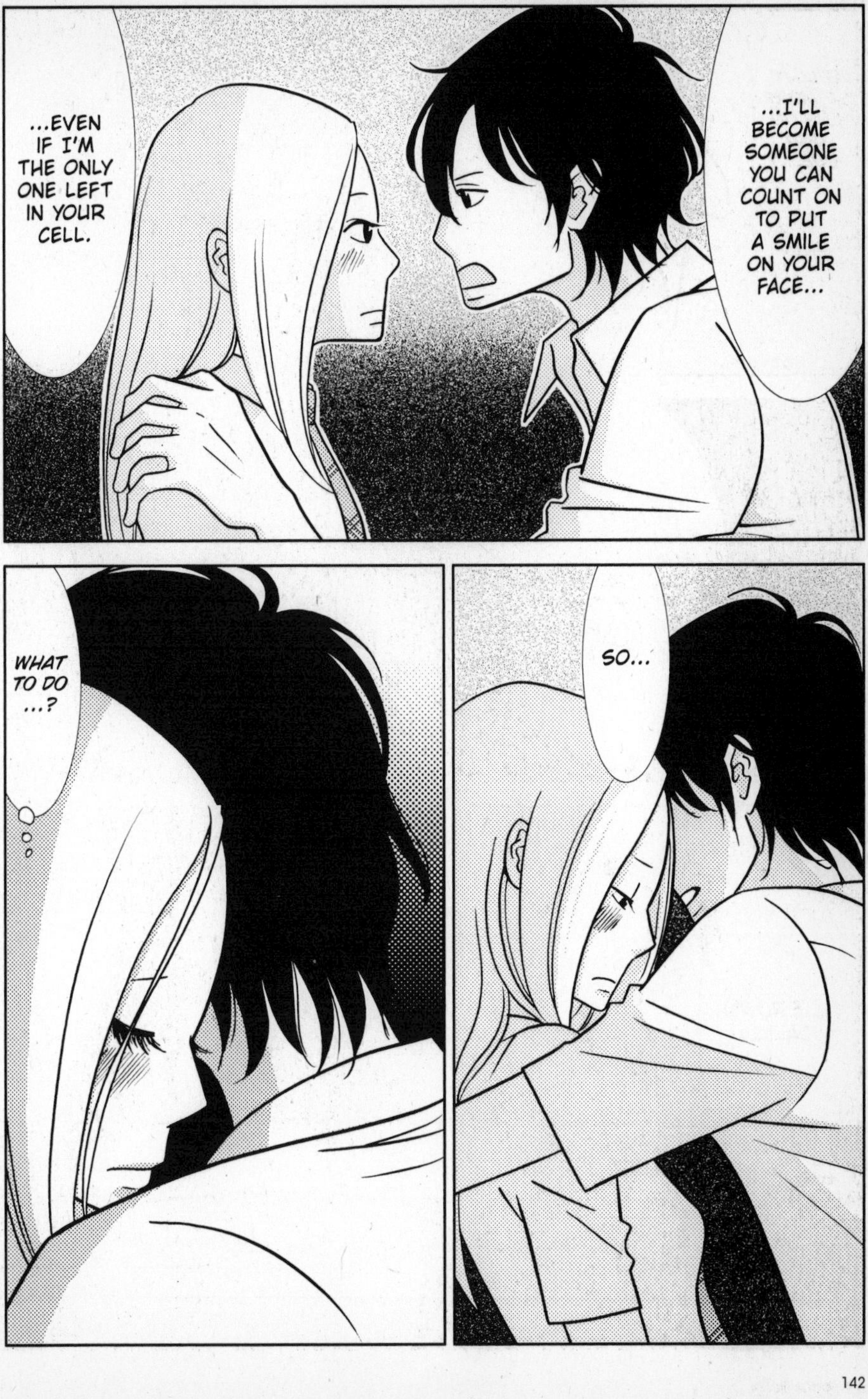
...I'LL BECOME SOMEONE YOU CAN COUNT ON TO PUT A SMILE ON YOUR FACE...
...EVEN IF I'M THE ONLY ONE LEFT IN YOUR CELL.
SO...
WHAT TO DO ...?

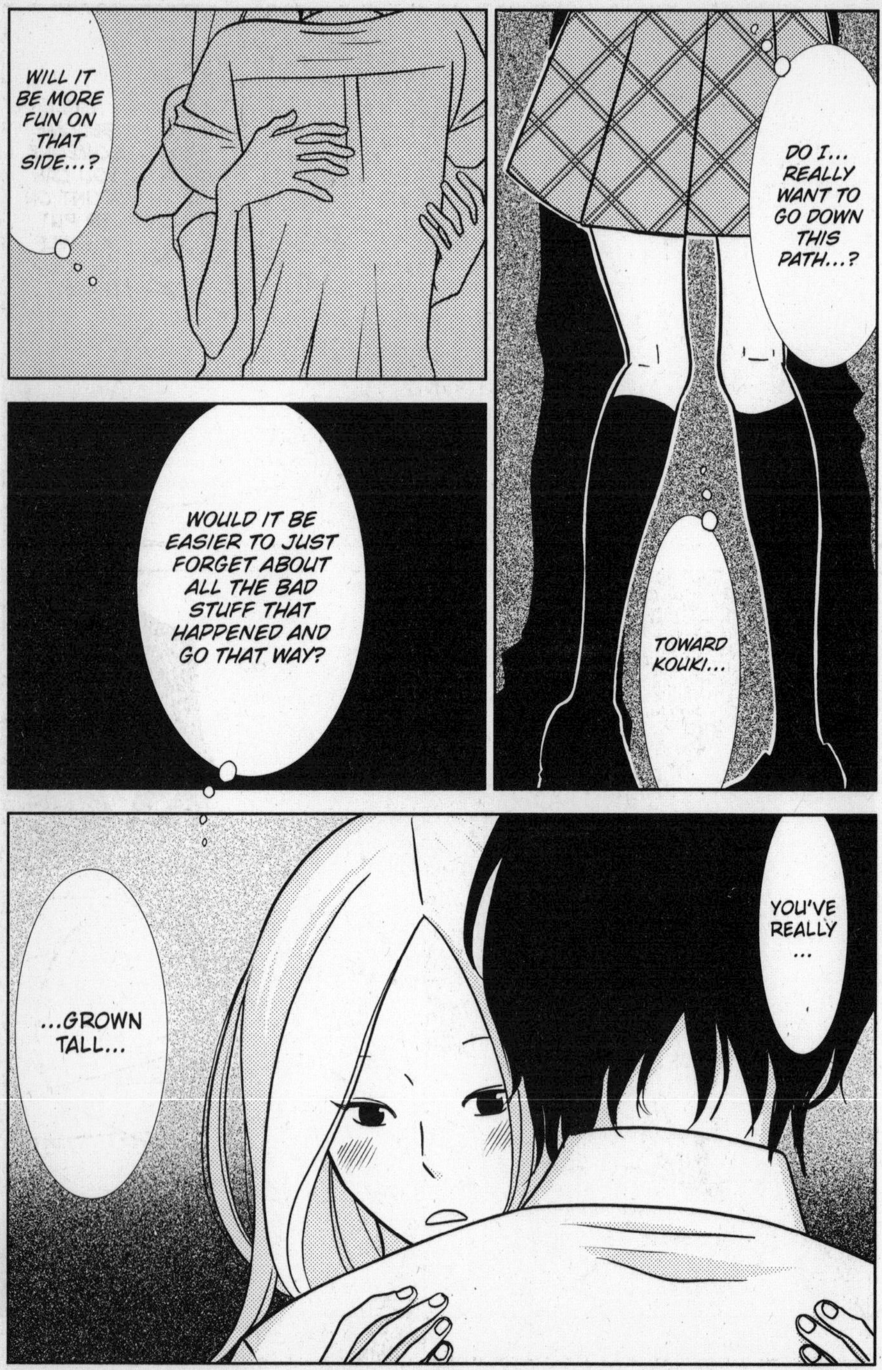
DO I... REALLY WANT TO GO DOWN THIS PATH...?
TOWARD KOUKI...
WILL IT BE MORE FUN ON THAT SIDE...?
WOULD IT BE EASIER TO JUST FORGET ABOUT ALL THE BAD STUFF THAT HAPPENED AND GO THAT WAY?
YOU'VE REALLY ...
...GROWN TALL...

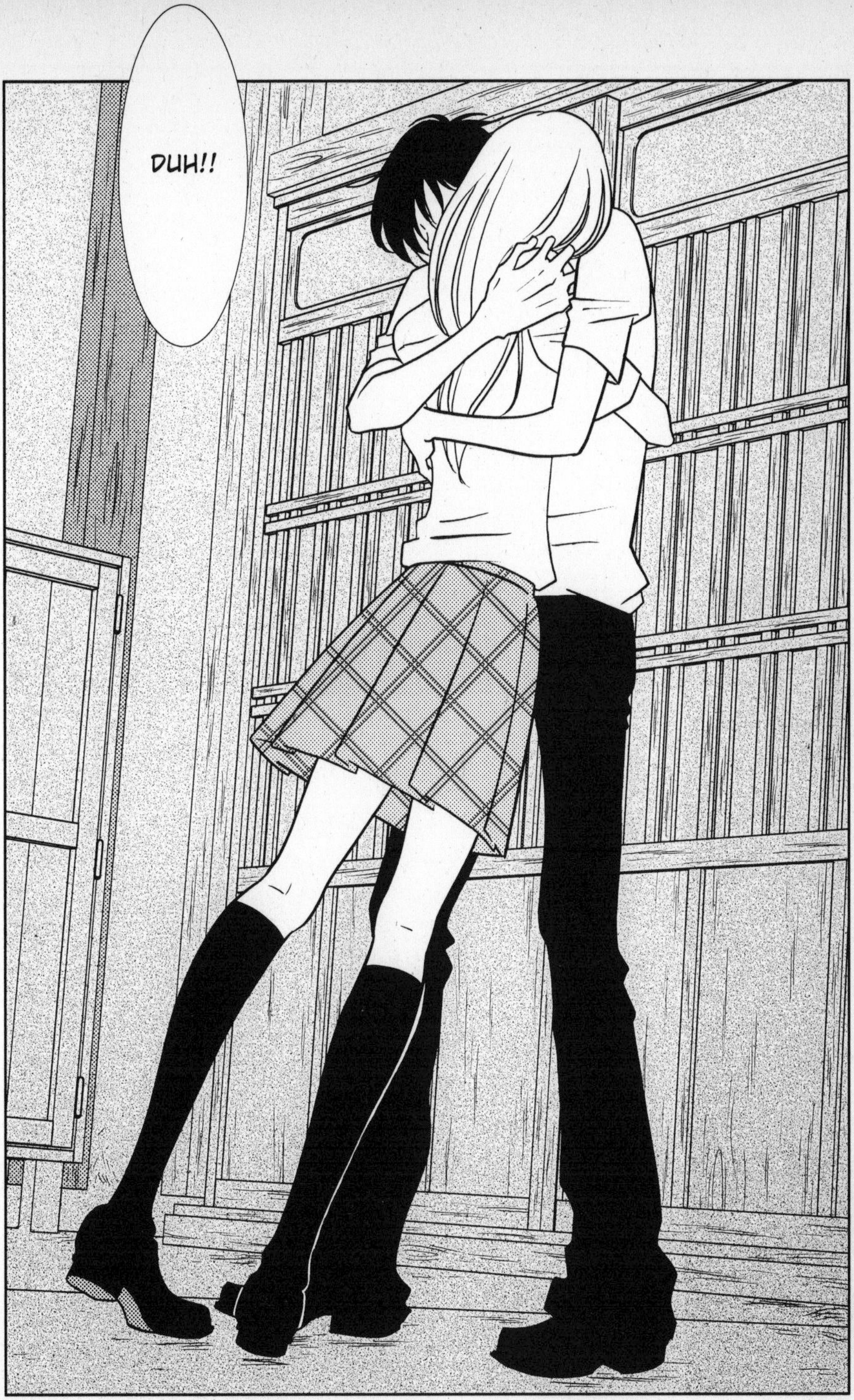
DUH!!

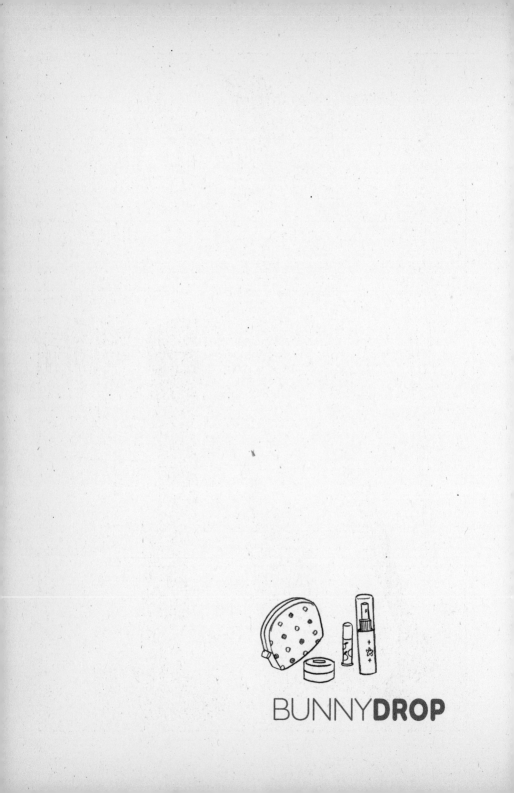

BUNNY**DROP**

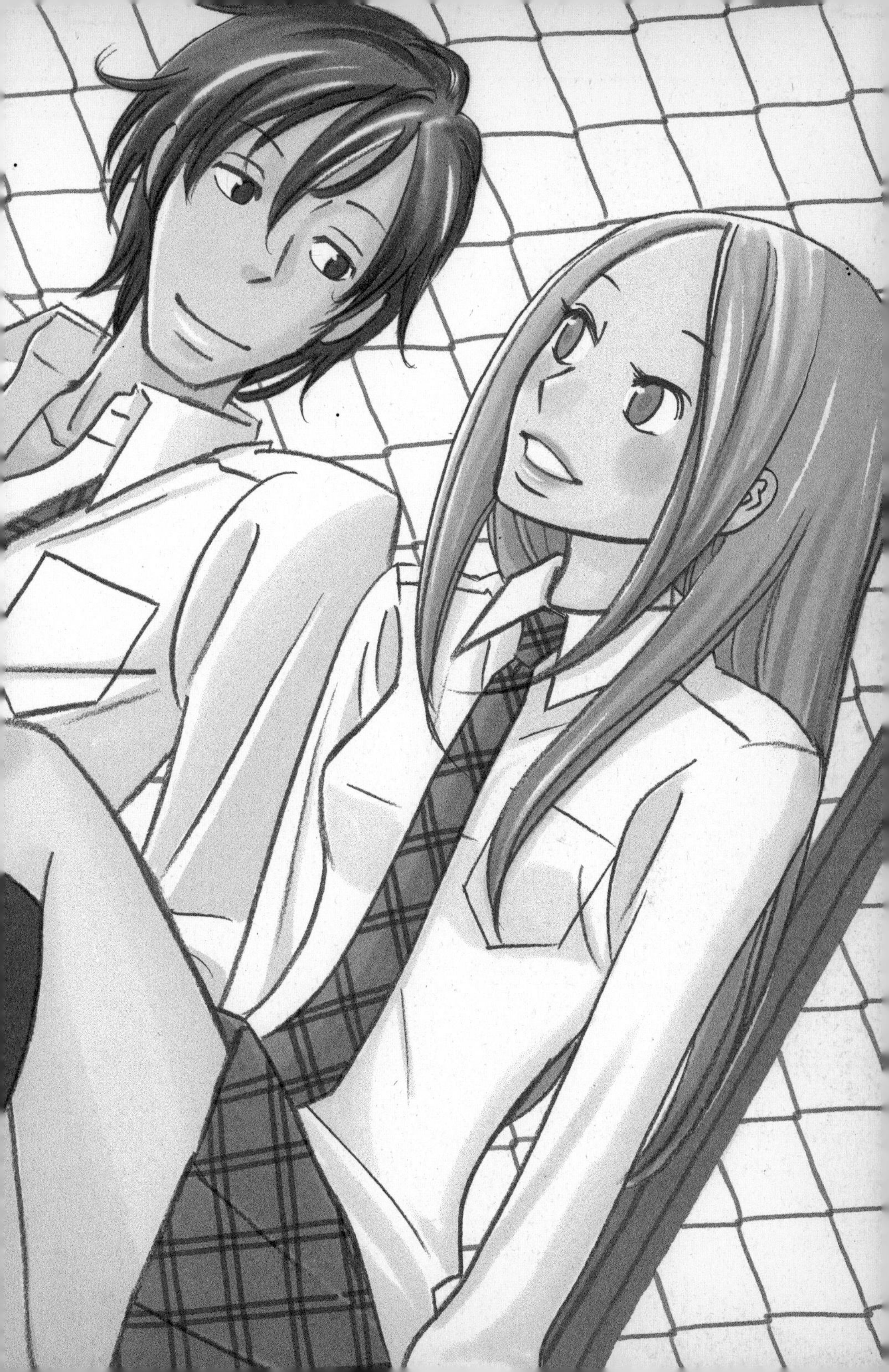

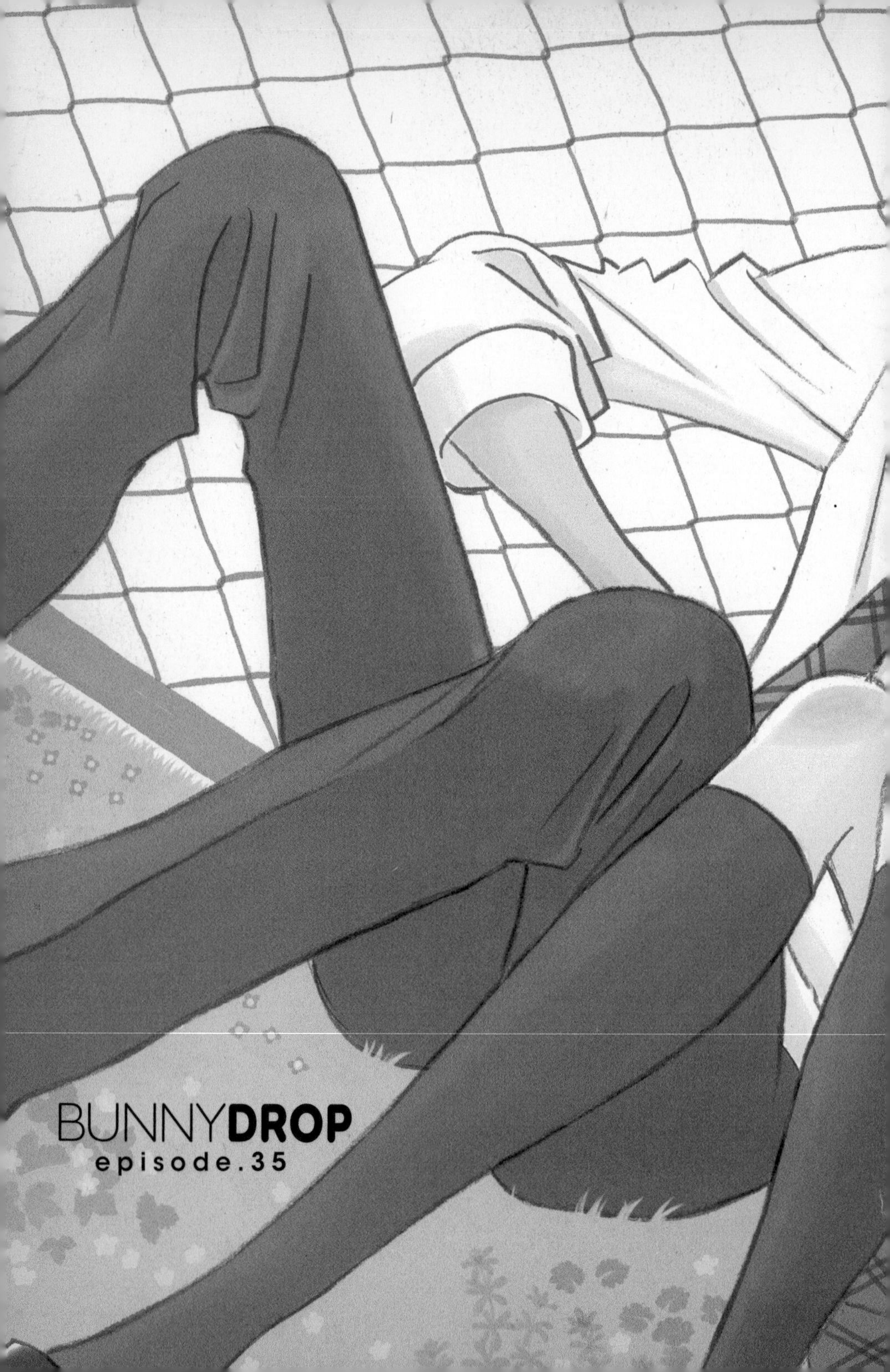
BUNNY DROP
episode.35

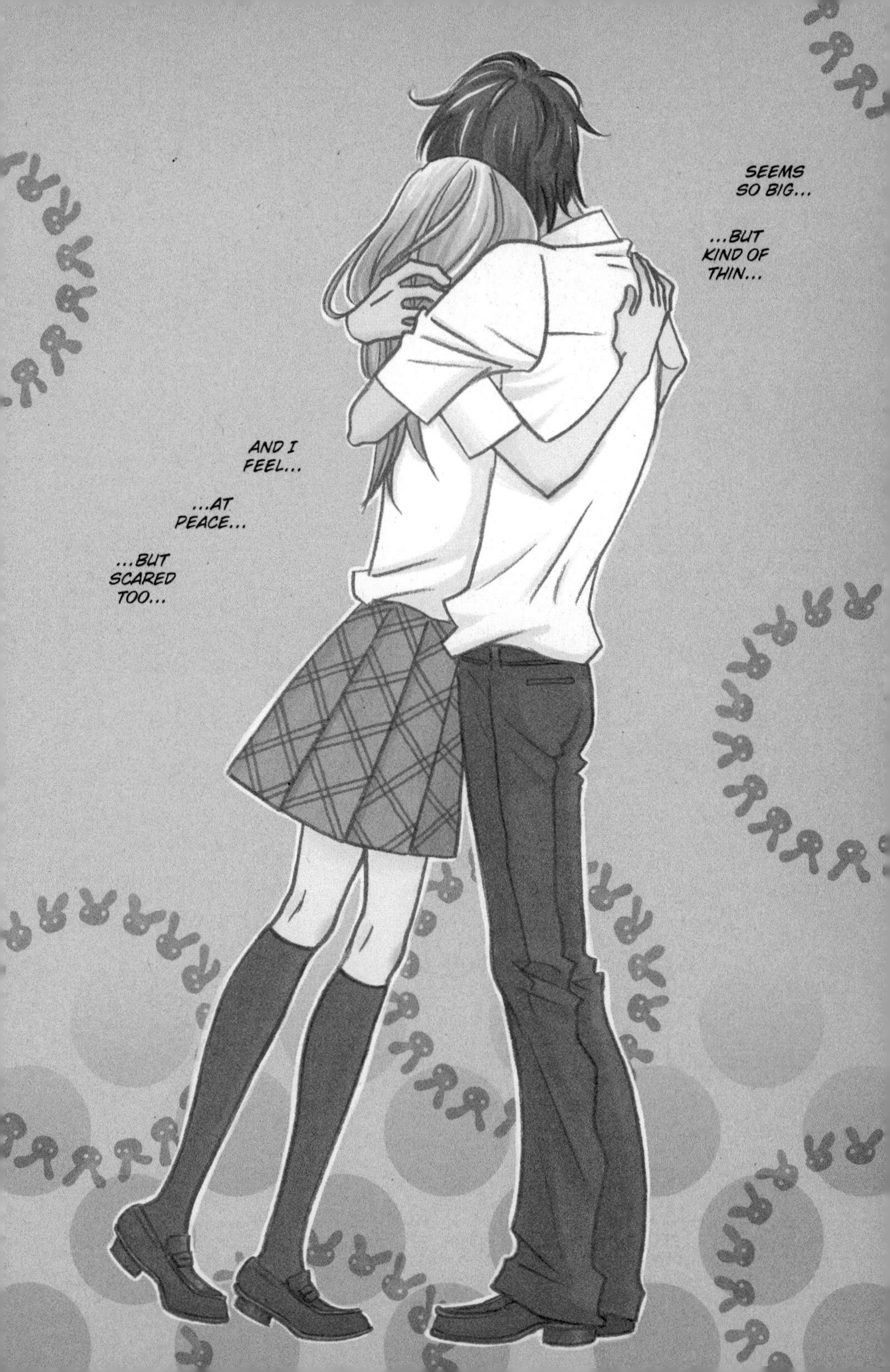
SEEMS SO BIG...
...BUT KIND OF THIN...
AND I FEEL...
...AT PEACE...
...BUT SCARED TOO...

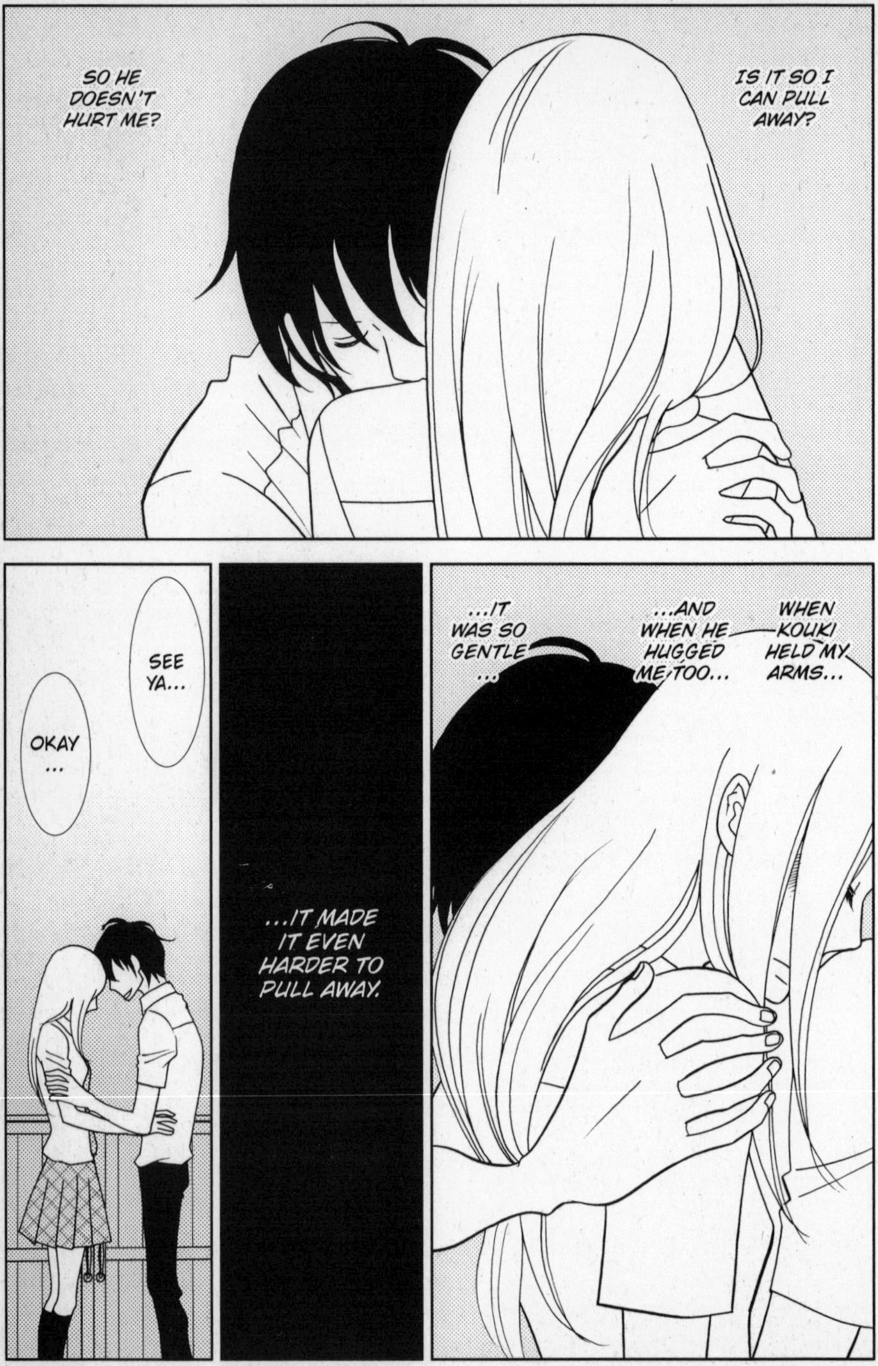
IS IT SO I CAN PULL AWAY?
SO HE DOESN'T HURT ME?
WHEN KOUKI HELD MY ARMS...
...AND WHEN HE HUGGED ME TOO...
...IT WAS SO GENTLE...
...IT MADE IT EVEN HARDER TO PULL AWAY.
SEE YA...
OKAY...

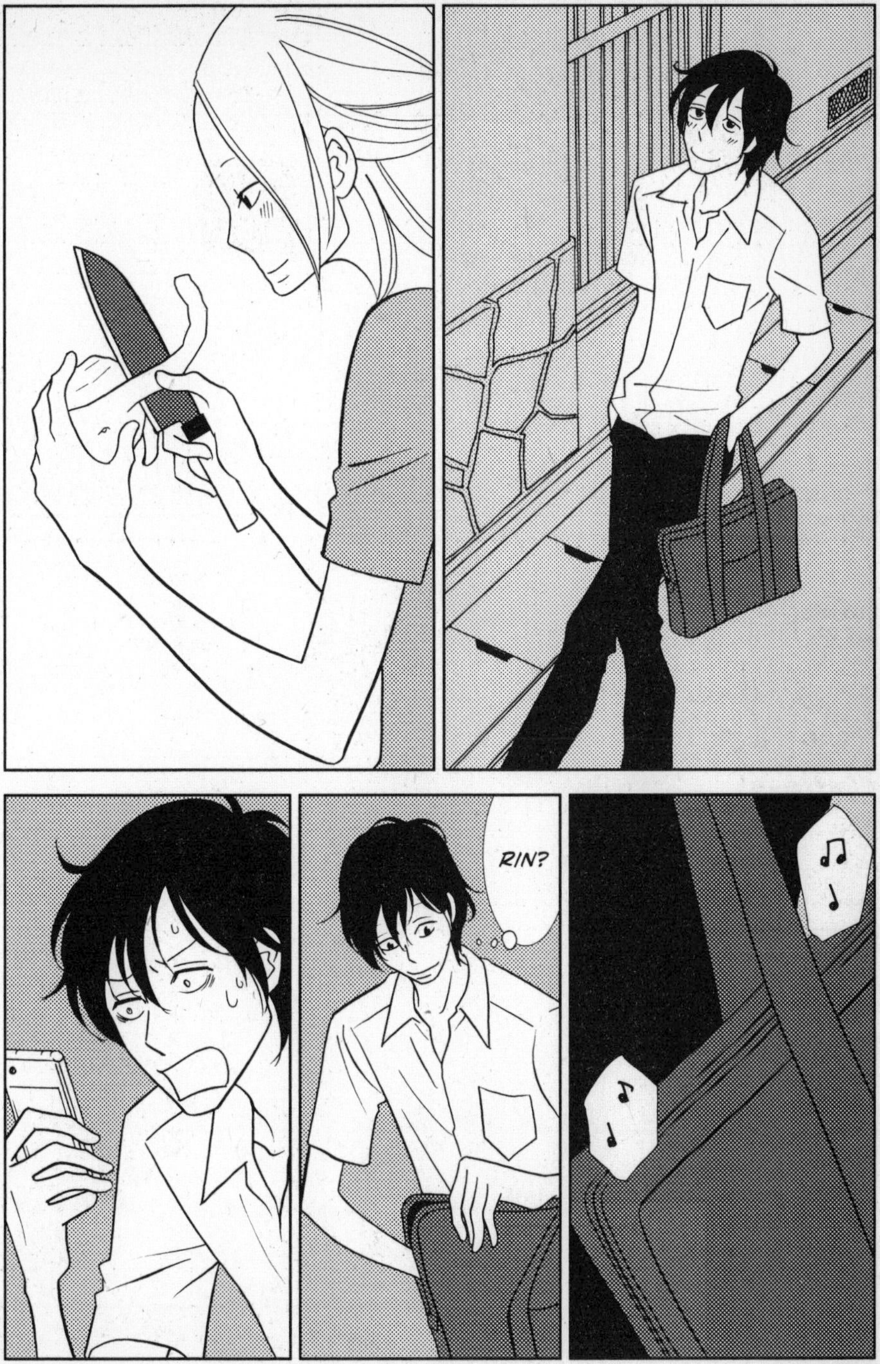
RIN?

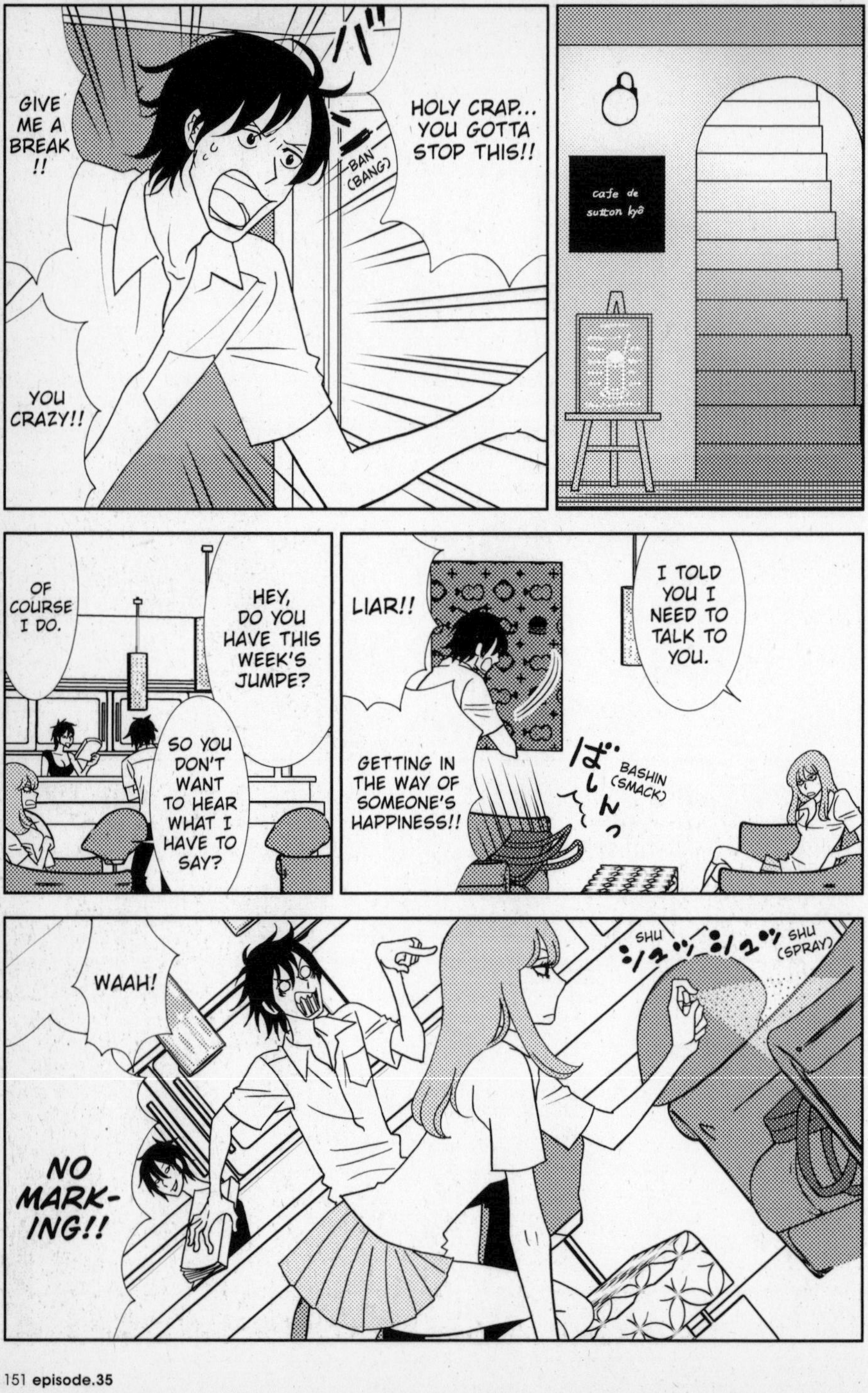
cafe de sutton kyô
HOLY CRAP... YOU GOTTA STOP THIS!!
BAN (BANG)
GIVE ME A BREAK !!
YOU CRAZY!!
I TOLD YOU I NEED TO TALK TO YOU.
LIAR!!
ばしんっ BASHIN (SMACK)
GETTING IN THE WAY OF SOMEONE'S HAPPINESS!!
HEY, DO YOU HAVE THIS WEEK'S JUMPE?
OF COURSE I DO.
SO YOU DON'T WANT TO HEAR WHAT I HAVE TO SAY?
シュッ SHU シュッ SHU (SPRAY)
WAAH!
NO MARKING!!

BOOK: SHONEN JUMPE, FULL MOON SUPER BONUS ISSUE

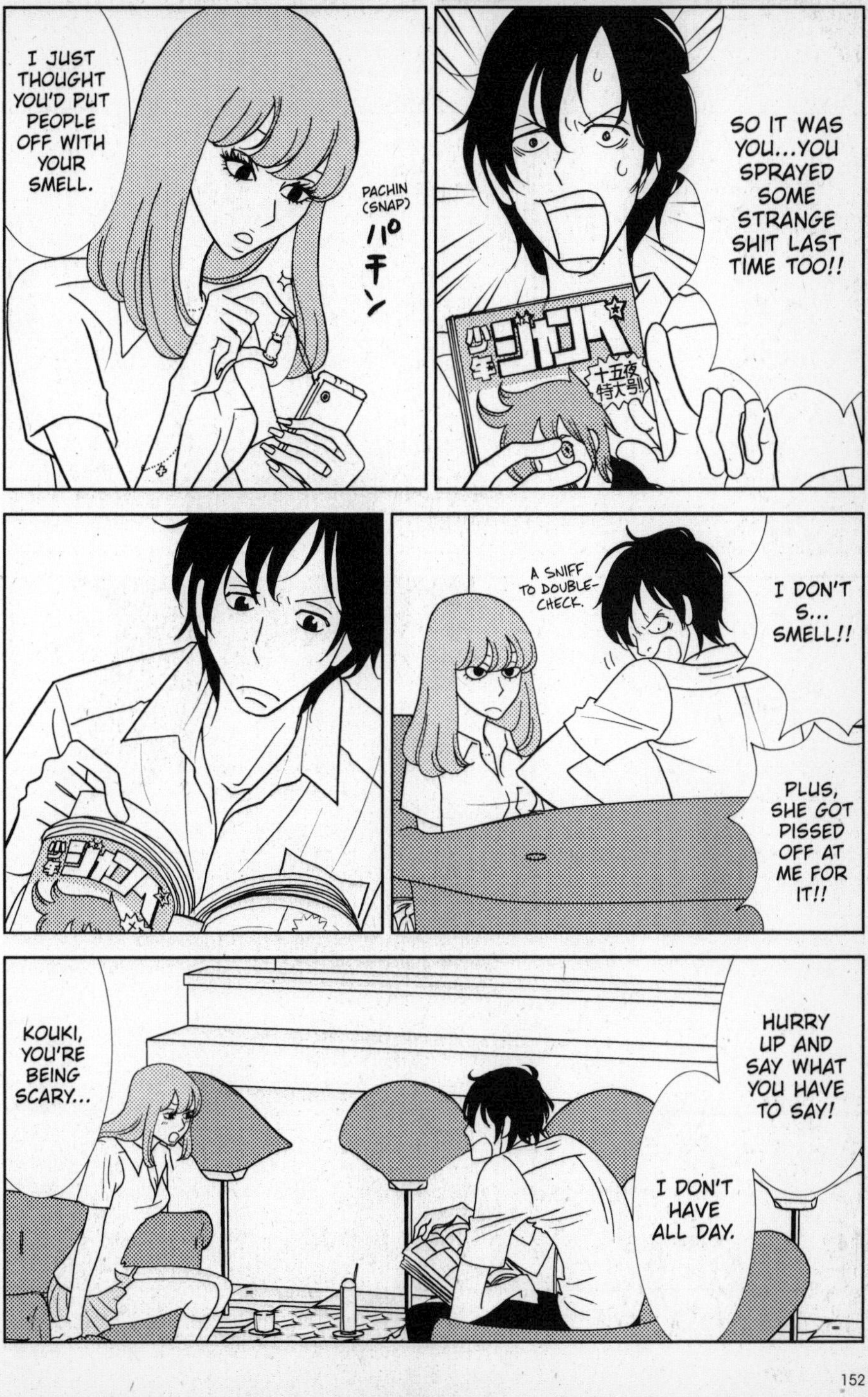
SO IT WAS YOU...YOU SPRAYED SOME STRANGE SHIT LAST TIME TOO!!
十五夜特大号!
I JUST THOUGHT YOU'D PUT PEOPLE OFF WITH YOUR SMELL.
PACHIN (SNAP)
パチン
I DON'T S... SMELL!!
A SNIFF TO DOUBLE-CHECK.
PLUS, SHE GOT PISSED OFF AT ME FOR IT!!
HURRY UP AND SAY WHAT YOU HAVE TO SAY!
I DON'T HAVE ALL DAY.
KOUKI, YOU'RE BEING SCARY...

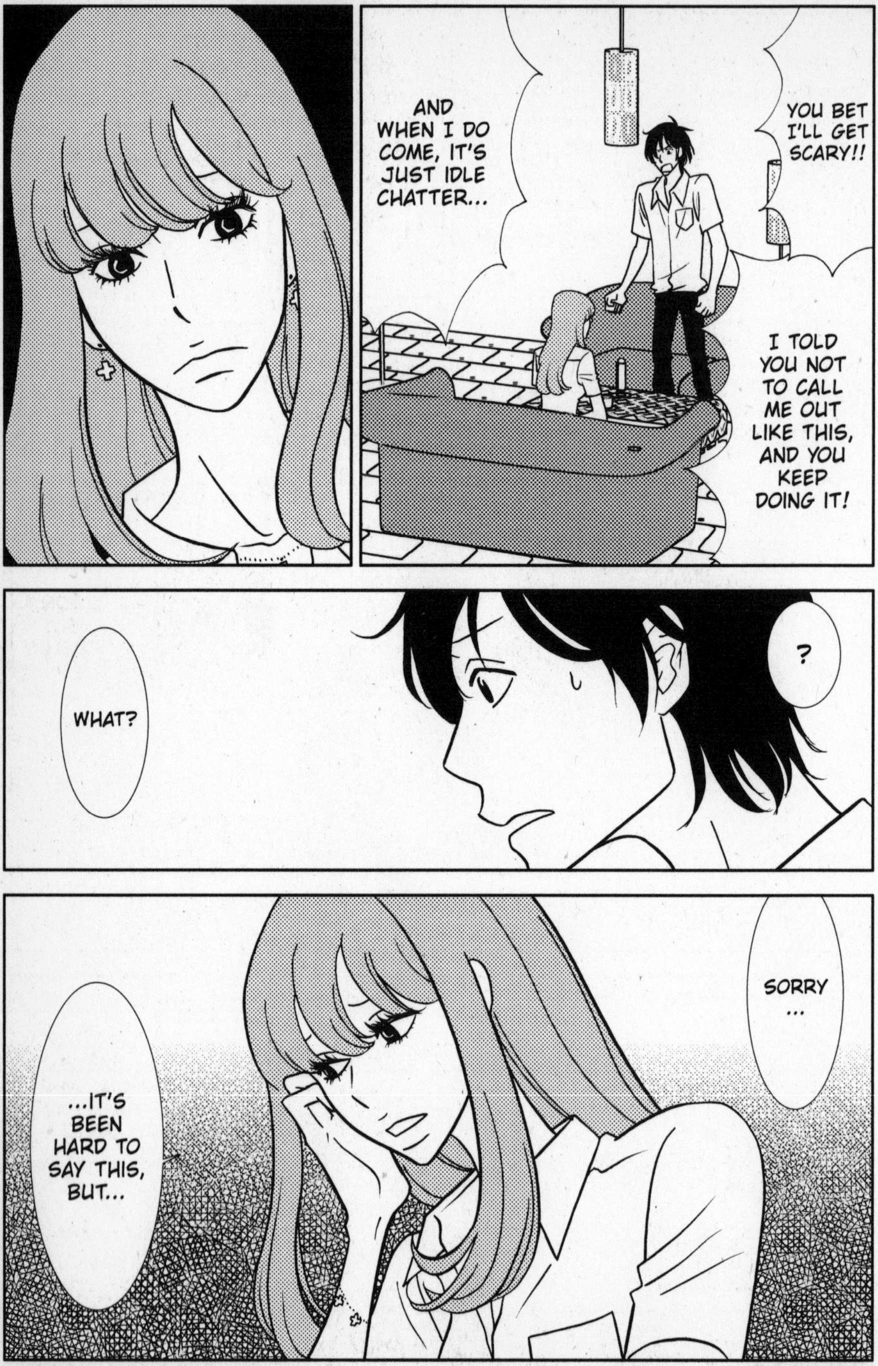
YOU BET I'LL GET SCARY!!
I TOLD YOU NOT TO CALL ME OUT LIKE THIS, AND YOU KEEP DOING IT!
AND WHEN I DO COME, IT'S JUST IDLE CHATTER...
?
WHAT?
SORRY ...
...IT'S BEEN HARD TO SAY THIS, BUT...

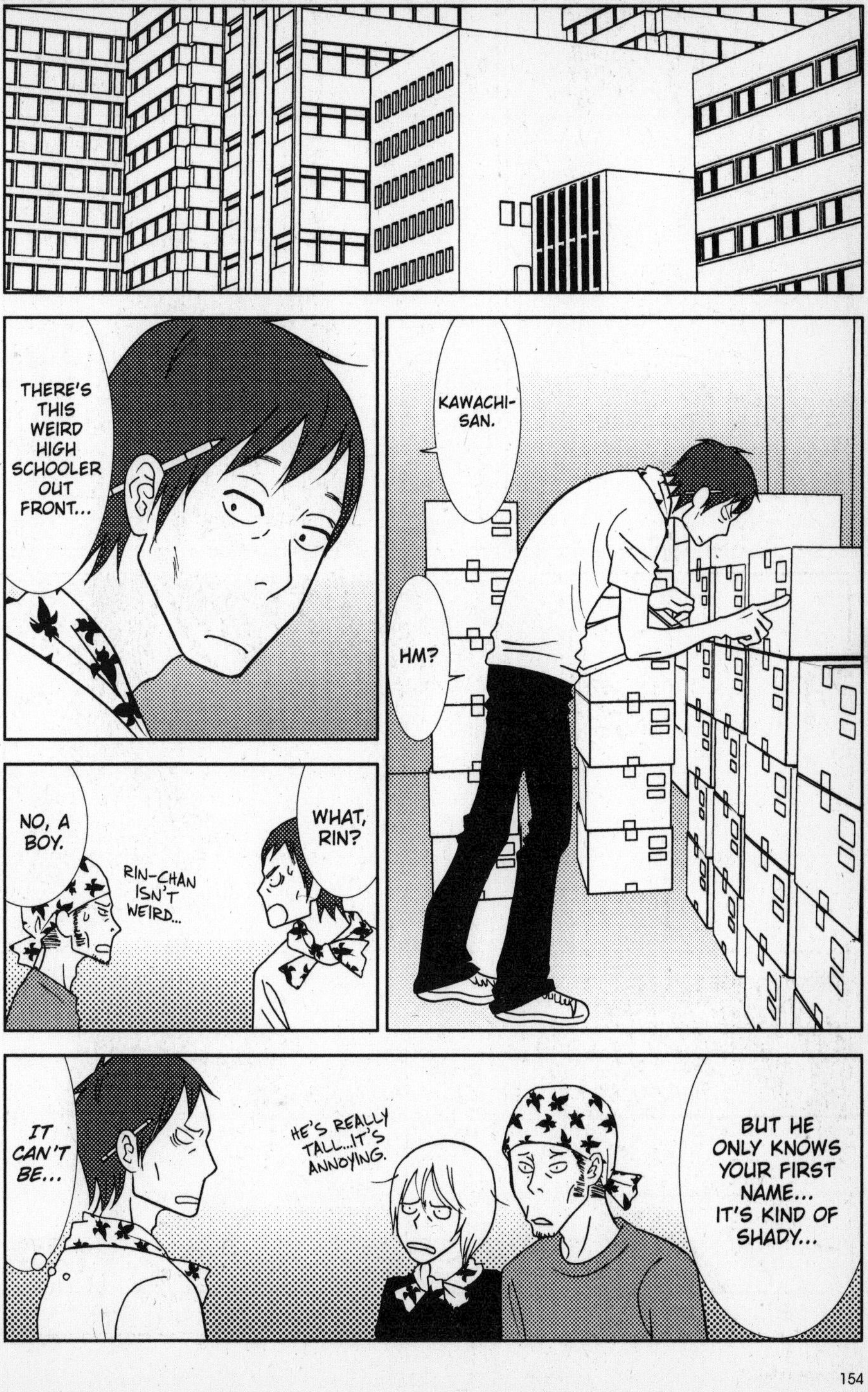
KAWACHI-SAN.
HM?
THERE'S THIS WEIRD HIGH SCHOOLER OUT FRONT...
WHAT, RIN?
RIN-CHAN ISN'T WEIRD...
NO, A BOY.
BUT HE ONLY KNOWS YOUR FIRST NAME... IT'S KIND OF SHADY...
HE'S REALLY TALL...IT'S ANNOYING.
IT CAN'T BE...

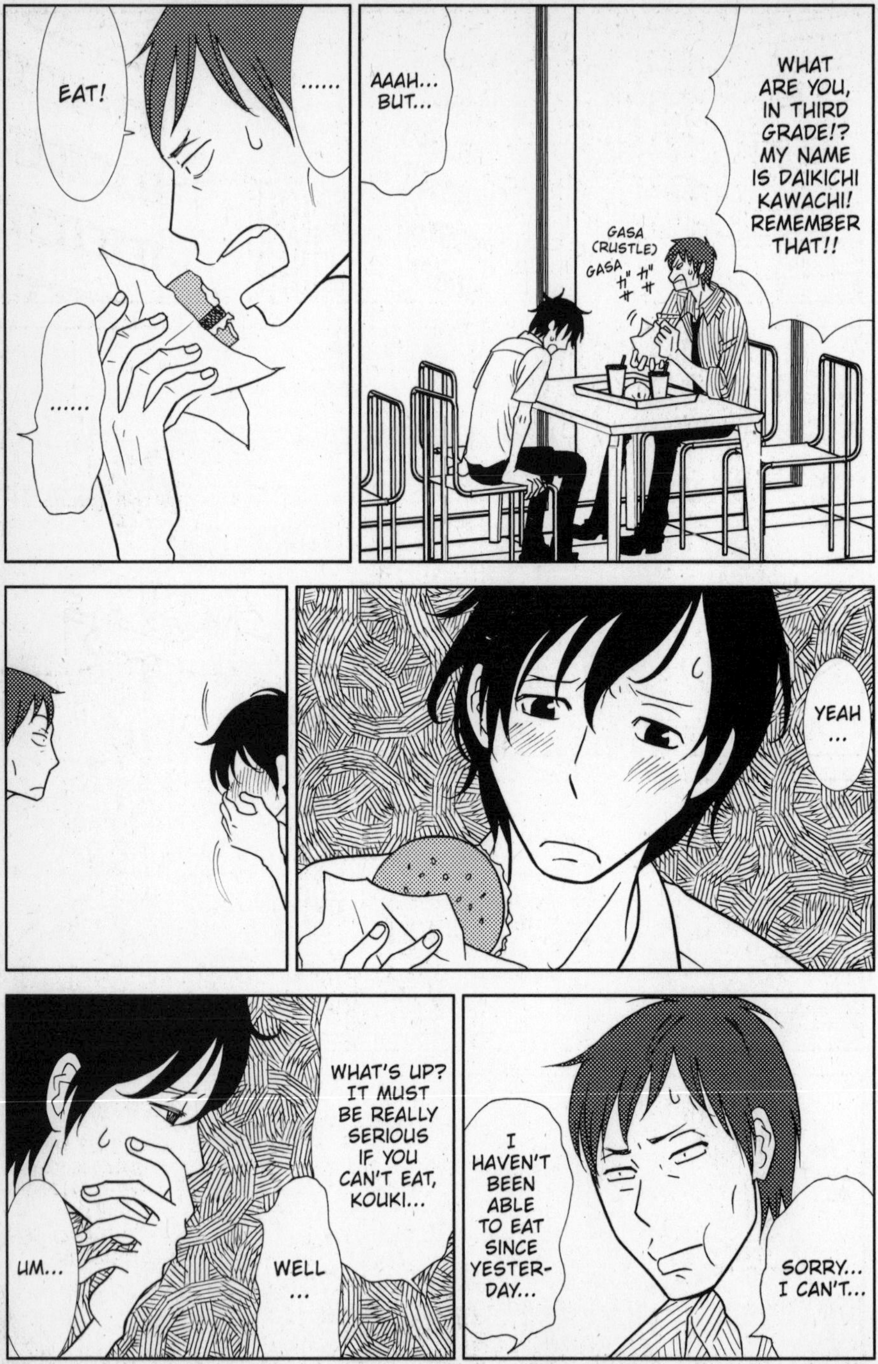
WHAT ARE YOU, IN THIRD GRADE!? MY NAME IS DAIKICHI KAWACHI! REMEMBER THAT!!
GASA (RUSTLE) GASA
AAAH... BUT...
......
EAT!
......
YEAH ...
SORRY... I CAN'T...
I HAVEN'T BEEN ABLE TO EAT SINCE YESTER-DAY...
WHAT'S UP? IT MUST BE REALLY SERIOUS IF YOU CAN'T EAT, KOUKI...
WELL ...
UM...

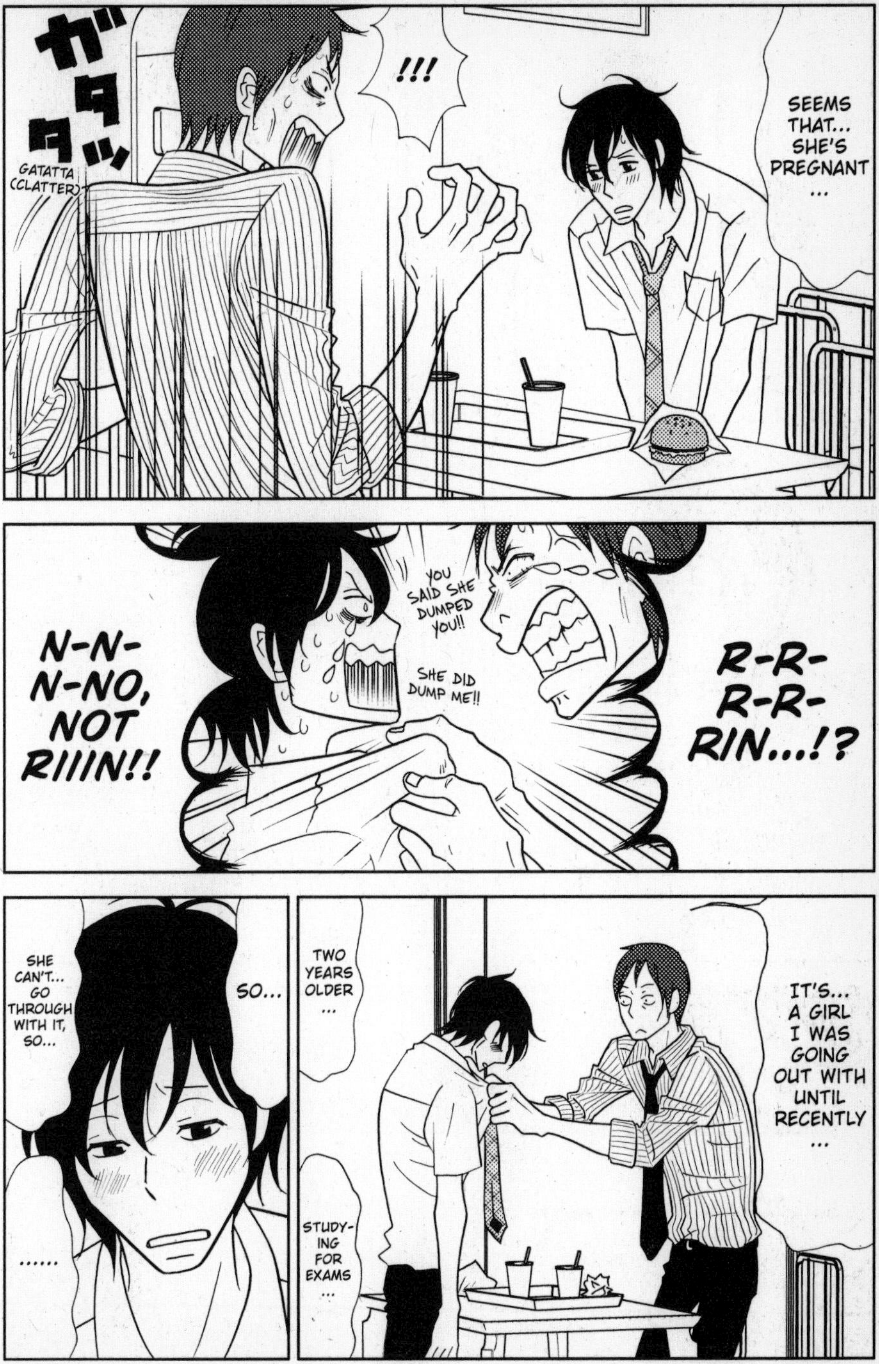
SEEMS THAT... SHE'S PREGNANT ...
!!!
ガタタッ
GATATTA (CLATTER)
R-R-R-R-RIN...!?
YOU SAID SHE DUMPED YOU!!
SHE DID DUMP ME!!
N-N-N-NO, NOT RIIIN!!
IT'S... A GIRL I WAS GOING OUT WITH UNTIL RECENTLY ...
TWO YEARS OLDER ...
STUDYING FOR EXAMS ...
SO...
SHE CAN'T... GO THROUGH WITH IT, SO...
......

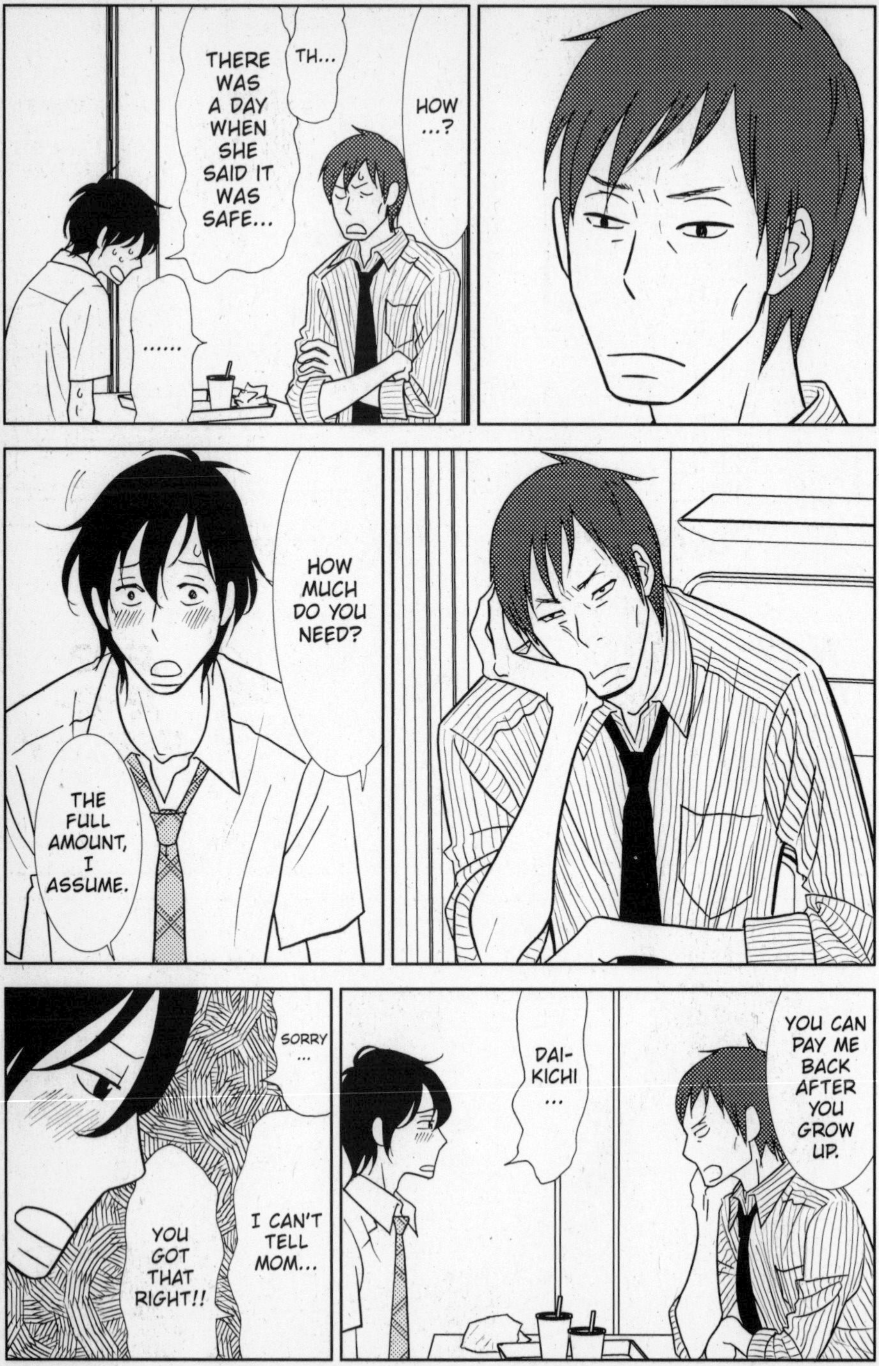
HOW ...?
TH...
THERE WAS A DAY WHEN SHE SAID IT WAS SAFE...
......
HOW MUCH DO YOU NEED?
THE FULL AMOUNT, I ASSUME.
YOU CAN PAY ME BACK AFTER YOU GROW UP.
DAI-KICHI ...
SORRY ...
I CAN'T TELL MOM...
YOU GOT THAT RIGHT!!

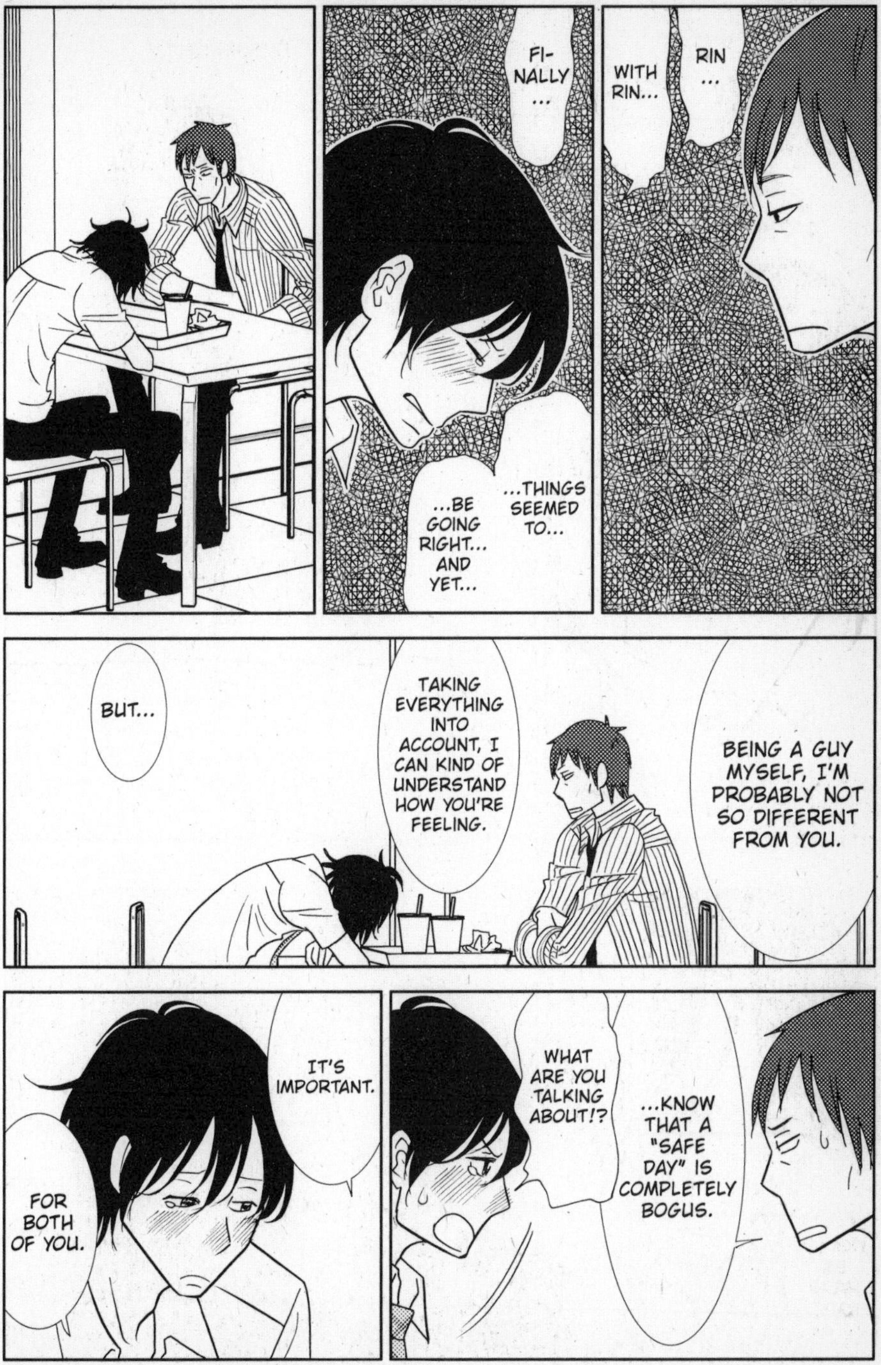
RIN...
WITH RIN...
FI-NALLY...
...THINGS SEEMED TO...
...BE GOING RIGHT... AND YET...
BEING A GUY MYSELF, I'M PROBABLY NOT SO DIFFERENT FROM YOU.
TAKING EVERYTHING INTO ACCOUNT, I CAN KIND OF UNDERSTAND HOW YOU'RE FEELING.
BUT...
...KNOW THAT A "SAFE DAY" IS COMPLETELY BOGUS.
WHAT ARE YOU TALKING ABOUT!?
IT'S IMPORTANT.
FOR BOTH OF YOU.

ぽん
PON (PAT)
DON'T CRY ANYMORE ...
ワサ
WASA (RUFFLE)
ワサ
WASA
YOU SURE? NOT SAYING ANYTHING IS ONE OPTION TOO.
NO...
THAT WOULD BE HARD TOO...

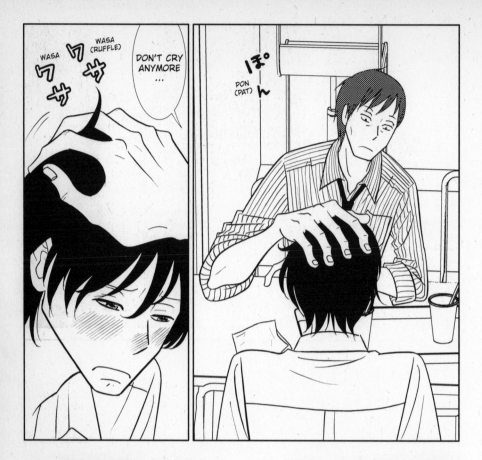

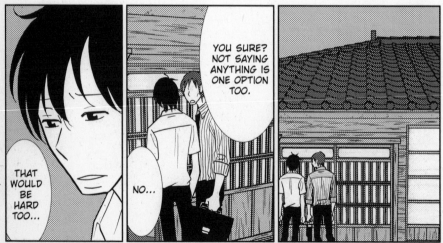

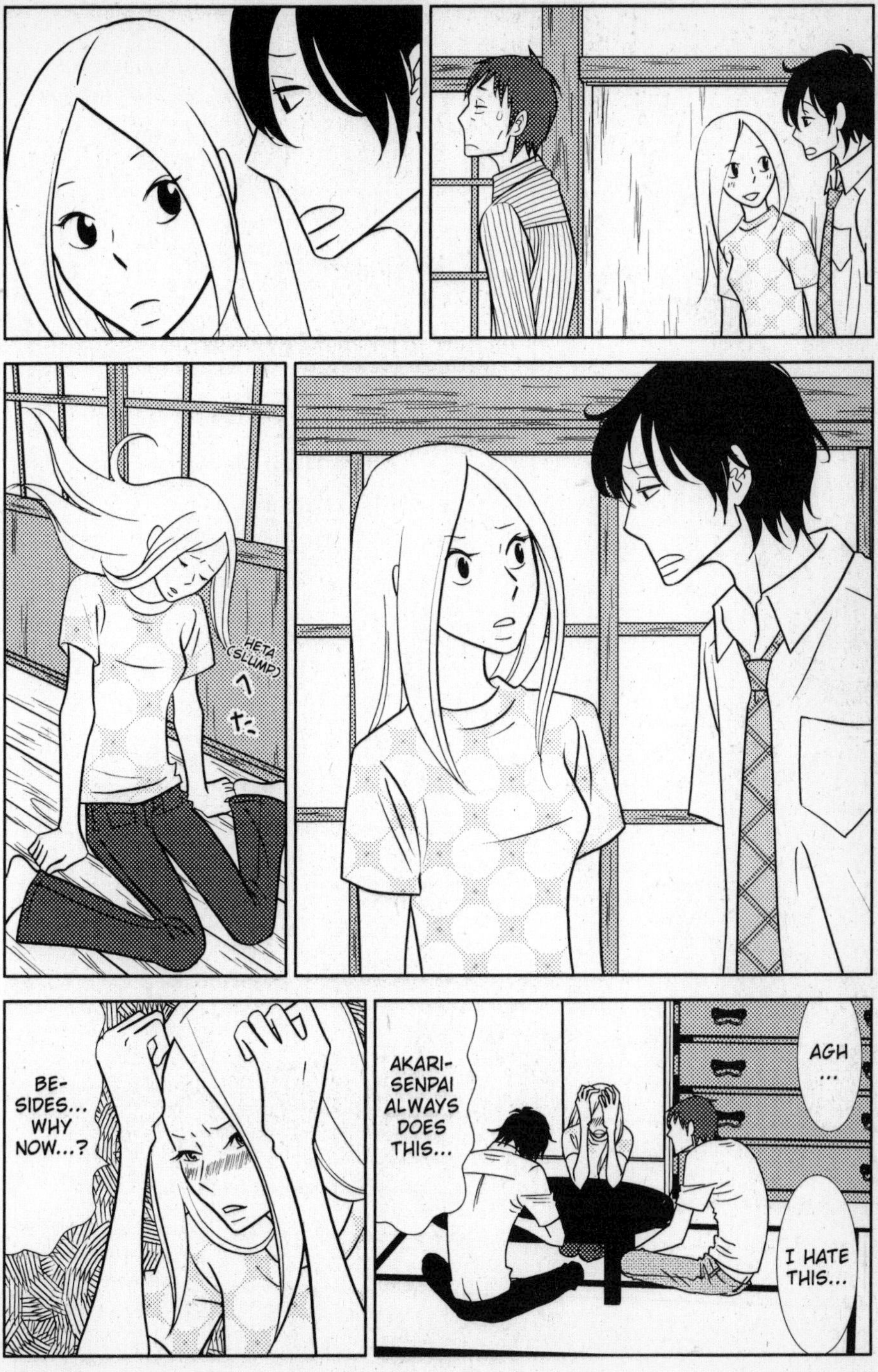
HETA (SLUMP)
AGH...
I HATE THIS...
AKARI-SENPAI ALWAYS DOES THIS...
BE-SIDES... WHY NOW...?

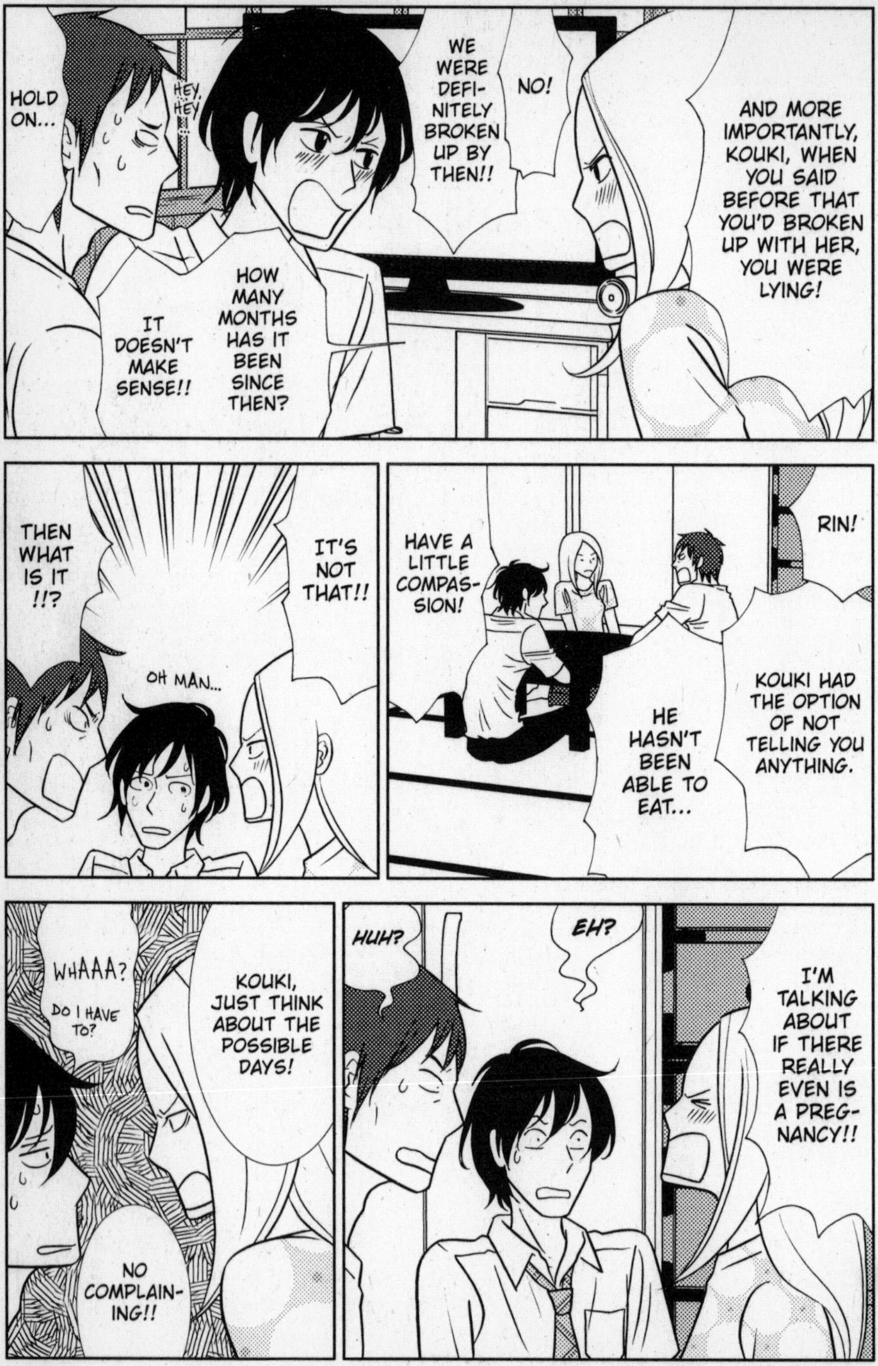
AND MORE IMPORTANTLY, KOUKI, WHEN YOU SAID BEFORE THAT YOU'D BROKEN UP WITH HER, YOU WERE LYING!
NO!
WE WERE DEFI-NITELY BROKEN UP BY THEN!!
HEY, HEY
HOLD ON...
HOW MANY MONTHS HAS IT BEEN SINCE THEN?
IT DOESN'T MAKE SENSE!!
RIN!
HAVE A LITTLE COMPAS-SION!
KOUKI HAD THE OPTION OF NOT TELLING YOU ANYTHING.
HE HASN'T BEEN ABLE TO EAT...
IT'S NOT THAT!!
THEN WHAT IS IT !!?
OH MAN...
EH?
I'M TALKING ABOUT IF THERE REALLY EVEN IS A PREG-NANCY!!
HUH?
KOUKI, JUST THINK ABOUT THE POSSIBLE DAYS!
WHAAA?
DO I HAVE TO?
NO COMPLAIN-ING!!

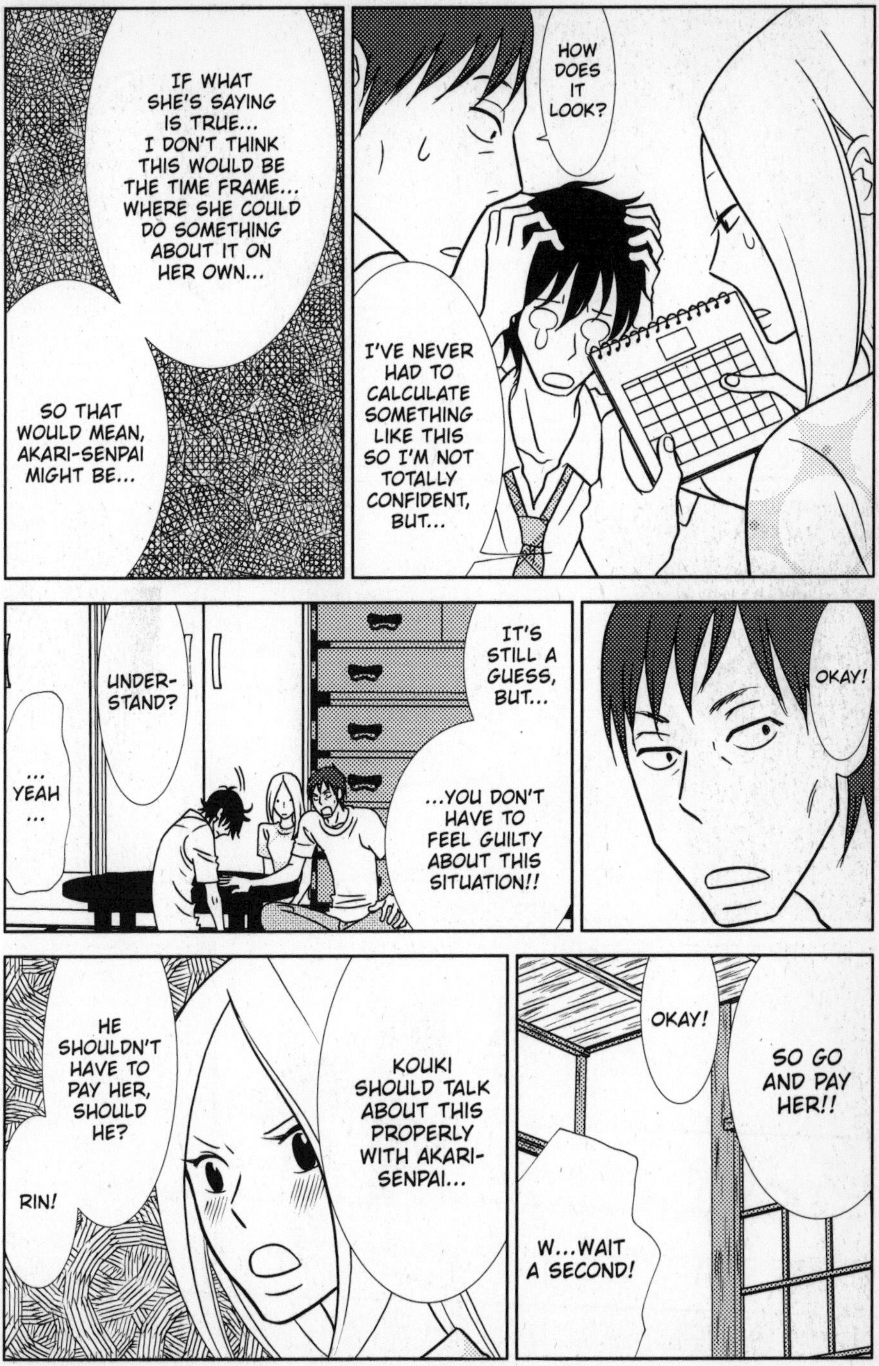
HOW DOES IT LOOK?
I'VE NEVER HAD TO CALCULATE SOMETHING LIKE THIS SO I'M NOT TOTALLY CONFIDENT, BUT...
IF WHAT SHE'S SAYING IS TRUE... I DON'T THINK THIS WOULD BE THE TIME FRAME... WHERE SHE COULD DO SOMETHING ABOUT IT ON HER OWN...
SO THAT WOULD MEAN, AKARI-SENPAI MIGHT BE...
OKAY!
IT'S STILL A GUESS, BUT...
...YOU DON'T HAVE TO FEEL GUILTY ABOUT THIS SITUATION!!
UNDER-STAND?
...YEAH...
SO GO AND PAY HER!!
OKAY!
W...WAIT A SECOND!
KOUKI SHOULD TALK ABOUT THIS PROPERLY WITH AKARI-SENPAI...
HE SHOULDN'T HAVE TO PAY HER, SHOULD HE?
RIN!

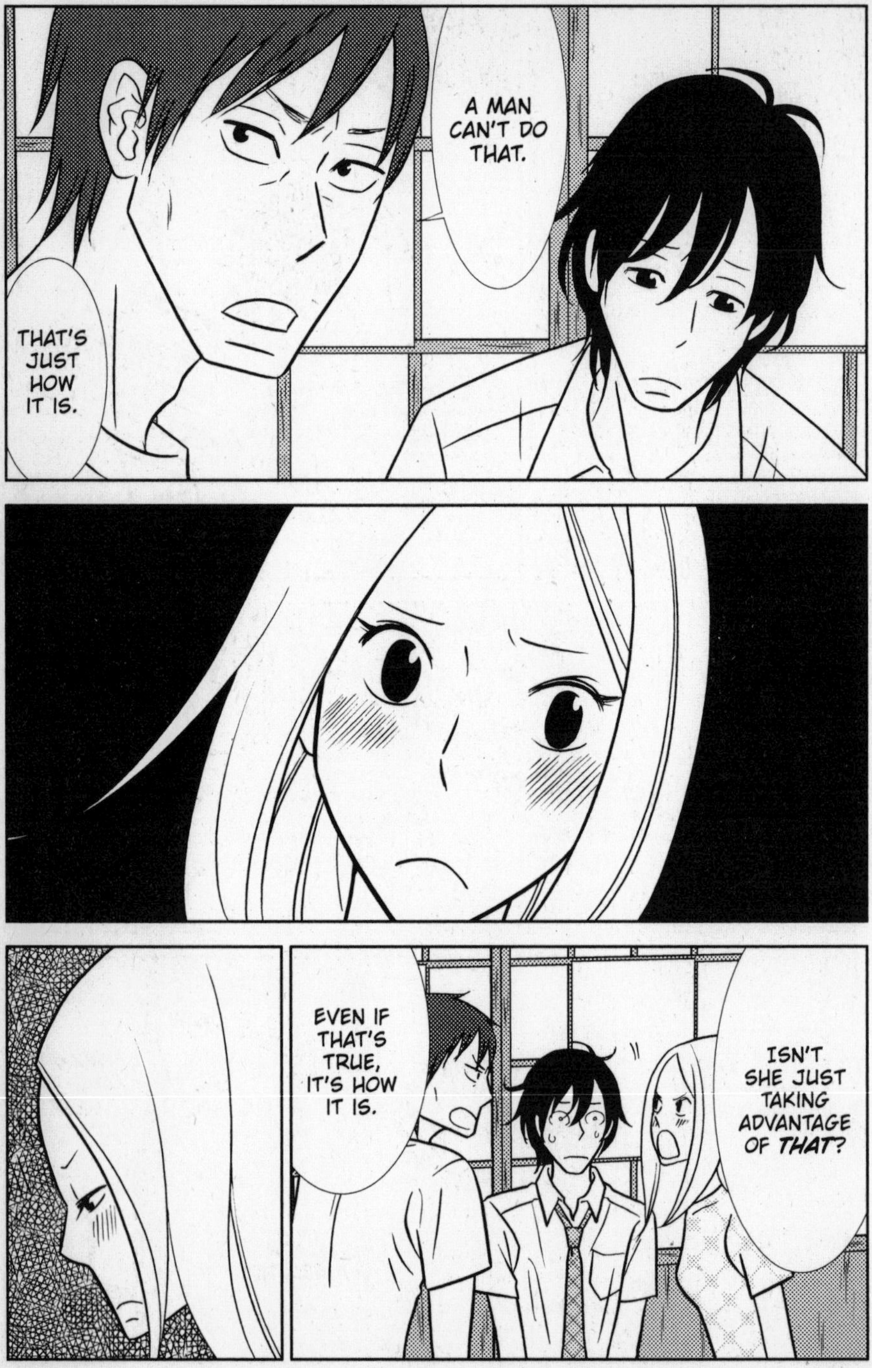
A MAN CAN'T DO THAT.
THAT'S JUST HOW IT IS.
ISN'T SHE JUST TAKING ADVANTAGE OF *THAT*?
EVEN IF THAT'S TRUE, IT'S HOW IT IS.

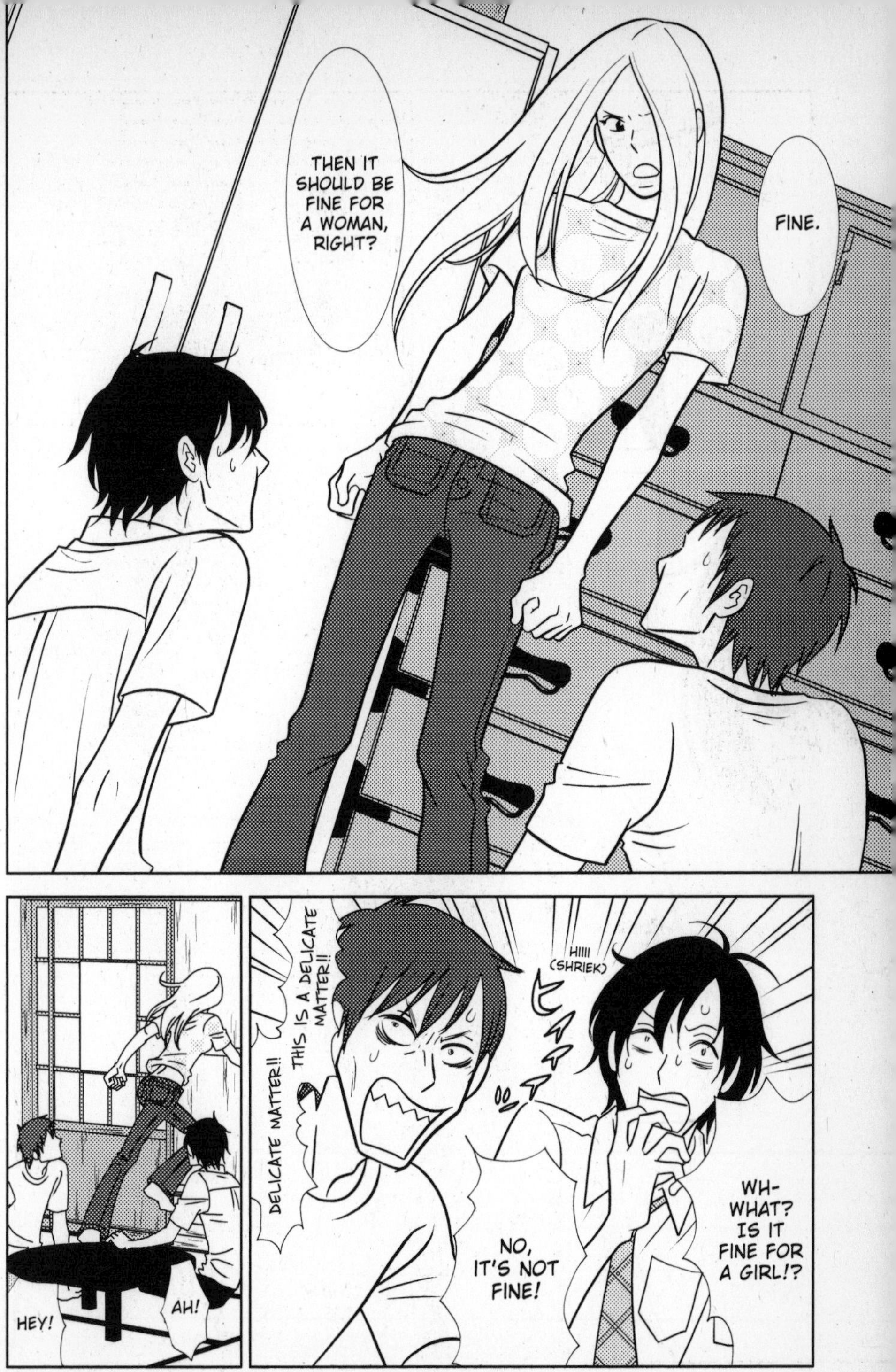
FINE.
THEN IT SHOULD BE FINE FOR A WOMAN, RIGHT?
HIIII (SHRIEK)
WH-WHAT? IS IT FINE FOR A GIRL!?
NO, IT'S NOT FINE!
THIS IS A DELICATE MATTER!!
DELICATE MATTER!!
AH!
HEY!

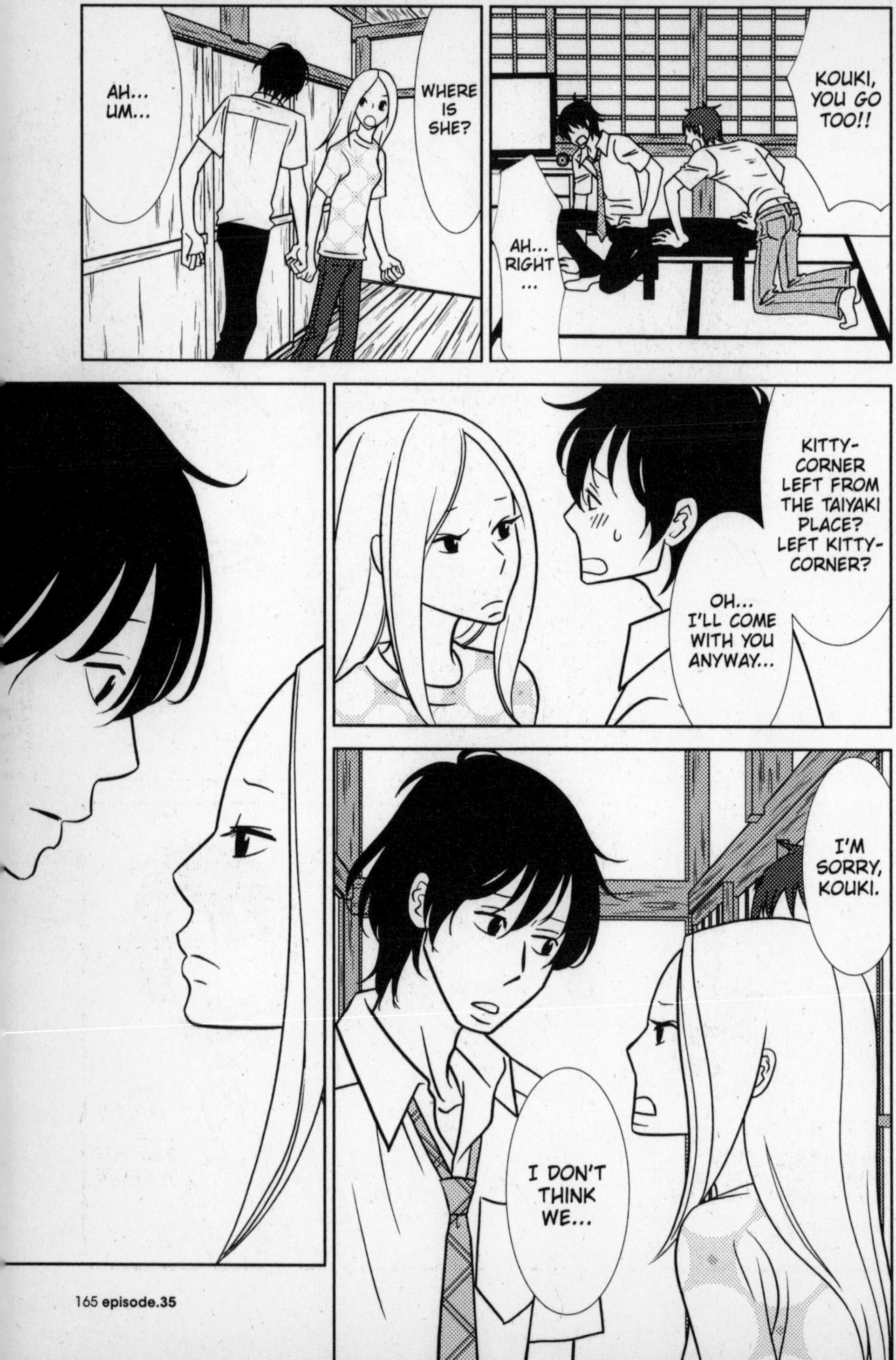
KOUKI, YOU GO TOO!!
AH... RIGHT ...
WHERE IS SHE?
AH... UM...
KITTY-CORNER LEFT FROM THE TAIYAKI PLACE? LEFT KITTY-CORNER?
OH... I'LL COME WITH YOU ANYWAY...
I'M SORRY, KOUKI.
I DON'T THINK WE...

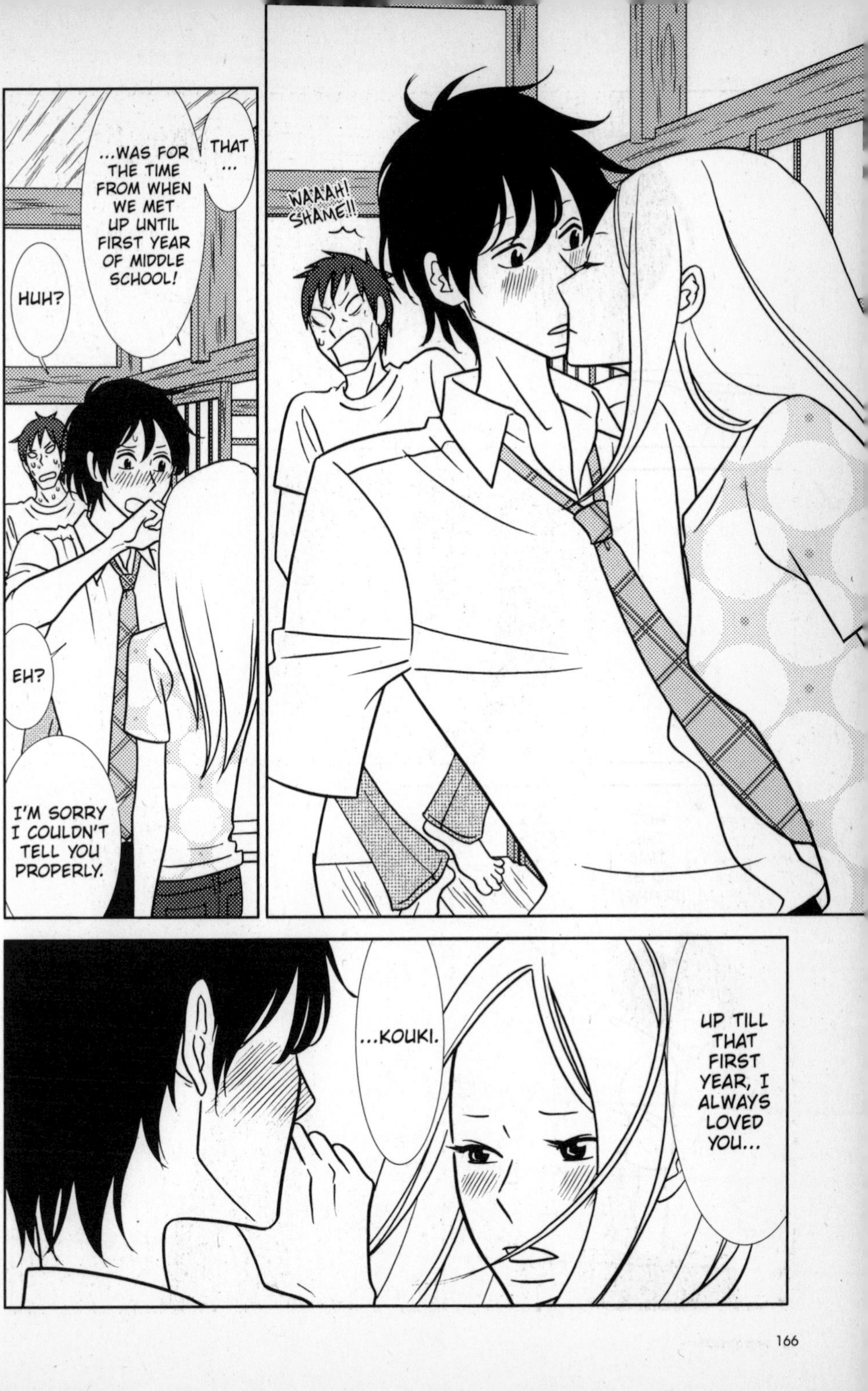
WAAAH! SHAME!!
THAT...
...WAS FOR THE TIME FROM WHEN WE MET UP UNTIL FIRST YEAR OF MIDDLE SCHOOL!
HUH?
EH?
I'M SORRY I COULDN'T TELL YOU PROPERLY.
UP TILL THAT FIRST YEAR, I ALWAYS LOVED YOU...
...KOUKI.

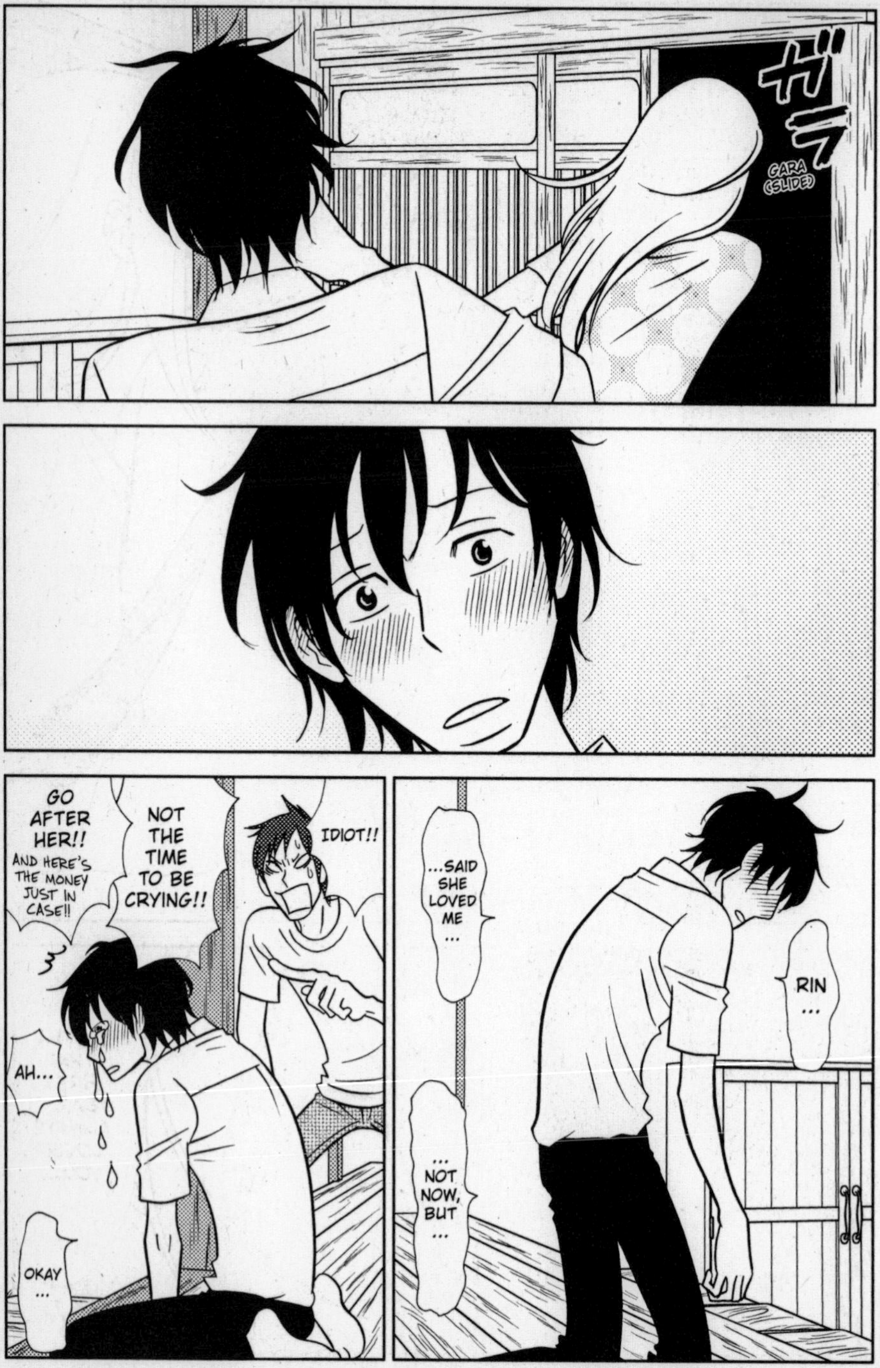

ガラ
GARA (SLIDED)
RIN ...
...SAID SHE LOVED ME ...
... NOT NOW, BUT ...
IDIOT!!
NOT THE TIME TO BE CRYING!!
GO AFTER HER!!
AND HERE'S THE MONEY JUST IN CASE!!
AH...
OKAY ...

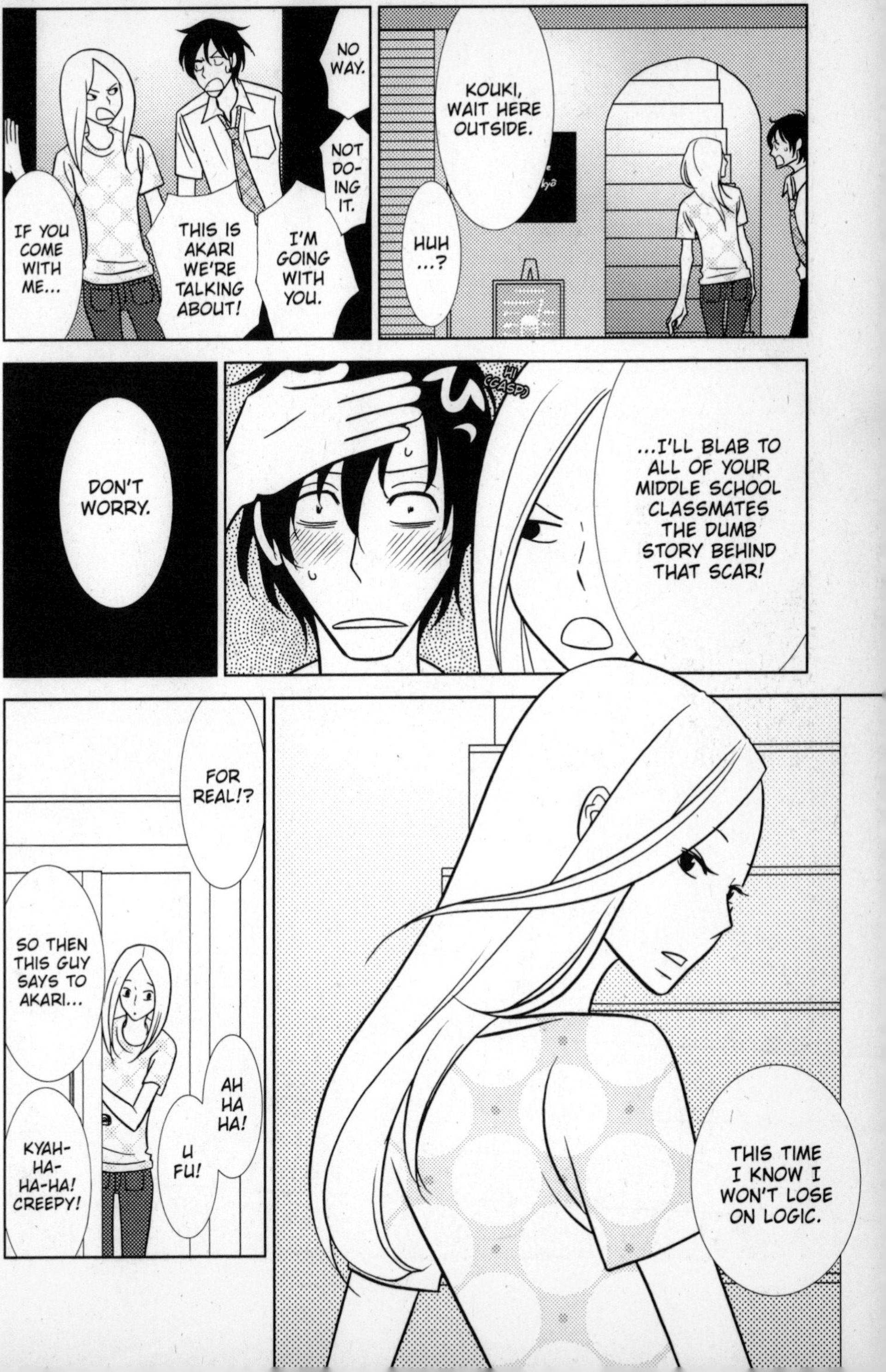
KOUKI, WAIT HERE OUTSIDE.
HUH...?
NO WAY.
NOT DO-ING IT.
I'M GOING WITH YOU.
THIS IS AKARI WE'RE TALKING ABOUT!
IF YOU COME WITH ME...
HI (GASP)
...I'LL BLAB TO ALL OF YOUR MIDDLE SCHOOL CLASSMATES THE DUMB STORY BEHIND THAT SCAR!
DON'T WORRY.
THIS TIME I KNOW I WON'T LOSE ON LOGIC.
FOR REAL!?
SO THEN THIS GUY SAYS TO AKARI...
AH HA HA!
U FU!
KYAH-HA-HA-HA! CREEPY!

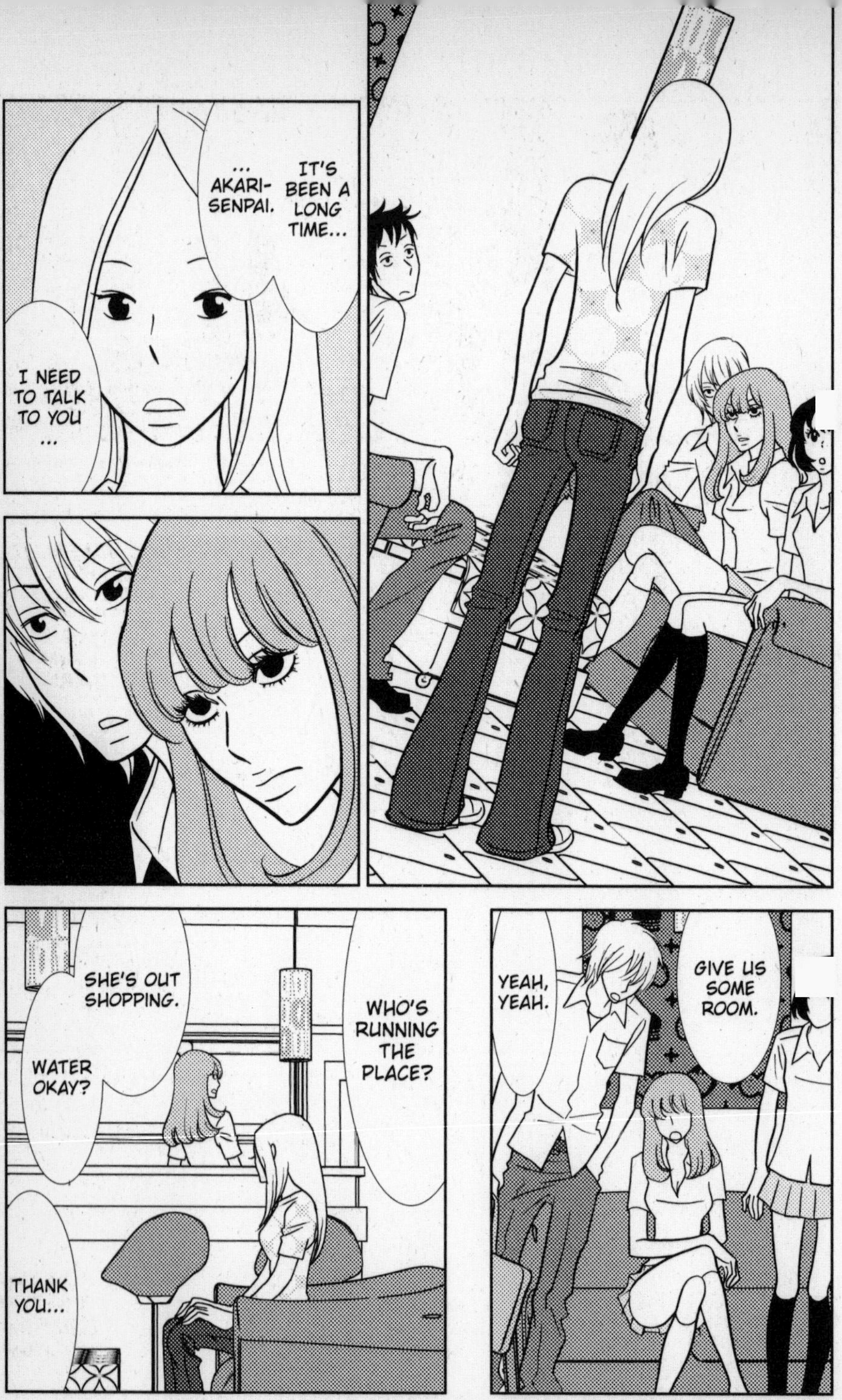
IT'S BEEN A LONG TIME...
... AKARI-SENPAI.
I NEED TO TALK TO YOU ...
GIVE US SOME ROOM.
YEAH, YEAH.
WHO'S RUNNING THE PLACE?
SHE'S OUT SHOPPING.
WATER OKAY?
THANK YOU...

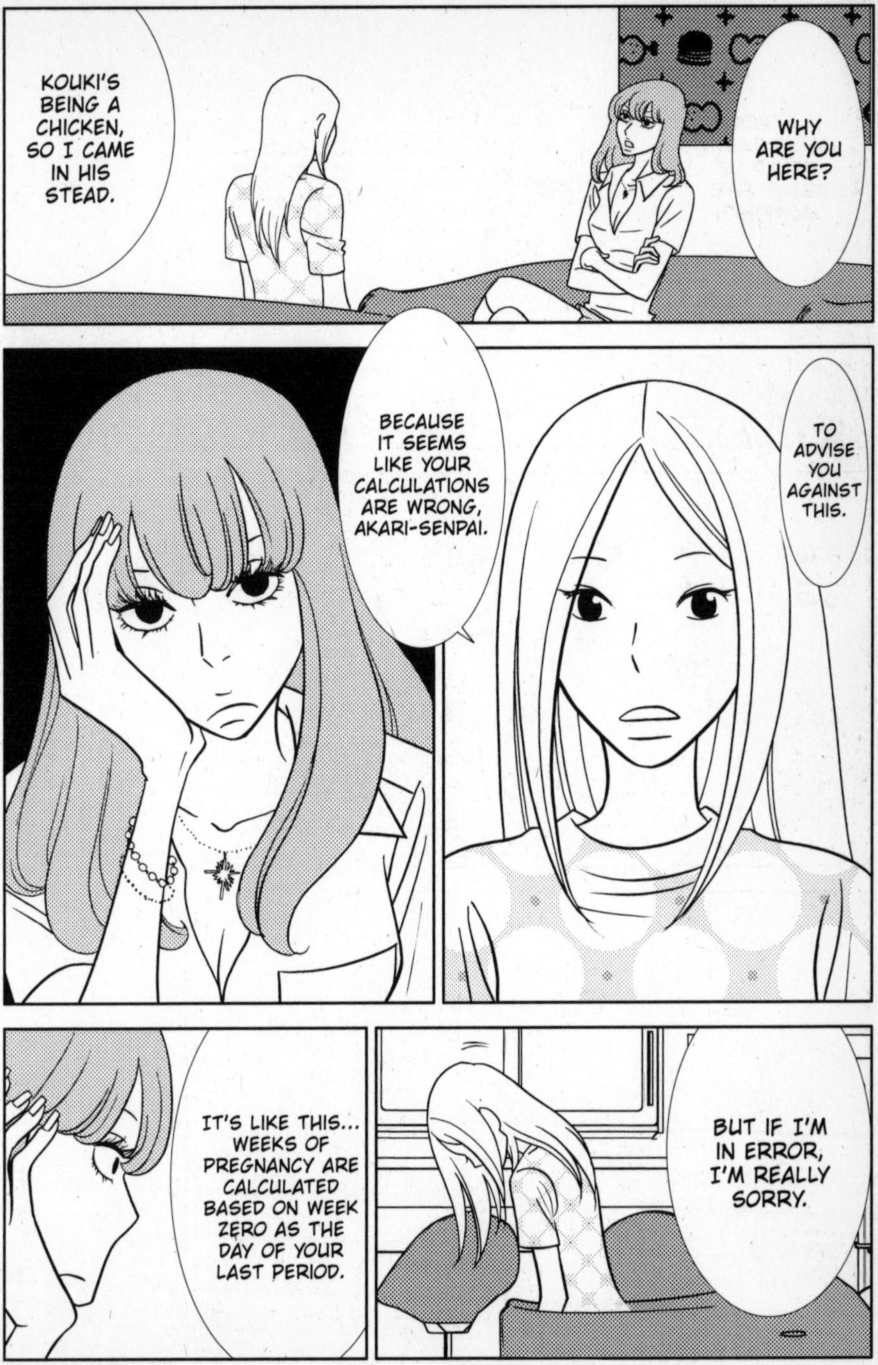
WHY ARE YOU HERE?
KOUKI'S BEING A CHICKEN, SO I CAME IN HIS STEAD.
TO ADVISE YOU AGAINST THIS.
BECAUSE IT SEEMS LIKE YOUR CALCULATIONS ARE WRONG, AKARI-SENPAI.
BUT IF I'M IN ERROR, I'M REALLY SORRY.
IT'S LIKE THIS... WEEKS OF PREGNANCY ARE CALCULATED BASED ON WEEK ZERO AS THE DAY OF YOUR LAST PERIOD.

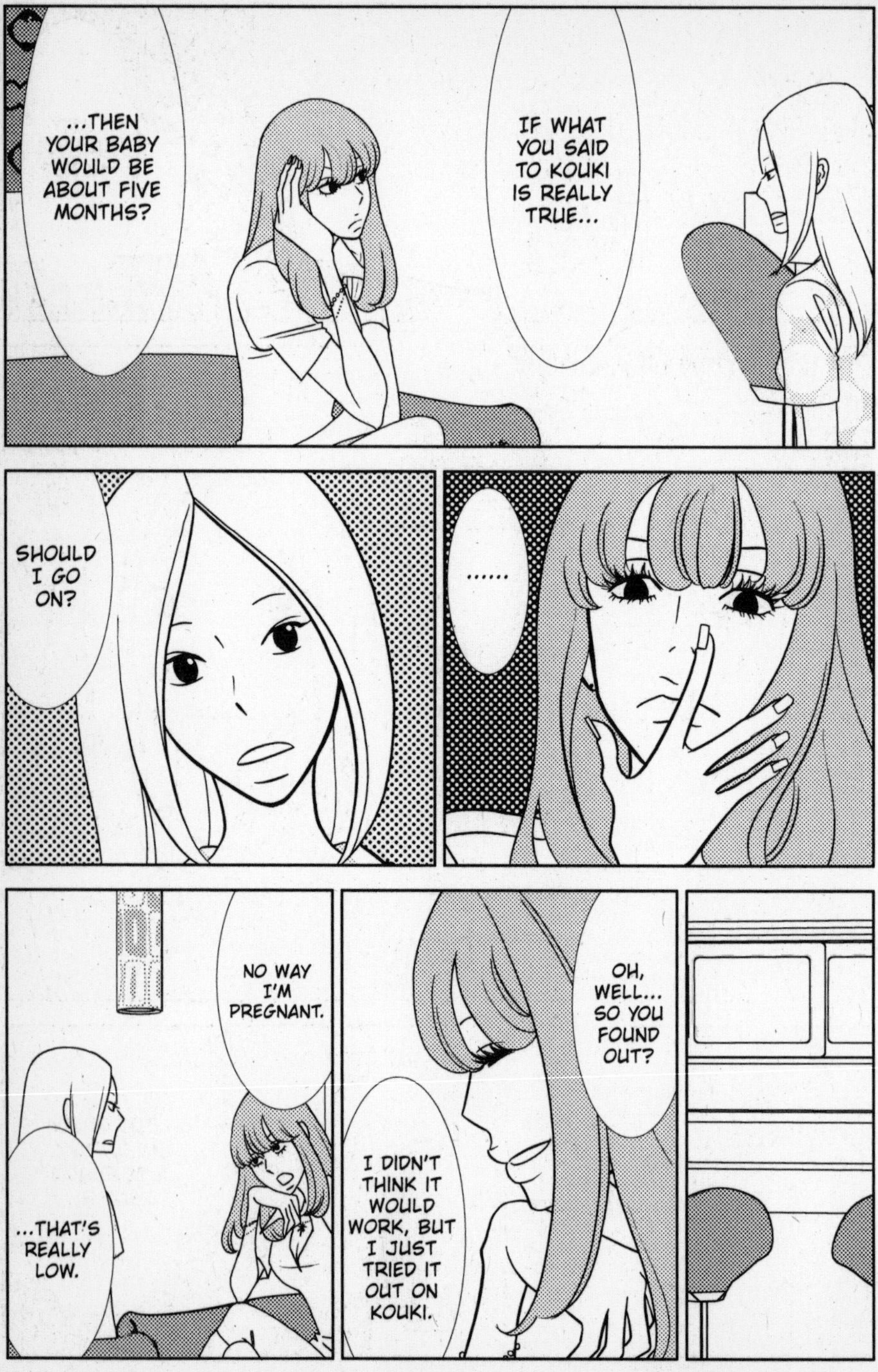
IF WHAT YOU SAID TO KOUKI IS REALLY TRUE...
...THEN YOUR BABY WOULD BE ABOUT FIVE MONTHS?
......
SHOULD I GO ON?
OH, WELL... SO YOU FOUND OUT?
I DIDN'T THINK IT WOULD WORK, BUT I JUST TRIED IT OUT ON KOUKI.
NO WAY I'M PREGNANT.
...THAT'S REALLY LOW.

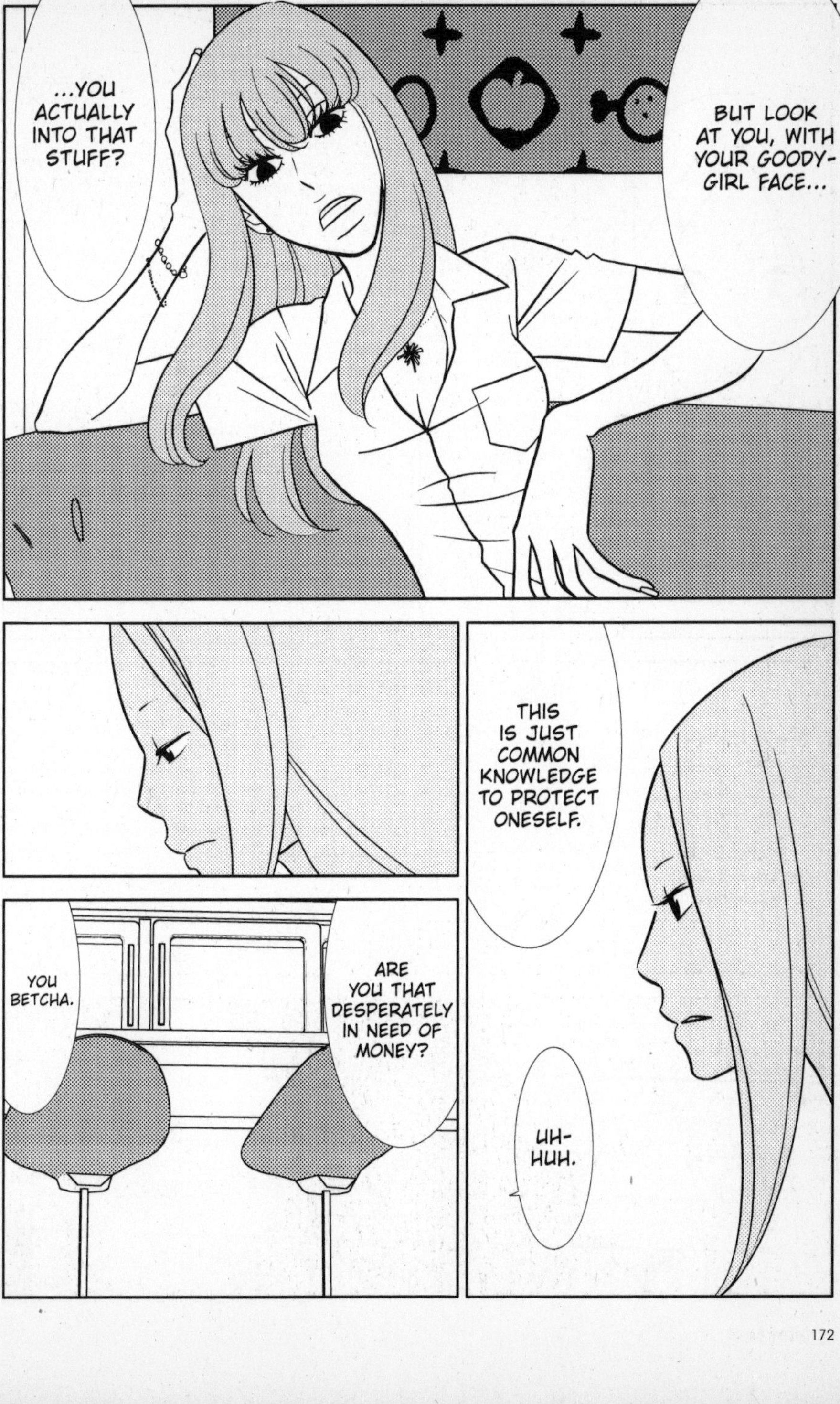
BUT LOOK AT YOU, WITH YOUR GOODY-GIRL FACE...
...YOU ACTUALLY INTO THAT STUFF?
THIS IS JUST COMMON KNOWLEDGE TO PROTECT ONESELF.
UH-HUH.
ARE YOU THAT DESPERATELY IN NEED OF MONEY?
YOU BETCHA.

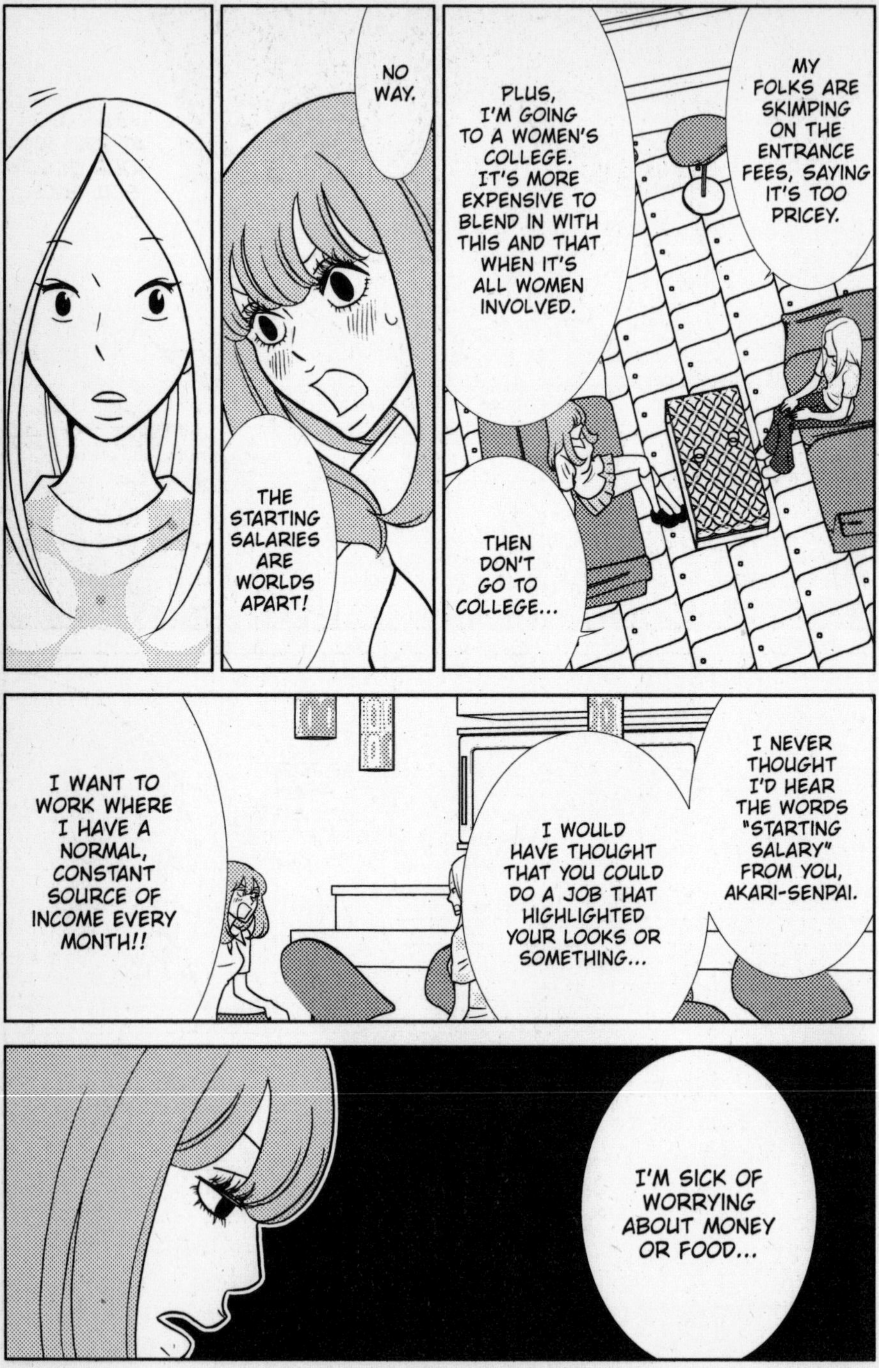
MY FOLKS ARE SKIMPING ON THE ENTRANCE FEES, SAYING IT'S TOO PRICEY.
PLUS, I'M GOING TO A WOMEN'S COLLEGE. IT'S MORE EXPENSIVE TO BLEND IN WITH THIS AND THAT WHEN IT'S ALL WOMEN INVOLVED.
THEN DON'T GO TO COLLEGE...
NO WAY.
THE STARTING SALARIES ARE WORLDS APART!
I NEVER THOUGHT I'D HEAR THE WORDS "STARTING SALARY" FROM YOU, AKARI-SENPAI.
I WOULD HAVE THOUGHT THAT YOU COULD DO A JOB THAT HIGHLIGHTED YOUR LOOKS OR SOMETHING...
I WANT TO WORK WHERE I HAVE A NORMAL, CONSTANT SOURCE OF INCOME EVERY MONTH!!
I'M SICK OF WORRYING ABOUT MONEY OR FOOD...

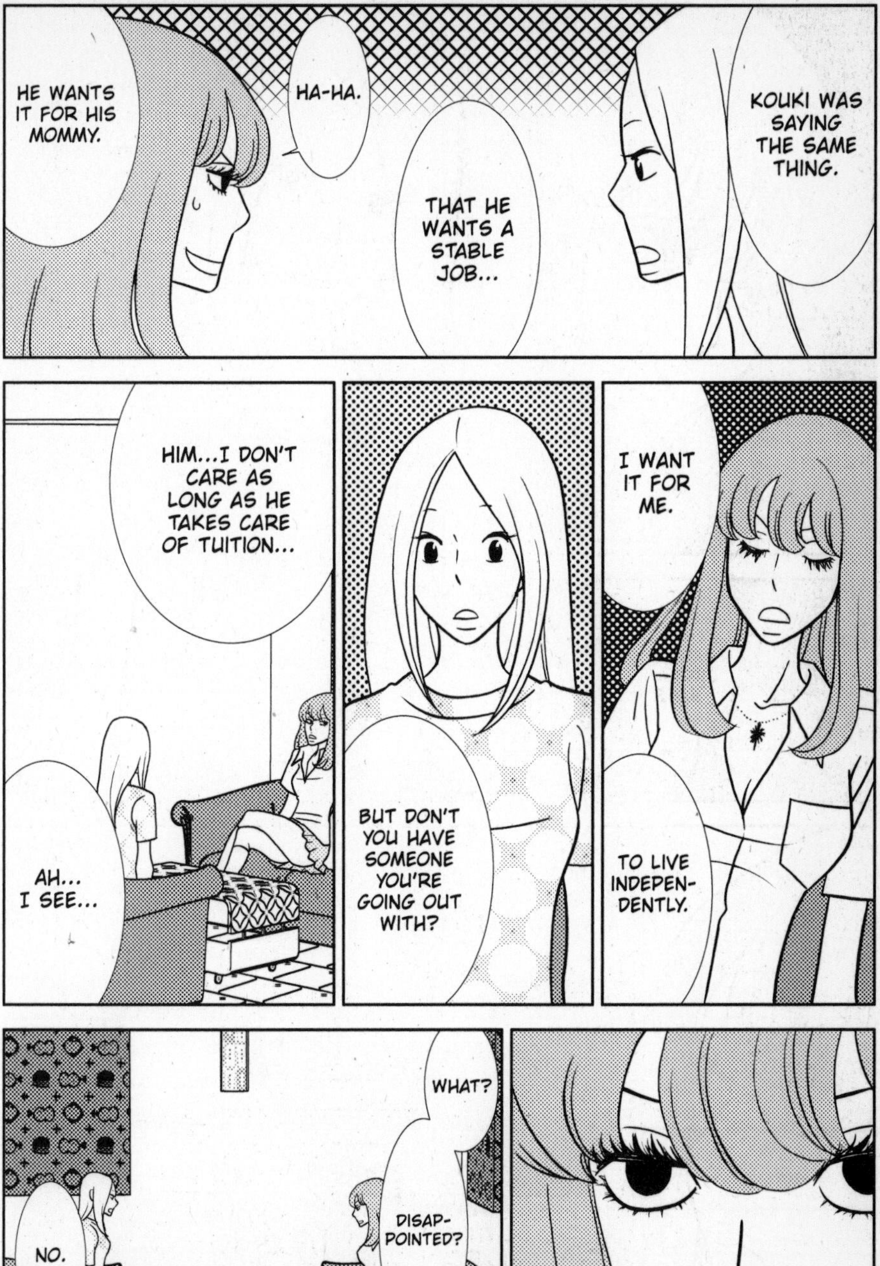

KOUKI WAS SAYING THE SAME THING.
THAT HE WANTS A STABLE JOB...
HA-HA.
HE WANTS IT FOR HIS MOMMY.
I WANT IT FOR ME.
TO LIVE INDEPEN-DENTLY.
BUT DON'T YOU HAVE SOMEONE YOU'RE GOING OUT WITH?
HIM...I DON'T CARE AS LONG AS HE TAKES CARE OF TUITION...
AH... I SEE...
WHAT?
DISAP-POINTED?
NO.

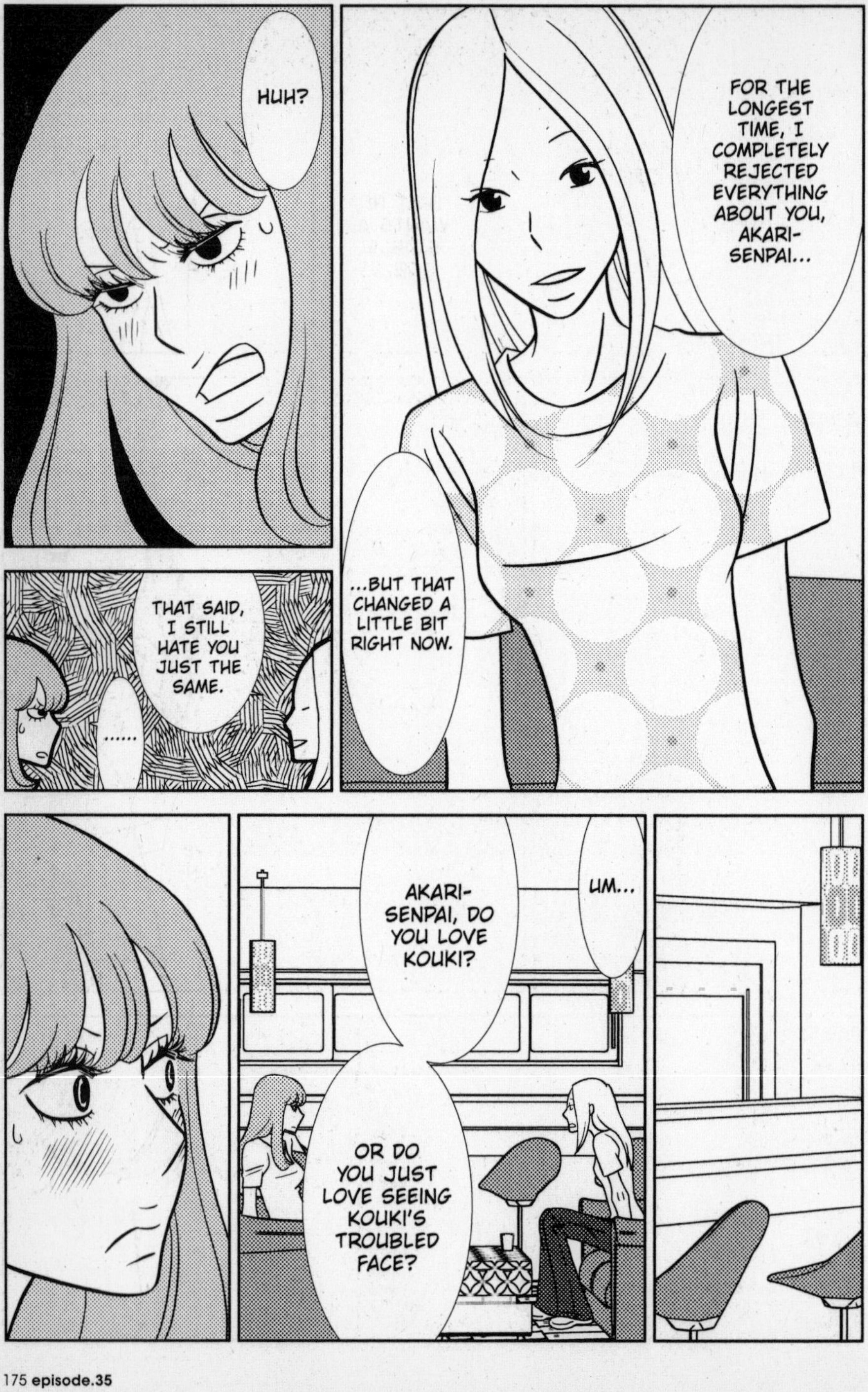
FOR THE LONGEST TIME, I COMPLETELY REJECTED EVERYTHING ABOUT YOU, AKARI-SENPAI...
...BUT THAT CHANGED A LITTLE BIT RIGHT NOW.
HUH?
THAT SAID, I STILL HATE YOU JUST THE SAME.
......
UM...
AKARI-SENPAI, DO YOU LOVE KOUKI?
OR DO YOU JUST LOVE SEEING KOUKI'S TROUBLED FACE?

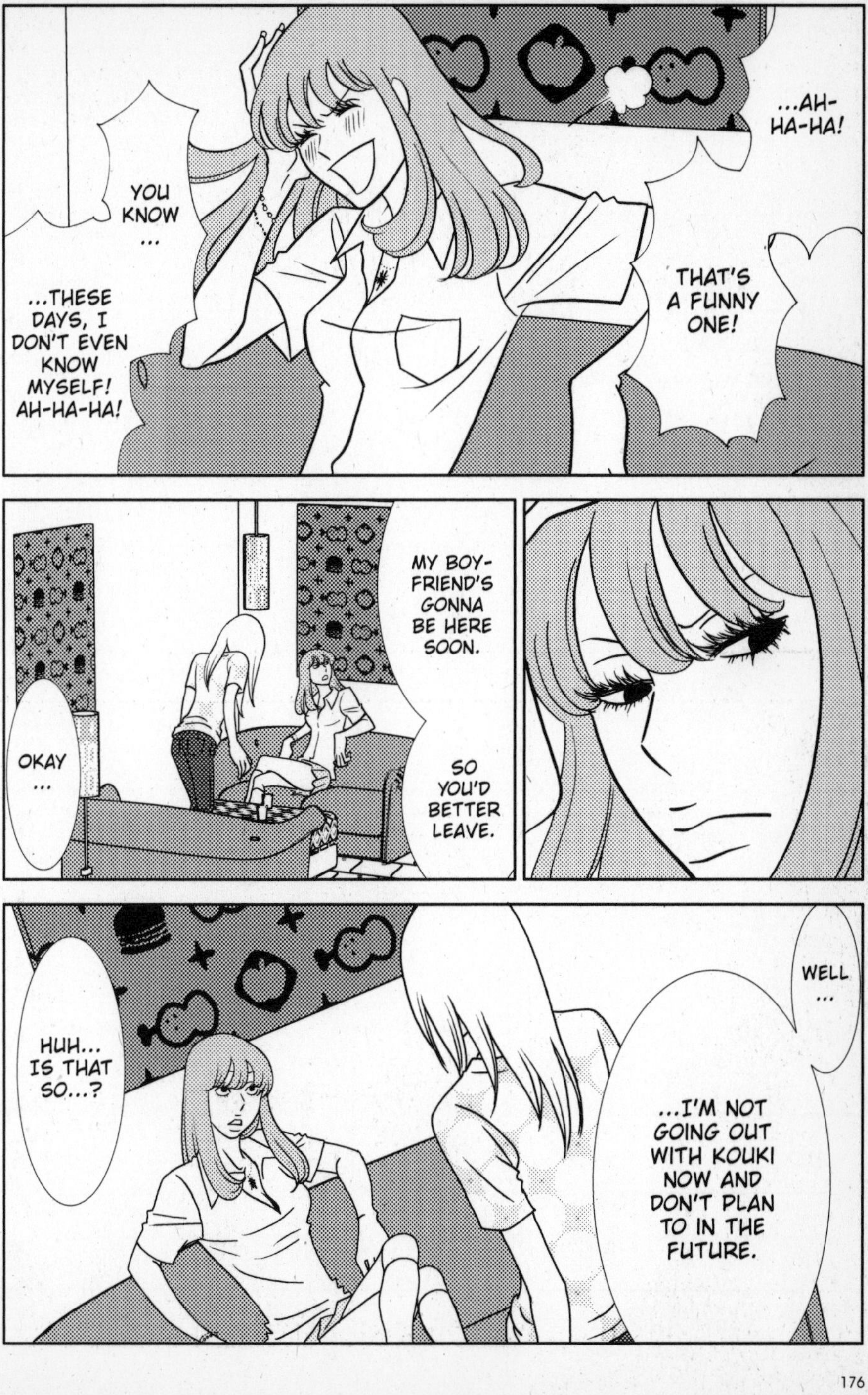
...AH-HA-HA!
THAT'S A FUNNY ONE!
YOU KNOW ...
...THESE DAYS, I DON'T EVEN KNOW MYSELF! AH-HA-HA!
MY BOY-FRIEND'S GONNA BE HERE SOON.
SO YOU'D BETTER LEAVE.
OKAY ...
WELL ...
...I'M NOT GOING OUT WITH KOUKI NOW AND DON'T PLAN TO IN THE FUTURE.
HUH... IS THAT SO...?

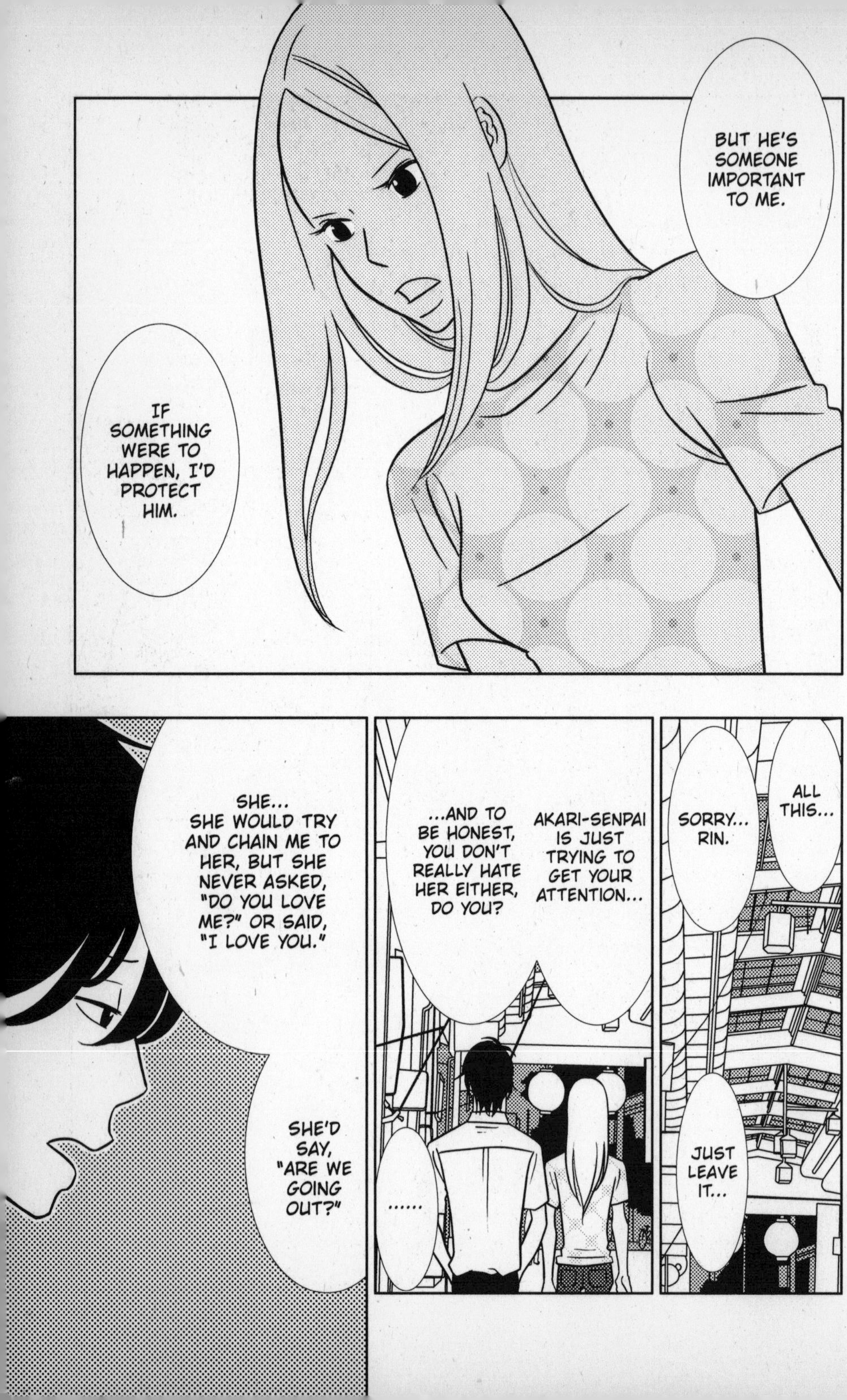
BUT HE'S SOMEONE IMPORTANT TO ME.
IF SOMETHING WERE TO HAPPEN, I'D PROTECT HIM.
ALL THIS...
SORRY... RIN.
JUST LEAVE IT...
AKARI-SENPAI IS JUST TRYING TO GET YOUR ATTENTION...
...AND TO BE HONEST, YOU DON'T REALLY HATE HER EITHER, DO YOU?
......
SHE... SHE WOULD TRY AND CHAIN ME TO HER, BUT SHE NEVER ASKED, "DO YOU LOVE ME?" OR SAID, "I LOVE YOU."
SHE'D SAY, "ARE WE GOING OUT?"

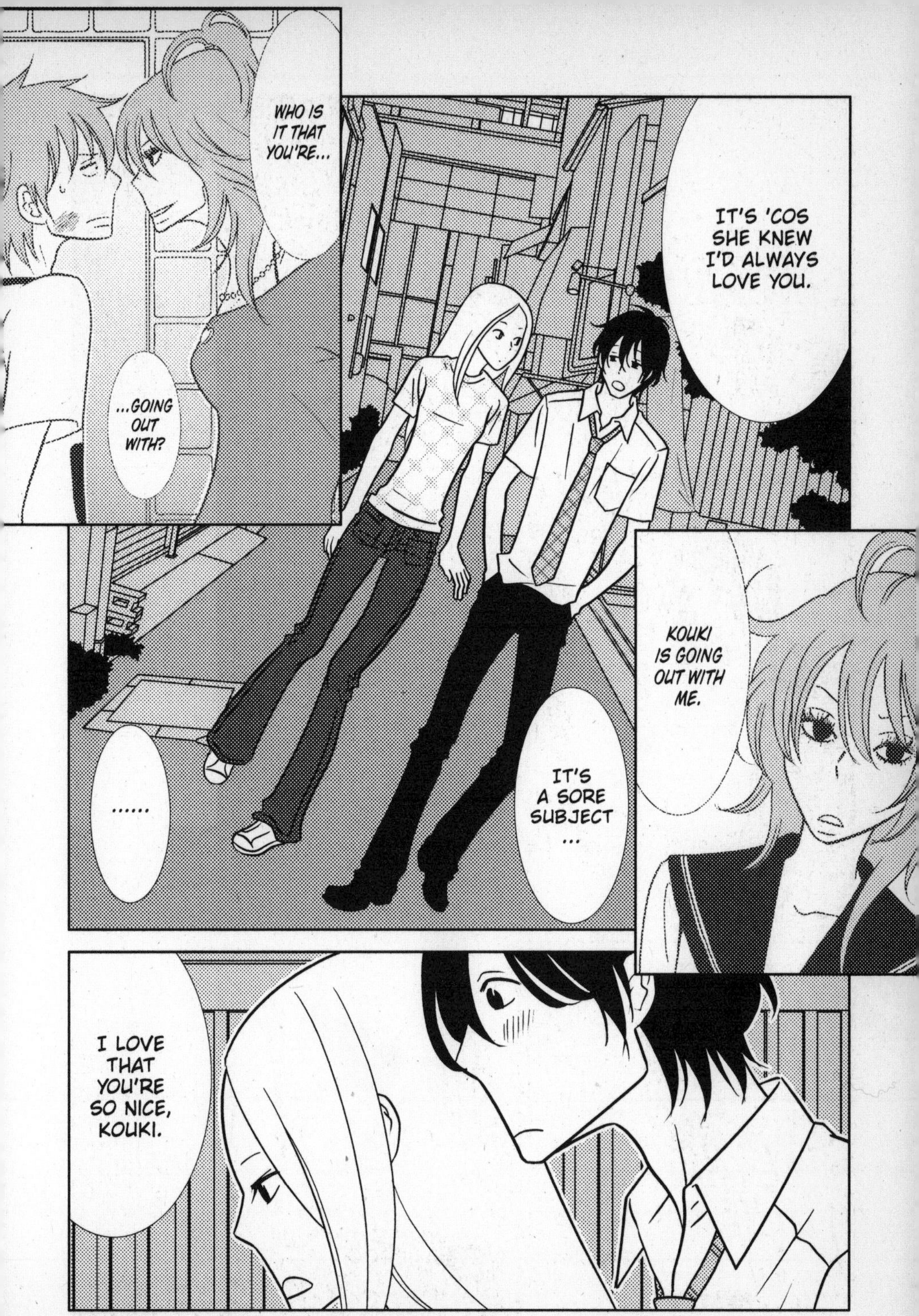

IT'S 'COS SHE KNEW I'D ALWAYS LOVE YOU.
WHO IS IT THAT YOU'RE...
...GOING OUT WITH?
KOUKI IS GOING OUT WITH ME.
IT'S A SORE SUBJECT ...
......
I LOVE THAT YOU'RE SO NICE, KOUKI.

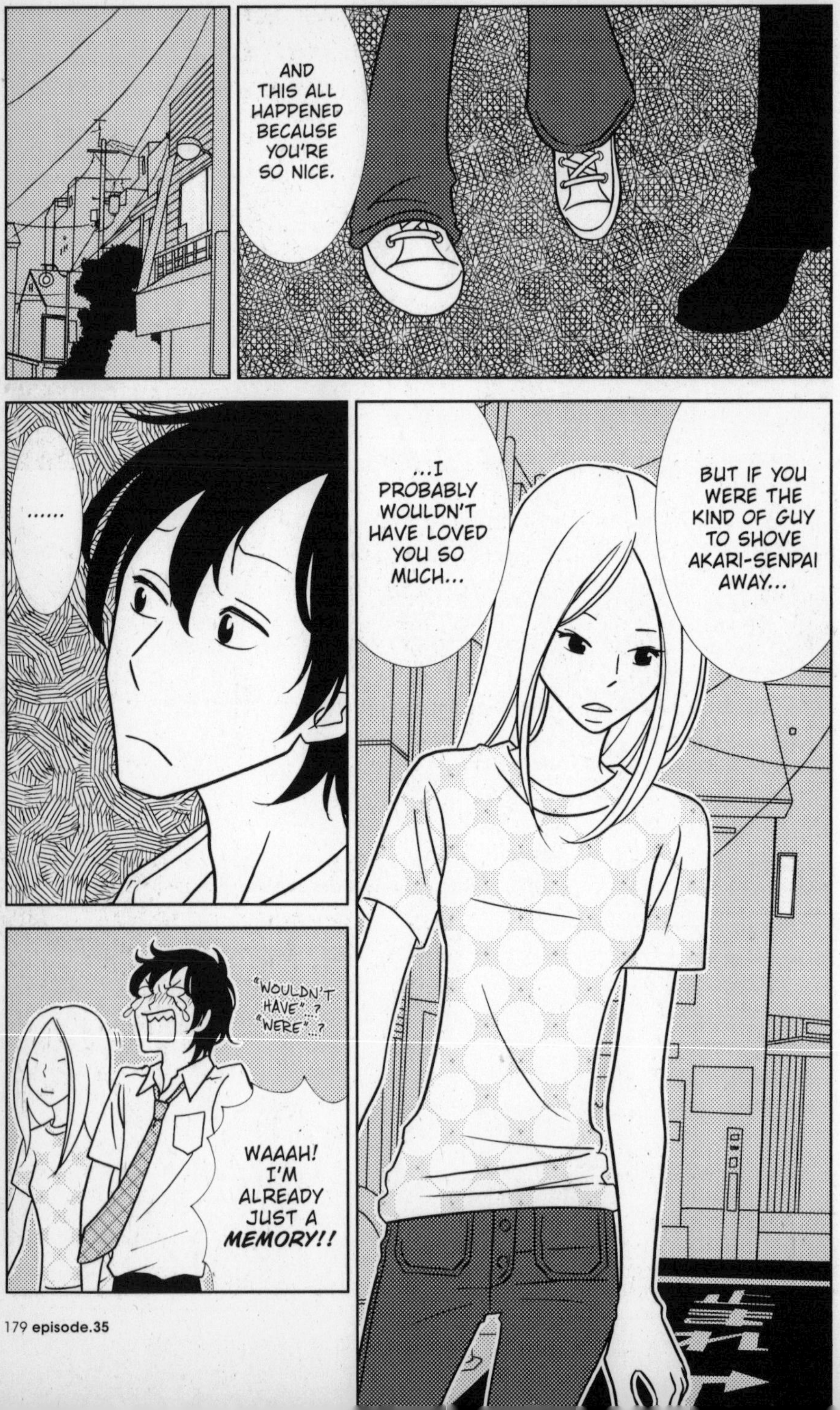
AND THIS ALL HAPPENED BECAUSE YOU'RE SO NICE.
BUT IF YOU WERE THE KIND OF GUY TO SHOVE AKARI-SENPAI AWAY...
...I PROBABLY WOULDN'T HAVE LOVED YOU SO MUCH...
......
"WOULDN'T HAVE"? "WERE"?
WAAAH! I'M ALREADY JUST A *MEMORY!!*

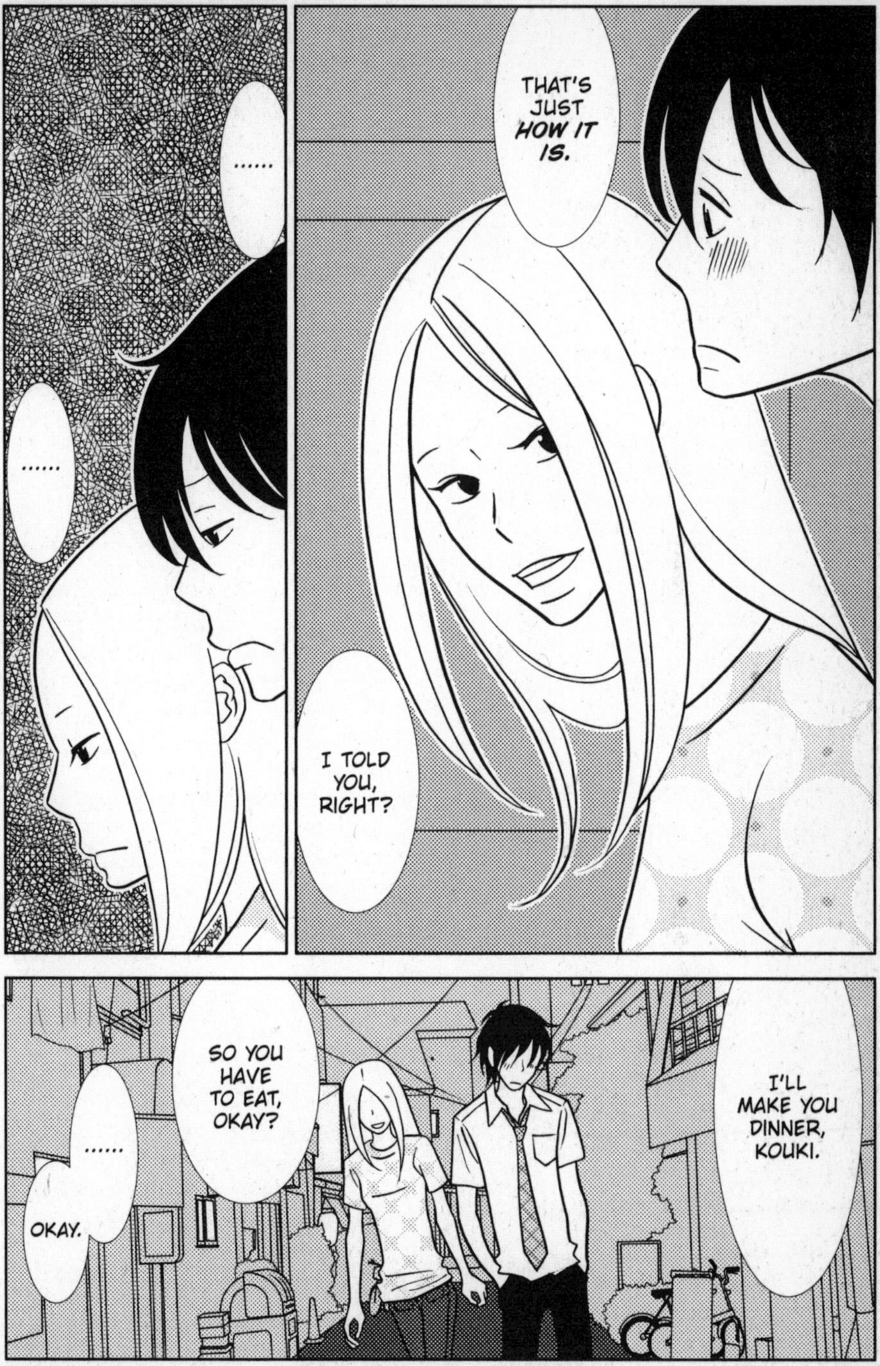
THAT'S JUST *HOW IT IS.*
I TOLD YOU, RIGHT?
......
......
I'LL MAKE YOU DINNER, KOUKI.
SO YOU HAVE TO EAT, OKAY?
......
OKAY.

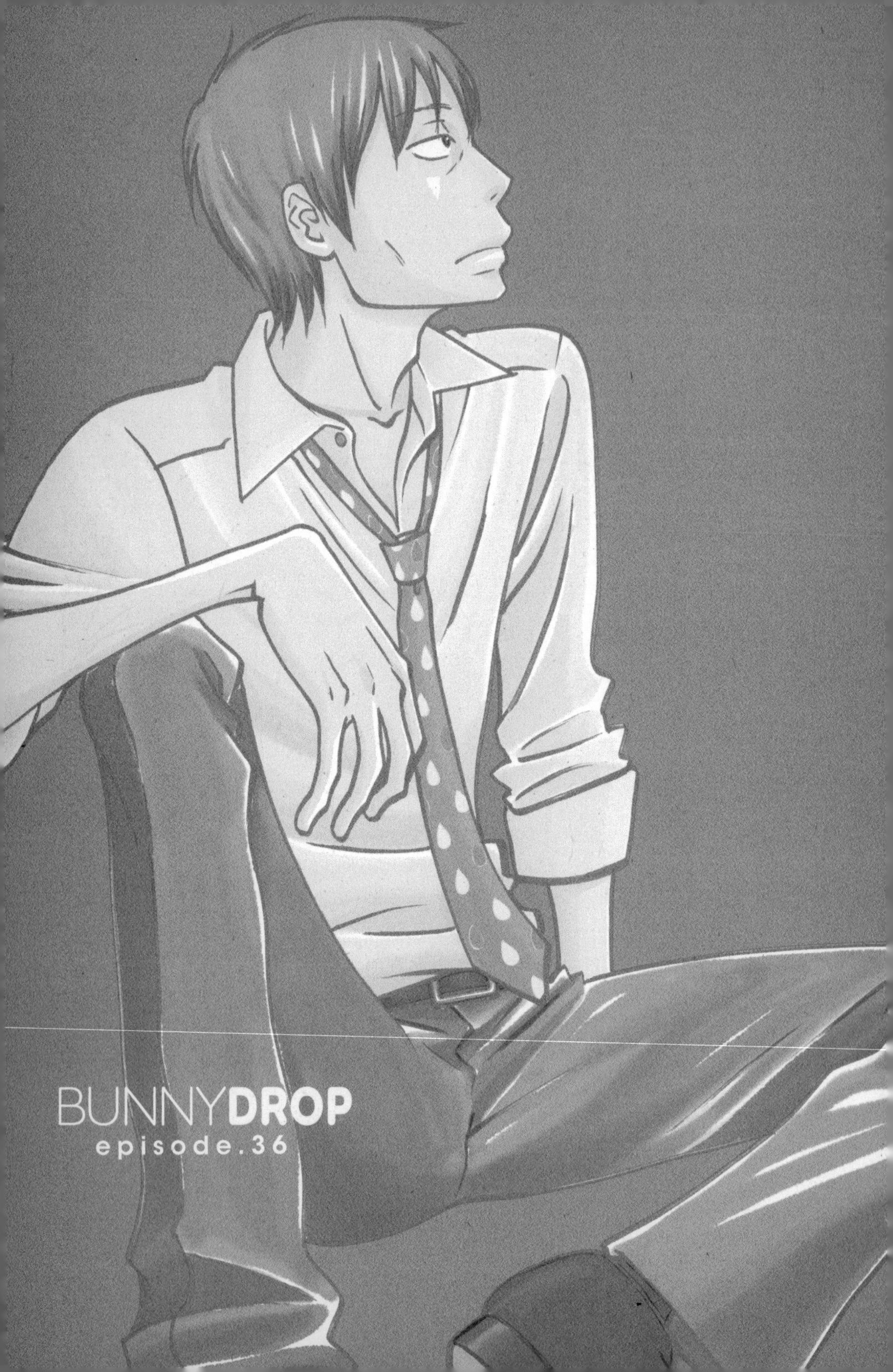
BUNNYDROP
episode.36

BUNNY**DROP**

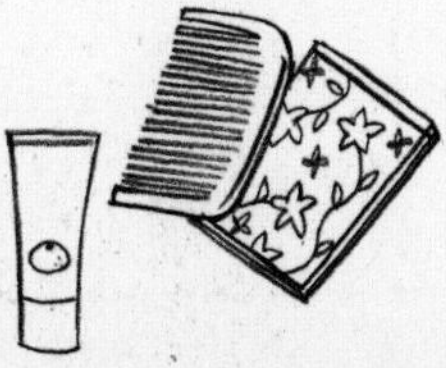

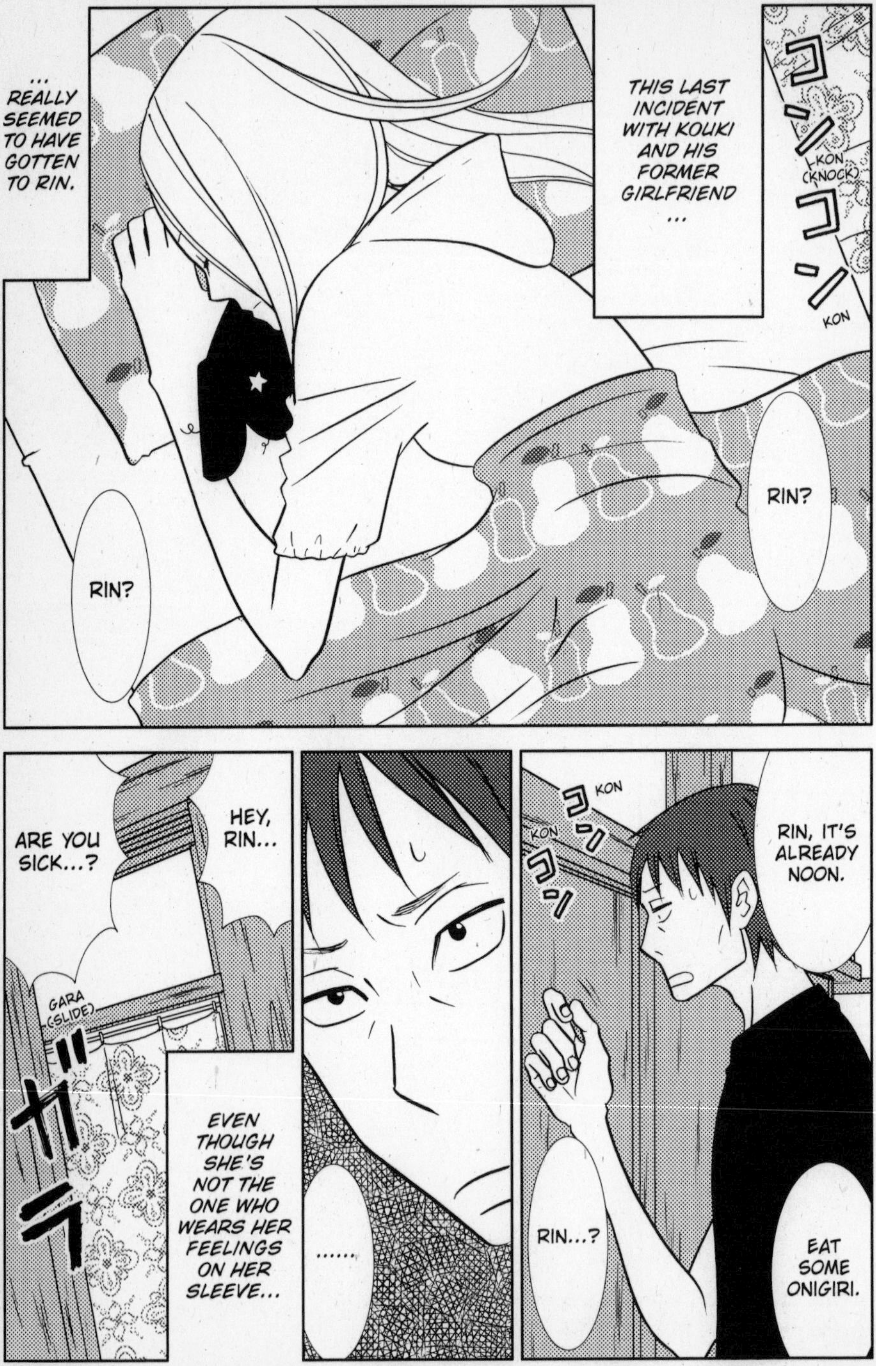
KON (KNOCK)
KON
THIS LAST INCIDENT WITH KOUKI AND HIS FORMER GIRLFRIEND ...
... REALLY SEEMED TO HAVE GOTTEN TO RIN.
RIN?
RIN?
KON
KON
RIN, IT'S ALREADY NOON.
EAT SOME ONIGIRI.
RIN...?
......
HEY, RIN...
ARE YOU SICK...?
GARA (SLIDE)
EVEN THOUGH SHE'S NOT THE ONE WHO WEARS HER FEELINGS ON HER SLEEVE...

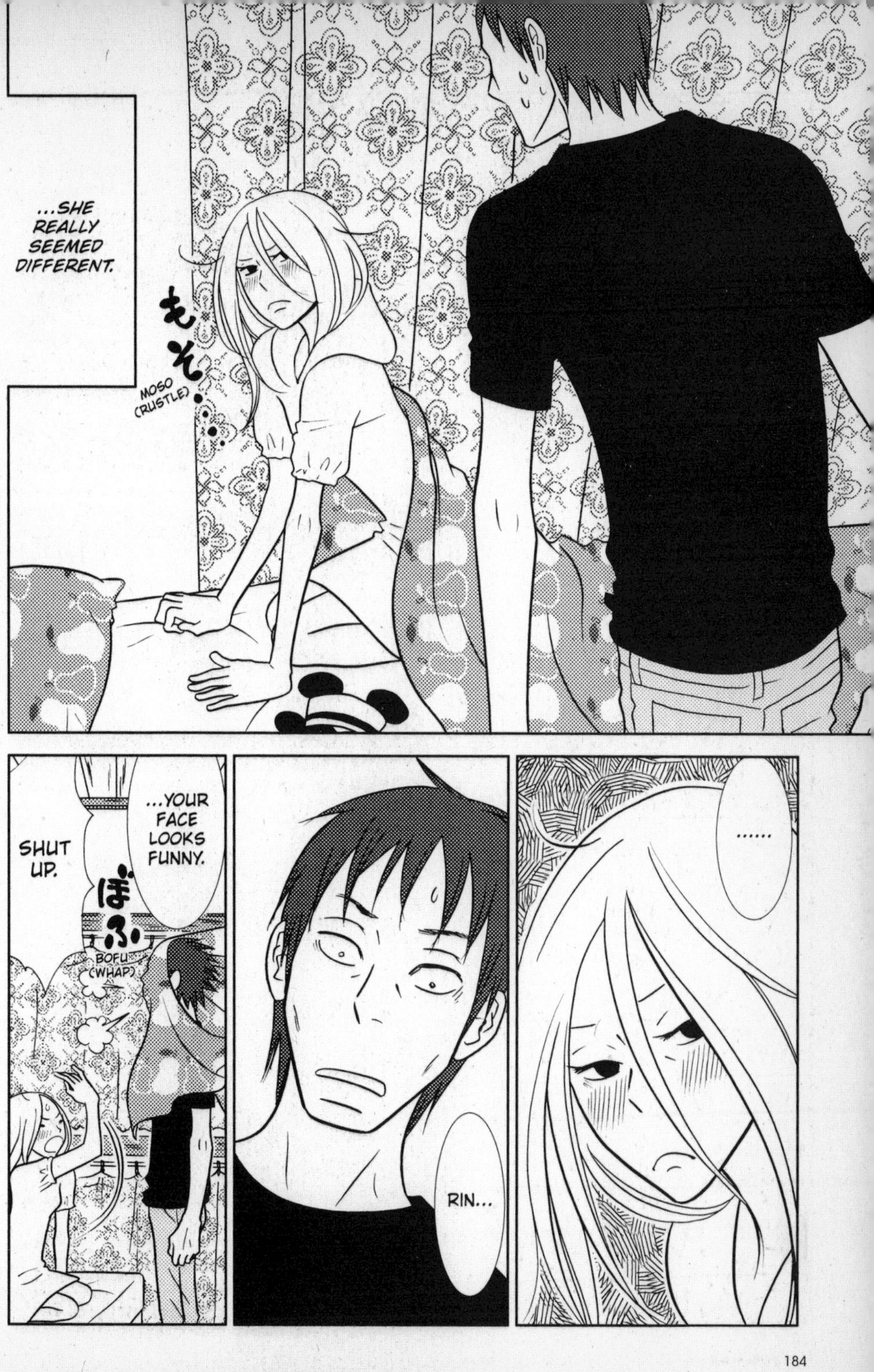
...SHE REALLY SEEMED DIFFERENT.
もそ
MOSO (RUSTLE)
......
RIN...
...YOUR FACE LOOKS FUNNY.
SHUT UP.
ぼふ
BOFU (WHAP)

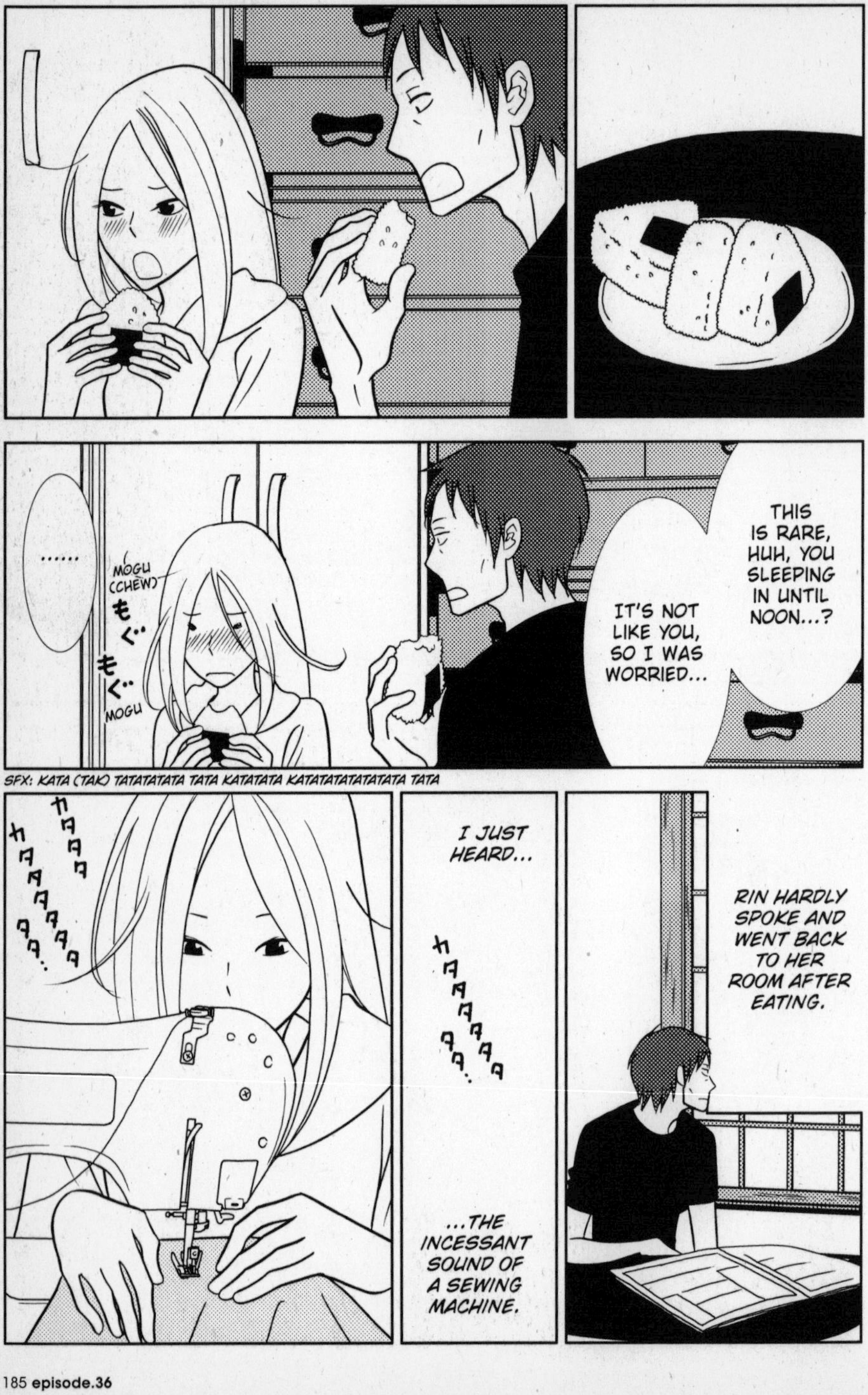
THIS IS RARE, HUH, YOU SLEEPING IN UNTIL NOON...?
IT'S NOT LIKE YOU, SO I WAS WORRIED...
MOGU (CHEW)
もぐ
もぐ
MOGU
......
SFX: KATA (TAK) TATATATATA TATA KATATATA KATATATATATATATA TATA
RIN HARDLY SPOKE AND WENT BACK TO HER ROOM AFTER EATING.
I JUST HEARD...
...THE INCESSANT SOUND OF A SEWING MACHINE.

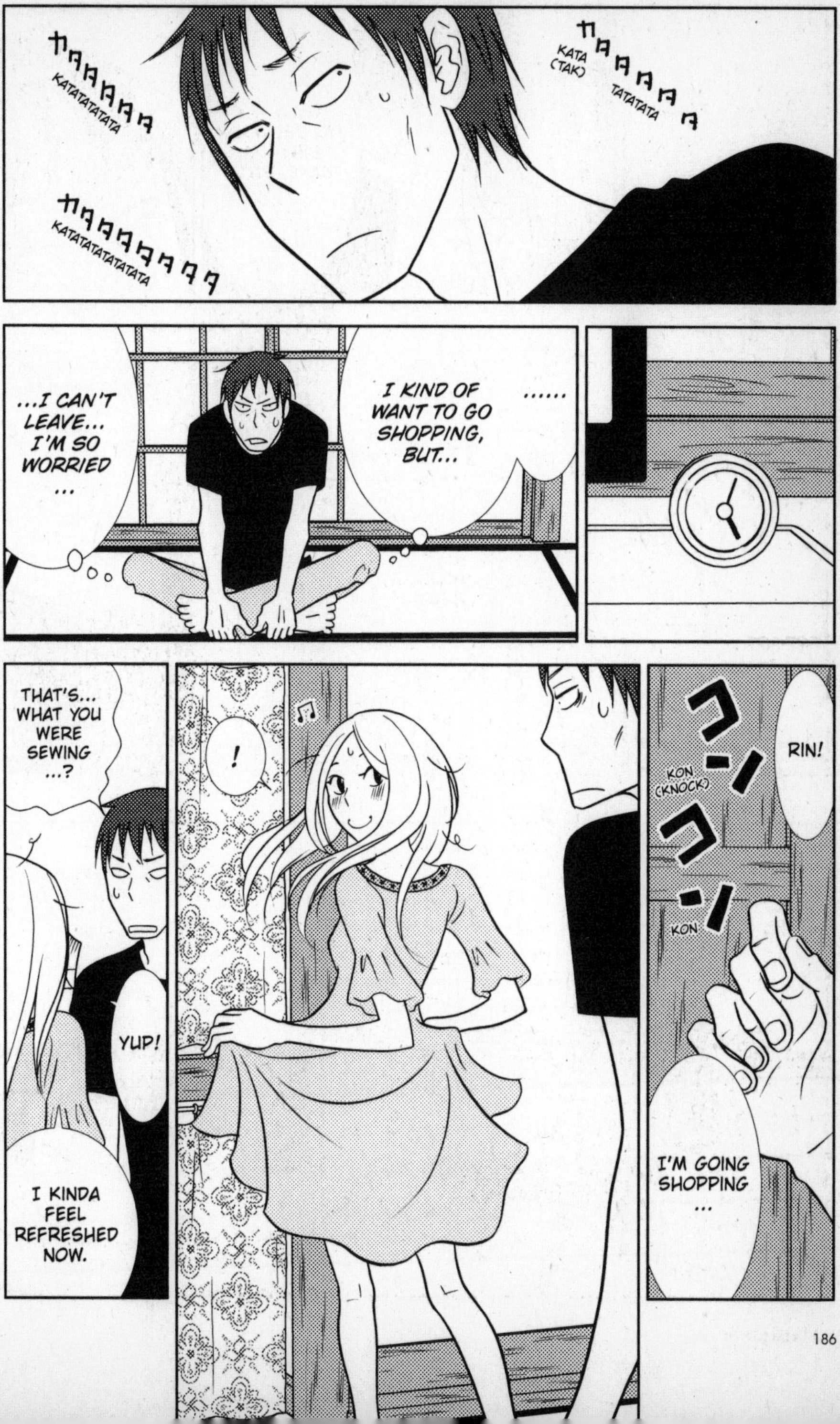

カタタタタタタ
KATA (TAK)
TATATATA
カタタタタタタ
KATATATATATA
カタタタタタタタタ
KATATATATATATATATA
......
I KIND OF WANT TO GO SHOPPING, BUT...
...I CAN'T LEAVE... I'M SO WORRIED ...
RIN!
コンコン
KON (KNOCK)
KON
I'M GOING SHOPPING ...
!
THAT'S... WHAT YOU WERE SEWING ...?
YUP!
I KINDA FEEL REFRESHED NOW.

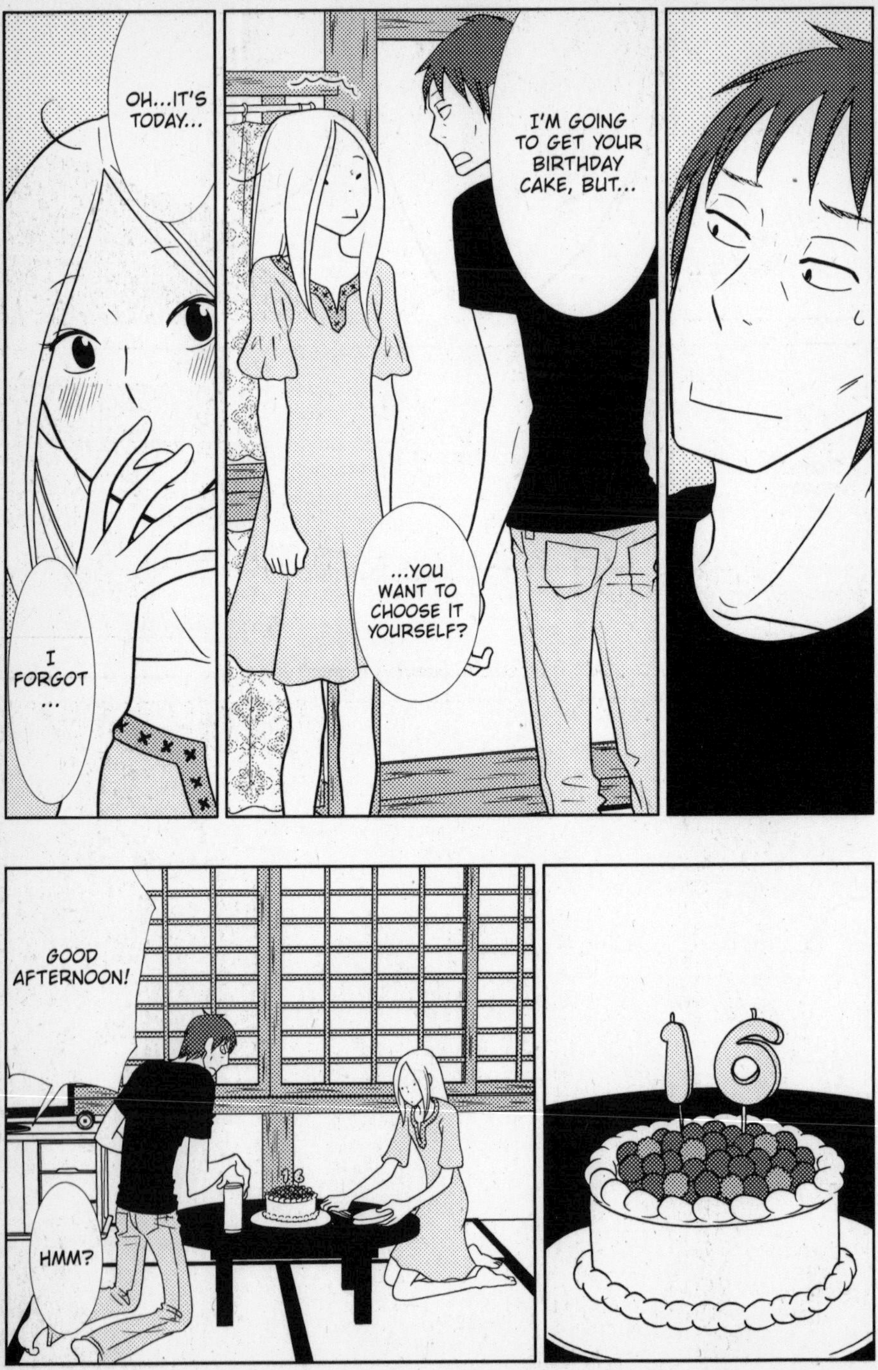
I'M GOING TO GET YOUR BIRTHDAY CAKE, BUT...
...YOU WANT TO CHOOSE IT YOURSELF?
OH...IT'S TODAY...
I FORGOT ...
GOOD AFTERNOON!
HMM?

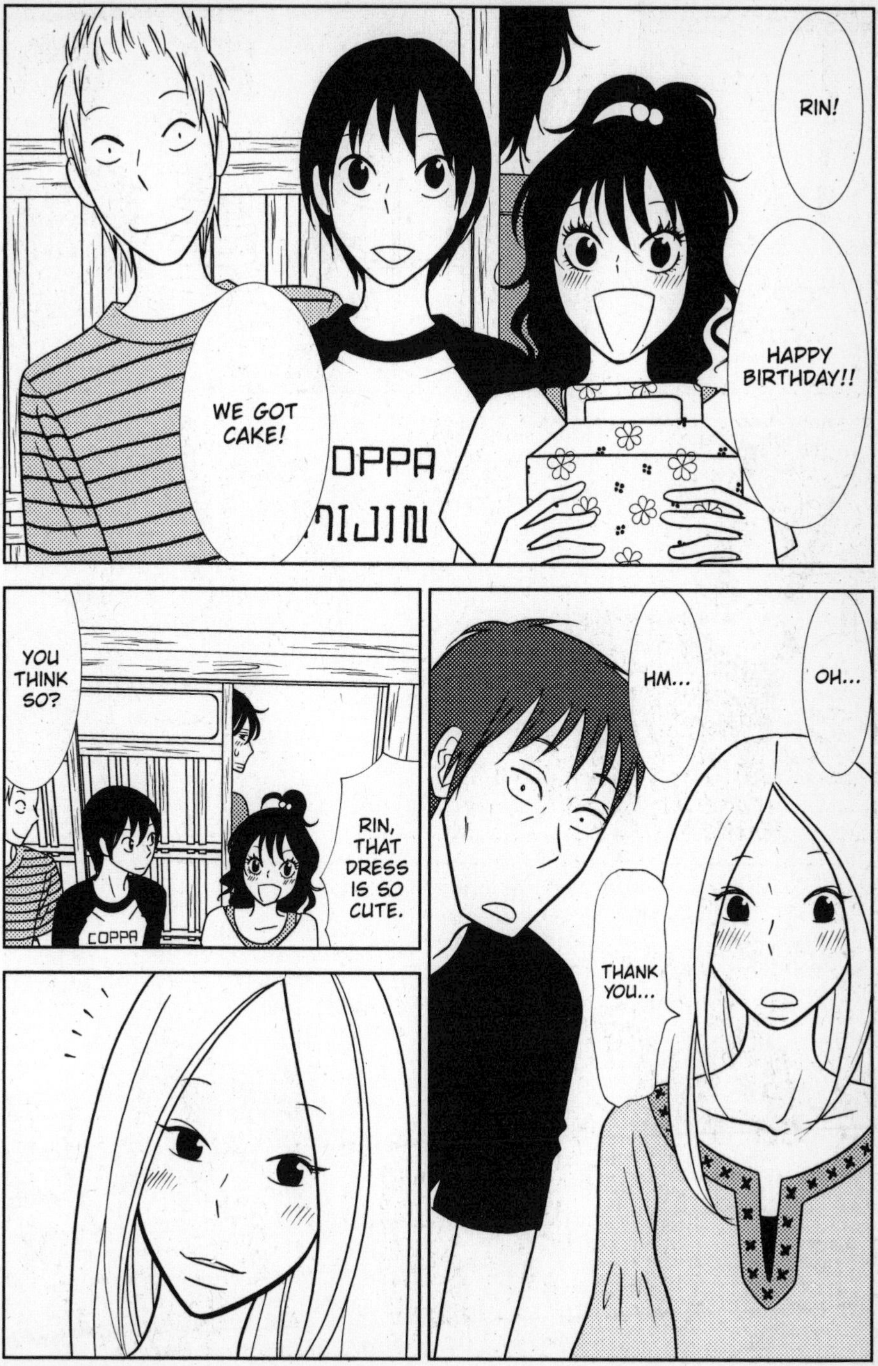
RIN!
HAPPY BIRTHDAY!!
WE GOT CAKE!
COPPA
OH...
HM...
THANK YOU...
RIN, THAT DRESS IS SO CUTE.
YOU THINK SO?
COPPA

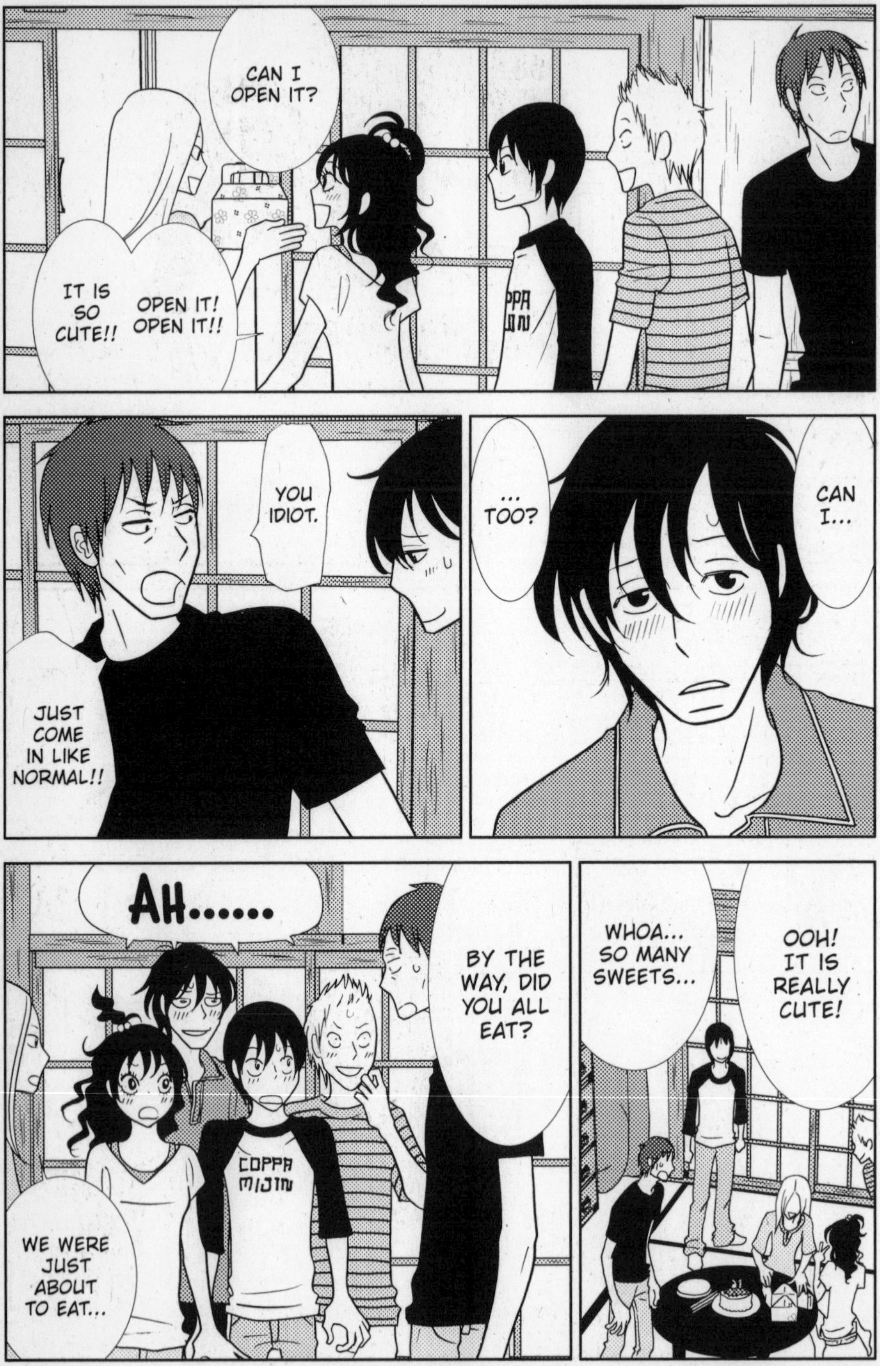
CAN I OPEN IT?
OPEN IT! OPEN IT!!
IT IS SO CUTE!!
CAN I...
... TOO?
YOU IDIOT.
JUST COME IN LIKE NORMAL!!
OOH! IT IS REALLY CUTE!
WHOA... SO MANY SWEETS...
BY THE WAY, DID YOU ALL EAT?
AH......
COPPA MIJIN
WE WERE JUST ABOUT TO EAT...

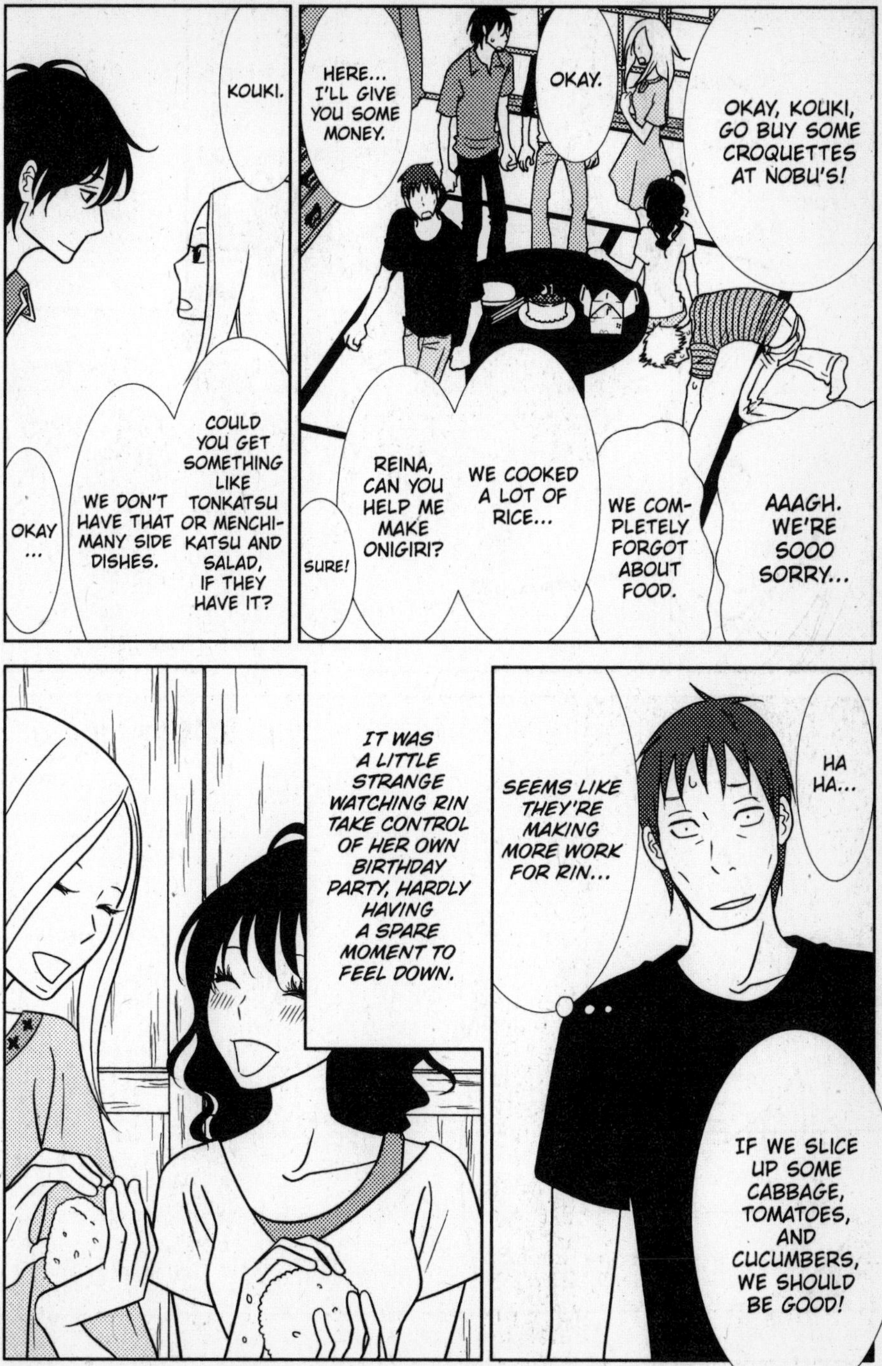
OKAY, KOUKI, GO BUY SOME CROQUETTES AT NOBU'S!
OKAY.
HERE... I'LL GIVE YOU SOME MONEY.
AAAGH. WE'RE SOOO SORRY...
WE COMPLETELY FORGOT ABOUT FOOD.
WE COOKED A LOT OF RICE...
REINA, CAN YOU HELP ME MAKE ONIGIRI?
SURE!
KOUKI.
COULD YOU GET SOMETHING LIKE TONKATSU OR MENCHI-KATSU AND SALAD, IF THEY HAVE IT?
WE DON'T HAVE THAT MANY SIDE DISHES.
OKAY...
HA HA...
SEEMS LIKE THEY'RE MAKING MORE WORK FOR RIN...
IF WE SLICE UP SOME CABBAGE, TOMATOES, AND CUCUMBERS, WE SHOULD BE GOOD!
IT WAS A LITTLE STRANGE WATCHING RIN TAKE CONTROL OF HER OWN BIRTHDAY PARTY, HARDLY HAVING A SPARE MOMENT TO FEEL DOWN.

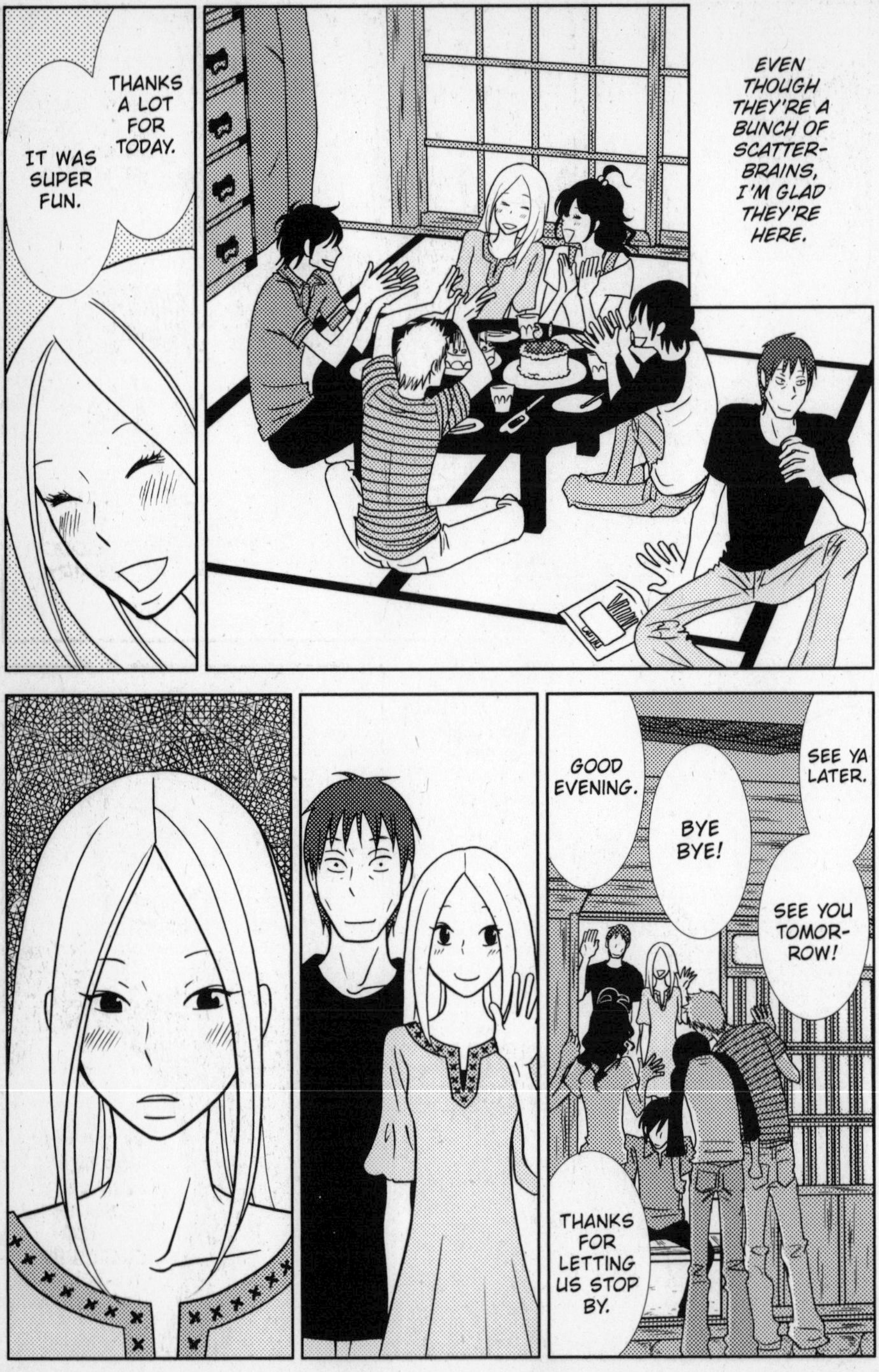
EVEN THOUGH THEY'RE A BUNCH OF SCATTER-BRAINS, I'M GLAD THEY'RE HERE.
THANKS A LOT FOR TODAY.
IT WAS SUPER FUN.
SEE YA LATER.
GOOD EVENING.
BYE BYE!
SEE YOU TOMOR-ROW!
THANKS FOR LETTING US STOP BY.

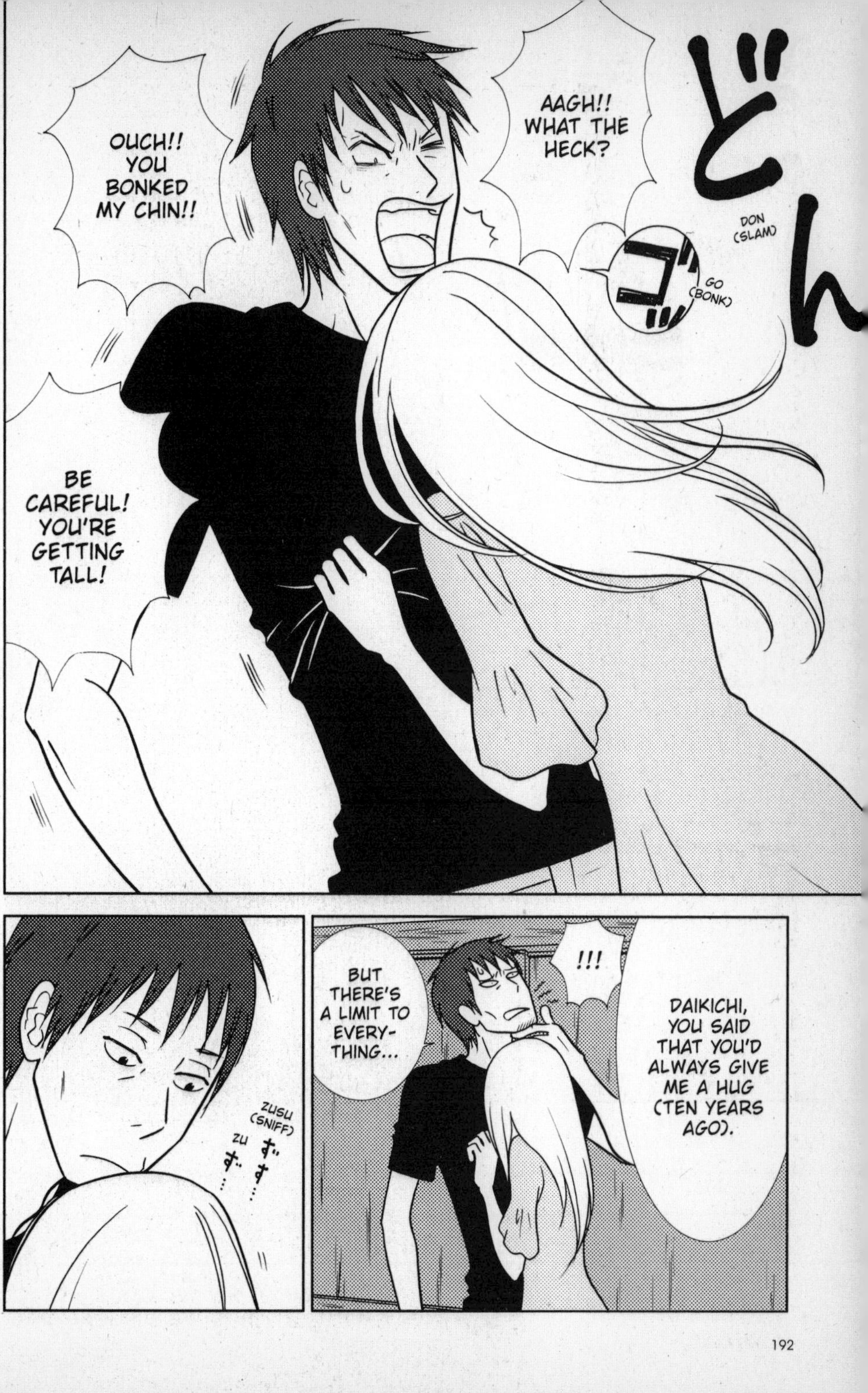

どん
DON (SLAM)
AAGH!! WHAT THE HECK?
ゴッ
GO (BONK)
OUCH!! YOU BONKED MY CHIN!!
BE CAREFUL! YOU'RE GETTING TALL!
!!!
DAIKICHI, YOU SAID THAT YOU'D ALWAYS GIVE ME A HUG (TEN YEARS AGO).
BUT THERE'S A LIMIT TO EVERY-THING...
ずす…
ず…
ZUSU (SNIFF)
ZU

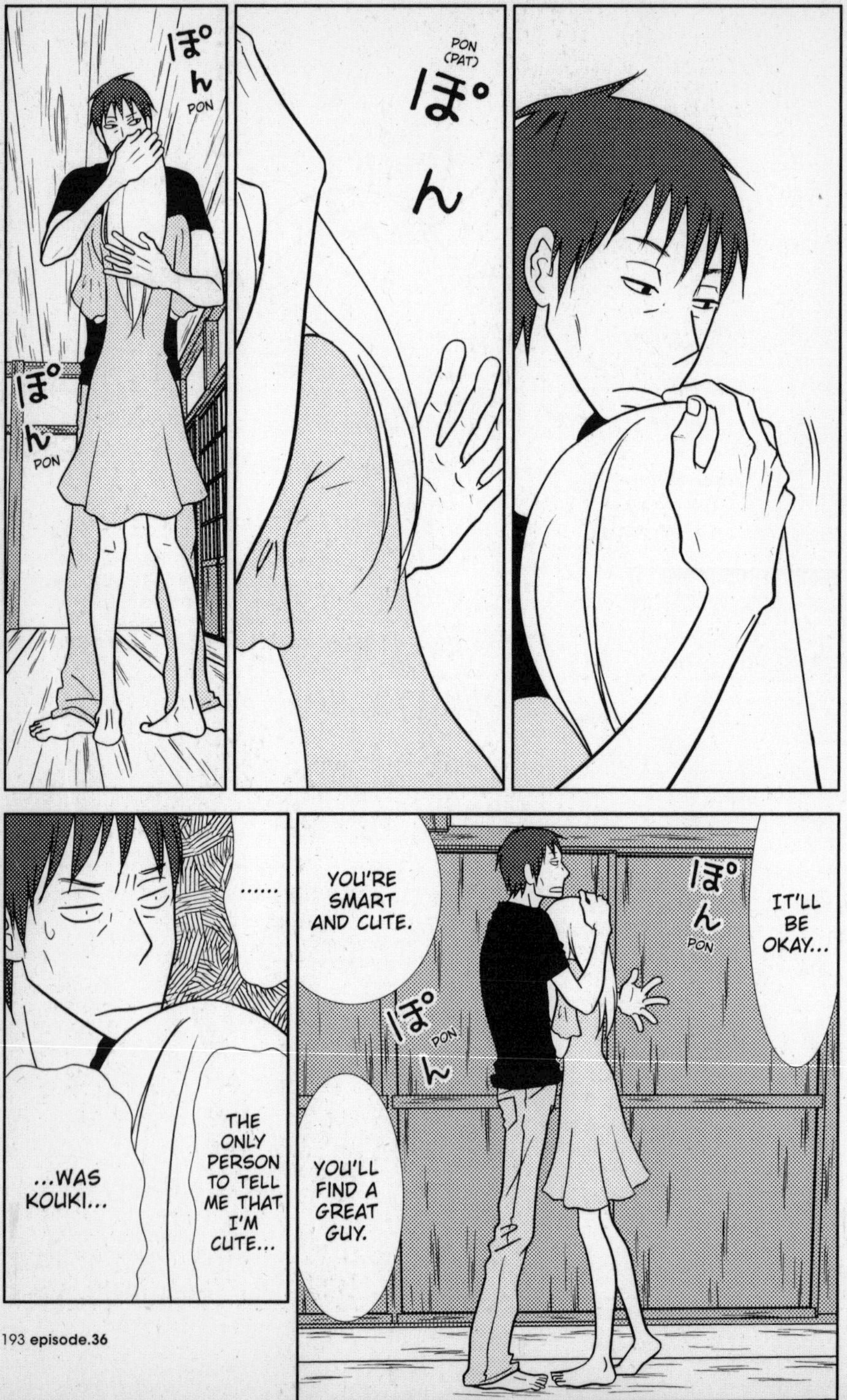
ぽん
PON (PAT)
ぽん
PON
ぽん
PON
IT'LL BE OKAY...
ぽん
PON
YOU'RE SMART AND CUTE.
ぽん
PON
YOU'LL FIND A GREAT GUY.
......
THE ONLY PERSON TO TELL ME THAT I'M CUTE...
...WAS KOUKI...

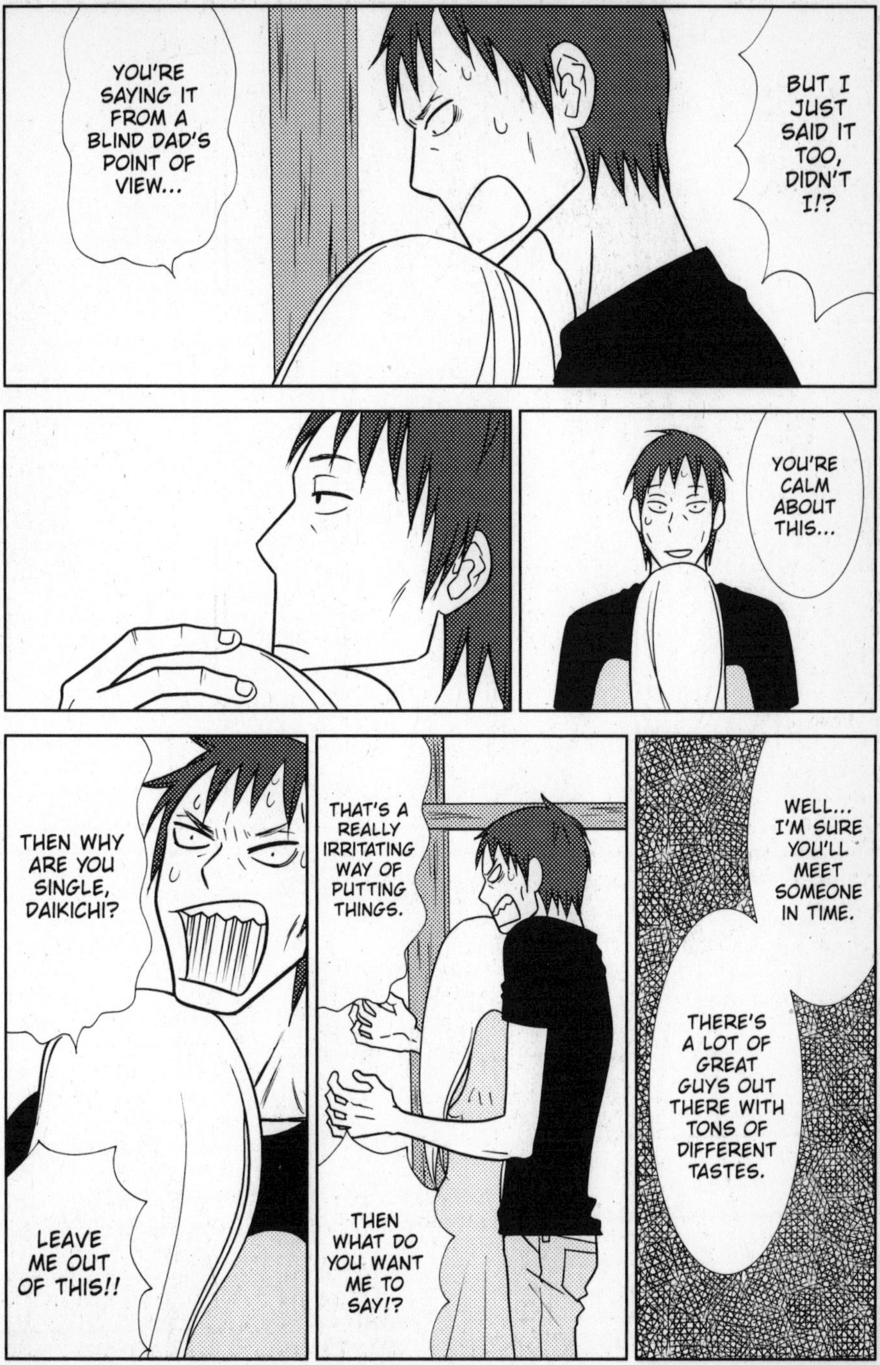

BUT I JUST SAID IT TOO, DIDN'T I!?
YOU'RE SAYING IT FROM A BLIND DAD'S POINT OF VIEW...
YOU'RE CALM ABOUT THIS...
WELL... I'M SURE YOU'LL MEET SOMEONE IN TIME.
THERE'S A LOT OF GREAT GUYS OUT THERE WITH TONS OF DIFFERENT TASTES.
THAT'S A REALLY IRRITATING WAY OF PUTTING THINGS.
THEN WHAT DO YOU WANT ME TO SAY!?
THEN WHY ARE YOU SINGLE, DAIKICHI?
LEAVE ME OUT OF THIS!!

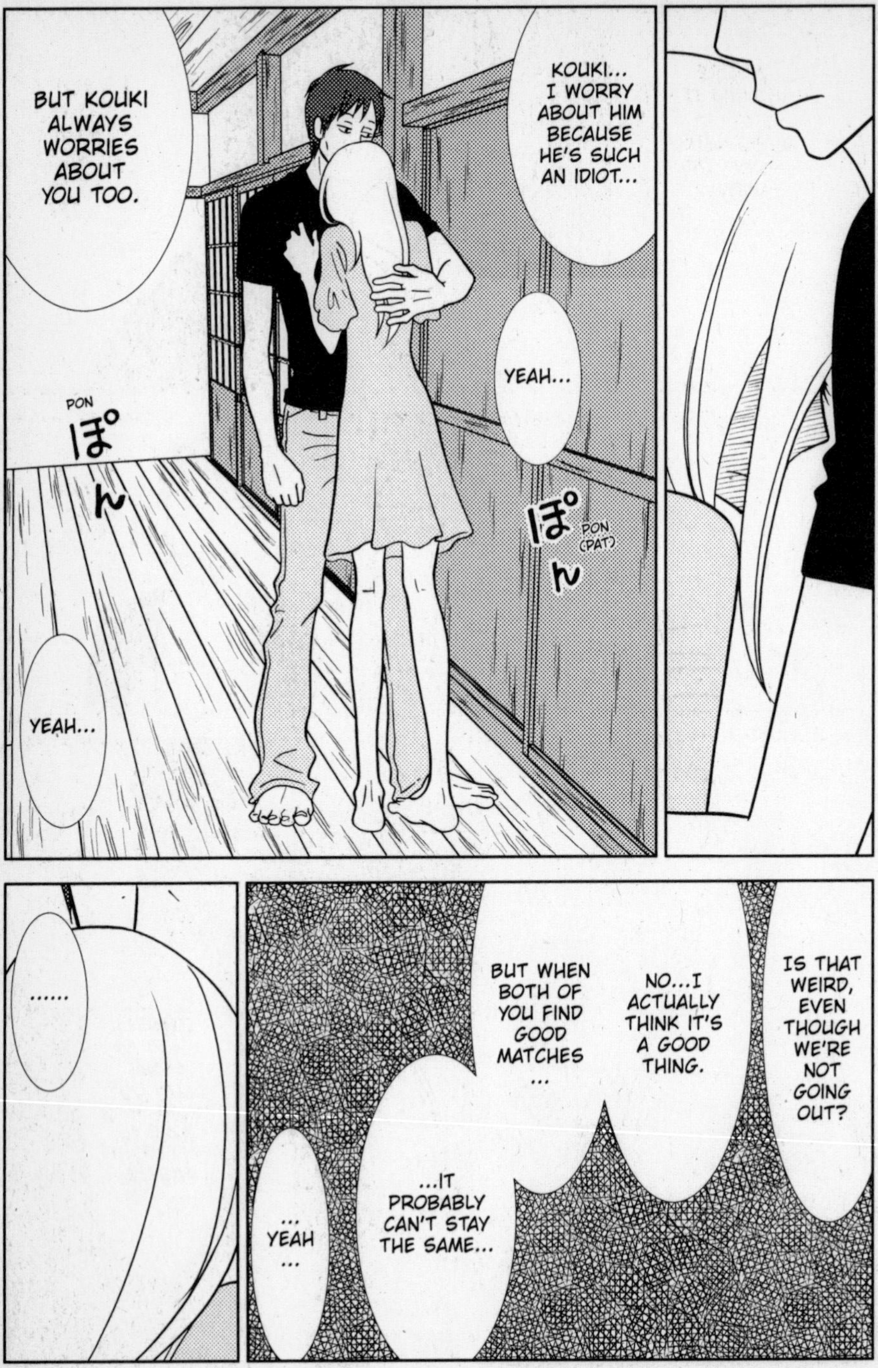
KOUKI... I WORRY ABOUT HIM BECAUSE HE'S SUCH AN IDIOT...
BUT KOUKI ALWAYS WORRIES ABOUT YOU TOO.
YEAH...
PON
ぽん
ぽん
PON (PAT)
YEAH...
IS THAT WEIRD, EVEN THOUGH WE'RE NOT GOING OUT?
NO...I ACTUALLY THINK IT'S A GOOD THING.
BUT WHEN BOTH OF YOU FIND GOOD MATCHES ...
...IT PROBABLY CAN'T STAY THE SAME...
... YEAH ...
......

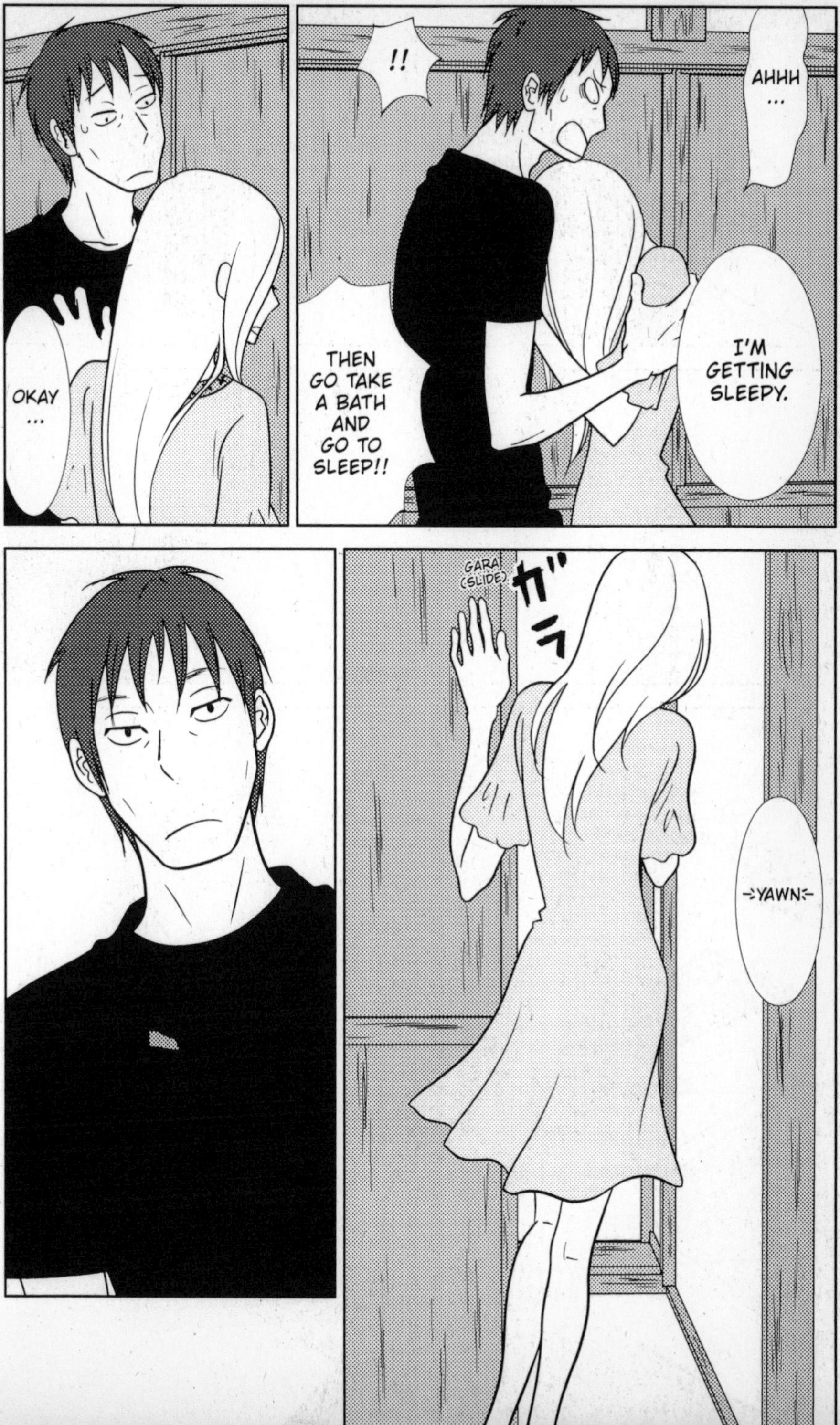
AHHH ...
I'M GETTING SLEEPY.
!!
THEN GO TAKE A BATH AND GO TO SLEEP!!
OKAY ...
ガラ
GARA (SLIDE)
-YAWN-

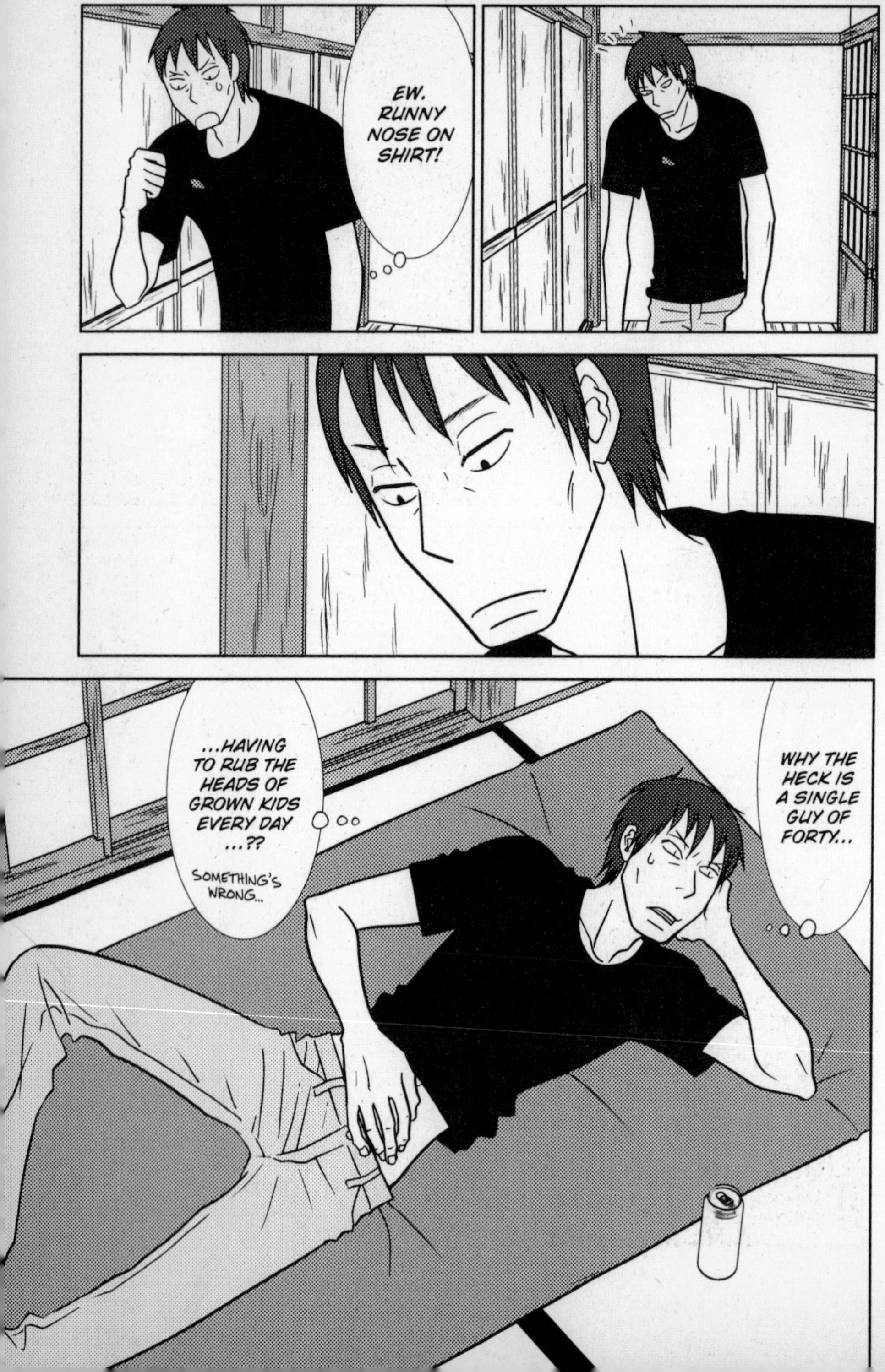
EW. RUNNY NOSE ON SHIRT!
WHY THE HECK IS A SINGLE GUY OF FORTY...
...HAVING TO RUB THE HEADS OF GROWN KIDS EVERY DAY ...??
SOMETHING'S WRONG...

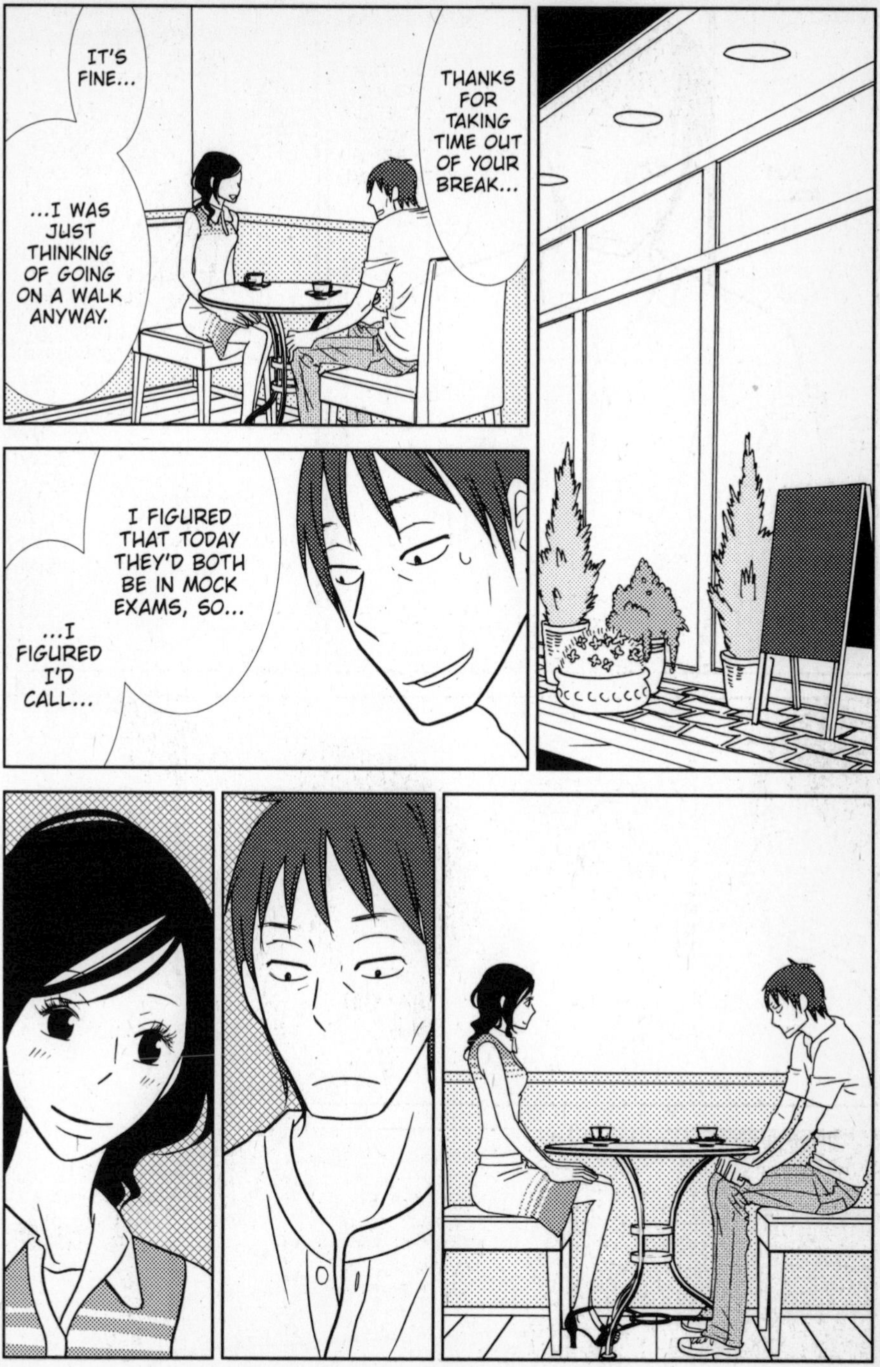
THANKS FOR TAKING TIME OUT OF YOUR BREAK...
IT'S FINE...
...I WAS JUST THINKING OF GOING ON A WALK ANYWAY.
I FIGURED THAT TODAY THEY'D BOTH BE IN MOCK EXAMS, SO...
...I FIGURED I'D CALL...

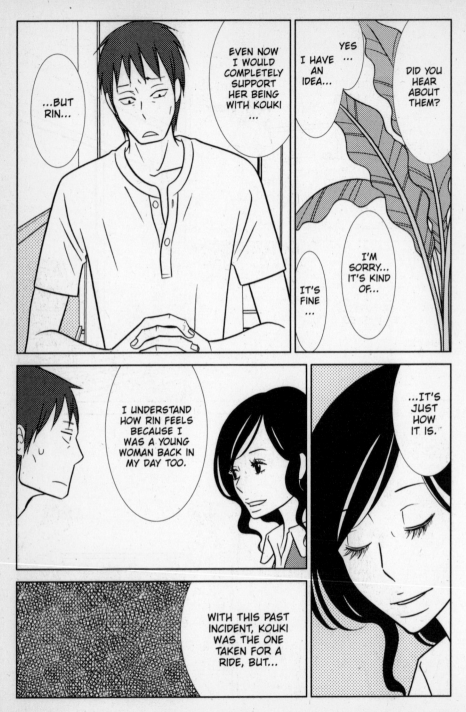

...BUT RIN...

EVEN NOW I WOULD COMPLETELY SUPPORT HER BEING WITH KOUKI...

YES... I HAVE AN IDEA...

DID YOU HEAR ABOUT THEM?

IT'S FINE...

I'M SORRY... IT'S KIND OF...

I UNDERSTAND HOW RIN FEELS BECAUSE I WAS A YOUNG WOMAN BACK IN MY DAY TOO.

...IT'S JUST HOW IT IS.

WITH THIS PAST INCIDENT, KOUKI WAS THE ONE TAKEN FOR A RIDE, BUT...

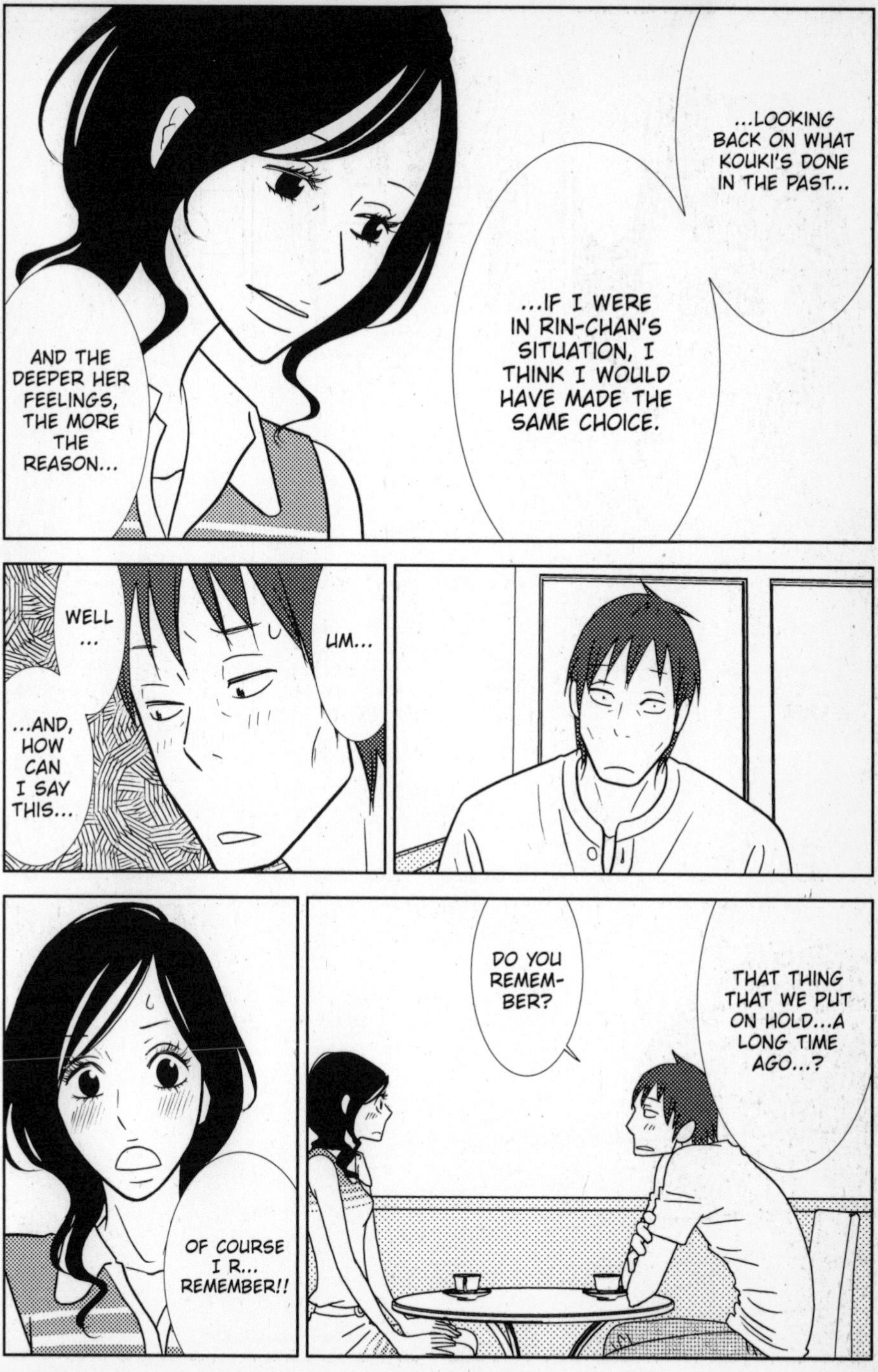
...LOOKING BACK ON WHAT KOUKI'S DONE IN THE PAST...
...IF I WERE IN RIN-CHAN'S SITUATION, I THINK I WOULD HAVE MADE THE SAME CHOICE.
AND THE DEEPER HER FEELINGS, THE MORE THE REASON...
UM...
WELL ...
...AND, HOW CAN I SAY THIS...
THAT THING THAT WE PUT ON HOLD...A LONG TIME AGO...?
DO YOU REMEM-BER?
OF COURSE I R... REMEMBER!!

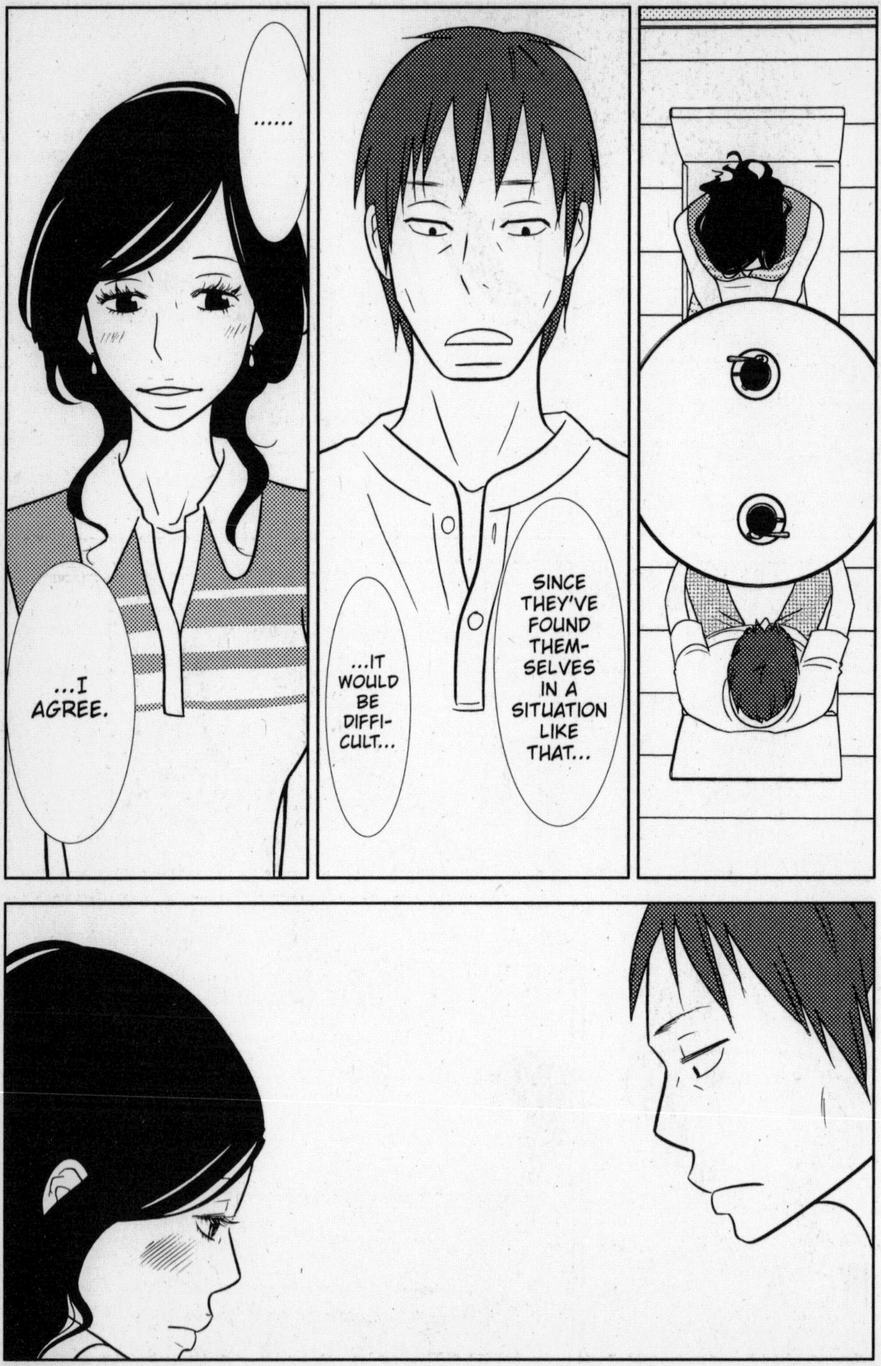
SINCE THEY'VE FOUND THEM-SELVES IN A SITUATION LIKE THAT...
...IT WOULD BE DIFFI-CULT...
......
...I AGREE.

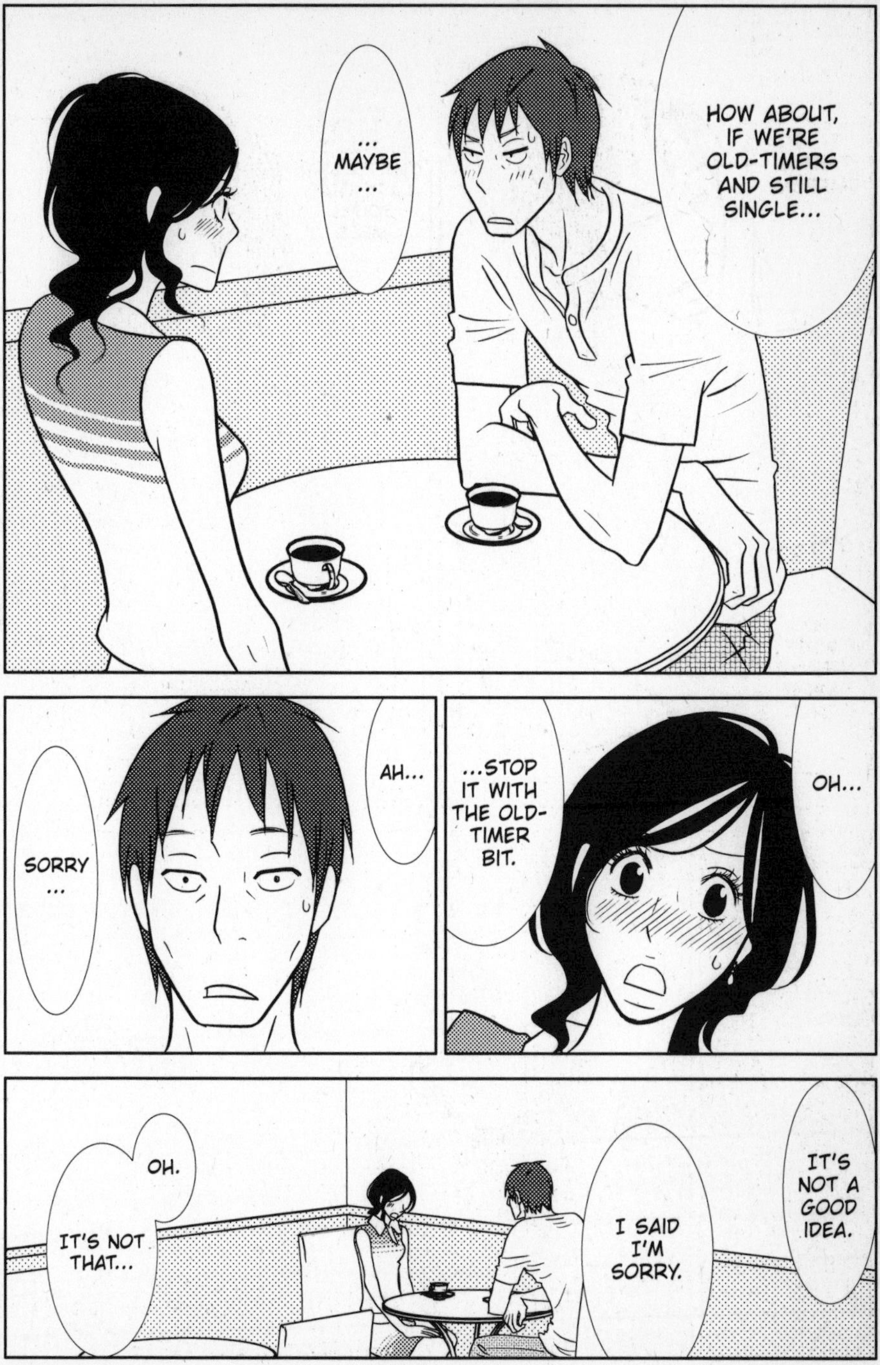
HOW ABOUT, IF WE'RE OLD-TIMERS AND STILL SINGLE...
... MAYBE ...
OH...
...STOP IT WITH THE OLD-TIMER BIT.
AH...
SORRY ...
IT'S NOT A GOOD IDEA.
I SAID I'M SORRY.
OH.
IT'S NOT THAT...

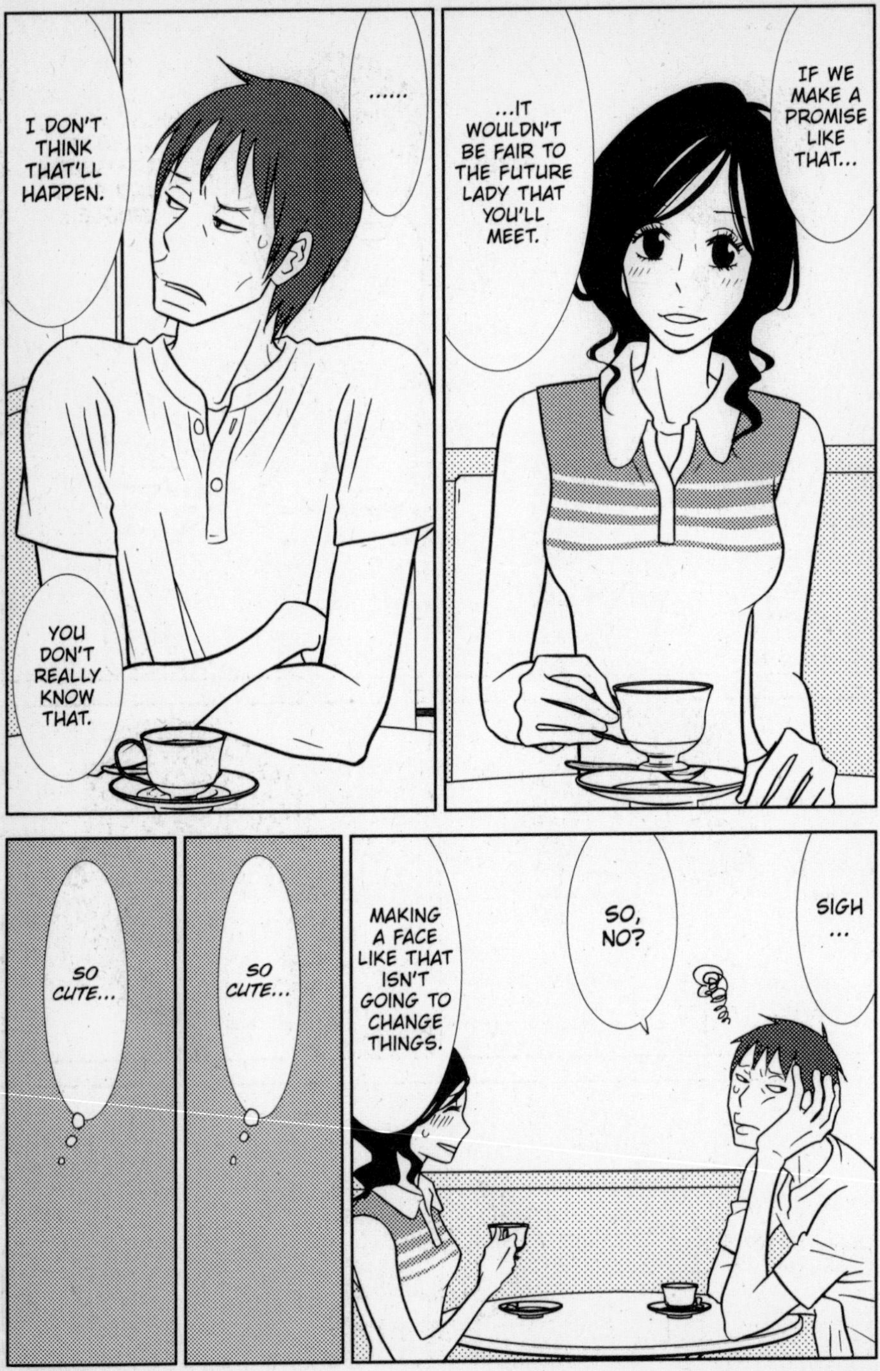
IF WE MAKE A PROMISE LIKE THAT...
...IT WOULDN'T BE FAIR TO THE FUTURE LADY THAT YOU'LL MEET.
......
I DON'T THINK THAT'LL HAPPEN.
YOU DON'T REALLY KNOW THAT.
SIGH ...
SO, NO?
MAKING A FACE LIKE THAT ISN'T GOING TO CHANGE THINGS.
SO CUTE...
SO CUTE...

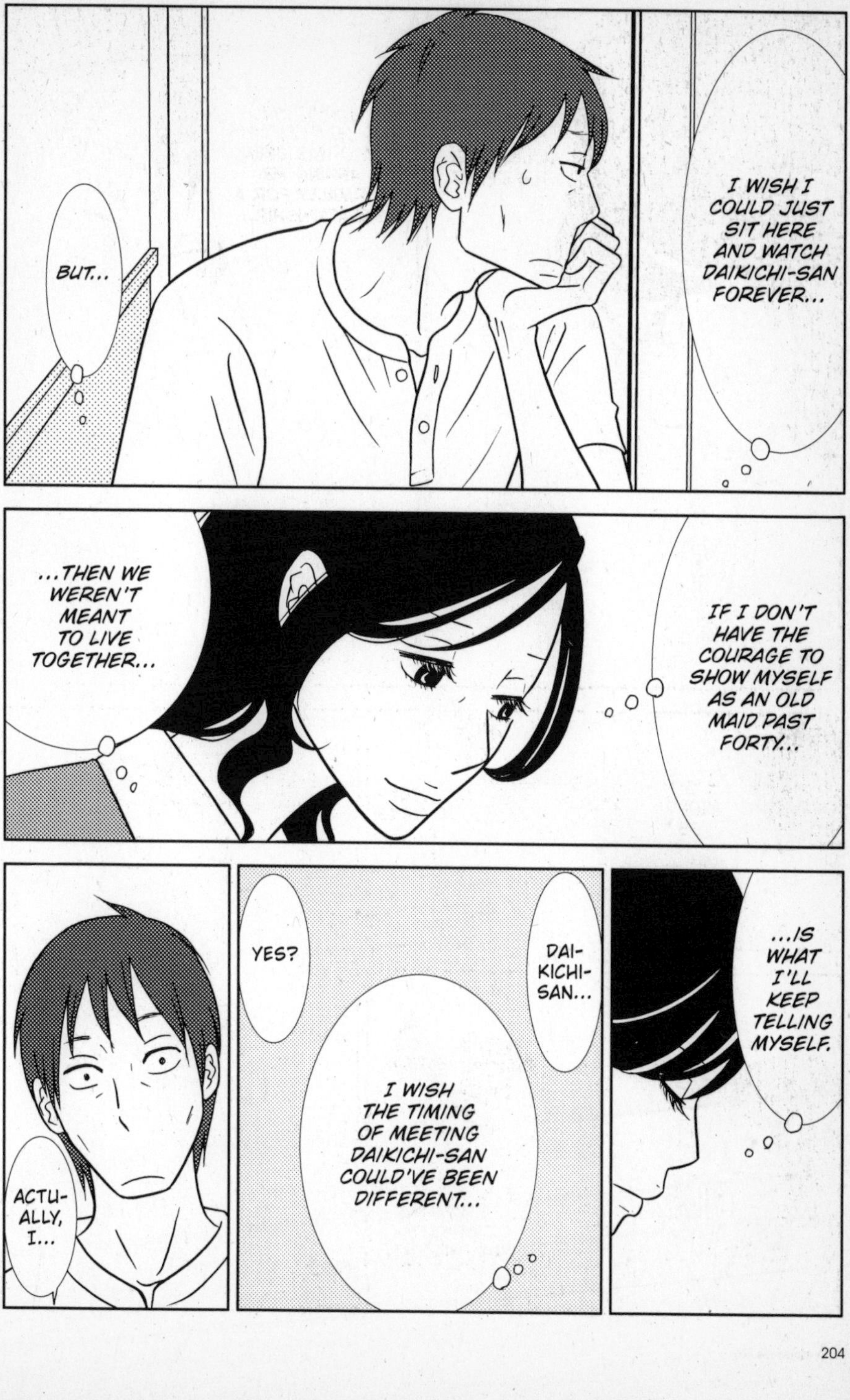
I WISH I COULD JUST SIT HERE AND WATCH DAIKICHI-SAN FOREVER...
BUT...
IF I DON'T HAVE THE COURAGE TO SHOW MYSELF AS AN OLD MAID PAST FORTY...
...THEN WE WEREN'T MEANT TO LIVE TOGETHER...
...IS WHAT I'LL KEEP TELLING MYSELF.
DAI-KICHI-SAN...
YES?
I WISH THE TIMING OF MEETING DAIKICHI-SAN COULD'VE BEEN DIFFERENT...
ACTU-ALLY, I...

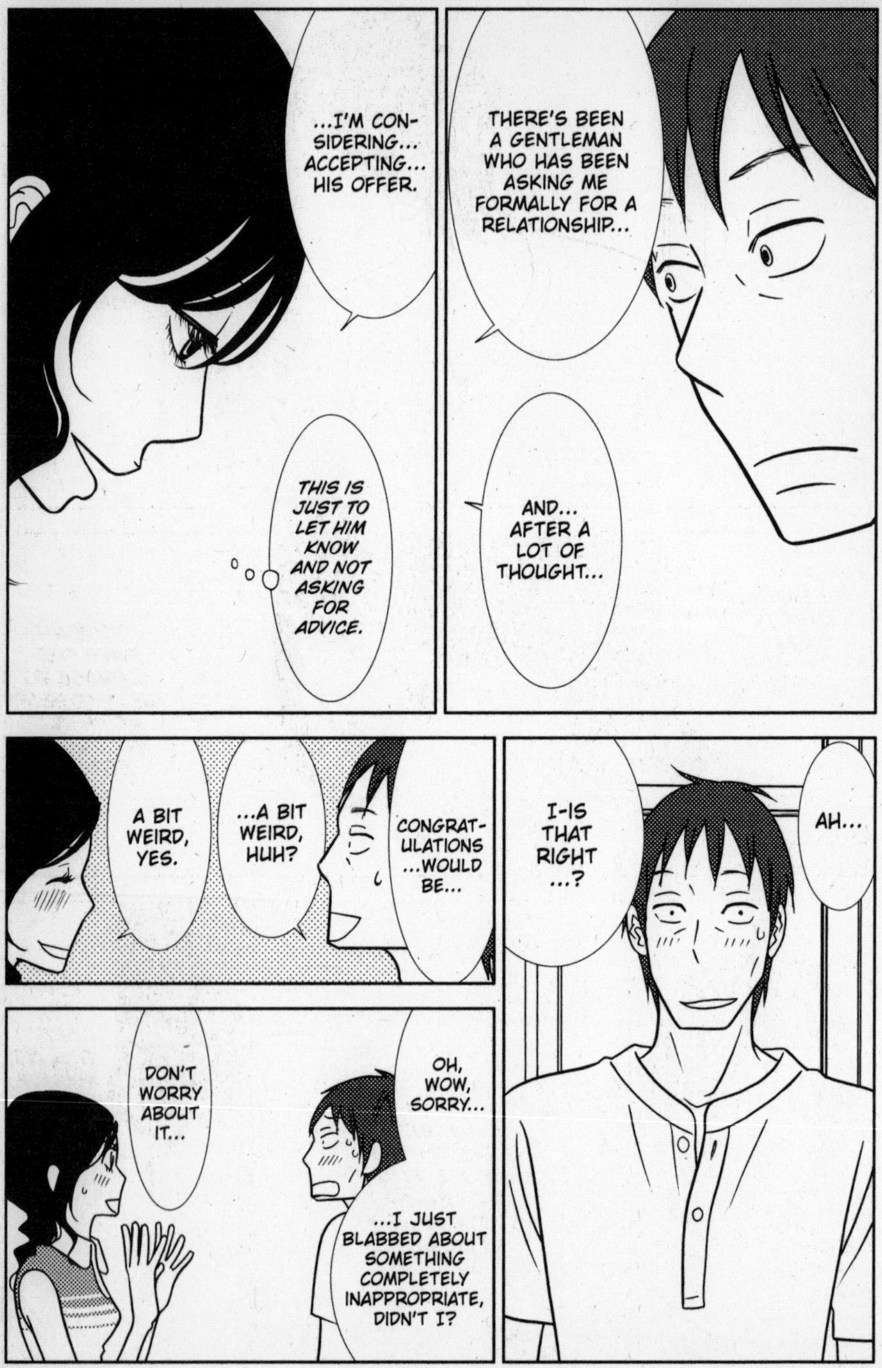
THERE'S BEEN A GENTLEMAN WHO HAS BEEN ASKING ME FORMALLY FOR A RELATIONSHIP...
AND... AFTER A LOT OF THOUGHT...
...I'M CONSIDERING... ACCEPTING... HIS OFFER.
THIS IS JUST TO LET HIM KNOW AND NOT ASKING FOR ADVICE.
AH...
I-IS THAT RIGHT ...?
CONGRATULATIONS ...WOULD BE...
...A BIT WEIRD, HUH?
A BIT WEIRD, YES.
OH, WOW, SORRY...
...I JUST BLABBED ABOUT SOMETHING COMPLETELY INAPPROPRIATE, DIDN'T I?
DON'T WORRY ABOUT IT...

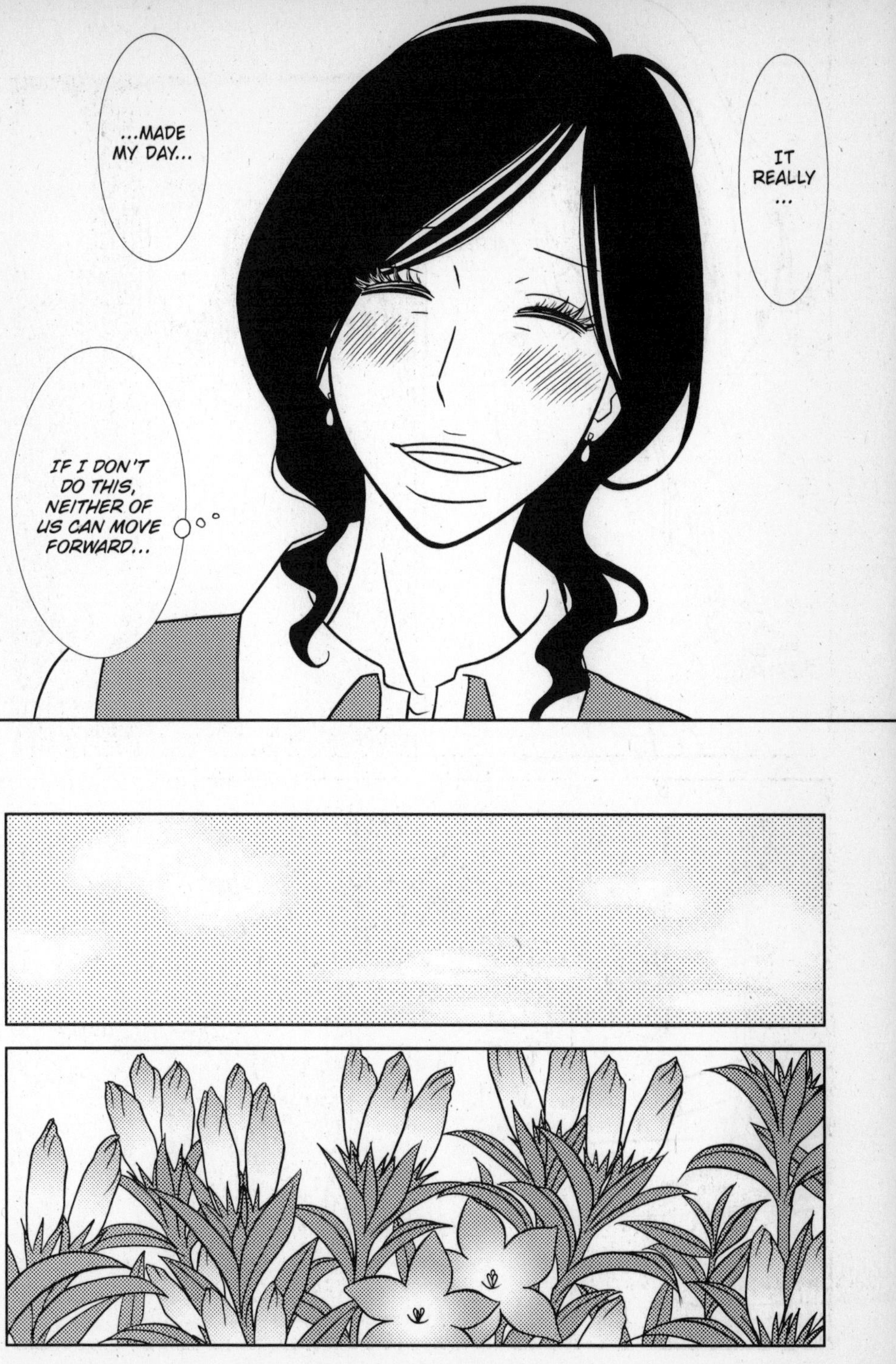
IT REALLY ...
...MADE MY DAY...
IF I DON'T DO THIS, NEITHER OF US CAN MOVE FORWARD...

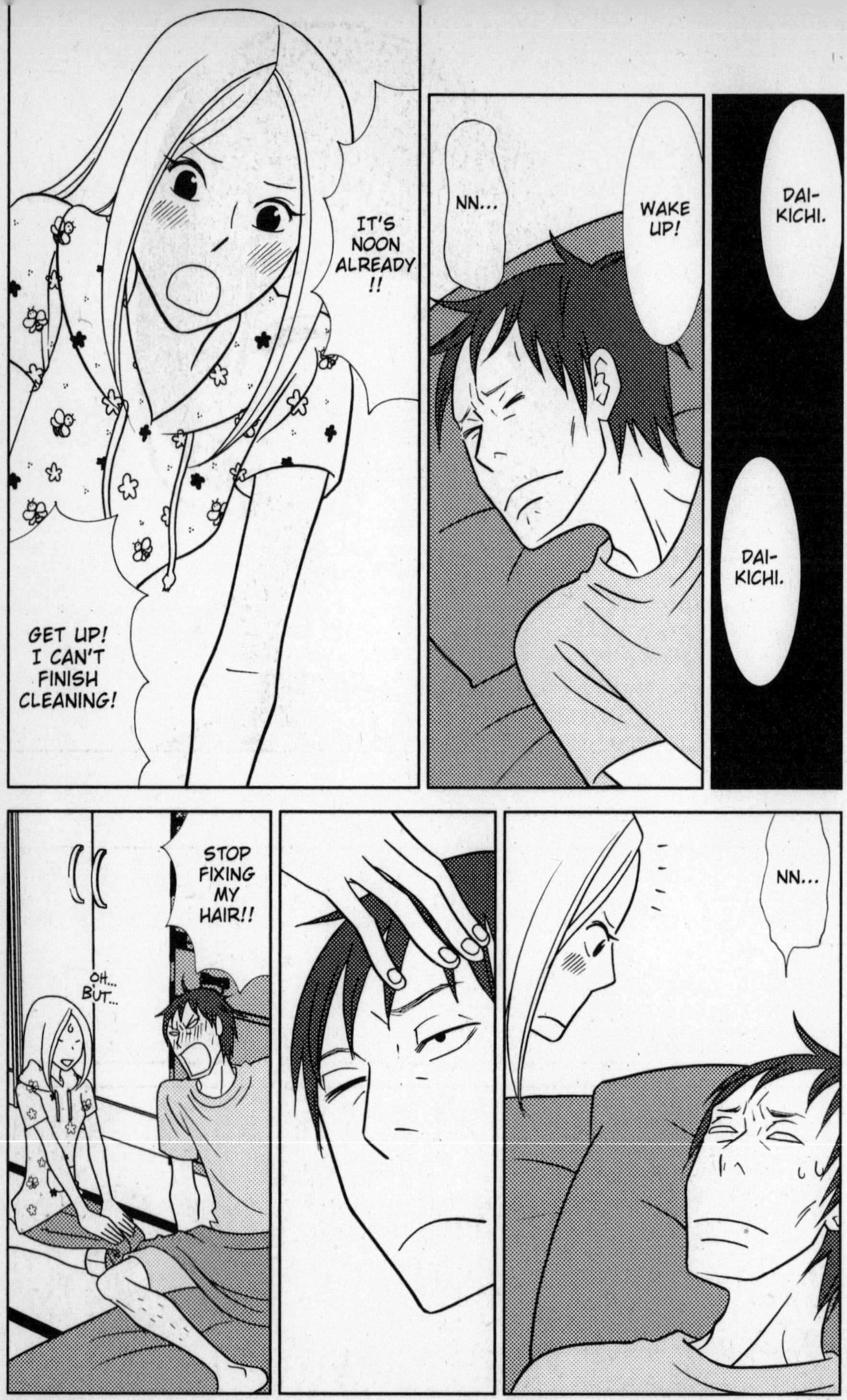
DAI-KICHI.
DAI-KICHI.
WAKE UP!
NN...
IT'S NOON ALREADY!!
GET UP! I CAN'T FINISH CLEANING!
NN...
STOP FIXING MY HAIR!!
OH... BUT...

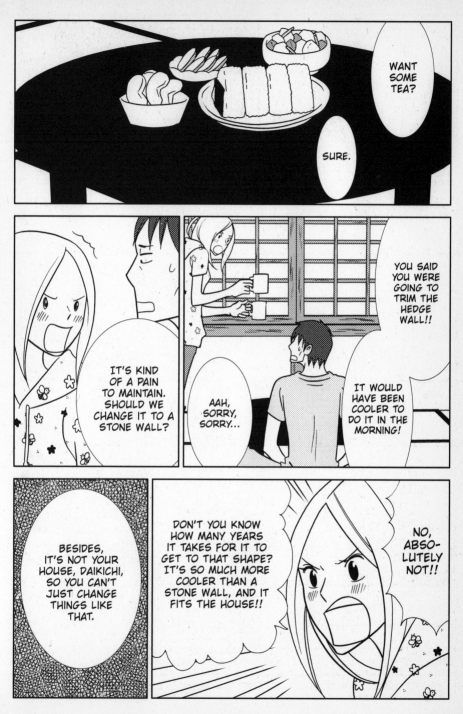

WANT SOME TEA?
SURE.
YOU SAID YOU WERE GOING TO TRIM THE HEDGE WALL!!
IT WOULD HAVE BEEN COOLER TO DO IT IN THE MORNING!
AAH, SORRY, SORRY...
IT'S KIND OF A PAIN TO MAINTAIN. SHOULD WE CHANGE IT TO A STONE WALL?
NO, ABSO-LUTELY NOT!!
DON'T YOU KNOW HOW MANY YEARS IT TAKES FOR IT TO GET TO THAT SHAPE? IT'S SO MUCH MORE COOLER THAN A STONE WALL, AND IT FITS THE HOUSE!!
BESIDES, IT'S NOT YOUR HOUSE, DAIKICHI, SO YOU CAN'T JUST CHANGE THINGS LIKE THAT.

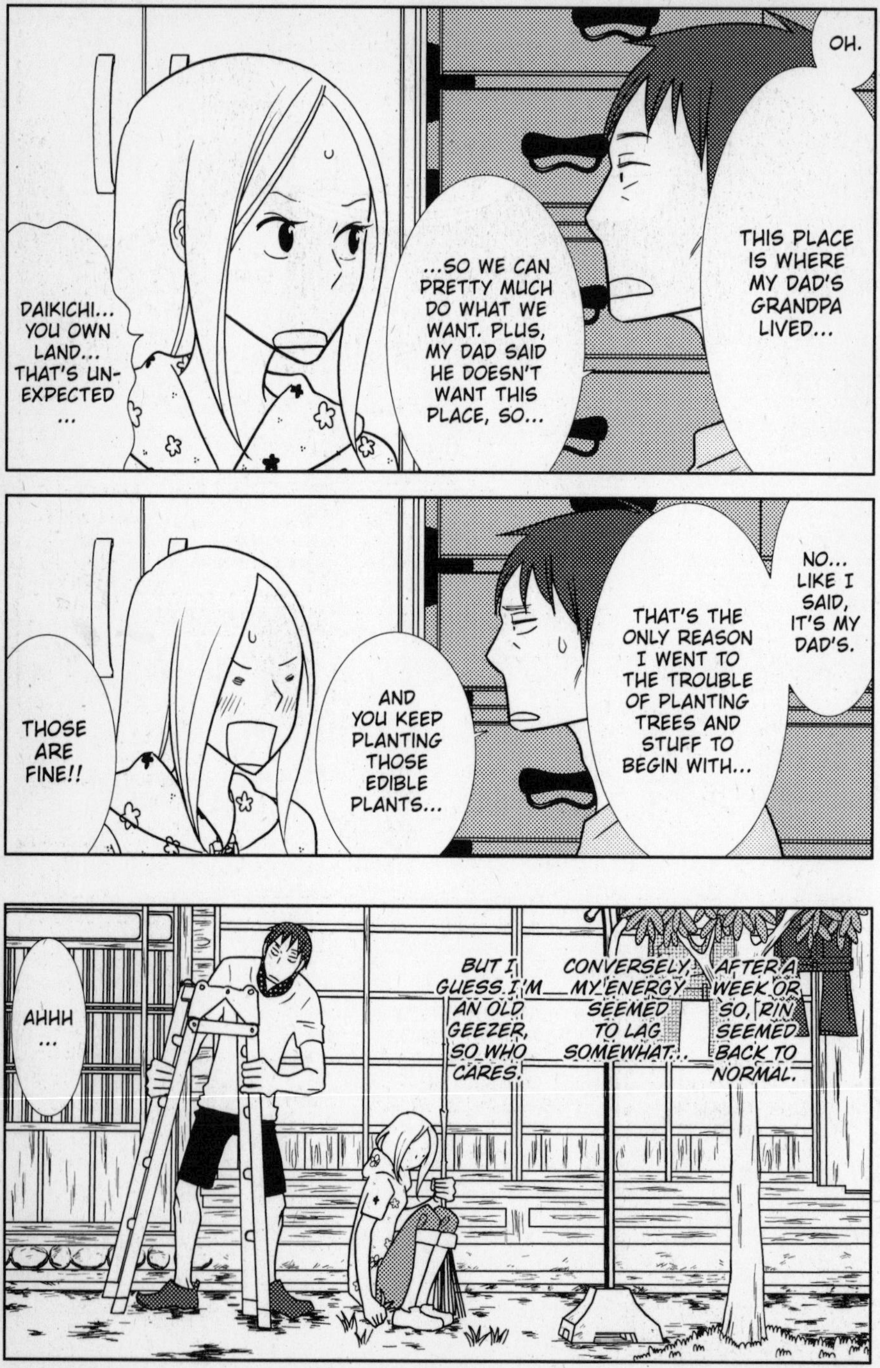
OH.
THIS PLACE IS WHERE MY DAD'S GRANDPA LIVED...
...SO WE CAN PRETTY MUCH DO WHAT WE WANT. PLUS, MY DAD SAID HE DOESN'T WANT THIS PLACE, SO...
DAIKICHI... YOU OWN LAND... THAT'S UN-EXPECTED...
NO... LIKE I SAID, IT'S MY DAD'S.
THAT'S THE ONLY REASON I WENT TO THE TROUBLE OF PLANTING TREES AND STUFF TO BEGIN WITH...
AND YOU KEEP PLANTING THOSE EDIBLE PLANTS...
THOSE ARE FINE!!
AFTER A WEEK OR SO, RIN SEEMED BACK TO NORMAL.
CONVERSELY, MY ENERGY SEEMED TO LAG SOMEWHAT...
BUT I GUESS I'M AN OLD GEEZER, SO WHO CARES.
AHHH...

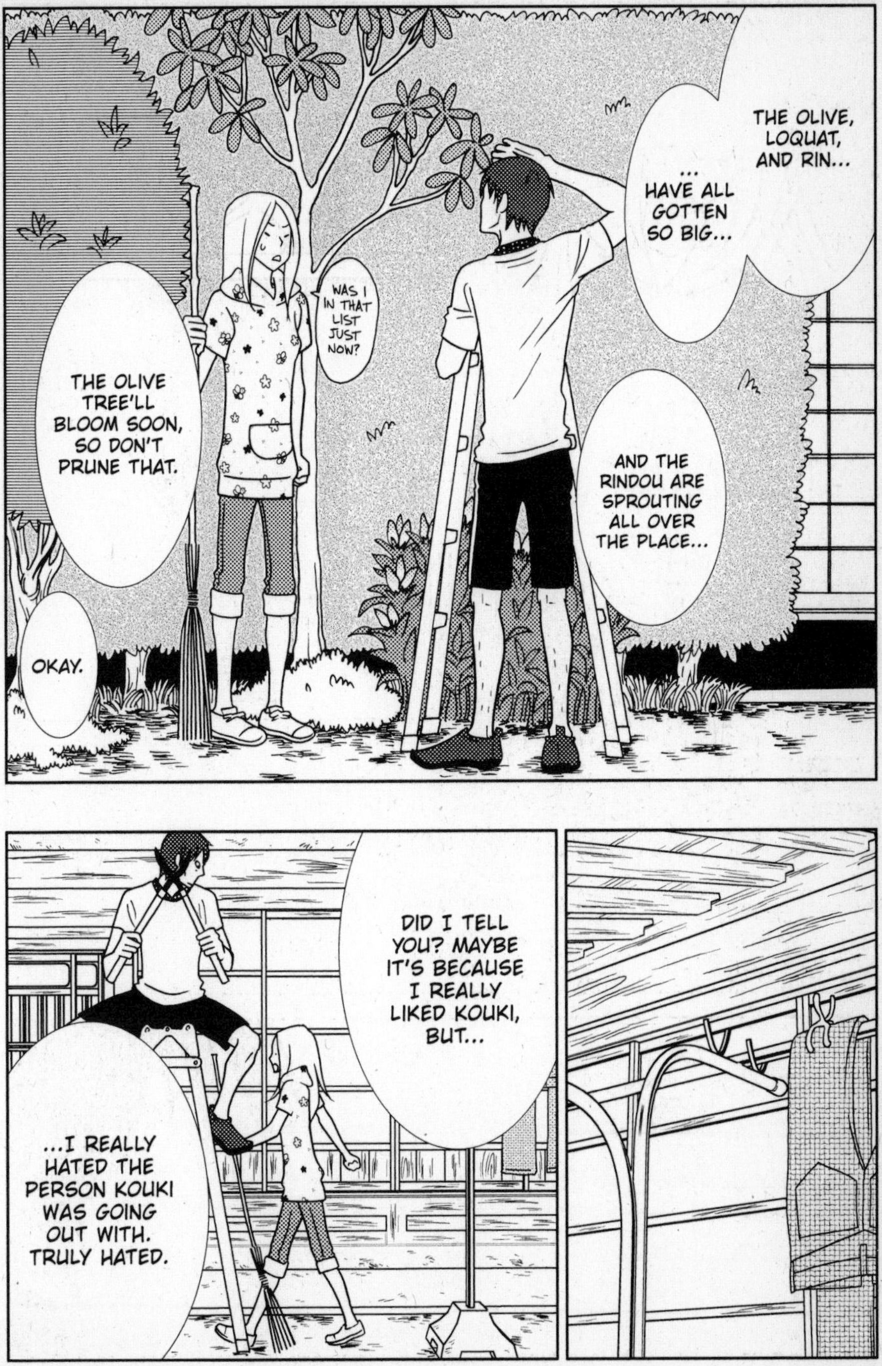
THE OLIVE, LOQUAT, AND RIN...
... HAVE ALL GOTTEN SO BIG...
AND THE RINDOU ARE SPROUTING ALL OVER THE PLACE...
WAS I IN THAT LIST JUST NOW?
THE OLIVE TREE'LL BLOOM SOON, SO DON'T PRUNE THAT.
OKAY.
DID I TELL YOU? MAYBE IT'S BECAUSE I REALLY LIKED KOUKI, BUT...
...I REALLY HATED THE PERSON KOUKI WAS GOING OUT WITH. TRULY HATED.

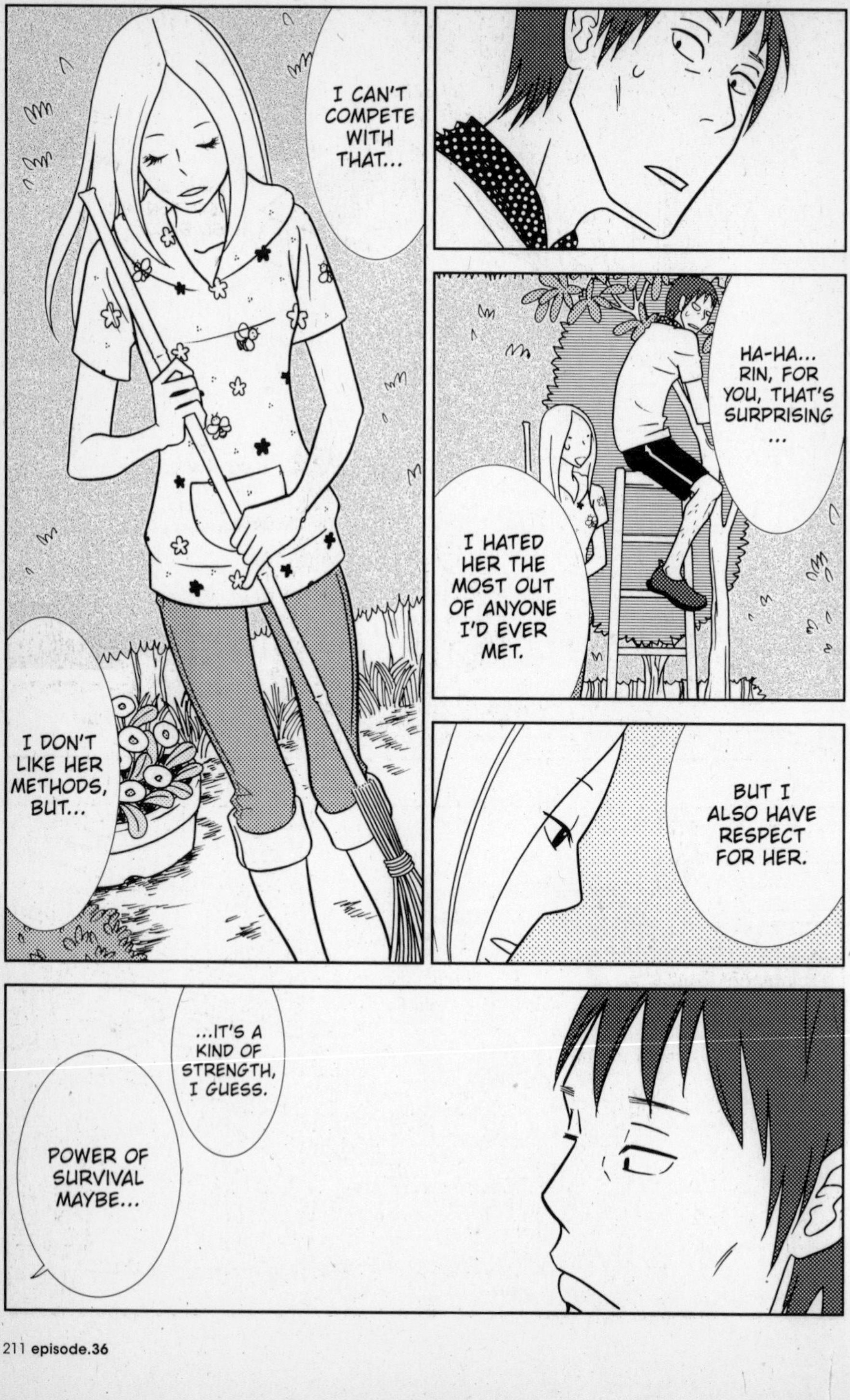
HA-HA... RIN, FOR YOU, THAT'S SURPRISING ...
I HATED HER THE MOST OUT OF ANYONE I'D EVER MET.
BUT I ALSO HAVE RESPECT FOR HER.
I CAN'T COMPETE WITH THAT...
I DON'T LIKE HER METHODS, BUT...
...IT'S A KIND OF STRENGTH, I GUESS.
POWER OF SURVIVAL MAYBE...

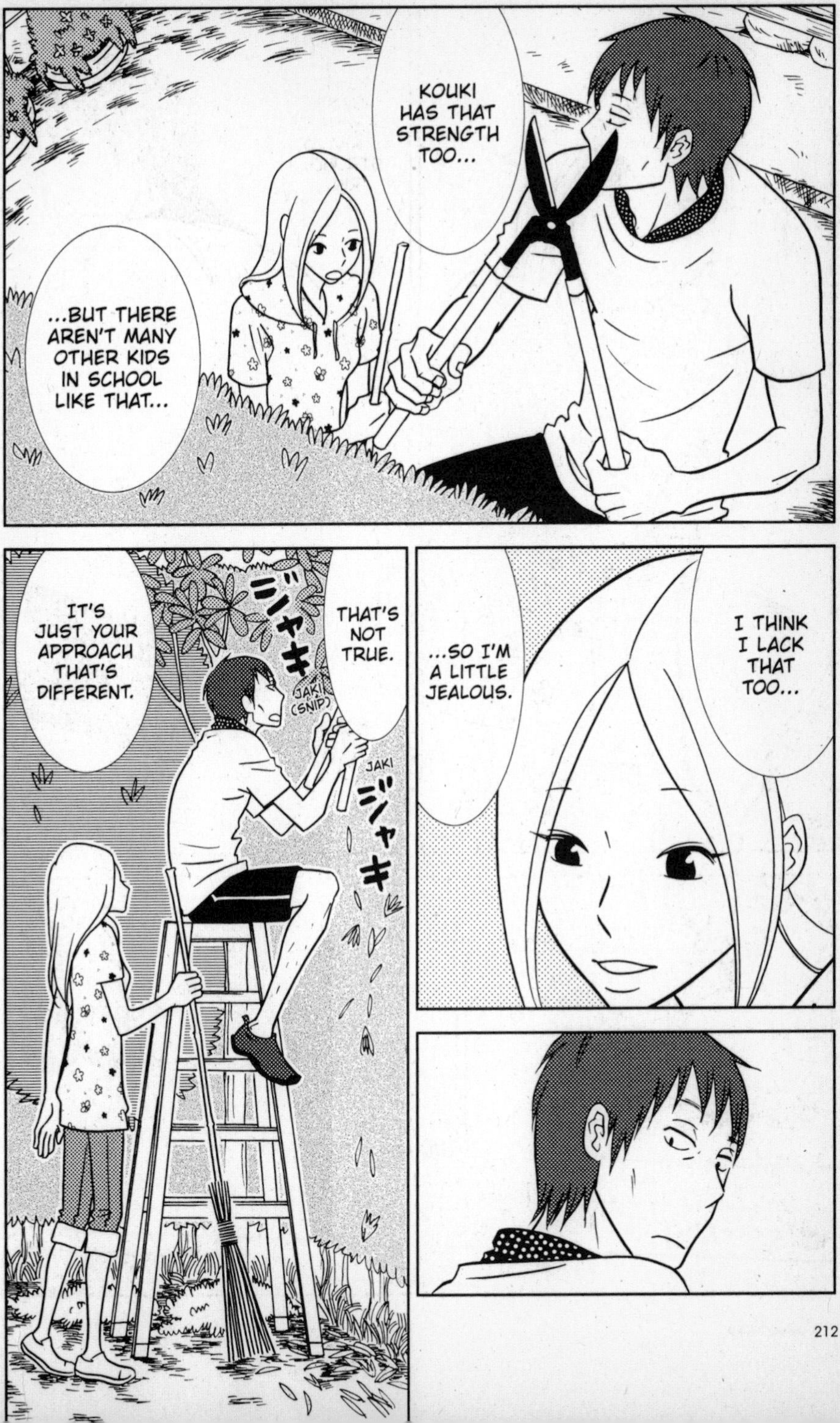
KOUKI HAS THAT STRENGTH TOO...
...BUT THERE AREN'T MANY OTHER KIDS IN SCHOOL LIKE THAT...
I THINK I LACK THAT TOO...
...SO I'M A LITTLE JEALOUS.
THAT'S NOT TRUE.
ジャキ
JAKI (SNIP)
JAKI
ジャキ
IT'S JUST YOUR APPROACH THAT'S DIFFERENT.

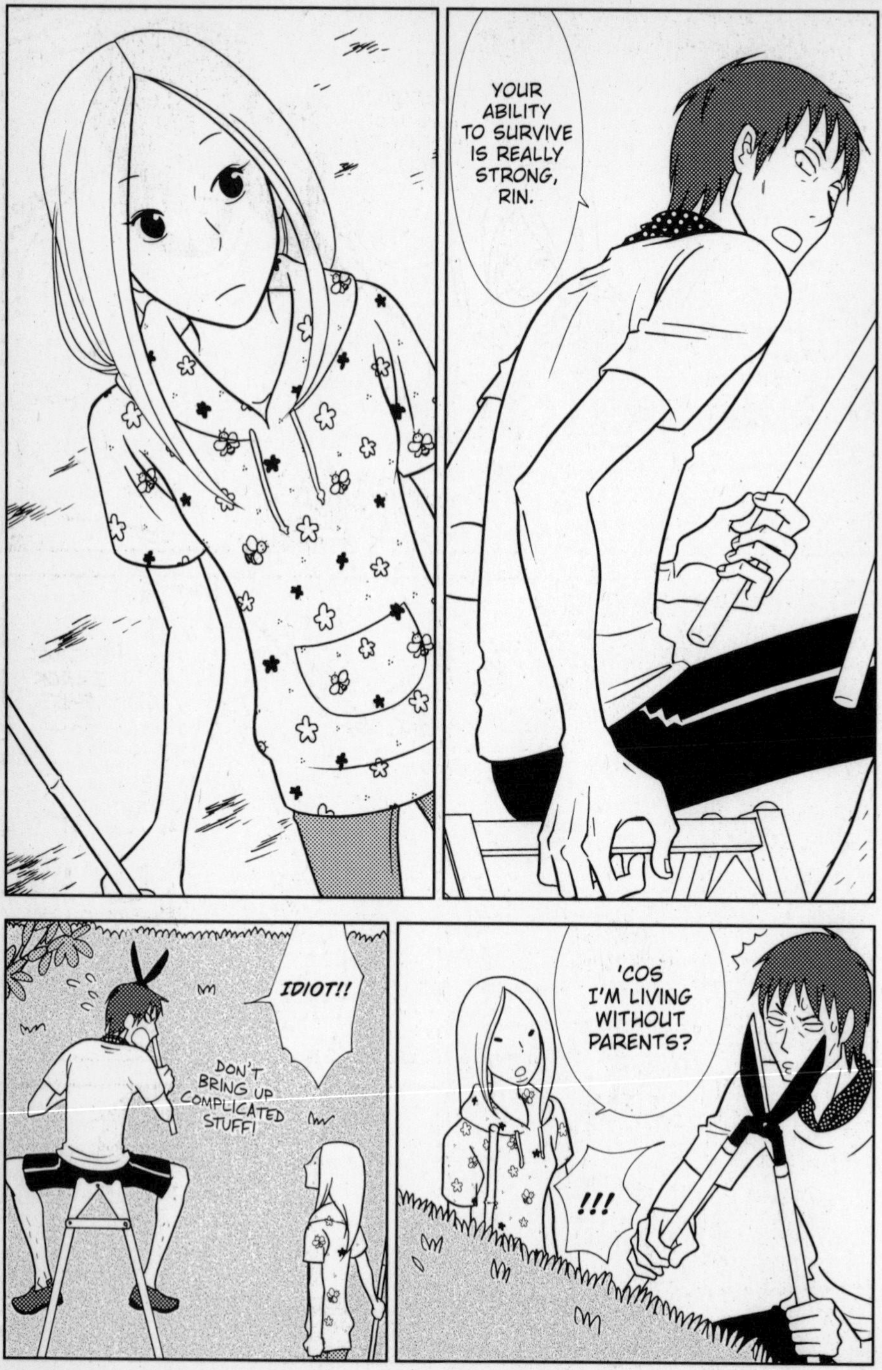
YOUR ABILITY TO SURVIVE IS REALLY STRONG, RIN.
'COS I'M LIVING WITHOUT PARENTS?
!!!
IDIOT!!
DON'T BRING UP COMPLICATED STUFF!

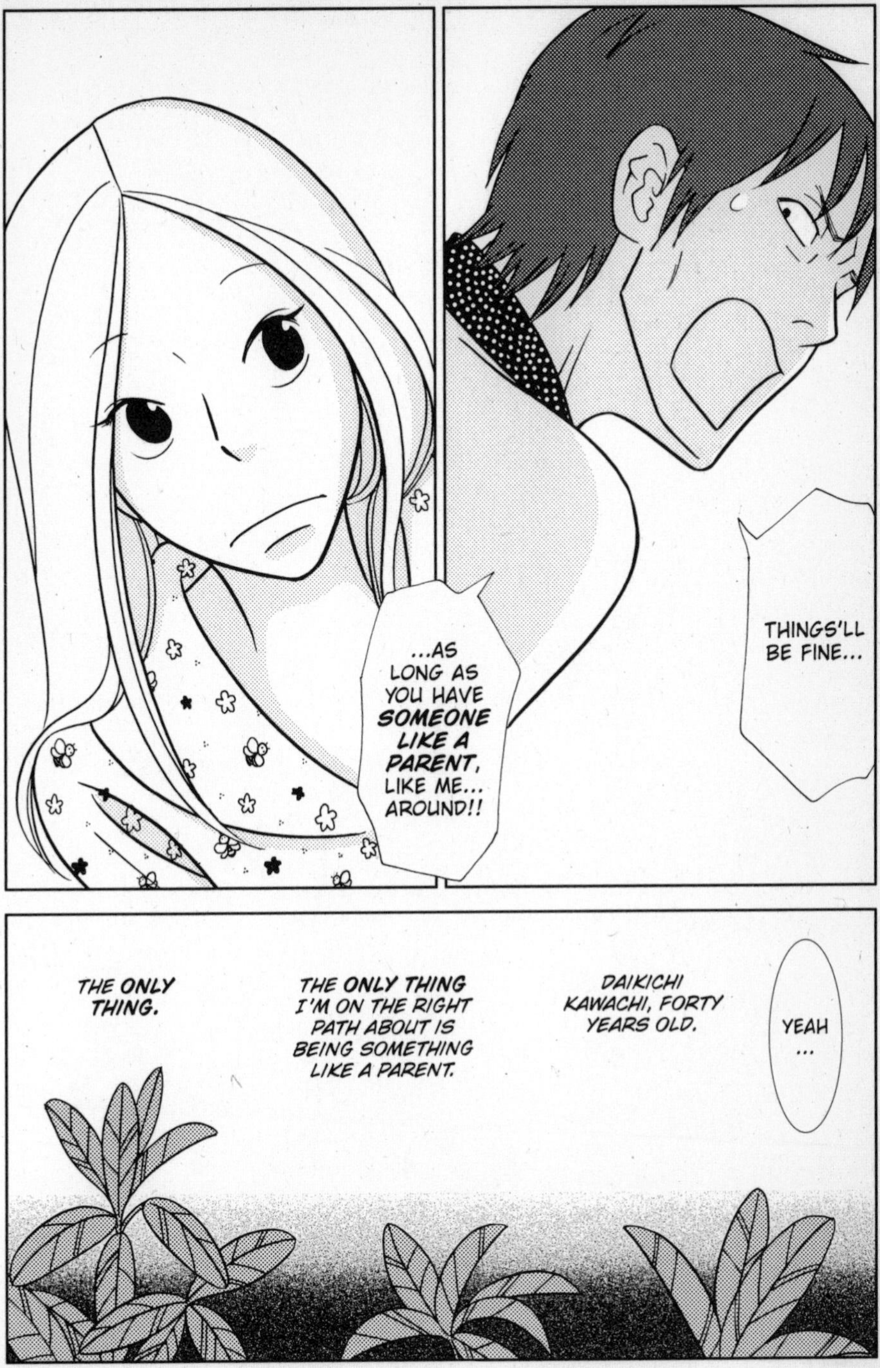
THINGS'LL BE FINE...
...AS LONG AS YOU HAVE **SOMEONE LIKE A PARENT**, LIKE ME... AROUND!!
YEAH...
DAIKICHI KAWACHI, FORTY YEARS OLD.
THE **ONLY THING** I'M ON THE RIGHT PATH ABOUT IS BEING SOMETHING LIKE A PARENT.
THE **ONLY** THING.

to be continued...

TRANSLATION NOTES

> **COMMON HONORIFICS**
> No honorific: Indicates familiarity or closeness; if used without permission or reason, addressing someone in this manner would constitute an insult.
> **-san**: The Japanese equivalent of Mr./Mrs./Miss. If a situation calls for politeness, this is the fail-safe honorific.
> **-kun**: Used most often when referring to boys (though it can be applied to girls as well), this indicates affection or familiarity. Occasionally used by older men among their peers, but it may also be used by anyone referring to a person of lower standing.
> **-chan**: An affectionate honorific indicating familiarity used mostly in reference to girls; also used in reference to cute persons or animals of either gender.

Page 9
Famicom: The Japanese name for the Nintendo Entertainment System released in Japan in 1983. Its name was taken from "family computer."
Invaders: *Space Invaders*, a classic Japanese-designed arcade game whose popularity exploded when it hit the market in the late seventies.

Page 14
Beef bowl: Called *gyuudon* in Japanese, a beef bowl primarily consists of simmered sliced beef over rice.

Page 24
Meat-and-potato stew: Called *nikujaga* in Japanese, this dish is a bit different from a Western dish that might have the same name. In Japan, it is a common comfort food dish of thinly-sliced meat, potatoes, onions, and other vegetables in a sweetened soy sauce-flavored broth.

Page 55
Daily journal: All students in a class take turns as daily monitors and are responsible for supervising the class during different periods of the day, and writing a daily journal to be submitted to the teachers.

Page 117
Yukata: A light cotton kimono worn during the summer.

Page 119
Liberal arts or science track: Students in academically-geared high schools are placed in these two tracks—*bunkei* (liberal arts) or *rikei* (science)—by the department of education (*monbushou*). Track placement is largely determined by the students themselves, but teachers also discourage students from seeking a track they feel is above their level of achievement. The amount of math and science in the liberal arts track is considerably less than in the science track.

Page 136
Super Saiyan: A term referencing the manga *DragonBall* by Akira Toriyama. It refers to an advanced level transformation by members of the powerful Saiyan race, beings from another planet.

Page 137
Goldfish scoop: A Japanese game often seen at summer festivals that requires the player to scoop up fish (live or fake) with a paper scooper.

Page 151
Jumpe: A reference to the weekly Japanese comic magazine, *Shonen Jump*.

Page 165
Taiyaki: Fish-shaped bun filled with sweet bean paste.

Page 183
Onigiri: A rice ball made with a variety of different fillings.

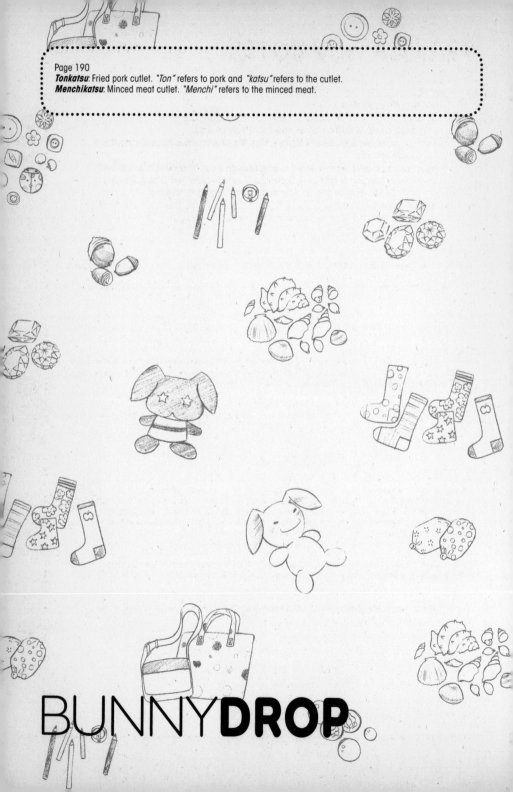

Page 190
Tonkatsu: Fried pork cutlet. "*Ton*" refers to pork and "*katsu*" refers to the cutlet.
Menchikatsu: Minced meat cutlet. "*Menchi*" refers to the minced meat.

BUNNY**DROP**

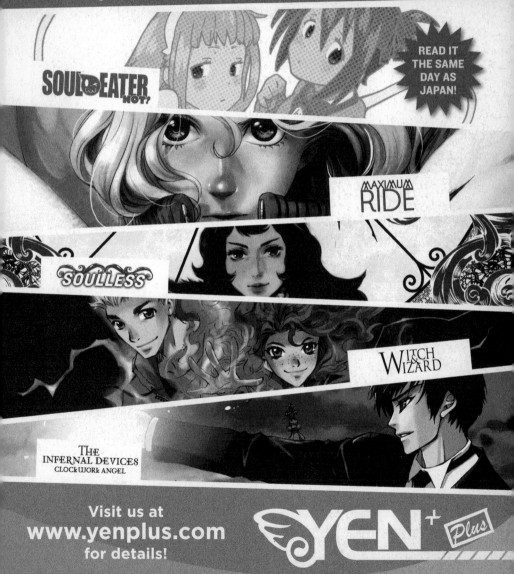

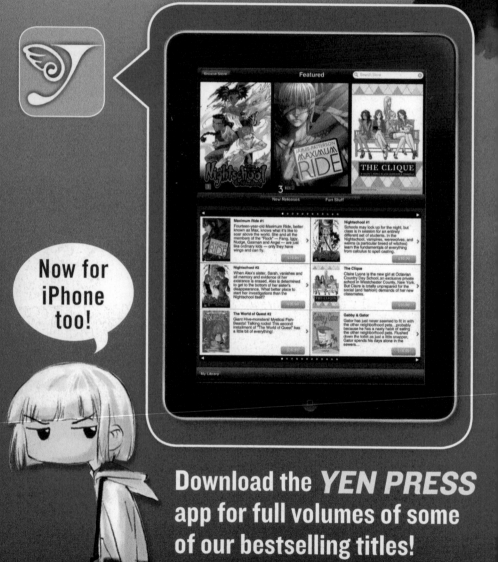

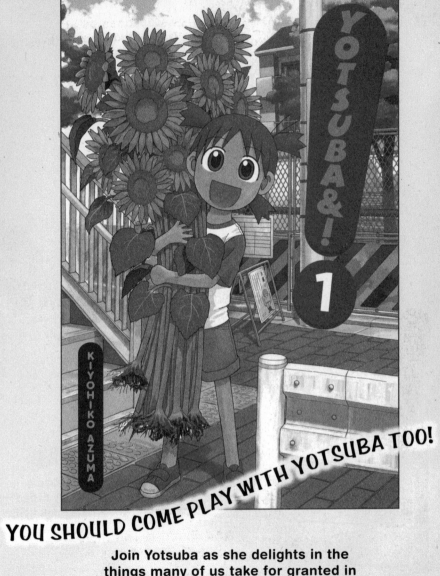

Hello! This is YOTSUBA!

Guess what? Guess what?
Yotsuba and Daddy just moved here
from waaaay over there!

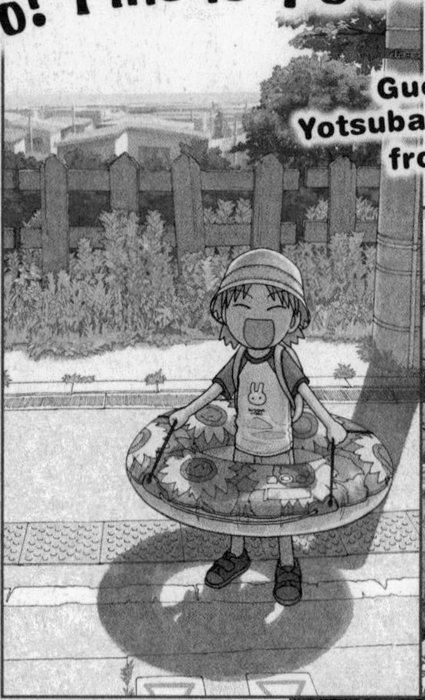

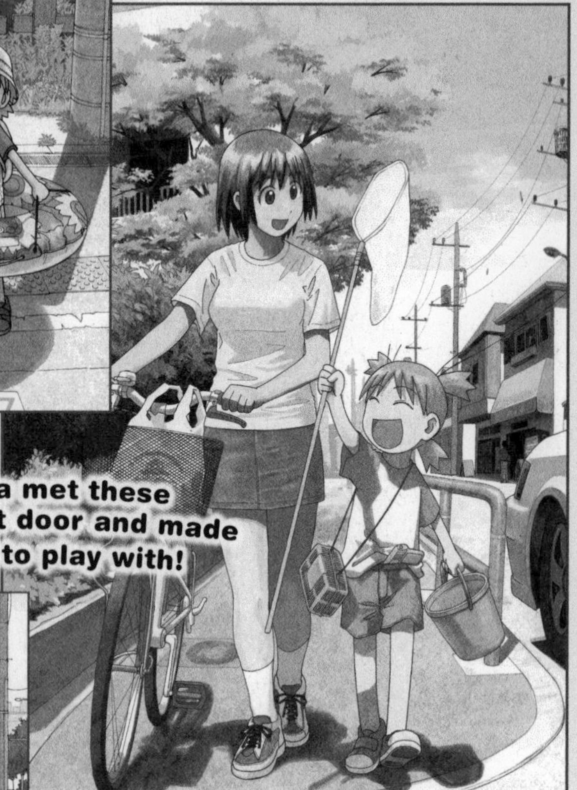

!

And Yotsuba met these
nice people next door and made
new friends to play with!

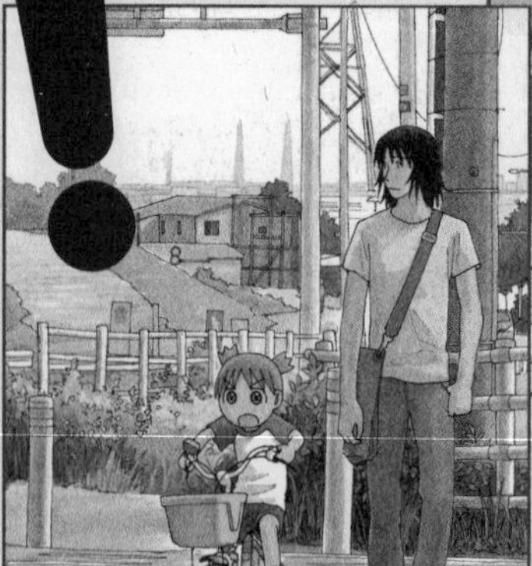

The pretty one took
Yotsuba on a bike ride!
(Whoooa! There was a big hill!)

And Ena's a good drawer!
(Almost as good as Yotsuba!)

And their mom always
gives Yotsuba ice cream!
(Yummy!)

And...
And...
OHHHH!

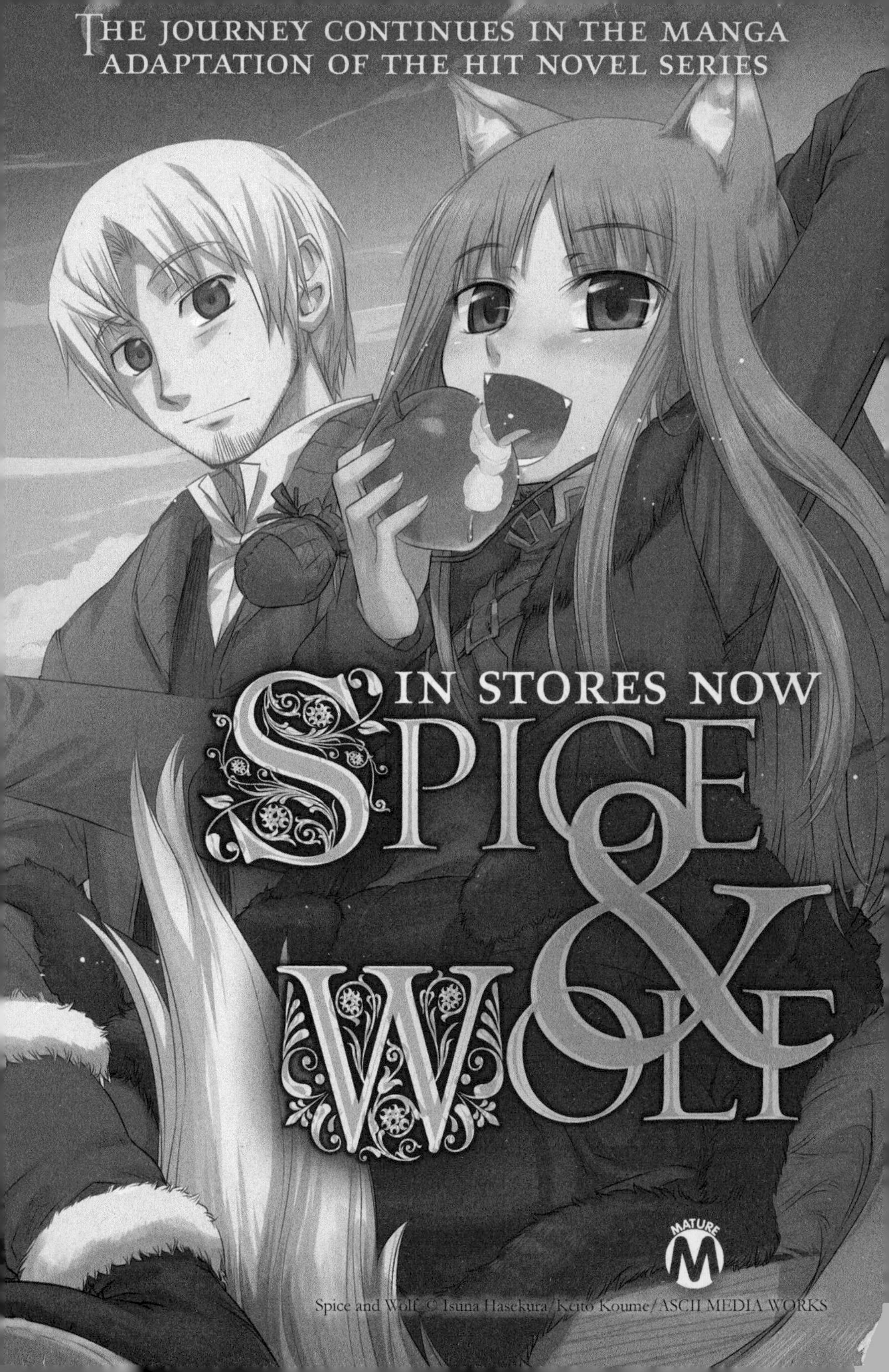
THE JOURNEY CONTINUES IN THE MANGA
ADAPTATION OF THE HIT NOVEL SERIES
IN STORES NOW
SPICE & WOLF
MATURE
M
Spice and Wolf © Isuna Hasekura/Keito Koume/ASCII MEDIA WORKS

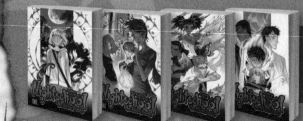

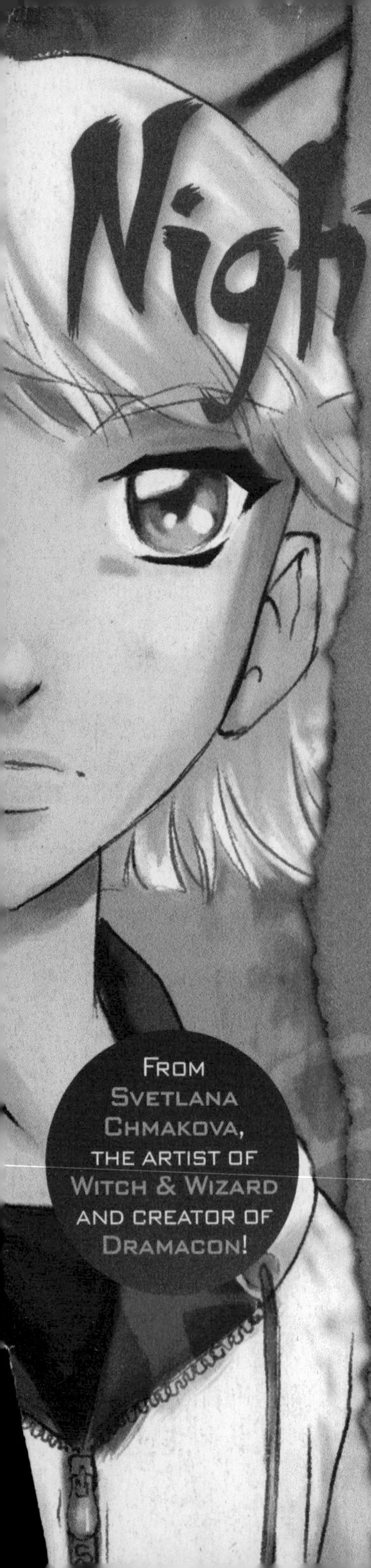

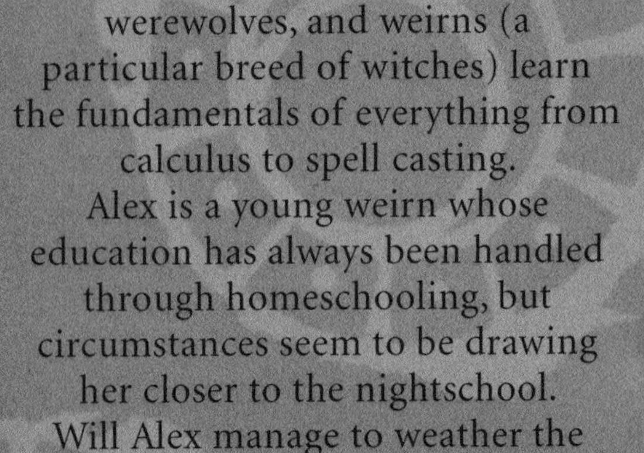

BUNNY DROP ⑥

YUMI UNITA

Translation: Kaori Inoue • Lettering: Alexis Eckerman

BUNNY DROP Vol. 6 © 2009 by Yumi Unita. All rights reserved. First published in Japan in 2009 by SHODENSHA PUBLISHING CO., LTD., Tokyo. English translation rights in USA, Canada, and UK arranged with SHODENSHA PUBLISHING CO., LTD. and Hachette Book Group through Tuttle-Mori Agency, Inc., Tokyo.

Translation © 2012 by Hachette Book Group, Inc.

Yen Press
Hachette Book Group
237 Park Avenue, New York, NY 10017

www.HachetteBookGroup.com
www.YenPress.com

Yen Press is an imprint of Hachette Book Group, Inc. The Yen Press name and logo are trademarks of Hachette Book Group, Inc.

First Yen Press Edition: August 2012

ISBN: 978-0-316-21719-4

10 9 8 7 6 5 4 3 2 1

BVG

Printed in the United States of America